AF723370

NEW DEVELOPMENT PARADIGMS AND CHALLENGES FOR WESTERN AND CENTRAL INDIA

About the Editors

R. Parthasarathy is HUDCO Chair Professor at School of Planning, CEPT University, Ahmedabad. Till recently, Parthasarathy was a Professor at the Gujarat Institute of Development Research, Ahmedabad. Email: rpsarathy@spcept.org.

Sudarshan Iyengar is Vice Chancellor, Gujarat Vidyapeeth, Ahmedabad. Iyengar was earlier the Director of Gujarat Institute of Development Research, Ahmedabad. Email: iyengars@icenet.net.

New Development Paradigms and Challenges for Western and Central India

VOLUME ONE

Editors

R. Parthasarathy
Sudarshan Iyengar

Published for

Gujarat Institute of Development Research,
Ahmedabad
by

CONCEPT PUBLISHING COMPANY, NEW DELHI-110059

Cataloging in Publication Data—DK
Courtesy: D.K. Agencies (P) Ltd. <docinfo@dkagencies.com>

New development paradigms and challenges for western and central India / editors, R. Parthasarathy, Sudarshan Iyengar.

p. cm.

Papers presented at the National Seminar on New Developmental Paradigms and Challenges in Western and Central India, held at Ahmedabad.

Includes bibliographical references.

Includes index.

ISBN 8180692809

1. India—Economic conditions—Congresses. 2. India—Economic policy—Congresses. 3. Sustainable development—India—Congresses. 4. India—Social policy—Congresses. 5. Natural resources—Co-management—India—Congresses.

I. Parthasarathy, R. II. Iyengar, Sudarshan, 1954-

DDC 330.954 22

All rights reserved. No part of this work may be reproduced, store in a retrieval system, or transmitted in any form or by any means, electronic, mechanical, photocopying, recording or otherwise, without the prior written permission of the copyright owner and the publisher.

The views and opinions in this book are those of the authors and not necessarily reflect the views of the organizations to which they belong.

ISBN 81-8069-280-9 (Set)
ISBN 81-8069-312-0 (Vol. I)
ISBN 81-8069-313-9 (Vol. II)

First Published 2006

© Gujarat Institute of Development Research

Published and Printed by
Ashok Kumar Mittal
Concept Publishing Company
A/15-16, Commercial Block, Mohan Garden
New Delhi-110059 (India)

Phones : 25351460, 25351794
Fax : 091-11-25357103
Email : publishing@conceptpub.com

Dedicated to

Professor Pravin Visaria

Foreword

Western parts of India, especially Gujarat and Maharashtra have, during the past 15 years, led the charge in India's economic growth. Gujarat, in fact, has been matching growth rates of China whose example many of us would like India to emulate. These regions are in the throes of a rapid socio-ecological transition. Aside from creating wealth for entrepreneurial agents and the educated-employed, however, what this transition has in store for the majority of the region's people is a growing hiatus between rising expectations and stagnant pool of opportunities. What the transition also holds in store is a growing conflict between economic growth and environment. In many ways then, the region is wading through a turbulent phase, presenting numerous challenges of transforming economic growth into wholesome, all-round and equitable development. Meeting these challenges requires deft handling of the economy and the political processes of public choice.

This collection, to which, I have the honour to write this foreword, brings together a collection of 25 writings and reflections which deal with variations on this overall theme of the development of Western and Central India during recent times. These writings were first presented in a 2003 workshop organized to commemorate half a century of development partnership between the Ford Foundation and India. These volumes, in many ways, is a tribute to the sterling catalytic role played by the Foundation during the early decades after independence and reflects a broad spectrum of the developmental issues with which the Foundation has engaged.

The collection is interesting because of the variety of concerns, perspectives as well as styles it seeks to accommodate. It includes essays as well as empirical research papers. It has erudite thought pieces on one hand and practical notes written by practitioners. Several authors write on alternative strategies of economic growth and their fall out. But others also share their views on the social sector and environmental issues. These volumes will disappoint a reader looking for a comprehensive treatise on economic growth and social transformation in Western and Central India. But with the variegated perspectives it presents, it will delight someone in search of a mosaic that attempts to address a huge diversity of issues and concerns that the society in this region is experiencing.

November 2005 **Tushaar Shah**

Preface

In the second half of 2001 in a meeting in Jodhpur between the Ford Foundation grantees and the representatives of the Ford Foundation, Delhi, there was a discussion on how to suitably commemorate the 50 years of partnership of the Foundation with India in the year 2002. The freewheeling discussions hovered on themes of varied hues from culture to economy and democratic governance to fortifying the mechanisms for social justice. For an academic who had the support of the Foundation for a number of research projects, the whole discussion initially looked a little gentle, however, when it picked up the significance of the dimensions of the Foundation's support to the institutions and processes in India and South Asia became clear. During the half-a-century ending 2002, the Foundation's first and oldest overseas office in New Delhi has played a key role in the establishment of institutions which have contributed to the development and often introduced some challenging processes of developmental discourse. The Foundation has been widely credited for the "Green Revolution" in India and more recently for introducing the concept of micro-finance. Further, it has supported many prestigious institutions in India including institutions of academic excellence, fundamental research, policy design, advocacy and action, besides, India's Planning Commission among others. The discussion lingered in the mind and led to the thought that these interventions would have introduced a new spin not only in the developmental processes but also in the multi-dimensional outcomes. It also led to a desire to assess how much of this support had been absorbed and how could the next phase of the Foundation's work in India could contribute in identifying a new agenda. The developmental stage of the States is to be looked at first, and the challenges of the future identified. Invariably, a mutually beneficial partnership evolves when the stakes are shared between the interested and the gains are also shared. Thus, the Ford Foundation-50—Gujarat Institute of Development Research (FF50-GIDR) partnership platform to undertake a commemorative journey in 2002-03 took shape. In this, the Surabhi Foundation and Mandala are partners besides the GIDR which hosted the *National Seminar on New Developmental Paradigms and Challenges in Western and Central India*. Surabhi organised a Film Festival on *Images of India: Traditions and Transitions,* and Mandala planned Theatre Productions and installations: *The Rivers of India, Voices and Dreams and Haasyaras*.

The Seminar's goal was to bring together academics, scholars, government officials and NGOs to share the progress and the processes, and to take stock of where we are in the changing developmental paradigms and to identify the challenges ahead. The participants and contributors of research papers to the Seminar focussed on a wider context of Indian Economic and Social Development.

The focus therefore was not on providing a treatise on economics or sociology but to identify the variety of issues and challenges in a developmental challenge perspective. Thus, an important contribution of this exercise is the conceptualisation of developmental paradigms in an identifiable ground of social and economic progress initiated by the government and civil society efforts. This, in the Editors' point of view, could henceforth be taught in the undergraduate to graduate courses as Indian Economic and Social Development in place of what the authors (and even the current students of economics) study as Indian Economic Development (popularly known as IED). This is not an imagined vision—the papers in these two volumes would bear testimony.

An ambitious task of this kind cannot obviously be achieved without kind support from many. First, we would like to thank the Chief Guest for the Seminar, Prof. Kirit Parikh, Chairman, GIDR and currently Member, Planning Commission, Government of India, who also helped the Editors immensely in the subsequent stages of the work. Prof. Yoginder K. Alagh, former Member, Planning Commission, and a Central Government Minister, inaugurated the Seminar and Mr. Jay Narayan Vyas, former Minister for Narmada Development, Government of Gujarat, chaired the panel discussion and delivered the Valedictory Address. Prof. Tushaar Shah willingly agreed to our request to write the Foreword for these volumes. Words of thanks cannot adequately express our gratitude to these eminent persons yet we would like to convey our deep sense of gratitude to each one of them.

Institutions and individuals are inextricably linked in the politico-economic fabric of the Indian society. One of the institutions that have been supported by the Foundation to come up is the Gujarat Institute of Area Planning (GIAP). The GIAP transformed itself into the Gujarat Institute of Development Research (GIDR) under the leadership of Prof. Pravin Visaria whose erudition and commitment to developmental paradigms is known. The Foundation supports to the Seminar came at a time when the GIDR—the host institution—had been, for a couple of years without Prof. Visaria. He died in 2001. The editors of these volumes who grew under the tutelage of Prof. Visaria dedicate these volumes to his memory.

In fact both the GIDR and the Editors of these volumes were only keen that a suitable commemorative academic event coincides with the Seminar. A *Professor Pravin Visaria Memorial Public Lecture* was organised and Prof. Tim Dyson of London School of Economics, delivered the lecture. The topic of the lecture, "India's Population: Past, Present and Future," held as part of FF50-GIDR seminar was also an occasion for the people, policy makers, politicians and social activists to take stock of the developments on the social front today. The lecture also helped in taking to the people the developmental contours of the region.

A Seminar of this scale and volumes would not have been possible but for the able support of the Director, the administration and the support staff at the GIDR: Mr G. G. Nair, Mr Upendra Upadhyay, Mr K.P. Solanki, Ms Kalpana Mehta, Mr Jignashu Yagnik, Mr Bharat Adhyaru, Mr Dixit Parmar, Mr Dinesh Parmar, Mr Niranjan Bhatt, Mr Shivsingh Rathod, Mr Joravar Singh and Mr Raju Vaghela. Ms Girija Balakrishnan, Ms V.A. Vasanthi and Ms Sheela Devadas word-processed the papers for the Seminar and subsequently for these volumes. The Director and members of the GIDR Faculty deserve a special mention and thanks for their encouragement and crucial support at all stages.

During the organising of the Seminar, in the follow-up with the authors and in brining out these two volumes, Ms Jharna Pathak, Mr Harish Joshi and Mr Jayanti Solanki played a significant supportive role. But for their enthusiastic and ungrudging support the task would have been unmanageable for the Editors. We express our gratefulness to all of them.

These volumes are envisaged with a plan, although the delay in giving it a final shape is inexplicable. Other commitments and some reticence in writing down the thought processes that finally appear as the overview were partly responsible for the time lapse. In fact Prof Leela Visaria, present Director, GIDR, persuaded the Editors to accomplish the task in the shortest possible time and we gratefully acknowledge her efforts. However, the timeliness of the publication is not optimistically lost, as the development processes that have unfolded in the past two years lend further credence to some of the diagnosis, prognosis and policy imperatives. The papers received for these volumes were reviewed and revised and in some cases re-reviewed before acceptance as a publishable material. A professional editor, Dr. Rohini Patel, subsequently edited these revised papers. We would like to credit immense gratitude to the paper writers, reviewers, and the Editor for their committed work and encouraging response.

It would indeed be knotty to suitably thank the Foundation for its support and the distinguished participants of the Seminar and the contributors to these volumes. A Seminar of this importance would not have been possible but for the strong, committed and responsive acknowledgement of all of them. It is with delight the editors express their gratitude to the Foundation, participants of the seminar and the authors contributing to these volumes. The Ford Foundation, New Delhi, was indeed generous to a fault as perhaps they were in the Indian context, to support what was originally an intellectual knowledge generating activity that turned out to be a fruitful discourse between the various stakeholders of the developmental debate.

We owe a great measure of deep gratitude to the Ford Foundation officials and staff: Dr Gowher Rizwi, the then Representative, Dr Steven Lawry, Dr Dorris Capistrano, Ms Roshmi Goswami, Ms Renuka Agarwala, Ms Mona Challu, Ms Soha Khan, Mr Tuhina Sunder, Mr Nagasubramaniam and Mr Deep Chand. Our special thanks to Mr Ganesan Balachandaran, the present Representative, and Dr Vasant Saberwal for showing concern, and giving support and encouragement to complete the remaining portion of the process culminating in this publication. In the collaborative exercise with Surabhi and Mandala we appreciate the help of Mr Siddharth Kak and Ms Mita Vasisht.

While we were in the process of bringing out these volumes, both of us moved out from GIDR: R. Parthasarathy to the School of Planning (CEPT), Ahmedabad, and Sudarshan Iyengar to Gujarat Vidyapeeth. Both these institutions provided excellent academic and accommodative atmosphere for our pursuit. We would like to place on record our gratitude to these institutions.

While organising the Seminar and subsequently bringing out these volumes, the aim and purpose was to learn from the past approaches, the emerging scenarios and the paradigm shifts informed by the New Institutional Economists. If, as we had hoped, the FF 50-GIDR Seminar and the collection of papers in these volumes bring about an intercourse of the developmental paradigms and challenges and the academics, policy-makers and practitioners, the efforts and the purpose would be well served. Lastly, we are grateful to Mr Ashok Mittal of Concept Publishing Company who readily agreed to our request to contribute towards the dissemination part of the process by publishing the collection of papers.

R. Parthasarathy
Sudarshan Iyengar

Contents

PART II

Urbanisation and Industrialisation

PART III

Social Sectors

VOLUME TWO

PART IV

Management of Common Property Resources: Institutionalisation and Innovations

PART V

Watershed Development: As If People Mattered?

PART VI

Participatory Irrigation Management: A Reform or a Programme?

List of Tables

List of Charts, Figures, Map, Graphs and Appendix Figures

Charts

Figures

Map

Graphs

Annex Tables and Appendix Figure

Tables

Figures

The Contributors

Bakshi, Nishita, Indian Institute of Forest Management, Bhopal.

Ballabh, Vishwa, Institute of Rural Management, Anand.
Email: vb@fac.irma.ernet.in

Bhende, M.J., Institute of Social and Economic Change, Bangalore.
Email: bhende@isec.ac.in

Biswas, P.K., Indian Institute of Forest Management, Bhopal.
Email: pkbiswas@iifm.org

Chatterjee, Mirai, SEWA, Ahmedabad.
Email: sewass@icenet.net

Deshpande, R.S., Institute of Social and Economic Change, Bangalore.
Email: deshpande@isec.ac.in

Dholakia, Archana, Gujarat University, Ahmedabad.
Email: archana_dholakia@hotmail.com

Dholakia, Ravindra H., Indian Institute of Management, Ahmedabad.
Email: rdholakia@iimahd.ernet.in

Duggal, Ravi, CEHAT, Mumbai.
E-mail: raviduggal@vsnl.com

Ghate, Rucha, The Institute for Research and Development, Nagpur.
Email: shodh@nagpur.dot.net.in

Hirway, Indira, Centre for Development Alternatives, Ahmedabad.
Email: hirwayad1@sancharnet.in

Iyengar, Sudarshan, Gujarat Vidyapeeth, Ahmedabad.
Email: iyengars@icenet.net

Khaitan, Neelima, SEWA Mandir, Udaipur.
Email: smandir@vsnl.com

Kundu, Amitabh, Jawaharlal Nehru University, New Delhi Email: Amitabh@jnuniv.ernet.in

Mahadevia, Darshini, School of Planning, Centre for Environment Planning and Technology, Ahmedabad.
Email: spceptad1@sancharnet.in

Marothia, Dinesh K., Dept. of Agril. and Natural Resource Economics University, Raipur Chhattisgarh.
Email: dkmarothia@yahoo.com

Mukhopadhyay, Pranab, Goa University, Goa.
Email: pm@thegym.net

Mukundan, K., World Bank, New Delhi.
Email: kmukundan@worldbank.org

Nair, Ramesh P.K., Indian Institute of Forest Management, Bhopal.

Parthasarathy, R., School of Planning, Centre for Environmental Planning & Technology, Ahmedabad.
Email: rpsarathy@spcept.org,

Ray, Sunil, Institute of Development Studies, Jaipur.
Email: sunil@idsj.org

Sarangi, Niranjan, Jawaharlal Nehru University, New Delhi

Shah, Amita, Gujarat Institute of Development Research, Ahmedabad
Email: amita@gidr.ac.in

Shah, Anil, Development Support Centre, Ahmedabad.
Email: dsc@satyam.net.in

Shah, Mihir, Samaj Pragati Sahayoj, Dewas, M.P.
Email: samprag@sifi.com

Singh, Katar, Chairman, India Natural Resource Economics and Management Foundation, Anand.
Email: inrem@earth.planet.net.in

Singh, Surjit, Institute of Development Studies, Jaipur.
Email: idsjaipur@sancharnet.in

Swamy, Shivananda, Centre for Environmental Planning & Technology, Ahmedabad.
Email: shivanand@spcept.org

Roy, Tirthankar, Gokhale Institute of Politics and Economics, Pune.
Email: tirthankar_roy@yahoo.co.in

Vijay, Shankar, P.S., Samaj Pragati Sahayoj, Dewas, M.P.
Email: samprag@sifi.com

Verma, Madhu, Indian Institute of Forest Management, Bhopal.
Email: mverma@iifm.org

PART I

ECONOMIC GROWTH AND SUSTAINABLE DEVELOPMENT

1

Introduction

Paradigms and Challenges

R. PARTHASARATHY and SUDARSHAN IYENGAR

The challenges of economic development in the last decade have been recast in India as they are elsewhere. The growth rate of the economy in the eighties had been somewhat higher than during the preceding 30 years. It had been shared—even if unequally—by most sectors and states. The beginning of the 1990s witnessed a crisis in the international trade environment of the country and the managers of the Indian economy made a dramatic shift from the state-controlled economy to market-friendly policies in the early 1990s. While the debate is on among the economists about the need and urgency for the second and later generations of economic reforms, there is a need to understand and discuss the variable impact of the new economic policies on the economic development of different regions and sectors.

In recent years, issues regarding management of natural resources have also assumed importance in addressing the stagnating agricultural productivity and in improving the livelihood of the people dependent on these resources. One oft-cited reason is that the existing systems do not adequately address the mismanagement and the serious disrepair of the infrastructures. The breakdown can be seen most vividly at the village level where government administration of the natural resources—be it water, forest or land—has become ineffective. Often, the magnitude of mismanagement is gross enough to give rise to the problems of waterlogging, salinity and soil degradation. Moreover, there is a growing consensus that the solution to these problems lies in transferring management of natural resources to the community itself where control over the resource is with the end-users. The creation of new institutions at the village-community level has become the central focus of recent governmental programmes.

The pattern of growth in the nineties indicates that although food production had been rising steadily, irrigation sector continued to have a substantial idle capacity. On the other hand, questions of land-use patterns, even as over-exploitation of groundwater creates serious problems threatening the survival of agriculture, are of no less import. The rural development programmes targeting the poor had been meeting with limited success till very recent times. The public distribution system was also not able to target the poor adequately. These events and trends have had an adverse impact on the rural communities which, in turn, exerted more pressure on the natural resource base of land, forest and water, the status of which had already been precarious The Watershed Development Programme through the people's involvement in 1997 has brought some relief. Its plans for drought-proofing and mitigation instead of drought relief and the institutional mechanism for implementing the programme have been amended to give the Panchayati Raj institutions an important role to play.

Some of these issues assume significance as they are also to be viewed in conjunction with the wider reform measures initiated by the Government of India and aimed at reducing governmental controls and subsidies. It is becoming apparent that reform measures affect various rural and urban regions of India differently. To add to the complexity, the reform and revitalisation of development, particularly rural development, are facing difficulty as they reach and evoke a response from millions of cultivators long dependent on governmental administration. In reviewing India's new strategies for management and planning we discover lessons in community-based natural resource management and the emerging scenarios. This is important as the new norms are aimed at transforming the developmental paradigm.

A number of studies have formed the basis for the focus of the national seminar. The literature on decentralisation of development initiatives by Korten (1990), Dholakia and Iyengar (1991), Dreze and Sen (1995), Bardhan (1996), Parthasarathy and Iyengar (1998) and Iyengar and Hirway (2001) underscores the challenge of developing a realistic understanding of the grassroots situation and generate data that could be used for planning with the help of people for whom the government bureaucrats have been taking decisions for years. They also highlight the importance of providing opportunities and incentives, training and capacity building, and demanding contributions from the communities in order to stimulate participation and inculcate a sense of ownership at both individual and community levels.

It is clear, therefore, that any investigation into the dynamics and challenges in the natural resource sector must be multi-disciplinary, involving not only understanding from social science point of view but also a grasp of the technological aspects of resource management. Further, there are clear links between the natural resources management and the quality of human capital that manages it. Therefore, it becomes imperative to look at the issues related to human resource development and other development aspects and issues. The collection of papers in this volume analyses many such interrelated issues and we have grouped them under different sub-themes.

Economic Growth and Sustainable Development

Maharashtra and Gujarat have been following a development strategy that had a clear focus on industrialisation and urbanisation. Industrialisation has yielded good dividends in both the states in western India (Iyengar and Oza 2002), but there are problems relating to the environmental status (Hirway *et al.* 2002). It may be partly due to the dominance of the state, which has been guilty of sins of commission and omission and has generated substantial negative externalities. It is difficult to say if the two economies would have generated relatively lower negative externalities in the proccss of fast economic growth under a free market situation. Three papers presented in the seminar discuss state-level growths and environmental problems.

Ravindra Dholakia in his paper "Economic Reforms and Development Strategy" examines the development strategy followed by the State of Gujarat during the nineties. It has continued the strategy of industrialisation and urbanisation with an open-door policy. Economic reforms of the Government of India with an explicit emphasis on trade and industry have considerably benefited Gujarat in making its economic performance outstanding. The state government facilitated only the growth of private enterprise since its strategy was already consistent with the changes in the policy reforms at the Centre. Dholakia points out that the states while competing for entrepreneurs offer tax concessions that have detrimental effects on the tax revenues. However, since the year 2000 fresh incentives have been cost-related that augment output and hence tax revenues. This strategy would not adversely affect the government's ability to spend on social sector programmes. Infrastructure improvement and development have also been undertaken in a big way. Gujarat has been able to achieve high growth rates in the value-added in both registered and unregistered manufacturing sectors. Abolition of urban land ceiling would bear sound results and the market prices will reflect the real scarcity and would help in an organised growth. In the context of liberalisation it is important to note that the acts and ordinances formulated in the past continue to act as obstacles in the smooth working of the private enterprises in the manufacturing and service sectors. As the focus of the development strategy has shifted from the organised manufacturing activity to the unorganised sectors, rationalisation of regulatory mechanisms also needs overhauling that should facilitate growth and not obstruct it.

In India, the states that have experienced industrialisation-based fast economic growth have also been affected to some extent by the environmental degradation. In Gujarat too, damage to the environment has been recorded, although the nature and extent of the environmental problems remain contentious issues. Indira Hirway, in her paper, "Challenges to Sustainable Development: Some Issues in the Context of Gujarat", studies the pattern of development in Gujarat to assess its sustainability. The author uses an integrated framework and examines the processes related to economic growth, poverty, environment and social development. The decadal growth rate of the State Domestic Product (SDP) has been impressive (between 5.0 and 5.5 per cent per annum) in Gujarat. The rate of poverty reduction has also been stable around 3.1 to 3.5 per cent per annum. Development in the social sector has slowed down and the sex ratio has come down in the 1990s. The 2001 data on the sex ratio is alarming in some talukas. Groundwater situation appears more serious than any other environmental indicator. Forests appear to have registered some improvement, in both area and quality. Salinity affected area has increased and area covered by mangroves has shrunk. Correlation matrix in the paper shows a negative association between environmental degradation and social development indicators. Strategy for sustainable development in Gujarat necessitates adopting an integrated approach in which economic development, social sector development and environmental concerns are treated in unison.

In a global perspective, the nexus between poverty and environment and hence sustainable development has been viewed only as a problem of poverty. In other words, the poor have largely been held responsible for degrading the environment and consequently their livelihood strategies and coping mechanisms have been viewed as generating negative externalities and making development unsustainable. Amita Shah, in her paper, "Poverty and Natural Resources: Understanding the Dynamics in the Context of Dry Land Regions in Western India", reviews the poverty scene in four western states contextualised in agricultural growth in arid and semi-arid areas and the hilly tracts. She argues that the relatively lower and diminishing level of poverty in the arid regions in the plains is a short-run phenomenon as extensive agriculture is generally practised when irrigation is made available. Marginal land parcels are brought under cultivation that would eventually lead to a high degradation of the environment. It would result sequentially, in even more severe poverty than what may be currently found in the tribal regions that have a degrading forest resource-base. Property rights over forest and groundwater hold the key to future sustainable development and redressal of poverty.

Pranab Mukhopadhyay, in his paper "Goa: Been There, Done That. Now What? Resource Management and Democratic Process", raises appealing issues with respect to the status and management of natural resources in rural Goa. Goa is economically one of the most advanced states in India in terms of per capita income. The main economic activity in the state is tourism. Since 2001, the number of annual tourists has been higher than the number of local residents. The situation is atypical in this state in India. The tourist- and trade-based economy has a large floating population that creates pressure on the resource-base of the region. Coastal Regulation Zone's rules violations, overdraw of groundwater, and entry of trawlers in marine fishing have created serious ecological and environmental problems in the state. It is argued that government-initiated and market-led development has created many problems and destroyed some strong local institutions that promised sustainable development. If some of these institutions are strengthened and the panchayats are made more capable of mobilising financial resources at their level, use and development of natural resources in the coastal state of Goa might become more sustainable.

Urbanisation and Industrialisation

Urbanisation has indicated a significant deceleration in its growth rates in recent decades. Excepting the period 1971-81, urban growth as a whole has registered a steady decline in the country. The paper, "Urbanisation and Growth Dynamics in India: An Analysis with Special Reference to Western and Central Regions", by Amitabh Kundu, Niranjan Sarangi, Shivananda Swamy and K. Mukundan analyses the results of the 2001 Census urban data and argues that there has been a more judicious and analytical understanding of the census criteria than in 1991. The 2001 Census has identified some new towns using more comprehensive criteria. The net addition to the total number of towns was 472, which is less than that of 1991. The reduction in the number of towns added is explained by the larger declassification and merging phenomenon that occurred in the 2001 Census.

Big cities are getting bigger. The dominance of Class I towns/ cities over other categories seen since 1941 has been maintained. Importantly, the study demonstrates that a spatial pattern of the level of urbanisation and urban growth is distinctly different. Since independence until 1991, the level of urbanisation has been generally high in the developed States like Maharashtra, Gujarat, Tamil Nadu and Haryana, although they experience medium or low urban growth. In contrast, high urban growth was registered in relatively backward States like Bihar, Uttar Pradesh, Rajasthan, Orissa and Madhya Pradesh that had low percentage of urban population. However, the 1990s make a significant departure from the earlier decades as many of the developed and highly urbanised states have registered urban growth above the national average. The backward states, in contrast, have experienced a growth rate either below the National average or equal to that. As a result the disparity in terms of growth of urban population across the states has gone up during the nineties.

Analysing the interdependences between the indicators of urbanisation and those of socio-economic development, the authors show that the percentage of urban population is higher in the economically better-off states than in the relatively backward ones. Further, the relationships between the indicators of economic development and the growth of urban population has improved significantly over time and have become significant in the nineties. The authors argue that the growth of urban population over the decades has led to an increase in the pressure on basic amenities and resulted in deterioration in the standard of living. The patterns of interdependence between urbanisation and socio-economic development assessed through district-level data are significantly different in the developed state of Maharashtra compared to the less developed State like Rajasthan during the last three decades. This implies that industrialisation has influenced a higher level of urbanisation in Maharashtra, which is not a relevant factor in the case of Rajasthan.

How do regional economies grow with industrialisation and how does this take place? Gujarat again offers answers to these questions. In the paper titled "Urban-Industrial Development Dynamics: Perspectives from Gujarat, India", Shivanand Swamy and Mukundan analyse the case of Gujarat (between 1971 and 2001) as a highly industrialised and constantly urbanising state. Financial incentives are not very effective in determining the location of a factory or development of an industry. Urban agglomerations offer better overall incentives to entrepreneurs in setting up manufacturing units. Thus, despite policy-level attempts to decentralise, the industries have continued to develop in clusters in and around major urban centres. Between 1991 and 2001, richer and urbanised regions have grown at a faster rate than the poorer regions. The state, although aware of such a trend, does not appear to have done enough in terms of investing in the urban infrastructure. As a result the fast-growing urban areas are generating large negative externalities potent enough to bring down the human development score.

An alternative policy option for reducing the concentration of productivity and high-income jobs in a few large or metropolitan cities has also been on the agenda of researchers and policy makers. However, a significant shift has taken place in the policy environment: the small and medium towns are nowadays expected to pursue their own growth through private participation. The urban local bodies are expected to generate both resources and partnerships. Darshini

Mahadevia, in her paper, "Municipal Finances and Development in Small Medium Towns: Gujarat", examines the scope of such a pattern of urbanisation with the example of Gujarat state. Swami has argued that despite the policies favouring decentralisation of industries there has been concentration and growth of industries near the metropolitan urban agglomerations, and Mahadevia points out that the existing urban development policies in Gujarat have already been skewed against the growth of small and medium towns. The per capita grant disbursed to the large cities has been higher than that to the small and medium towns. Low per capita income and low per capita expenditure patterns in small and medium towns have restricted the scope of faster development of smaller towns in Gujarat. Had the policies to promote decentralisation of industries worked and had the new industries spread around the small and medium towns, the process of urbanisation would have been harsher and the inadequacies in budget provisions for development of infrastructure would have hit harder.

Financial sector reforms have been debated time and again in the country. Lending portfolios, interest rates, and non-performing asset ratios in the commercial and cooperative banks are important discussion points. Rajasthan is one of the drought-prone states and had a relatively lower level of commercial bank network at the time when the concept of social banking began to be institutionalised in 1969. The state experienced good growth in commercial banks, cooperatives and other lending institutions between 1969 and 1991. But the period also shows an escalating burden of outstanding loans with the pubic sector financial institutions. It is only post-1991 that bad debts came down in absolute terms. Surjit Singh, in his paper, "Institutional Finance in Rajasthan: The Recent Trends", provides a panoramic view of the growth of financial institutions in Rajasthan and their status in terms of deposit mobilisation, advances and bad debts. Interestingly, the debt situation among the households in Rajasthan has been worse than the national averages for the three time points: 1971, 1981and 1991. Persistent indebtedness is also evident partly due to frequent droughts. The author argues that the formal financial institutions are not able to tackle the short duration but frequent credit requirements of the households and that micro-finance has shown some promise in this regard. He, however, observes that in this sub-sector too, the situation in Rajasthan is not as good as in the south Indian states. The formal credit scene has shown some improvement in terms of both deposits and advances but falling credit-deposit ratios do not augur well for the Rajasthan economy. Dependence on informal credit sources appears high as in the case of western states and thus the high cost of investment, especially in agriculture. There would be a disincentive to invest in agriculture if it does not come down.

Social Sector

In the process of economic development the role of human resource development has assumed importance only in recent times. Even though human resources have been a focus of inquiry of social scientists, economists have treated human resources only as a factor of production to increase the total output in an economy. The per capita income has been the main indicator of economic development and studies on the social sector have largely focused on the public expenditure by the governments on education, health and social welfare. After 1980, however, a paradigm shift seems to have occurred in the social sector theory largely informed by the empirical situation that obtained from sub-Saharan Africa and some of the Latin American countries in the post-economic-reform periods. The International Monetary Fund (IMF) and the World Bank (WB), the two Brettonwoods Conference progeny, promoted the economic reforms worldwide. The IMF promoted and supported stabilisation in the international economic dealings focussing on fiscal policy changes and Balance of Payments, which the WB translated as Structural Adjustment Programmes (SAPs). One aspect of the SAP was to prune the public expenditure but it has come under attack from some renowned economists such as Amartya Sen.

Improvement in human resource specifically in the formation of skills for producing goods and services was to be achieved through investments in the social sector. But since the returns accrue in the long run and are rather intangible, pruning expenditure in the social sector was generally advised. As a result, in the process of economic reforms, expenditure in the social sector was reduced in some economies and consequently marginal sections—the poor and the socially disadvantaged—in the developing countries suffered. The situation sharpened the analysis of social sector and emphasis shifted from development of human resource as a "capital stock" needed for higher production to human development for a dignified and healthy life. The shift was from human resource as a means to economic development to human development as an end in itself. Contribution of the UNDP has been phenomenal in effecting the paradigm shifts at the policy and programme levels in the member countries. Social sector thus became a broad rubric to include education, health, poverty alleviation programmes, rural development and social security. Human development issues are now considered in the framework of basic rights approach and the role of state in the human development field has been enhanced. Even in social security there has been a paradigm shift from mere protective social security that centred on protection against frictional unemployment, old age, infirmities and destitution to promotional social security, the concept introduced by Amartya Sen and Jean Dreze. The concept includes empowerment through improved endowments, exchange entitlements, employment generation programmes, and public distribution systems (for a comprehensive treatment of the subject, see Prabhu 2001).

When we invited research scholars to contribute to the Seminar on various aspects of the social sector, we hoped that some of them would trace the links between the state-level experiences in formulating and implementing programmes on health, nutrition, education and social security. The papers on the theme, to a large extent, forge many additional linkages as well.

Archana Dholakia and Ravindra Dholakia in their paper, "Expenditure Allocation and Welfare Returns to Government Expenditure Efforts : A Suggested Model and its Implication," develop a theoretical model that considers government budget allocation and illustrate its implication on the economic and social sectors. They argue that, at the margin, changes in expenditure allocation are determined not by the magnitude of marginal productivities of government effort, but by the behaviour of marginal returns in relative terms. Nine indicators of education, health, nutrition and other social sectors measure the index of basic welfare as the output of government efforts. This Basic Welfare Index (BWI) constructed by the authors is an alternative to the earlier indices used by other scholars to measure the welfare of the people and encompasses the three components of minimum desirable welfare, namely, health, education and nutrition and others. The results demonstrate that an increase in the Expenditure on Human Capital (EHK) by the government increases the basic welfare at an increasing rate and that on the physical capital (EPK) increases welfare at a decreasing rate. Based on the findings, Dholakias recommend the government should put the money where the mouth is, that is, to spend more on the social sector than what has been the case in the recent past.

On the critical sector of health, Ravi Duggal's paper, "Health and Healthcare in Western and Central India: The Criticality of Public Finance", is a comprehensive analysis of the western-central states. He brings out an interesting contradiction in the state's interest in the health and healthcare sector. Maharashtra and Gujarat, the states that perform well on the SDP and per capita income fronts and rank higher than other states such as Madhya Pradesh and Rajasthan, also performed well with respect to investment in the public health programme prior to economic reforms. He thus recognises economic growth as a favourable condition for higher and better investment in public health. However, in the post-reform period which, according to him, had set in during the 1980s, Gujarat and Maharashtra seem to have withdrawn somewhat and reduced public investment. He attributes this to the central policies in the health sector wherein the programme content itself eventually encourages privatisation of the sector. On the basis of the analysis of the National Sample Survey (NSS) data he argues that private expenditure for healthcare by the poor is so high that it leads them into indebtedness. Referring to the international experience, he finds that the share of public expenditure to total health expenditure is substantial in most of the developed countries and even in the developing countries such as China and other Asian countries. He has observed an improvement in public investment in the post-reform period in the economically backward Indian states and finds it desirable. Duggal states that there is ample scope for public-private partnership, but the state's interest and investment have to be dominant because the ultimate goal in the social sector is to achieve human development in the basic rights framework. He recommends integration of healthcare programmes with other social sector programmes and suggests a strategy of strong public action and stringent regulations as a pedestal for implementation. Like

Dholakias, Duggal too underscores the role of the government in accelerating a basic welfare system.

Mirai Chatterjee, in her paper, "Human Resources for the Twenty-First Century: The Contribution of Traditional Birth Attendants (Dais)", presents a grassroots case as against the macro-level analysis of Duggal. Unfolding the Self-Employed Women's Association's strategy for development in general and human development in particular in Gujarat, she focuses on the traditional birth attendants' training in conducting safe deliveries and providing primary maternal and child healthcare to the rural population as a case in point for capacity building and human development. The approach is through membership-based mobilisation and organisation of women and empowering them with appropriate capacity-building exercises in healthcare at village and community levels. The long-term goal of the *dai* training programme is achieving health security for client groups and building a human resource pool. A trained *dai* is an innovation and could become a low-cost standard alternative for promoting better healthcare in rural areas.

Labour and employment security has become a contentious issue in the wake of economic reforms in India. Western India, particularly Maharashtra and Gujarat with a large share of formal industrial sector, is obviously in focus. Even in labour and employment security there has been a paradigm shift initiated by the ILO-ARTEP studies which view employment and employment security within the basic rights framework rather than only as demand-supply equations. Labour and related issues are discussed in the human development perspective rather than in a resource perspective. In a refreshing analysis Tirthankar Roy, in his paper, "Liberalisation and Labour in Indian Industry", has made a fine and important point that in the conventional labour market framework and media dominated concerns, the problems and prospects of new entrant firms and informal labour markets are neglected, in both analysis and policy advocacy. The tendency among the scholars is to view the impact in terms of the polarisation model-ascent on markets and withdrawal of State. They then infer that the process has strengthened the capital and weakened the labour, which is a very simplistic view of the situation. Using old-new and formal-informal distinctions as analytical devices, Roy builds a framework of variable imact of market reforms on employment and industrial relations.

Taking up two case studies of textile and jute industry he argues that in the old firms the social contract between labour and management broke down, and the few surviving, profitable mills devised decentralised bargaining institutions. The paper's significant contribution is the observation that in the case of old firms in the formal sector, capital has been weakened because new entrants have the distinct advantages of modern technology and skilled labour. The employment terms for labour have also become weakened because of the breakdown of the contractual arrangements leading to what he terms disempowerment. Secondly, he points to the loss of state support suffered by the old informal sector due to the impact of globalisation on its markets. With the renewed emphasis on small and tiny sector in an informal unorganised environment in the western-central states in India, Roy's suggestion to study more closely the changes in labour markets appears relevant and appropriate.

Management of Common Property Resources: Institutions and Innovations

Commitment towards a Welfare State and a resultant appropriation of property rights of the natural resources by the governments has had differential impacts on development and management of the Common Property Resources (CPRs) in India. Jodha (2002) has drawn attention to this aspect and Iyengar and Shukla (2002) have illustrated this in their review of the development and management of common property resources in Gujarat. The number of the players and stakeholders in using, developing and managing the natural resources of land, water and forests has risen and thus a mix of management systems is in operation under different property regimes. However, under most property rights regimes, natural resources have been degrading at a rapid rate.

The literature on the management of common property resources provides a wealth of ideas and an array of problems that bear on community-based management. Ostrom (1990), Vaidyanathan (1999), Kadekodi and Chopra (1989), Jodha (1992), Sengupta (1991), Shah (1993) and others have approached the "tragedy of the commons (albeit, tragedy of open access)" dilemma from a variety of perspectives and methodologies. The on-going debate on the issue of linking land ownership with water rights has not resolved the problem of multiple claims on water exercised by those who want it for uses other than crop cultivation, such as home consumption, animal, urban and industrial use, and power generation. Little has been written about the fact that village communities inevitably find themselves nested in a wider context of powerful stakeholders for all of whom the state must find accommodation. Little has been written about the politics of resolving localised water resource disputes and how the community based institutions deal with competing claims.

What does the term "community" mean anyway? First, it must be noted that in the jurisdiction of a Water User Association for water management or Joint Forest Management committee it may vary from one village to several of them. Thus, the "community" in a particular village is integrally part of larger communities defined by different institutional parameters governing the natural resource management. Therefore, while referring to a "community of users", one must recognise that they may have a common interest in, or may be in conflict over the use of the resource. Therefore, the proponents of decentralisation must confront the issue of how marginalised groups, including women, disadvantaged castes or tribes, tenants, the land-poor, and the landless will be treated under the new system. The vast literature on India's rural sociology has developed several new foci: gender and equity analysis (Agarwal 1994; Meinzen-Dick *et al.* 1997; Shiva 1988; Mosse 1994; Moench 1998; van Koppen *et al.,* 2002; Zwarteveen 1997) the political economy of caste relationships and mobilisation (Kohli 1987, 1990; Wood 1987; Mendelsohn and Vicziany 1998) as well as changes in landuse and labour patterns in the post-liberalisation era (Agarwal 1994; Bhalla 1976). Within the field of irrigation management there is a substantial literature focused on community participation and conflict resolution (Chambers 1988; Chambers, Saxena and Shah 1989; Mosse 1994; Brewer *et al.* 1999; Maloney and Raju 1994; Sengupta 1991; Parthasarathy 2000; van Koppen, Parthasarathy and Safiliou 2002).

Women's categorical marginalisation in decision-making has to be understood in the wider context of hierarchical gender relations that shape society. Women's exclusion from productive assets such as land, credit and technologies underlies their exclusion from other inputs in agrarian production. The developmentalist school points to consumption imperatives and argues that environmental problems are amenable to innovative solutions. The protectionist school, including Gadgil and Guha (1992, 1995) and Agarwal and Narain (1997), argues that it is local citizens, as heirs to a conservationist tradition, who are most likely to utilise their resources rationally and sustainably. Therefore, common property resource management is intimately linked with environmental analysis and appropriation mechanism. There is a burgeoning literature that provides warnings regarding the overuse or misuse of natural resources. One of the concerns expressed by different authors in this volume is with the impact of new institutions like WUAs, watershed committees and JFM committees on resource sustainability amidst increasing demands and usage.

Dinesh Marothia, in his paper titled "Alternative Institutional Structures for Sustainable Development for Common Pool Resources: Lessons from Chhattisgarh", analyses the status of different common pool resources in what he has insightfully termed as "distributed governance". The central concept is that the governance can be shared among the state, the community and the private interest groups with respective property right regimes for the same resource. Arrangements, interactions, interface and technical factors under the distributed governance would influence one another in both static and dynamic situations. All this helps or hampers the sustainable use of natural resource and this should be the point of examination. In Chhattisgarh, the newly formed state (formerly part of Madhya Pradesh) cases of micro-minor irrigation tanks, village woodlots, community fishponds, non-timber forest products and participatory irrigation management have been examined. The lessons are very insightful. Distributed governance in most cases is initiated by the state without necessarily understanding the socio-economic profiles or traditional customs and practices or conventional property rights. More than help regeneration or sustained use of natural resources, there has been degradation all around: be it fisheries, non-timber forest produce, village woodlots, or irrigation management. Marothia argues for a better understanding and management of institutional arrangements and the importance of political and bureaucratic determination to share power with the farmers. This transformation is necessary to help improve not only the performance but also to promote the goals of sustainable management of the scarce irrigation water resource. To achieve this, he suggests the policy designers gather in-depth understanding of the strengths and weaknesses of alternative property rights regimes while developing institutional arrangements for the CPRs. Decentralised governance, which the Seventy-third and Seventy-fourth Constitutional Amendments aim to bring about, has to be informed more elaborately with in-depth analysis of the local situation. Prescriptions and programmes without this essential exercise are going to have a very limited and in some cases even negative impact on decentralised and distributed governance (Dholakia and Iyengar 1991).

"Management of Forest as CPR for Sustainable Rural Development" by P.K. Biswas first traces the contribution of forest in development and goes on to outline the present status of forests in India. For the philosophy of decentralised governance to succeed, he feels the need for people's involvement in the decision-making process. To achieve this, he says the tenure rights of the rural people should be secured. Secure tenure rights and the development of systems of regulation and enforcement based on local-level decision-making are the prime issues emerging from the analysis. Interestingly, Biswas links up these issues with a stress on the need to formalise community-based management systems at both the local and higher levels. He believes that the culture of indigenous people and the dynamics of social processes have to be understood properly since sustainable forest management is the key to sustainable rural livelihood. An alliance has to be forged among government, non-government and local-level organisations—perhaps a hint that the present system is below par (for the rise and decline of these partnerships, see Anil Shah's paper in this volume). There has to be an effective partnership among all the stakeholders for capacity building, monitoring and evaluation. To achieve this task, Biswas too like Marothia believes that sociological/ social anthropological insights, perceptions and knowledge are essential in bringing about reforms.

Biswas's views on the long-debated issue of "people in forest" are important because very few scholars take a stand. While stressing that rural livelihood is integrated with the management of forest as a CPR, it is imperative to involve communities and then empower them. The government's role is to facilitate communities and grant legal sanction to the village forest committee/forest protection committee. Reiterating his earlier position about legalising the partnerships, he argues that it is crucial to have a memorandum of understanding signed between communities and government. His strong argument is that granting powers to the communities should legitimise forests as CPRs. He points out that the National Forest Policy already asks for community empowerment and this needs to be backed by appropriate legislation.

The need for community participation in forest management has been felt during the last one-and-a half decade or so. Regimented departmental management has not given any hopes of arresting the fast degradation of natural resources. Some concessions have been granted to the communities living in and near forests for managing them. Some communities have already been managing forests, especially in the areas that were covered at one time with thick forests. Rucha Ghate, in her paper titled "Leadership in Community Initiated Forest Management", examines how these communities are faring. She concludes that a leader requires an in-depth understanding of the local situation and the ability to tackle day-to-day situations to succeed in taking community initiatives and actions to manage forests; the leader does not have to be charismatic or political. Utilising the existing social capital and developing social capital are important in this endeavour. In distributive governance, role clarity and clear and negotiable property rights at different levels assume special importance.

Growing trees outside forestland is an area in which some fresh efforts have gone in the country. The Anand group, which has a relatively significant venture in milk with the massive back-up of the cooperative sector, has introduced this innovation in tree-growing and wasteland development. Katar Singh's paper, "A New Paradigm of Development Based on Afforestation of Wastelands through Tree Growers' Cooperative and Other Village Institutions" examines the economic rationale of tree plantation on wastelands and reviews major public policies and programmes of afforestation of wastelands in India. He analyses the experience of tree growers' cooperative societies exploring the problems and prospects of scaling up this innovative institutional model. "Tree growing" is not a completely successful attempt. One of the major constraints recorded has been an inordinate delay in the transfer of degraded revenue wasteland to the tree growers' cooperative society. Obviously, the issue is one of a change in the property regime. The state is unwilling to transfer the property even to a cooperative society that has been recognised as the most appropriate vehicle for rural development. It is interesting to note that the Forest Department can exercise complete control over any tree-growing in a forest or on private land! Even the cooperative society cannot cut trees without an express permission of the Forest Department. There is no credit available for growing trees either. At times, market prices of the wood have not yielded remunerative returns to the tree growers. One has to agree with the author that this grand experiment does not seem to have a bright future. If wastelands are to be regenerated, the constraints will have to be removed. Regenerated wastelands have the potential to improve the microclimate, employment opportunities, and produce raw materials for wood-based industries.

Property rights, especially in land ownership, are so vital that a majority of experiments with natural resource development have got mired in the issues of rights and tenures in holding and using land. Even with their commitment made long ago and long-drawn efforts, the non-government organisations (NGOs) have been able to make only a limited impact in improving the vegetative cover and livelihood regeneration. Neelima Khetan's paper, "Land Ownership Patterns: Implications for Natural Resources Development and Governance", attempts to share the experiences of Seva Mandir, an NGO, as it took up natural resource development in Southern Rajasthan. She contends that the potential for a sustainable development of natural resources and community participation is significantly defined by the nature of land tenure prevailing in the area. The paper describes the historical and social context including patron-client relationships. However, post-independence, the region has witnessed weakening of the resource base of the poor due to discretionary policies of the state which are often arbitrarily implemented. She regards lack of appropriate institutions and social capital as the major barrier to wasteland development. Private land parcels are treated first, and despite higher incentives for treating the community or large and pooled tracts of wastelands there are few takers. The NGO has found that it is difficult for the people to come together to treat community land, let alone act on a watershed basis. Of course, an important aspect that has been brought out in this matter is that there has been severe encroachment on community land parcels. This feature is prevalent not only in the study area, but its presence has also been documented extensively in many arid and semi-arid regions (Iyengar and Shukla 2002). The government's authoritative attitude, she points out, has emasculated local institutions so much and eroded social capital to such an extent that the peasants have lost their associational capacity. Khetan's observation is a sad commentary on the way in which, under distributive governance, the domineering state with its bureaucracy has led to the wilting of local institutions. One of the major issues highlighted in the paper is the need for revitalising the people's interest in NRM work, which can be accomplished only by building on their existing stake in land and using this engagement for addressing the more contested areas of the NRM.

In arid and semi-arid regions, management of grasslands rested with those communities that survived on livestock. However, over a period of time occupation diversification has led the people who were earlier solely depending on livestock or agriculture for livelihood to take up multiple activities. This has created pressure on land in general and particularly on the common pool lands in arid and dry areas. While many villages and communities suffered in Rajasthan due to this trend, there are cases where the community institutions have been renovated for the better. Sunil Ray in his paper, "Institutional Renovation for Pastureland Development in a Village of Rajasthan", analyses the way in which institutional renovation helped the village community to grow and conserve its grasslands and generate economic gains. He traces the development of local institutions for management of local resources and examines what potentials these institutions have for development in economically diverse and socially divided conditions. Clarity of property right helps in institutional arrangements immensely. In this case, the government agreed to transfer part of the revenue land to the village common land for grassland. The transfer infused a new confidence in the informal group that had been formed to tackle the grass and fuelwood scarcity. It must be noted that more than one NGO helped the village community to build their capacities for mobilising and organising themselves. Nevertheless, they framed the rules of the game based on their traditional understanding and social norms that prevailed.

Historically, wetlands are also common property resources. Attention towards wetlands has grown since the Ramsar Convention in 1971. Wetlands act as a continuum between land and water. They support important ecosystems and with the rise in population and development of economic activities, wetlands have come under pressure, they are fast disappearing too. Madhu Verma, Nishita Bakshi and Ramesh Nair present in their paper, "Role of Multiple Stakeholders for Sustainable Management of Water Resources: The Case of an Urban Wetland of Madhya Pradesh", on Bhoj which is the largest lake in western-central India. Over time, the Bhoj wetland has been shrinking. International organisations have shown interest in restoring it to its past status. People living in the city of Bhopal, where the lake is located, have also shown interest in protecting it from further degradation. The authors have undertaken an extensive study using contingent valuation method and shown that there is willingness to pay to restore the ecological and environmental services of the wetland. The discussion is an exhaustive exercise in applied environmental economics. One of the important requirements, as the papers on land issues have argued, is to achieve stakeholders' participation at multiple levels. The authors attempt to conceptualise the model with causes, impact and feedback control strategies by using Oakerson's Basic Interaction Model for Common Property Resource Management. The paper also assesses the impact of economic, ecological, social and technological factors on the lake's ecosystem and suggests control strategies through a feedback mechanism and by following a holistic approach toward sustainable management. The authors rightly state that the critical need is to recognise the inter-linkages and benefits that could be obtained if the wetland is managed in an integrated manner and is used sustainably.

Watershed Development : As if People Mattered

Government programmes for natural resource regeneration, especially in arid and semi-arid areas, brought back the watershed approach with full vigour after 1994, with an important shift in paradigm. The programmes envisaged participation of people in the planning and implementation. Mihir Shah and P.S. Vijay Shankar in their paper, "Watershed Reforms in India", argue that policy makers do not adequately focus on the need for and scope of reforms in programmes that directly influence the livelihood of disadvantaged people.

Watershed programmes, aimed at increasing productivity of small and marginal farmers in the dry lands, hold the key to future agricultural development, employment generation and poverty alleviation in India. They emphasise the need to focus attention on technologies that help reduce evaporation and make productive use of soil moisture. The paper also reflects on the importance of carefully designed strategies for implementation and minimising the weaknesses of programmes implemented by NGOs and government agencies. This stems from the recognition that, as an approach, a participatory watershed programme is indeed a departure from the past. The paper brings out the need for sustainable groundwater harvesting as an integral part of watershed programmes. They make a pertinent observation, namely, that the problem in India's watershed programme is the overly concern with the modalities of fund allocation, while the weakest links are equity and people's involvement and empowerment. The recognition of the lack of an alternative implementation mechanism that can match the operational scale of the government is underscored in the paper, which concludes with an outline of macro-economic model of a reformed watershed programme in India.

One reason why participation is the weakest link is that it is mostly sought at the end of the project and from above. Deshpande and Bhende, in their paper, "Participatory Approach in a Resources Centred Programme: A Review of the Socio-Economic Issues", complement Shah and Shankar's paper with their focus on participation of stakeholders in a resource-centred programme, taking stock of the socio-economic aspects of the process. The paper deals with the concept of participation based on the review of theoretical and empirical studies. It is clear that for a successful implementation of the watershed development programmes, cohesive groups are the prime requisite. Five major areas of conflicts that act as stumbling blocks in the process of participation have been identified: (i) social politicisation, (ii) illegal use of resources, (iii) lack of positive discrimination, (iv) conflict between upper and lower reaches in the accrual of benefits, and (v) displacement to accommodate different watershed structures. Methods of organising people for watershed management are discussed and the institutional, attitudinal, and other socio-economic constraints relating to the policy, information and interagency coordination are listed which make it difficult to obtain and sustain participation of beneficiaries. They wonder why the participation sought in the government-run programmes fails to last and works against the very design of the development intervention. The authors believe that the socio-psychological aspects of group participation are extremely important and show that some processes in the government programmes are designed in a way that are destined to fail. The government programmes have generally failed to take into account the factors that ensure meaningful and sustained participation of stakeholders from the beginning to the end. They find that the involvement of NGOs in the process has shown more promise in making the watershed programme successful. There seems to be an agreement that resource-centred programmes have a better potential to succeed with a genuine and well-designed participation.

Participatory Irrigation Management: A Reform or a Programme?

Parthasarathy's paper, "Objects and Accomplishments of Participatory Irrigation Management Programme in India: An Open Pair of Scissors", acknowledges that years of community management of water resources has led to the belief that it has the potential to address problems of stagnating agricultural productivity in the command areas of major irrigation projects. One frequently cited reason for this is that the existing irrigation systems are mismanaged and in a state of serious disrepair. The breakdown, it is argued, could be seen most vividly at the village level where government administration of water delivery has become so ineffective that in most cases farmers do not receive assured, adequate and timely supply. The participatory irrigation management programme, set up as a prelude to irrigation management transfer to users, is seen as a step in the direction of involving users in the management of the resource. Though it is recognised that the government should no longer be in the business of retailing water to individual consumers, the paper argues that the PIM policy or Act as an instrument lacks the sharpness to catalyse farmer management as a cutting edge to irrigation sector reforms. In fact, as the analysis shows, the objectives of the reform measures and the actual achievement have been moving in the opposite directions so far. As is well known most systems, whether large or small, have serious problems relating to water distribution and use-efficiency. Therefore, it is argued that just a shift in the responsibility of the day-to-day management, though necessary, will not be sufficient to improve the performance of the system. Further, the evolution of water distribution protocols that are temporally or spatially sensitive cannot be achieved in the short run, unless an enabling environment is created. Given these constraints, the author attempts to understand why the physical achievement of management transfer programme in its six years of existence in Gujarat is slow.

The paper highlights some of the measures that are required to close the gap between goals and practices. Regarding the participatory approach to what is essentially a reform process, the paper points out that the governmental indifference to the implementation of the irrigation management transfer is largely due to the approach itself; and, in no small measure, due to having to fulfil the obligations like repairing the systems before transferring. The author underscores the need to assess critically the shortcomings of the programme and recognise the four areas, the political establishment, policy makers, NGOs, and communities as critical to the success of the programme.

Vishwa Ballabh discusses one of the grey areas in water management in his paper, "Politics of Water Management: Missing Links in the Debate". He presents the broad political debate and politics of water management and argues that the politics in water should be understood at different levels. His analysis identifies interest groups in the water sector, defines their objectives, and examines whether they have succeeded in achieving their goals or not. Overall, interests of these groups appear to coincide which helps maintain the status quo in the water sector. This, in a way, helps the water resources department to maintain its power and authority and remain dominant in the water sector. The powerful interests subscribe to those strategies and policies, which promise an increased supply of water, possibly free of cost. Ballabh believes that the dominant rationality and legitimacy continue to focus on increasing the water supply and finds that the alternative that focuses on decentralised management of limited water and devolution of power to the local level is often being ignored. He argues that the strategy of creating a new infrastructure in the sector is not an answer to the current problem. On the other hand, a real reform in the water sector can be brought about only through reorienting of water resources departments in such a way that space is created for a meaningful participation of the local bodies. Without this reorientation, according to Ballabh, problems will be compounded.

In many respects, the short paper by Anil Shah, "Fading Shine of Golden Decade", sums up the problems that have been raised by the various authors in the volume and goes on to put the changes in the governmental perspective on participatory approaches in a chronological order. Shah points out that in the 1990s three major programmes in the sectors of forestry, land management and water were launched, namely, Joint Forest Management (JFM), Watershed Development Programme (WDP) and Participatory Irrigation Management (PIM). He terms the decade of the 1990s as the *golden decade* when a number of programmes of participatory management in natural resources were initiated. In fact, in 1990, JFM—a watershed in the history of forest management—was implemented. As far as water management is concerned, the paper describes Watershed Development Programme of 1994 as a silent revolution. In 1997 Andhra Pradesh took a historical step in resource management when it adopted the model of transferring the government canals to farmers' organisations. The paper draws on the positive aspects and effects of the government policies. At the same time, the analysis also points out the weaknesses and flaws of watershed development. Later on, the shine of the golden decade had begun to fade by the time the discussion on the proposals for the Tenth Five Year Plan took place. Instead of reaping the benefits of earlier policies by providing them more support and encouragement, the government tried to strangle the system with the introduction of rigid and stringent measures. In the Watershed Development Programme, the stranglehold of Panchayat Raj institutions has increased, which has deprived the local community and non-government organisations (NGOs) of their command over financial and other resources. The Panchayati Raj institutions are yet to attend satisfactorily to their mandatory duties of governance, let alone take over the management of development programmes like watershed. In any case they are ill equipped to manage development programmes. The question is, just when the user groups are learning to function well, why lose momentum? In the opinion of Shah, the newly introduced Swajaldhara Programme violates the very principles on which the WDP is based. The National Afforestation

Programme has also put the JFM in the reverse gear. The scope for genuine participation of people in resource planning, development and conservation therefore appears to be in jeopardy. By not adequately supporting the new system, the government ensures that it performs poorly thus proving the case for state management. The "benevolent" mask of the establishment would, thus, once again, come off.

Evidently, the state of development in the Western and Central states of India shows considerable dynamism and as expected throws up certain challenges. The foci of planning strategies and implementation have been varied and that many actors have chipped in to make the recent economic and social developmental mosaic. Some of the issues that the authors of this volume have brought to the fore are: role of government, state of natural resources and social sector. Repeatedly, scholars have pointed out that the neglect of the social sector has led not only to declining social benefits but also perpetuated the existing inequities. That the trend is more evident after the liberalization era is no coincidence. Perhaps it is the dynamic process that is unleashed by the forces of private-public differences in investment expectations. Conversely, the declining government role and the expectation that it would necessarily contribute positively to development of the sector also does not seem to hold water. The cases of irrigation management turnover and watershed programmes show that public participation, when enlisted, fails. Alternatively, it is also suggested that enlisting of participation is only a phase in the development state! Where does the contradiction begin? It is true that developmental paradigms are not static yet strategies for development ought to have consistency of both plan and action. If the theory of "fading shine of the golden decade," is true, as it seems, then, the developmental planning and strategies for or toward resources seem nebulous at present. At this juncture, this collection of papers offers insights in to a variety of interrelated issues. The issues raised by the scholars in some cases and alternatives suggested, we hope, they would be useful various actors involved in the perspective planning of the state.

REFERENCES

Agarwal, Anil and Sunita Narain, eds. (1997): *Dying Wisdom: Rise, fall and Potential of India's traditional water harvesting systems.* New Delhi: Centre for Science and Environment.

Agarwal, Bina (1994): *A Field of One's Own: Gender and Land Rights in South Asia.* Cambridge: CUP.

Bardhan, Pranab (1996): "Decentralized Development," *Indian Economic Review* 31:2, pp. 139-56.

Bhalla, S. (1976): "New Relations of Production in Haryana Agriculture," *Economic and Political Weekly* (Review of Agriculture) 11:13, 27 March, pp. A23-A30.

Brewer, J., S. Kolavalli, A.H. Kalro, G. Naik, S. Ramnarayan, K.V. Raju, R. Sakthivadivel (1999): *Irrigation Management Transfer in India: Policies, Processes and Performance.* New Delhi: Oxford & IBH Publishing.

Bruns, Bryan Randolph and Ruth Meinzen-Dick (2000): *Negotiating Water Rights,* New Deihi: Vistar Publications.

Chambers, Robert (1988): *Managing Canal Irrigation: Practical Analysis from South Asia.* New Delhi: Oxford & IBH Publishing.

Chambers, Robert, N.C. Saxena and Tushaar Shah (1989). *To the Hands of the Poor: Water and Trees.* New Delhi: Oxford & IBH Publishing.

Dholakia, Ravindra, and Iyengar, Sudarshan (1991): *Planning for Rural Development: Issues and Case Studies.* Bombay: Himalaya Publishing Company.

Dreze, Jean and Amartya Sen (1995): *India: Economic Development and Social Opportunity.* New Delhi: Oxford India Paperbacks.

Gadgil, Madhav and Ramachandra Guha (1992): *This Fissured Land: An Ecological History of India.* Delhi: Oxford University Press.

Gadgil, Madhav and Ramachandra Guha (1995): *Ecology and Equity: The Use and Abuse of Nature in Contemporary India.* New Delhi: Penguin.

Hirway, Indira; Kashyap, S.P.; and Shah, Amita (2002): *Dynamics of Development in Gujarat.* New Delhi: Concept Publishing Company.

Iyengar, Sudarshan, and Oza, Digant (2002): *Gujarat Ek Sarvayyu* (in Gujarati), Mumbai and Ahmedabad: Navbharat Sahitya Mandir.

Iyengar, Sudarshan, and Shukla, Nimisha (2002): "Common Property Land Resources in India: Some Issues in Regeneration and Management", in Dinesh K. Marothia (ed.) *Institutionalising Common Pool Resources.* New Delhi: Concept Publishing Company.

Iyengar, Sudarshan, and Hirway, Indira (2001): *"Introduction"* in S. Iyengar and Indira Hirway (ed.) *In the Hands of the People: Selected Papers of Anil C. Shah.* Ahmedabad: Gujarat Institute of Development Research, Centre for Development Alternatives and Development Support Centre.

Jodha, N.S. (1992): *Common Property Resources: A Missing Dimension of Development Strategies.* World Bank Discussion Paper No. 169, Washington: World Bank.

Kadekodi, Gopal, Kanchan Chopra and M.N. Murthy (1989): "Peoples' Participation and Common Property Resources", *Economic and Political Weekly,* December 23-30, A 189-95.

Kohli, Atul (1990): *Democracy and Discontent: India's Growing Crisis of Governability.* Cambridge: CUP.

Kohli, Atul (1987): *The State and Poverty in India: The Politics of Reform*. Cambridge: CUP.

Korten, David C. (1990): *Getting to the 21st Century: Voluntary Action and the Global Agenda*. West Hartford, Conn: Kumarian Press

Maloney, Clarence and K.V. Raju (1994) *Managing Irrigation Together: Practice and Policy in India*. New Delhi: Sage.

Meinzen-Dick, Ruth S., L. Brown, H.S. Feldstein and A.R. Quisumbing (1997): "Gender, Property Rights and Natural Resources," *World Development* 25:8, pp. 1303-1315.

Mendelsohn, Oliver and Marika Vicziany (1998): *The Untouchables: Subordination, Poverty and the State in Modern India*. Cambridge: CUP.

Moench, Marcus (1998): "Allocating the Common Heritage: Debates Over Water Rights and Governance Structures in India," *Economic and Political Weekly* 33:26, June 27, pp. A46-A53.

Mosse, David (1994): "Authority, Gender and Knowledge: Theoretical Reflections on the Practice of Participatory Rural Appraisal," *Development and Change* 25:3, pp. 497-526.

Ostrom, Elinor (1990): *Governing the Commons: The Evolution of Institutions for Collective Action*. Cambridge: CUP.

Parthasarathy, R (2000): "Participatory Irrigation Management Programme in Gujarat: Institutional and Financial Issues", *Economic and Political Weekly*, 35: 35&36, pp. 3147 - 3154.

Parthasarathy, R and S. Iyengar (1998): "Participatory Water Resources Development in Western India: Influencing Policy and Practice through Process Documentation Research", in Mosse, Farrington and Rew (ed.) *Development as Process: Concepts and Methods for Working with Complexity*. London: Routledge.

Prabhu, Seeta K. (2001): *Economic Reforms and Social Sector Development: A Study of Two Indian States*. New Delhi: Sage Publications.

Sengupta, N. (1991): *Managing Common Property: Irrigation in India and the Philippines*. New Delhi: Sage Publications.

Shah, Tushaar (1993): *Groundwater Markets and Irrigation Development: Political Economy and Practical Policy*. Bombay: Oxford University Press.

Shiva, Vandana (1988): *Staying Alive: Women, Ecology and Development*. London and New Delhi: Zed Books Ltd., and Kali for Women.

Vaidyanathan, A. (1999): *Water Resource Management: Institutions and Irrigation Development in India*. New Delhi: Oxford University Press.

van Koppen Barbara, R., Parthasarathy and Constantina Safilou (2002): *Poverty Dimensions of Irrigation Management Transfer in Large Scale Canal Irrigation in Andhra Pradesh and Gujarat, India*. Research Report 61. International Water Management Institute: Sri Lanka.

Wood, John R. (1987): "Reservations in Doubt: The Backlash Against Affirmative Action in Gujarat, India," *Pacific Affairs* 60:3, pp. 408-430.

Zwarteveen, Margreet S. (1997): "Water: From Basic Need to Commodity: A Discussion on Gender and Water Rights in the Context of Irrigation, *World Development* 25:8, pp. 1335-134.

2

Economic Reforms and Development Strategy in Gujarat

RAVINDRA H. DHOLAKIA

In a multilevel federal democracy a state often represents a middle level between the central government and the local bodies. Gujarat had all these three layers of government efficiently functioning ever since its inception in 1960. The Constitution of India provides a reasonably clear division of the rights and duties of different layers of governments for achieving an overall development of the country. Within these broad constraints, different state governments in India have been following their own specific development strategies (*see*, Dholakia 1994). During the process of economic policy reforms and liberalisation, the constraints and regulation on economic activities by the centre in the different segments of the economy got relaxed. The states found more freedom and flexibility to pursue their own socio-economic agenda. It is not surprising that different states took advantage of this increased flexibility according to their physical capabilities, economic environment and ability to evaluate opportunities and risks involved. States were required to respond dynamically and compete with each other to attract the private sector activities by providing the most conducive economic environment. During the initial phase of the economic reforms, i.e. 1991-92 to 1997-98, Gujarat outperformed all other states in the country in terms of economic growth, according to the then member, Planning Commission (*see,* Ahluwalia 2000). It is, therefore, interesting to examine in detail the case of Gujarat, particularly the economic reforms and the development strategy it has followed during the nineties.

Development strategy in Gujarat state has been very clear and unambiguous ever since its inception in 1960 in according a high priority to industrialisation as can be seen from various state plans documents and the socio-economic reviews carried out annually. The state had made a clear choice of encouraging the secondary sector activities over the primary and tertiary sectors' activities (Dholakia 1994). It is a well-known fact that Gujarat lags behind several states in the country in terms of human capital and related indices. Between the human capital and physical capital related government expenditures also, the Gujarat government had consistently accorded higher priority to the latter (Archana Dholakia 1990). Thus, the development strategy of Gujarat state for industrialisation has been unbalanced growth with emphasis on Directly Productive Activity (DPA) rather than on creating Social Overhead Capital (SOC). While this has its own limitation for the overall development of the state, it has advantages in terms of clarity and consistency of objectives. Since Gujarat is well connected to other states, it has an access to their highly skilled technical and professional manpower, financial capital and physical infrastructure like ports, airports and means of communication. Gujarat has followed an open door policy with regard to the factor mobility—particularly the labour mobility in and out of the state irrespective of the political party in power. The endeavour of the Gujarat government has all along been to provide as far as possible the most conducive environment to promote business and industry in the state irrespective of who provides and owns them. In this sense, Gujarat did not have to make any major shift in its basic strategy in the wake of the liberalisation and policy reforms at the central level.

In the next section, we briefly discuss the concept of economic reforms and liberalisation and their possible impact on the level of economic activity in an economy. The specific instruments used by Gujarat state to promote economic growth through the private sector are then discussed in the four subsequent sections. Concluding observations are made in the last two sections of the paper.

II. Role of State and Economic Reforms

From 1955 to 1991, India as a nation followed the ideology of socialism and interventionist policy of direct state participation and control and regulation of economic activities. However, the process of a shift in the ideology from state intervention to market orientation initiated and speeded up since 1991 implies restoration of the functioning of the market forces in all markets by

(a) Removing or reducing quantity restrictions on supply;
(b) Removing price controls or other distortions; and
(c) Reducing unjustified or unnecessary market interventions by the government.

Liberalisation is a process of relaxing or reducing direct restrictions, regulations and controls on and participation in the economic activities by the government. Such direct interventions existing prior to liberalisation are conceptually similar to the quantitative restrictions. As against this, the government can also control and regulate the economic activities by imposing tariffs, charging fees, levying taxes, etc. These are conceptually similar to the price-based interventions. In a federal structure, the price-based reforms in the excise and customs duties, exchange and interest rate structure, or administrative price mechanism typically fall under the jurisdiction of the Central Government. State governments can exercise control only in matters pertaining to sales tax, minor taxes and user charges and fees on services provided by them. While State governments largely provide approvals and registration to smaller enterprises, restricting entry and exit of enterprises through licensing, reservation and specific legislations is largely under the control of the Central Government. The role of a State government to achieve faster economic growth under the existing federal structure is limited to what is feasible at the state level in terms of liberalisation and economic policy reforms on the one hand, and an effective resource base and socio-cultural environment in relation to the rest of the country on the other. It can be argued that the latter also depend on the policies of the state government vis-à-vis other states over a long period of time. The process of economic policy reforms and liberalisation at the state level, therefore, assumes special significance in providing a conducive environment in attracting and promoting private sector activities in the state. The dimension of inter-state competition in this regard makes the issue more complicated.

Generally, economic reforms are linked to the restoration of the functioning of the market forces in (a) goods markets, (b) services markets, and (c) factor markets that are likely to promote the growth of the private sector by encouraging it (i) to expand its existing activities in terms of scale and scope, and (ii) to participate in newer activities. These reforms usually apply uniformly to the existing and also new participants. However, competition among states often compels them to discriminate between these two sets of participants over varying periods of time. As a result, these measures do not represent policy reforms. Very often they actually contradict or negate the reforms. Prudence of ensuring sufficient revenue generation to be able to afford to offer various sops to attract industry into the state is often sacrificed with disastrous fiscal consequences in several states. These are not very uncommon outcomes in the framework of non-cooperative games.

Keeping this context in view, we can review the efforts made by the Gujarat government during the nineties to promote the private sector in the state. Like several Indian states, Gujarat also used the following three instruments (Sengupta 1996): (1) providing tax-and cost-related incentives; (2) provision of infrastructure and input supplies; and (3) granting various approvals and clearances particularly to the small-scale, cottage and tiny sector units (since these sectors are effectively under state control). For Gujarat, we may also add the fourth distinct instrument, viz., restoring the market forces in the land market in the state. These instruments are reviewed briefly in the following four sections.

III. Tax and Cost Related Incentives

In the industrial policy of Gujarat state during the nineties, the major instrument used by the state until recently was reduction, exemption or deferment of sales tax by the new business and industry to encourage them to locate in the state. Such measures resulted in reduced sales tax revenue collection by the state. It was estimated that during 1991-95, on an average, the state lost Rs. 2.10 billion per annum on account of such incentives. This loss increased to Rs. 13.43 billion during 1998-99, Rs.17.76 billion during 1999-2000, Rs.41.19 billion during

2000-01 and Rs.37.11 billion during 2001-02. Nevertheless, such sales tax-related incentives were thought to be very powerful to attract the private sector units to locate in their territory and so all the states entered into the race of offering greater incentives. This was a harmful competition because sales tax has been the single most important source of tax revenue for almost all the states in India, and over-time this adversely affected Gujarat state's buoyancy. Moreover, serious doubts have been expressed about the efficacy of such tax-related incentives to attract the private sector activities in the state (Dholakia and Dholakia 2000; Marvania 1995, *et al.*).

So external intervention to foster cooperation among the states became necessary. And in a forum of the Finance Ministers and Finance Secretaries of all the states, it was decided through consensus to implement some sales tax reforms simplifying the rate structure by reducing the number of slabs, accepting uniform floor rates and allowing no exemptions from January, 2000. This was specifically intended to remove the unhealthy and harmful competition to attract industries to a state from another state.[1] Gujarat was the first state to implement the floor rates and remove all exemptions. However, if other states do not follow such a joint decision, the leaders would be forced to bear the cost. Since several other states found excuses to delay the implementation of the decision, Gujarat was almost forced to have a fresh look at its industrial policy in terms of increasing several cost reduction incentives or subsidies to the private sector. Thus, subsidies substituted the tax exemption and tax reduction. However, the major advantage of the shift from the tax-related to cost-related incentives is that the budgetary process becomes more transparent. Previously, the subsidies were hidden and would not appear in the state budget, whereas now, they are explicit in the state budget. Other than this, there are hardly any significant benefits of such a shift in the policy.

Gujarat's Industrial and Agro Industries Policies, 2000, have attempted to provide cost related incentives to the private sector by increasing subsidies in various forms to attract them to Gujarat and "to make the industries globally competitive". Some of these measures are listed as an illustration in the Box.

Box 2.1: Incentives in Gujarat Industrial and Agro Industrial Policies, 2000

(a) *Interest Subsidy:* For new units in the small-scale and service sector industries, interest subsidy is offered @ 5 per cent p.a. up to a cumulative maximum of Rs. 2.5 million and Rs. 0.5 million respectively. For expansion and diversification of existing units, the interest subsidy is @ 3 per cent p.a. up to a cumulative maximum of Rs.1.5 million.

(b) *R & D Subsidy:* Financial assistance is offered up to Rs. 50 million per industrial cluster for establishing common facilities covering quality improvement, technology upgradation, market promotion and technical skills. Similarly, subsidy @ 50 per cent of the expenses up to Rs. 0.5 million for filing patents on the research by industries or R&D institutions is offered.

(c) *Quality Improvement Assistance.* Industrial units obtaining quality certification from approved institutions/research laboratories are offered subsidy @ 50 per cent of the expenditure up to a maximum of Rs. 0.2 million.

(d) *Backward Area Development:* Industrial units coming up in the identified backward talukas are offered additional incentives @ 25 per cent under all schemes.

(e) *Capital Subsidy:* For self-financed new SSI units, a subsidy @ 10 per cent of the fixed capital investment (max. Rs. 1 million); for employment park with employment in excess of 2,500, subsidy @ 10 per cent of the capital investment (max Rs. 20 million); for hi-tech park, subsidy @ 50 per cent of the capital investment (max. Rs. 25 million); for investment park with an investment in excess of Rs.5 billion; for share capital contribution @ 10 per cent of paidup capital (max. Rs. 25 million); for trade centres of more than 500 sq.mt. Construction, subsidy up to Rs. 5 million, etc. are offered.

(f) *Environmental Protection Assistance:* Interest subsidy for the industrial units undertaking environment protection measures is offered.

(g) *Land Provision:* Priority accorded to allocation of required land to industrial units with the "Deemed NA" concept is made more effective.[2] Land is proposed to be offered at affordable prices to industrial units.

(h) *Airfreight Subsidy:* For agri-industries and food industries, subsidy (max. of Rs. 1 million per exporter) and subsidy for market development abroad (maximum of Rs. 50,000 per exporter) are offered.

(i) *Project Report Preparation Assistance:* A subsidy @ 50 per cent of the cost of project proposal preparation for agri-industries is offered.

Several observations/comments can be made on the policy of the state to offer such subsidies with a view to attracting the private sector to the state. These are:

1. There are no in-depth studies or analyses justifying the quantitative extent of various subsidies and their internal consistency.
2. The direct subsidies are essentially substituted for the exemptions, reductions and deferments of the sales tax[3] given earlier and now discontinued under the cooperative agreement among the state finance ministries in the country. It seems that the extent of the various subsidies also derived so as to ensure neutrality of the net impact of the two alternatives on the state budget.
3. The replacement of the hidden subsidy in the form of tax sops by the above-mentioned explicit subsidies shows that there is no change in the basic philosophy, theory or approach of the state government for attracting private sector activities in the state. Under both the policies, the government believes in first allowing the Directly Productive Activity (DPA) and leave the infrastructure development to the felt need or shortages or political pressures rather than first creating the Social Overhead Capital (SOC) and wait for its utilisation. The advantage of such an approach for the policy-maker is that the government never becomes irrelevant and inconsequential. Under both these policies, discretion is retained with the bureaucrats and politicians. As a result, replacement of hidden subsidies by explicit subsidies does not adversely affect the illegal but private market for favours and discretion where the players are the bureaucrats, politicians and the potential beneficiaries of the subsidies. These are, however, the immediate or short-run implications. In the long run, since the extent of subsidies (and, hence, price of favours) becomes more transparent under explicit subsidies than under hidden subsidies, the pay-offs in the game become more estimable and competition among the players may lead to a decline in the extent of subsidies.

4. Most of these state subsidies are offered to the Small Scale Industries (SSI), which are defined as those having an investment in plant and machinery not exceeding Rs. 10 million. Questions may arise whether they are designed to promote the SSI or encourage the existing industrial units to break into SSIs leading to a disincentive for economies of scale. Such questions are no doubt very appealing theoretically but, considering the economic environment, technical possibilities of economies of scale, extent of relevant markets and the current definition of SSI, they sound impractical and far from reality. In a recent survey of SSIs in the state (1999-2000), it is found that out of 0.25 million SSIs, only 3 per cent have investment in plant and machinery in excess of Rs. 2.5 million. In fact, a closer examination of the list of subsidies would lead us to believe that their primary explicit objective is to protect the SSI rather than to promote them. This is also politically important because, like everywhere in the world and particularly in the developing world, SSIs are seen to be providing major employment opportunities to the local population outside the agricultural sector. Theoretically sound and practically acceptable arguments in terms of (1) imperfection of capital market, (2) unequal access to credit and labour, (3) underdeveloped local markets, (4) underdeveloped entrepreneurial skills, (5) fear of predatory practices by non-SSIs, and (6) consumers' concerns, are sufficient to justify the special concern of the state for SSIs.
5. Subsidies provided to a cluster of units in the form of employment park, hitech park and investment park aim of encouraging exploitation of external economies of scale—both pecuniary and technical. As pointed out earlier, it is not seriously examined whether such subsidies are absolutely essential or inevitable in Gujarat. Such policies are hardly ever decided independently. Very often they are imposed due to inter state competition.

Another tax-related measure the state government implements in 1997 was to abolish the turnover tax. Similarly, Octroi is a major issue in the state. It is an effective barrier on the movement of goods but puts an additional burden on the goods produced outside the city limits but are consumed in the city. This leads to adverse effects on resource allocation, efficiency and consumption. Moreover, it involves delays and inconvenience to the private sector ultimately giving rise to corruption. The Gujarat government abolished octroi in 143 towns and 14,000 villages in May, 2001. These municipalities, Nagar Panchayats and Village Panchayats collected Rs. 2.08 billion from octroi during 2000-01. This amount is now raised through a surcharge on the sales tax on petroleum products. The major proportion of the octroi revenue (above 80 per cent), however, accrues not from these 143 towns and 14000 villages, but from the six major municipal corporations in the state in which so far octroi has not been abolished in the absence of any viable alternative yielding a stable income. States of Karnataka and Rajasthan had to revert back to octroi after abolishing it because the alternative means could not generate the same amount of stable income for the local governments. The State Public Finance Reform Committee (SPFRC) for Gujarat (2000) had strongly recommended immediate abolition of octroi and suggested as alternative revision and realistic rates for water tax, property tax, health tax, education cess and user fees for various municipal facilities and services. The Gujarat Government has, however, not shown any determination so far to abolish octroi from the 6 municipal corporations in the state nor force them to revise their local taxes and user fees as per the recommendation of SPFRC (2000).

IV. Provision of Infrastructure and Input Supplies

In the second half of the nineties, there were major liberalisation initiatives in Gujarat in terms of providing infrastructural support and input supplies to the productive units in the state. Following recommendations in the report of the Gujarat State Finance Commission (1994), major reforms in the power sector were initiated around 1995-96 though not in a correct sequence. For instance, without addressing the root cause of the problems of the Gujarat Electricity Board (GEB), viz., inefficiencies in administration, production, distribution and inadequate tariff rates, the power sector was opened up to the private sector (Morris 2000). The policy statements on the Captive Power Policy (CPP) for the own-use and Independent Power

Projects (IPP) for the suppliers to the grid showed eagerness of the state government for private sector participation by providing guarantees against demand risks and losses. The policy succeeded in attracting several IPPs to produce and sell power to the GEB, but failed to make them cost efficient. As a result, (1) within a period of three years 2,300 MW additional power generation capacity was installed in the state out of the target of 5,000 MW in 10 years and Gujarat did not experience any major power cut in the past four years; (2) Gujarat, which used to face severe shortage of power, experienced marginal oversupply of electric power in 1999 and the state government introduced the *Tatkal Yojana* with high registration fees for new agricultural connections; (3) the GEB's financial situation started deteriorating seriously because it had to buy power at relatively high prices from the IPPs and it could not force tariff revisions nor remove inefficiencies in terms of Transmission and Distribution (T&D) losses which were of the order of 34 per cent. The state government started experiencing an unprecedented fiscal drag on account of the GEB and decided to impose a ceiling of Rs 11 billion per annum as subsidy limit to the GEB.

This led to the formation of an independent regulatory body in February, 2000 called Gujarat Electricity Regulatory Commission (GERC). It monitors the functioning of both GEB and IPPs and is empowered to take pricing and investment decisions in the power sector. The GEB is now required to take prior approval of the GERC for any new Power Purchase Agreements (PPA) and IPPs have also to refer their expansion plans to the GERC. Installation of meters for the customers of electric power by June, 2002 was made obligatory. This necessitated installing of six lakh new meters at a cost of Rs. 3 billion in about two years. With droughts and major earthquake, this target has not been met. The trifurcation of the GEB into production, transmission and distribution units was targeted to be over by 2004 and thereafter the possibility of privatisation was likely to be explored. The tariff revision for the agricultural use and industrial use was made by the GERC in early 2001 with the agricultural rates increasing five-fold times and the industrial rates by 4 per cent to 15 per cent. The implementation, however, is far from satisfactory on account of political reluctance and opposition. The GEB is also seriously exploring the possibilities of cutting down the cost of raw materials and downsizing its staff strength by about 50,000. These measures, if implemented quickly, would certainly help reduce the financial crises of the GEB and thereby the fiscal drag on the state government. As of now, however, neither the installation of meters and subsequent tariff revisions nor the ceiling on the subsidy to the GEB has been effectively implemented in the state on account of political reluctance. Future growth of the state economy depends critically on how this sector is handled in the state.

In the other infrastructural sectors like ports and roads, private participation is now encouraged. The Build-Operate-Transfer (BOT) policy on the lines of the Philippines and Chilean experiences is being adopted. Concepts of private ports and private companies owning their jetties are being implemented at the Pipavav Port. Similarly, out of 10 new port projects signed recently, 6 are planned to be in the private sector and the remaining 4 in the joint sector. The Gujarat Maritime Board is also being bifurcated and unbundled. Air cargo complex at Ahmedabad and such other complexes with private participation in the matter of storage of specialised cargo are proposed under the industrial policy of Gujarat, 2000. The road network to link the port and construction of underground pipes to transport commodities to and from ports are an important infrastructural development where clearer policy initiatives are expected (see Gujarat Chamber of Commerce and Industries 1998). Gujarat envisages 389 projects on infrastructure upto the year 2010 for implementation with private sector participation. For this, an Asset Management Fund has been introduced in Gujarat Infrastructural Investment Corporation (GIIC) covering the debt and equity funds to provide financial assistance to these projects. Moreover, subsidy at 25 per cent of infrastructure cost (subject to a maximum of Rs. 10 million) is offered to medium and large industrial projects coming up in the rural areas or extending the linkage facility to the rural areas. Similarly, Critical Infrastructure Fund (CIF) is introduced through the recent state budget to provide financial assistance up to 50 per cent of the investment on critical infrastructure requirement on a case-to-case basis in the industrial area of the state.

Gujarat Industrial Development Corporation (GIDC) has been providing comprehensive infrastructural facilities to the industrial units through their estates and sheds in selected locations in the state. It has now started handing over the management of these estates to the users. In four major industrial estates in the state, Notified Area Authorities are formed and, generally the association of shed-holders in a particular location is given the responsibility. The shed-users do not own the sheds but are given long-duration leasing rights (up to 99 years). Such associations work as usual by collecting membership fees and democratically electing representatives. Thus, the GIDC has started transferring the operation and management of the estates to the private sector after building the same. Similarly, since 1998-99, there has been a systematic effort to involve representatives of the private sector from the Gujarat Chamber of Commerce and Industries on the boards of the state government entities playing a vital role in the infrastructure and related matters of importance to the industry and trade in the state, e.g. Gujarat Electricity Board, Gujarat Infrastructure Development Board, Gujarat Pollution Control Board, Gujarat Environment Management Institute, etc.

In terms of Input Supplies, the State governments in India have a limited yet significant role to play. The most critical inputs where the policies of the Gujarat state Government can have a definite impact are water and coal. Gujarat is highly deficient in terms of both these basic inputs. For enhancing the effective supply of water to its productive users, there are two options: (i) increase the supply by building irrigation dams and harnessing water through better water conservation practices; and (ii) increase user charges to reflect the scarcity value of the resource. While the Gujarat Government has vigorously followed the policy of building irrigation dams, it has seriously lagged behind on other fronts. Even the Operation and Maintenance (O&M) of the irrigation schemes are not satisfactorily managed, nor are the charges for water supplied by such schemes revised regularly and adequately. After 1981, the water rates were revised upward only in 1999 for industrial uses and in 2001 for the agricultural use. Prior to the revision of the water rates, the cost recovery was hardly 15 per cent of the O&M expenditure and 1 per cent return on capital. The water rates had, therefore, to be revised substantially and sharply. For instance, the agricultural water rates have been raised 2.5 times on an average from their present level in January, 2001 and with an annual increase ranging from 15 per cent to 25 per cent for the next five years. These rate revisions are expected to ensure almost 100 per cent cost recovery (as defined earlier) after five years. However, the domestic and municipal uses of water are still highly subsidised in Gujarat considering the extent of water scarcity. This is, however, the subject of local bodies and not the state government. Moreover, the government of Gujarat also encourages private sector participation in the irrigation management by involving local bodies and Non-Governmental Organisations (NGOs). In spite of all these, Gujarat is still far from introducing a volumetric basis for water charges.

As far as coal is concerned, the Indian coal is of inferior quality and together with the heavy transport cost it becomes doubly expensive for Gujarat to use for power generation. Gujarat is seriously exploring the possibility of importing better quality coal from abroad to improve the efficiency and reduce its cost. Similarly, other industrial raw materials are also now available from the international markets since the quantitative restrictions on imports are relaxed at the national level. The State government has offered subsidies for the improvement of quality of products including industrial raw materials through the R&D efforts by the private sector as seen earlier.

The discussion of infrastructure and input supplies would remain incomplete without considering the Human and Social Infrastructure. In terms of the primary education and literacy, Gujarat's performance has been moderate. There are serious weaknesses in the state's secondary and tertiary education system. The students of the state are weak in communicating in the English language, a serious handicap in the modern IT and globalised environment. The domestic supply of technical and professional personnel in the state is also inadequate compared to the likely demand. The remedial action by the state government in this regard is not sufficient to meet the challenge. However, allowing private participation, accreditation and recent revision of user charges have a potential to go a long way to improve the situation. Similarly, healthcare is a weak area in Gujarat. Again, in this sector the major issues of revision of user charges, proper investment in facilities, quality of services and efficiency of the healthcare system need to be addressed seriously. However, very good healthcare services at a high cost are available selectively in the state.

The entertainment and hospitality sector has recorded a significant growth of late on account of rationalisation of the state's policies. The entertainment tax on cinema in the state was rationalised recently with only one uniform rate of 100 per cent replacing a complex rate structure. Several other forms of entertainment such as water parks, fun-fares, exhibitions, etc., are largely exempt under one or the other pretext. Similarly, the prohibition law is considerably relaxed on a selective basis for the star hotels to accommodate the liquor demands of foreign tourists and guests from outside the state. Although the physical environment in the large cities in the state is considerably polluted, it is very liveable on the periphery of cities and in smaller towns and villages. Moreover, Gujarat has the least disturbance in industrial peace among all the states though the average industrial wage rate in Gujarat is lower than in many states in the country. The state has a low crime rate relative to the comparable states and very often it is considered very safe and liveable state socially and culturally. Out of the two minor vices of the consumption of alcohol and tobacco (both of which are addictive and are injurious to health if consumed excessively), the Government of Gujarat has followed the policy of prohibition of the consumption of alcohol ever since its inception. Regarding tobacco, now the orders of the Supreme Court prohibit its consumption in public places and the free sale of tobacco products. The policy of prohibiting consumption of tobacco results in the loss of tax revenue (excise) to the Centre, but the policy of the alcohol prohibition leads to the loss of tax revenue (state excise) to the State itself. Perhaps this explains the enthusiasm of several states on the prohibition of tobacco consumption but considerable reluctance and unwillingness on the prohibition of alcohol although both have substantial benefits in terms of public health and social environment. While both these policies are operating in Gujarat, neither is effective in practice. On the whole, the human and social infrastructure existing in the state has not only been conducive but positively attractive for the highly skilled migrant labour to settle down in the state and be an integral part of its growth and development.

V. Approvals and Clearances for Industries

Gujarat has continued to achieve high annual growth rates of value added at 1993-94 constant prices during the nineties in the registered (10 per cent) and unregistered (8.9 per cent) manufacturing sectors. In terms of the number of new SSI units registered, the growth is impressive but has been declining of late, e.g. 14,631 (or 7.3 per cent) during 1997-98; 14,761 (or 6.8 per cent) during 1998-99; 14,437 (or 6.3 per cent) during 1999-2000; 13,325 (or 5.5 per cent) during 2000-01, and 5.6 per cent during 2001-02. The cumulative SSI registration in Gujarat as on October 31, 2001 stands at 263 thousand units

(Government of Gujarat, 2002). From these figures of growth rates of real value added in the registered manufacturing sector and of the number of new registered units in the SSI sector, it should be fairly clear that (i) the large scale units are growing faster than the SSI units in Gujarat; (ii) the SSI policy in the state does not seem to have encouraged the investors to break down their size into fragmented smaller units; and (iii) the annual growth in the registration of SSI units is came down fast during the latter half of the nineties. Moreover, as per, the 2000-01 census of the SSI, about 76 per cent of the 223 thousand registered units were found working and majority of them producing the products not reserved for the SSI sector. Since there is no restriction on the exit from the SSI sector, survival of 76 per cent units reflects very positively on the existing environment for the SSIs in the state. The regional spread of the new SSI units registered in the state during 2000-01 shows that hardly 6.2 per cent of the units are located in the metropolitan areas; about 60.6 per cent of the new units are located in the urban areas excluding the metropolitan areas, and about 33.2 per cent of the new units are located in the rural areas (Government of Gujarat 2001). The emerging urban centres, smaller towns and villages are largely attracting the new SSI units in the state. The district and Nagar Panchayats and municipalities are, therefore, likely to play an important role in attracting the industry and trade. Removal of octroi from these towns and villages would further strengthen this trend. The state industrial policy accords priority to promote identified thrust industries including electronics, engineering, ancillaries, garments, gems and jewellery, food and agri-processing industries, leather goods, other labour intensive industries and 100 per cent Export-Oriented Units (EOU). A separate incentive scheme including speedy approval has been introduced to promote such thrust industries in the state.

At the district level it is the District Industries Centre (DIC) that plays a pivotal role in the promotion of industries. The principal objective of establishing the DIC is to provide all assistance under one roof to the entrepreneurs engaged in different types of industries and to those proposing to establish small and cottage industries in the district (Government of Gujarat, 1999). The state government has made the DICs more effective and operational by delegating the powers concerning registration for several developmental and subsidy purposes. Thus, registration for cash subsidy, SSI registration certificate for sales tax exemption, recommendation of loans and loans under artisan schemes, etc., have been delegated to the DICs. This not only simplifies procedures but also effectively decentralises the developmental decisions providing further incentives to the administration to become people-oriented. As a result, District Industrial Executive Committee under the chairmanship of either of the Member of Parliament from the district or the Collector meets periodically to discuss and resolve problems of industrialists to the extent possible with the help of the DIC. Similarly, to ensure better co-ordination among various agencies working in the district, a Single Window Industries Follow-up Team (SWIFT) was constituted in 1996-97 in each district under the chairmanship of the district Collector. Moreover, at the state level a monitoring cell is established in the office of the Industries Commissioner to monitor the working of the DICs on a monthly basis.

The DICs provide registration for both the tiny sector and the small-scale sector. The validity for registration under tiny sector is for five years. Thereafter, the unit has to either renew the registration or get conversion to the SSI registration. Since January, 1999, there has been a major simplification introduced to expedite the registration of small and tiny sector units. Units with an investment up to Rs. 4 million in plant and machinery can now be registered without inspection. Officials at the DICs feel that more than 90 to 95 per cent of the small and tiny sector units would be covered here. This would cover not only the new units but also the hitherto unregistered existing units. There is a drive to register small entrepreneurs, rural artisans, cottage industries, etc., to enable them to get incentives available for such activities and also to strengthen the database in the sector.

For registration under the SSI sector, the procedures are also fairly simplified with only the following papers required to be submitted in general: (a) application form in duplicate; (b) notarised declaration on Rs. 20 stamp paper; (c) copy of rent receipt and of municipal tax bill in urban area; (d) copy of the partnership deed or memorandum of articles; (e) copy of the licence under Shops and Establishment Act; (f) power NOC or copy of the power bill; (g) sales tax number; (h) affidavit of machinery ownership or the list of machinery; and (i) copy of the first sales bill. Moreover, the SSI registration is now available almost on the same day of application. However, if the unit is in the following specified sectors, the necessary approval/permission is additionally required from the respective authority:

Sr. No.	Sectors	Authority Granting Approval
(i)	Pharmaceutical	Food and Drug Control Administration
(ii)	Chemical	Pollution Control Board
(iii)	Explosives	Department of Explosives, Faridabad.
(iv)	Pesticides/Insecticides	Central Insecticide Board

For larger units the states in India have a limited role. After liberalisation in this sector, approvals are needed only for six groups of strategic industries. For the rest, the procedures for environmental clearance are also simplified. Similarly, for 100 per cent Export Oriented Units, a letter of permission is needed from the Secretariat of Industrial Approval (SIA) in the Ministry of Industry, Government of India, to claim any type of benefits. Gujarat's new industrial policy proposes to set up an Export Park with 100 per cent EOUs to overcome delays involved in such approvals and permissions and derive external economies of scale in terms of administration of incentives to the 100 per cent EOUs. Moreover, the large-scale industries require non-agricultural land, power connection and several other infrastructural clearances. The DICs and the Office of the Industries Commissioner at the state level assist these large industries in getting what they want. DICs also perform the task of follow-up and monitoring the progress in such cases.

A major step was taken in Gujarat in 1999 to prepare and publish a citizens' charter for all the DICs. In this all procedural requirements are listed and the time limits prescribed for various clearances and approvals if the applicants have provided the necessary documents. Moreover, this is also monitored strictly by the Industry Commissioner almost every week since all these are computerised. Thus, unnecessary delays and harassment in undertaking of productive activity in the state are likely to reduce and quick disposal of applications and cases can be expected. All ready the efficiency and effectiveness of such measures can be judged by the growth of economic activities in this sector in the state as noted earlier.

The trade and industry often bitterly refer to the inspection visits by different government officials to the units during the year. The Confederation of Indian Industry (CII), Gujarat chapter, has estimated that on an average about 46 visits of government officials take place during a year to a registered manufacturing unit for "inspection" purposes. Out of these, about two-thirds are from the Central Government offices and the remaining one-third are from the State Government offices. For an unregistered manufacturing unit the number of visits is estimated to be about 28. This excessive number of visits point to the continuation of the "inspector raj" and a high degree of regulation and control leading often to unproductive but otherwise avoidable "transaction costs". Although the state government recognises the point made by the trade and industry, the government bureaucracy has not made any significant effort to reduce these visits by the inspectors. This is also the area where the Central Government has not made any progress. This is a complicated issue because the inspections are necessary for (a) enforcement of certain standards and laws, and (b) development and entitlement for incentives based on assets, production, etc. Those units where incentives are either claimed or sought, most of the approvals and several of the inspections become necessary. Otherwise, several of the approvals/ permissions and inspections are not necessary. The government officials at the state and the district levels in Gujarat, however, are not very clear about the proportion of the inspection visits between enforcement and development.

Currently, the following Acts and Ordinances need inspection for their satisfactory enforcement in a production unit: Provident Fund Act, Boiler Act, Employees State Insurance Act, Factory Act, Labour Act, IDR Act, Pollution Control Act, Food and Drugs Control Act, ISO/ISI Act, Agmark/FPO Act, Essential Commodity Act, Lubricating Oil and Grease Control Order, Molasses Control Order, Explosive Act, etc. Similarly for development and incentives, the inspection visits are required from banks, financial institutions, sales tax department, excise department, etc. Although it is generally agreed that duplication in inspection visits should be avoided, everybody feels that the inspection visits by the government officials cannot be reduced to zero. Even the concept of a Single Inspection Unit is not generally considered feasible under the prevailing conditions. Selective random inspection visits require a very strict and heavy punishment for the guilty and non-conforming units. Given the legal environment and aspects of the law enforcement prevailing in the state, this does not seem to be an effective option. Deregulation and liberalisation in the matters of inspection visits will require to be innovative and bold because the objective of inspection for enforcement is the welfare and safety of the people and workers, and for developmental incentives is the reduction of costs to the entrepreneurs. An effective solution of this problem could be found only when the developmental incentives do not remain discretionary but more general and objective rather than selective.

VI. Land Market Reforms

Another major liberalisation initiative is the abolition of the urban land ceiling in the state from April, 1999. This measure is expected to restore the legitimacy of the transactions in the land market in the urban areas. Now, the land can be freely transacted. It is hoped that the excess land locked up with several industrial units in the state can now be released for sale and development purposes. The effective land prices in the urban areas may, therefore, fall in the short run and housing and construction activities in the urban areas may boom. Moreover, the sale of excess land with industries in deep trouble can provide a very vital doze of fresh resources for their rehabilitation. However, it is feared that several industrial units located inside the city limits possess excess land not under their ownership, but on long-term lease. Thus, the excess land cannot be sold easily. The original owner in most cases is the state government or the municipal body. The decision to sell these lands or allow their sale is not being taken because it has a potential for malpractices and so the issue is deadlocked.

The Gujarat Government also simultaneously amended the Town Planning Act in 1999. It now requires the buyer of a barren and undeveloped land under the urban development authorities of different metropolitan areas to keep or surrender 50 per cent of the land for various infrastructural developments like roads, hospitals, parks, green land, etc. Previously the proportion was 35 per cent. The buyer retains the ownership of the land and can develop the necessary facilities on it charging the members joining the scheme a fee. Alternatively, the government or the urban development authority can buy the specified land from the buyer and develop the facilities if required. As it can be seen, this Act affects only the buyer on the periphery, which is undeveloped. There are already some protests and controversies regarding this Act from the owners of the new development schemes, but they are being settled. The purpose of this amendment was to avoid excess cost and disputes in the matters of providing the required infrastructure in future as well as make the users pay for the cost of infrastructure—at least a large proportion of it. This policy is quite consistent with the overall direction of reforms in the state.

On October 31, 2001, the state government took a bold decision to amend the Rent Control Act to tackle the problem of vacant premises and to encourage building construction in the urban areas. It was estimated that only in five major cities of Ahmedabad, Surat, Rajkot, Bhavnagar and Jamnagar, more than 0.8 million houses (dwelling units) are lying vacant. On the other hand, there is a tremendous scarcity of houses available on rent. This was ascribed to the Bombay Rent Control Act (1947) in force. The Act is now suitably amended so that for the new houses constructed or the ones under possession of the owners are exempted from the provisions of the Act for a period of 10 years. This will encourage renting of the premises lying vacant and encourage investments in the housing and hotel sectors. This is a major initiative taken by the Gujarat Government in reforming the land and property markets in the urban areas.

In the matter relating to making the land available to industries, the unique measure taken by the Gujarat Government in 1997 is to grant permission to convert agricultural land in to non-agricultural (NA) uses up to 10 hectares almost automatically. This cuts down the elaborate process and delays in obtaining the NA permission for land from the District Collectorate and encourages rapid industrialisation. This measure is particularly aimed at the large-scale industries. Considering, the low agricultural productivity and high density of industries with necessary infrastructural support in the state, this measure may be justified. However, of late, the state government has realised the urgency to activate the Land Use Board and put in place a realistic long-term Land Use Policy for the state since a significant decline of about 10 per cent in the net cropped area has been noticed over the past 20 years in the state

VII. Concluding Remarks

Table 2.1 presents the trend rates of growth in the different sectors of the Gujarat economy for the periods 1980-92 and 1991-01 based on the semi-logarithmic trend regressions on the GSDP at 1993-94 prices by sectors. The table helps us examine the shift in the implicit emphasis on different sectors in the development strategy followed by Gujarat after the reforms were initiated at the national level in 1991-92.

It can be readily seen that out of the 17 sectors, 11 sectors show statistically significant acceleration or deceleration in the basic trend rate of growth after 1991-92 in the State. The six sectors that do not show any statistically significant acceleration/deceleration in the growth include agriculture, registered manufacturing, electricity, railways, other transport, and storage. On the other hand, forestry, unregistered manufacturing, construction, trade and hotels, communication, public administration, and other services have experienced significant acceleration in their growth after 1991-92. These are the sectors where the emphasis in the development strategy of Gujarat seems to have shifted during the reform period. Surprisingly, the fishing, mining and quarrying, banking and insurance, and real estate sectors in Gujarat are experiencing a significant deceleration in their growth during the reform period. The first two of these are the natural resource-based sectors where Gujarat has a considerable potential, whereas the other two are the modern financial service sectors in which Gujarat should have substantial advantage given its emphasis on manufacturing and trade. However, a significant deceleration in the growth in these sectors implies that the focus of the development strategy in Gujarat is shifting away from the organised manufacturing and services to the unorganised sectors of the economy after 1991-92.

The private sector in Gujarat responded quickly and firmly to the policy changes signalling liberalisation and globalisation at the national level after 1991-92. It is clearly captured in the total collection of the customs duty by the Commissionerates in Gujarat over the years. The total customs duty collected from Gujarat increased more than five-fold during 1990-91 to 1999-00 at the annual compound rate of 20 per cent (Dholakia 2003). The share of Gujarat in the national customs revenue increased from 7 per cent in 1990-91 to 15.7 per cent

Table 2.1: Growth and Acceleration in GSDP at Constant (1993-94) Prices in Gujarat (1980-01)

Sr. No.	*Dependent Variable*	*Intercept* A	*Basic Trend Rate* b_1	*Acceleration* b_2	R^2
1	Agriculture	13.7580	0.0091	0.0175	0.1537
		(88.6330)	(0.4790)	(0.4560)	(1.6350)
2	Forest and Log	10.6620	-0.0023	0.0224	0.8010
		(608.8430)	(-1.087)	(5.1640)	(36.2440)
3	Fishing	10.0320	0.0926	-0.0670	0.9499
		(172.2000)	(12.9570)	(-4.634)	(170.7050)
4	Mining and Quarry	11.1910	0.0611	-0.0480	0.9603
		(339.8300)	(15.1430)	(-5.935)	(217.7400)
5	Registered Mfg.	12.6790	0.0779	0.0220	0.9670
		(205.5301)	(10.2990)	(1.4440)	(267.8435)
6	Un-Registered Mfg.	11.9830	0.0692	0.0196	0.9813
		(290.4290)	(13.6830)	(1.9200)	(472.9050)
7	Elect, Gas, Water, Sup.	10.3710	0.1028	-0.0150	0.9903
		(283.6550)	(22.9210)	(-1.657)	(924.6720)
8	Construction	11.5950	0.0439	0.0252	0.9475
		(233.1319)	(7.1928)	(2.0432)	(162.7330)
9	Trade, Hotel, Rest.	12.4700	0.0521	0.0268	0.9781
		(339.7560)	(11.5750)	(2.9456)	(403.4360)
10	Railway	10.7680	0.0258	0.0039	0.9075
		(318.5230)	(6.2350)	(0.4680)	(88.3304)
11	Other Trans.	11.1850	0.0820	-0.0130	0.9187
		(128.3820)	(7.6700)	(-0.627)	(101.7820)
12	Storage	7.0447	0.0138	0.0058	0.4664
		(104.4090)	(1.6706)	(0.3520)	(7.8670)
13	Community	10.1200	0.0591	0.0947	0.9947
		(353.7940)	(16.8490)	(13.3620)	(1704.8340)
14	Banking Insurance.	10.6740	0.1435	-0.0500	0.9848
		(183.0020)	(20.0530)	(-3.490)	(586.2330)
15	Real Estate	12.2320	0.0302	-0.0034	0.9998
		(8196.4060)	(165.2190)	(-9.0779)	(49563.8400)
16	Pub. Admin	11.2530	0.0476	0.0338	0.9372
		(180.6310)	(6.2280)	(2.1900)	(134.4450)
17	Other Services	11.6950	0.0504	0.0336	0.9939
		(596.2060)	(20.9700)	(6.9260)	1478.575)
	Total GSDP.	14.7490	0.0466	0.0243	0.9644
		(348.8210)	(8.9810)	(2.3230)	(244.4120)

Note: (1) The Regression Equation is: $Y = a + b_1 t + b_2 (t-t^*)D$ where $t^* = 12$ corresponding to the year 1991-92; and D is dummy such that D = 0 for t < 12 and D=1 for t >= 12.

(2) For cols. 3 to 5, figures in parentheses are t-values; and for col.6, the figures in parentheses are f-values.

(3) The critical values of t-stat are 2.09 and 1.73 for respectively 5 per cent and 10 per cent level of Significance.

in 1999-00. This should have arguably led to a corresponding increase in the export activity in the state over the decade. This is reflected in a recent estimate which puts the exports originating from Gujarat at Rs.49,496 crores or 20.75 per cent of the national exports in the year 2000-01 (GITCO 2002). This remarkable performance of Gujarat on the export front could be on account of the encouragement to the export activity from both the state government through several specific policies discussed in the previous sections and the national policies of liberalisation and globalisation since 1991-92. It seems that the strategy of development of the state economy through the export orientation has been effective in Gujarat. The GITCO (2002) study found that almost 50 per cent of the exporters in Gujarat were private proprietors or partnership concerns. More than 80 per cent were producers and exporters and about two-thirds of the exporters were small and medium enterprises. More than 40 per cent of the exporting units had come up only after 1991-92. Thus, the export orientation in Gujarat would imply a shift in the development strategy towards the unorganised sectors in the state.

To sum up the discussion, we can say that Gujarat has made subtle and significant changes in its policies to supplement the economic reforms initiated at the Central Government level. During the initial phase of liberalising the industrial sector by the Centre, Gujarat did not have to make any major changes in its policies. The changes in the economic environment made its strategy and policies followed till that point very relevant and attractive for the growth of the private enterprise in the state. However, after 1996 when the reform process at the Centre slackened considerably, Gujarat started its major efforts at state-level liberalisation. In this, the state government was constrained by the political consideration to protect the small and medium enterprises from the adverse effects of the liberalisation and globalisation. Of late, Gujarat seems to be facing some confusion over its development strategy. Within the overall strategy of "export growth through private enterprise," the state wants to achieve a high efficiency and productivity growth of resources employed in the state and simultaneously desires to protect some of the less efficient small and medium enterprises from the global competition with all kinds of subsidies. This confusion must end sooner than later. And when this happens the national reform process will be on the track and Gujarat would realise its benefits. The focus of the development strategy has, however, shifted away in the meantime from the organised manufacturing activity to the unorganised sectors in the state.

NOTES

1. Of course, such rationalisation of the sales tax within and across states has several well-known advantages for efficient public finance. It was required also as a necessary preparation for the introduction of the Value Added Tax (VAT).
2. NA refers to Non-Agricultural use of land. Previously, the District Collector's permission was required in order to acquire the piece of agricultural land to start an industry on it. Now the industry is required to inform the Collector within one month of starting the project after acquiring the land.
3. It may be noted that corporate income tax or any similar direct tax on industry and trade is not under the purview of the state governments in India.

REFERENCES

Ahluwalia, Montek Singh (2000): "Economic Performance of States in the Post-Reform Period," *Economic & Political Weekly,* Vol. 35, No. 19, May 6, pp. 1637-48.

Dholakia, Archana R. (1990): *Benefits from Government Expenditure in India—A Welfare Indicator Approach,* Bombay: Himalaya Publishing House.

Dholakia, Archana, R. (2000): "Fiscal Imbalance in Gujarat—Non-Tax Revenues and Subsidies," *Economic & Political Weekly,* Vol. 35, No. 35, August 26, pp. 3217-27.

Dholakia, Archana and Dholakia, Ravindra (2000): "Macroeconomic Performance and Tax Revenue—The Case of Gujarat State," in *Journal of Indian School of Political Economy,* Vol. 12, No. 1, Jan-March, pp. 21-34.

Dholakia, Ravindra H. (1994): "Spatial Dimension of the Acceleration of Economic Growth in India", *Economic & Political Weekly,* Vol. 29, No. 35, August 27, pp. 2303-9.

Dholakia, Ravindra H. (2003): "Measurement Issues in Comparing Fiscal Performance of States," (IIMA W.P. No.2002-01-05) appearing in *Economic & Political Weekly,* February/March.

District Industries Centre, Ahmedabad. (1999): *Nagarik Adhikar Patra* (Citizen's Charter), Office of Industries Commissioner, Government of Gujarat, February.

GITCO (2002): A Study of Exports from Gujarat—Final Report, prepared for Indext-B, Gujarat, March.

Government of Gujarat (1994): *Report of The Gujarat State Finance Commission,* April.

Government of Gujarat (2000 and 2001): *Gujarat State: Socio-economic Review,* 1998-99, 1999-2000 and 2000-01, Budget Publication No. 30.

Gujarat Chamber of Commerce and Industry (1998): "Proposal for Discussion in Sectoral Meetings", Gujarat Trade and Industry Conference 1998 held in Ahmedabad on 28th March.

Industries Commissionerate (2001): *Survey of Industrial Units (SSI, 1999-2000—Preliminary Results,* Government of Gujarat, Gandhinagar.

Marvania, P.G. (1995): *Pattern of Urban Industrial and Regional Development in Gujarat,* Ph.D. Thesis, Saurashtra University, Rajkot.

Morris, S. (2000): "Regulatory Strategy and Restructuring Model for Gujarat Power Sector", in *Economic & Political Weekly,* Vol. 35, No. 23, June 3-9, pp. 1915-1929.

Sengupta, D.N. (1996): "Deregulation at the State Level", *IIMA Working Paper No. 1327,* August.

State Public Finance Reforms Committee (SPFRC), Gujarat State (2000): *Report on Fiscal Consolidation in Gujarat—A Medium Term Plan, Gandhinagar,* Government of Gujarat, December.

3

Challenges to Sustainable Development

Some Issues in the Context of Gujarat

INDIRA HIRWAY

This paper examines the concept of sustainable development and presents some critical indicators of sustainable development for operationalising the concept, and it studies the pattern of development in Gujarat to assess its sustainability. It uses the analysis to draw relevant issues for promoting sustainable development for Gujarat. Part 1 examines the concept and indicators of sustainable development while Part 2 examines the extent of sustainability of development in Gujarat. The paper is based on several research studies conducted by us and it presents some work in progress on this subject.

1. Sustainable Development

The term sustainable development is frequently criticised as *a fashionable term* or as a *slogan without much stuff in it*. The term is also seen as a vague and weak term or as an umbrella concept that encompasses all good ideas on development. To an ecologist, sustainable development is *maintaining biodiversity*; to a sociologist, it is *maintaining cultural diversity and social harmony*; to an economist it is *self-sustaining economic development* and to a common man it is *conservation of resources*.

A critical question that arises in this context is what is it that needs to be sustained? Two broad answers that emerge from the literature are environmental resources and human well-being which include economic growth and social development in the context of the prevalent values like justice and equity. Eco-fundamentalists argue that resources must be sustained for maintaining intergenerational equity and sustainability of well-being. This approach, however, frequently does not take care of the following phenomena:

(a) Technological changes may generate more well-being from the same resources. For example, the New Report to the Club of Rome (i.e. Factor Four: Doubling Wealth and Halving Resource Use) argues that it is possible to double the total wealth by reducing use of resources by half.
(b) New technology in the areas of Cleaner Production, Pollution Prevention, Integrated Production Policies, etc., are able to reduce pollution, and as it is claimed sometimes, the reduction could reach a level that could be within the national abatement limits.
(c) It is possible to substitute environmental resources by man-made resources, at least to some extent.

Daly has given a good starting definition in this context. According to him, there are three simple rules for development to be sustainable: (i) those resources which are renewable are not used at a rate which exceeds the rate of their regeneration, (ii) those resources which are not renewable are not used at a rate which exceeds the rate at which a substituting resource becomes available, and (iii) the rate at which polluting materials are disposed of does not surpass the carrying capacity of the environment (Daly 1990). It needs to be noted that this is a dynamic concept, subject to technological changes.

However, sustainable use of resources does not necessarily assure maximisation or sustainability of well-being. The well-being approach, therefore, argues that one has to sustain human well-being for sustainable development. Sustained level of Gross Domestic Product (GDP) is not adequate for this, as it needs an addition of several critical factors that determine the level of well-being in a society. In a country like India well-being must include reduction in poverty along with a sustainable growth of production. In general, sustainable well-being must incorporate equity and justice which depends on the value system of the society on the one hand and institutions (for example, market, community and government) on the other. Neither the resources approach nor the well-being approach by itself is adequate. One has to combine both into a single approach of sustainable development.

The World Commission on Environment and Development (1987) has put it very well: "Sustainable development is a process of change in which exploitation of (environmental) resources, the direction of investments, the orientation of technological developments and institutional changes are all in harmony and enhance both current and future potential to meet human needs and aspirations".

In short, the focus of sustainable development is on a process which links resources, investments, technology and institutions with human needs and aspirations. One has to conceptualise this process in an integrated framework to understand sustainable development in a comprehensive fashion. Several environmental economists have presented models to explain the economic-ecological relationships. These models are formal or analytical and empirical or applied; evaluative (cost benefit analysis, cost effective analysis, environment impact analysis, etc.) and descriptive models (predictive models, economy-cum-environment models, or environment-cum-economic models), general equilibrium models, etc. (Chopra and Kadekodi 1999). These models are useful in their own way. However, a comprehensive theory of sustainable development is still not available.

The objective of this paper is not to present or discuss these models. What the paper wants to underline is that the concept of sustainable development is a highly complex concept or a process that involves a number of dimensions of development. Development is sustainable when these dimensions are taken care of.

Since there is still no precise definition of sustainable development, indicators have been developed to show whether an economy is moving in the right direction towards sustainable development or not. The indicators provide the required information to the policy-makers to formulate the right policies for achieving sustainable development (United Nations 2002). In other words, indicators help to operationalise this concept as they make it easier to talk about sustainable development. They translate the concept of sustainable development into numerical terms, descriptive measures and action-oriented signs and signals. As expected, these indicators combine social, economic and environmental trends.

Several sets of indicators of sustainable development have been developed by global and national organisations such as the International Institute of Sustainable Development (IISD), Commission on Sustainable Development for the United Nations (CSD-UN), and World Resources Institute (WRI), and by other research centres and scholars. The main problem in compiling these indicators has been one of balancing the complexity of sustainable development with the need for simplicity. Though the Bellagio Principles have tried to lay down the principles that should govern these indicators, the number of indicators presented by scholars has been very large, including the indicators presented at the recent International Summit on Sustainable Development.[1]

Working List of Indicators

The Working List of Indicators of Sustainable Development as designed by the UN (UN 2002) for the Johannesburg Summit on Sustainable Development primarily covers the subjects covered under Agenda 21. The indicators, which are presented in the Driving Force-State-Response framework, cover four broad areas, namely, social, economic, environmental, and institutional. There is a chapter related to the following indicators:

(a) *Social Indicators:* Combating Poverty, Demographic Sustainability, Promoting Education and Awareness, Protecting and Promoting Human Health and Promoting Sustainable Human Development;
(b) *Economic Indicators*: Share of Exports/Imports in the GDP, Changing Consumption Pattern, Financial Resources and Mechanisms and Transfer of Environmentally Sound Technology, and Capacity Building;
(c) *Environmental Indicators:* Water Resources, Seas and Coastal Areas, Land Resources, Fragile Eco-systems, Forest Resources, Sustainable Agriculture and Rural Development, Management of Waste, Biodiversity and Atmosphere; and
(d) *Institutional Indicators:* Integrating Environment and Development in Decision-making, Science for Sustainable Development, International Cooperation through Institutions, National Mechanisms—legal and other instrumental and NGOs.

The framework is presented in the Appendix. Though these indicators are fairly comprehensive, they are not satisfactory for understanding sustainable development for several reasons; (i) They are descriptive and are presented more or less independently of each other without showing their interrelationships; (ii) There are too many indicators with diffused focus—they do not identify correctly the important characteristics of sustainable development; (iii) The indicators are a mixed bag; they include input indicators, process indicators and output indicators; and (iv) The indicators do not question the established paradigm which may not be capable of leading to sustainable development.

There is therefore, a need to move a step forward to an alternative framework which presents indicators in an integrated manner. We propose the following framework for presenting the indicators.

(a) Interrelationship or association between economic growth, social development and environmental status in the long run,
(b) Impact of economic growth on environmental resources in the long-term prospective,
(c) Impact of economic growth on poverty reduction, including human poverty, in the long-term prospective, and
(d) Impact of changing environmental status on human development.

The above interrelationships and impact could be viewed in terms of the output-based parameters under this framework. This approach has the following advantages:

(a) It views sustainable development as a process that is related to economic growth, poverty, environment and social development;
(b) Though the parameters are descriptive, they do analyse the process that matters in sustainable development;
(c) One may develop these indicators into a composite index by using appropriate weights.

2. Assessing Sustainable Development in Gujarat

Using the above framework, an attempt has been made to assess the status of sustainable development in Gujarat. This empirical exercise uses secondary data and, in some cases, the available studies in the state. Since sustainable development is to be viewed in a long-term prospective, the analysis refers to the last two decades of the last century, approximately the period from 1980-81 to 1999-2000.

Economic Growth and Poverty Reduction

The growth rate of the State Domestic Product (SDP) and the rate of reduction in income poverty go hand in hand as shown in Table 3.1.

Table 3.1: Economic Growth and Income Poverty Reduction

CARG	*1970-71 to 1979-80*	*1980-81 to 1989-90*	*1990-91 to 1999-2000*	*1980-81 to 1999-2000*
NSDP	4.95	4.98	5.53	5.28
Per Capita SDP		2.84	3.38	3.53
Agricultural SDP	4.22	-0.81	0.72	
	1972-73 to 1993-94	*1983-84 to 1993-94*	*1993-94 to 1999-2000*	*1983-84 to 1999-2000*
Reduction in Income Poverty	-3.1	-3.2	-3.5	-3.3

- During the 1970s and 1980s when the state economy grew at about 5 per cent Compound Annual Rate of Growth (CARG), the poverty declined by about 3 per cent compound annual rate.
- During the 1990s when the rate of economic growth jumped to 5.53 per cent the rate of decline in poverty was 3.5 per cent compound annual rate.[2]
- It is clear that the relationship between economic growth and poverty reduction became much weaker in the 1990s.
- The per capita rate of growth is important in poverty reduction, but it appears to be less important than the overall growth rate.

Performance in Social Development

Performance of the state in the major areas of social development is given in a summary form in Table 3.2. Some of its highlights are as follows:

Table 3.2: Performance in Social Development

CARG	*1981-1991*	*1991-2001*	*1981-2001*
Population Growth	1.94	2.05	1.99
Sex Ratio	941	934 (1991)	921
	(1981)		(2001)
Decline in points	-7	-13	-20
	(1981-91)	(1991-2001)	(1981-2001)
CARG	-0.07	-0.14	-0.11
	(1981-91)	(1991-2001)	(1981-2001)
IMR	111	64	62
	(1981)	(1991)	(2001)
Decline in points	-47	-2	-49
	(1981-91)	(1991-2001)	(1981-2001)
CARG	-5.36	-0.32	-2.87
LEB	59.7	62.9	63.5
Increase in Points	+3.2	+0.6	+3.8
	(1981-1991)	(1991-2001)	(1981-2001)
CARG	0.52	0.09	0.31
	(1981-1991)	(1991-2001)	(1981-2001)
TFR	4.3	3.1	3.1
	(1981)	(1991)	(2001)
Decline in Points	-1.2	0	-1.2
	-3.22	0	—
Literacy Rate	52.21	61.29	69.97
	(1981)	(1991)	(2001)
Increase in Points	+9.08	8.68	17.76
	(1981-1991)	(1991-2001)	(1981-2001)
CARG	1.62	1.33	1.47
Children Attending School	—	63.85	79.52
		(1991)	(1998-99)
CARG	—	2.22	—
		(1991-2001)	

- In some areas the State has shown a negative trend, particularly in the 1990s. The compound annual growth rate of population has increased from 1.94 during 1981-1991 to 2.05 during 1991-2001; and the sex ratio has consistently declined during 1981-2001; the rate of decline during 1991-2001 was higher.
- The three major health indicators have shown lower progress during 1991-2001 than during 1981-1991. This deceleration

has been observed in IMR, LEB and TFR, with TFR remaining almost stagnant during the 1990s.

- The rates of increase in literacy have been very low during 1981-1991 (CARG 1.62) and 1991-2001 (CARG 1.33). What is worth noting is that the rate has declined in the 1990s.
- The compound rate of increase among the school-going children has been very low (2.2 per cent)

In short, (i) the rate of improvement in social development has been much lower than the rate of growth of the SDP, and (ii) The rate of improvement has decelerated (even stagnated and shown a reversal) in the 1990s when the rate of growth of the SDP has shown an increase. The weak association between economic growth and social development has become weaker in the 1990s.

Performance in the Environment Sector

The changing status of major environmental resources in the last two decades of the twentieth century is presented in Table 3.3. The table indicates the following:

- All the major resources have experienced depletion and degradation during the last two decades of the last century: Utilisable ground-water supply has declined at a compound annual rate of 2.29 per cent, and per capita availability of water has declined by 1.86 CARG. While the forest areas have diminished by 0.28 CARG, actual forest cover has gone down by 0.29 CARG, and dense forest by 1.25 CARG[3]. Land under wasteful use has increased by 0.53 CARG, while the area under DPAD and DDP has increased by 3.44 CARG; the area under mangroves has declined roughly by 7.77 CARG in the long-term prospective.
- In some cases the situation has improved marginally during the 1990s, but other regions, especially North Gujarat, Tribal Gujarat and Kuchchh-Saurashtra have experienced severe depletion and degradation in the long run (1980-2000).

Table 3.3: Environmental Status of Gujarat

Groundwater Resources				*CARG in % per year*		
	1984	*1991*	*1997*	*1984-91*	*1991-97*	*1984-97*
Utilisable GW Supply	17365.4	12277.6	12848.3	-4.84	0.76	-2.29
Per capita availability of w/s (m3)	1450	1322	1137	-1.3129	-2.49	-1.86
Number of non-white talukas	21	62	99	16.74	8.13	12.68
Forest Resources				*CARG in % per year*		
Decline in forest area (in sq. km.)	*1980-81*	*1990-91*	*1990-00*	*1980-90*	*1990-00*	*1980-2000*
	19655	18847	18590	-0.42	-0.14	-0.28
Decline in Actual Forest Cover (in sq. km.)	*1983-85*	*1991*	*1999*	*83-91*	*91-99*	*83-99*
	13600	11907	12965	-1.65	1.07	-0.29
Area under Dense Forest (in sq. km.)	7900	6224	6430	-2.94	0.41	-1.25
Area under Scrub Forest (CD<10)		*1995*	*1999*		*1995-99*	
		2647	2948		2.73	
Land Resources				*CARG in % per year*		
Land under wasteful use	*1980-81*	*1990-91*	*1996-97*	*1980-90*	*90-96*	*80-96*
	19275	19806	20983	0.272	0.99	0.53
Area under DDP / DPAP	*1980-81*	*1995-96*		*1980-95*		
	64129.2	104000		3.44		
Salt affected Area (in sq. km.)	*1980*	*1988*	*2001*	*80-88*	*88-01*	*80-2001*
	16900 (KLDB)	35984	50638	9.91	12.05	5.41
Coastal Resources				*CARG in % per year*		
Area under Mangroves	*1980*	*1999*		*1980-99*		
	2069	991		-7.78		

In short, economic growth, income poverty reduction, social development and environmental situation have not been in harmony during the last two decades in Gujarat. In fact, economic growth has not been translated adequately into social development, and it has had a very negative impact on the environmental health of the state.

The link between economic growth and poverty reduction on the one hand and social development on the other became very weak in the 1990s.

Economic Growth and Environmental Resources in Gujarat

Our studies on environmental resources in Gujarat indicate that the state has experienced severe depletion and degradation of its major environmental resources. The studies also show that the pressures exerted by the economic growth process in the state have been largely responsible for the depletion and degradation. No effective measures were designed to counter these pressures; the environmental resources were largely mismanaged.

As far as water resources are concerned, the major pressures emanating from the economic growth have been as follows:

(a) Agricultural growth, which largely depended on groundwater for irrigation in most areas, was a major drain. Free or subsidised power as well as subsidised construction of wells and tube-wells resulted in a massive extraction of groundwater which was done without paying proper attention to recharge.

(b) Neglect of local and traditional water harvesting structures for providing water for drinking and domestic use and dependence on a massive transfer of water from one region to another, coupled with almost free supply of water, resulted in a severe decline in the local water augmentation on the one hand and extraction of ground water on the other.

(c) Construction of medium and large dams on most rivers created obstacles in the natural water flows in many areas, particularly in downstream areas.

(d) Low water-use efficiency in agriculture caused by the from irrigation practices resulted in low returns per unit of water supply in agriculture on the one hand and waterlogging and salinity ingress on the other.

(e) Indiscriminate disposal of industrial wastewater, urban sewerage, agricultural water, etc., affected the quality of water adversely.

As far as *forest resources* are concerned, the pressures exerted by the economy may be listed as follows:

(a) Acquisition of forest areas for mega-infrastructural projects such as irrigation dams, roads and power lines and for cultivation has resulted in a decline in the forest area in the state. Illegal encroachment has further reduced the forest area.

(b) Extraction and collection of timber by felling trees (legally and illegally), mining and quarrying, gathering fuelwood and grazing of animals by local residents have led to depletion and degradation of the forest resources. The failure to make the tribals and the locals stakeholders in forest development has aggravated the problem.

As regards *land resources,* the degradation has been the result of the following pressures:

(a) Agriculture practices like overuse of water in irrigation, irrigation with saline water, overuse of chemical inputs and over-drafting of groundwater (leading to sea-water intrusion in coastal areas) have resulted in degradation of agricultural lands.

(b) Deforestation, scarcity of water resources, overgrazing of lands (including Common Property Land Resources), neglect of common lands, cutting of trees and exposing lands to water and wind erosion, etc., have led to desertification in some regions and severe land degradation in several other regions.

Coastal resources also have experienced severe pressure from economic growth processes in the coastal region.

(a) Construction of ports, jetties, ship-breaking and ship-building industries, growth of urban centres and rise in the urban population in the coastal region have affected coastal eco-systems adversely in many places.

(b) Setting up of industrial estates, industrial parks and mega-industries in the coastal region in the 1990s has exerted tremendous pressure on the coastal ecosystems. Oil spills, quarrying in coastal zones, indiscriminate disposal of hazardous industrial waste, etc., have adversely affected the coastal ecosystems.

(c) Overwithdrawal of groundwater, growth in the number of saltpans and salt industry, destruction of mangroves, etc., have increased coastal salinity of land and water in the region.

In short, the major cause of the widespread decline and degradation of natural resources in the state is the faulty development path chosen by the state through its various policies, programmes, subsidies, incentives and other interventions. The various interventions are basically aimed at economic growth—increase in SDP without worrying much about the composition and consequences of this growth. Water resources were developed by the government as well as by farmers (through direct interventions or through supportive and promoting policies) for raising agricultural production; industries were invited and promoted through very attractive policies to raise industrial growth; and the use of mines and minerals was encouraged to raise the gross production from minerals and mineral-based industries. The focus on raising SDP, almost at any cost, has been the main factor responsible for the gross negligence of natural resources in the state.

Impact of Economic Growth on Income Poverty and Social Development

The above analysis indicates that economic growth does not automatically lead to social development, in the sense that there is no one-to-one relationship between economic growth and social development. The elements that strengthen the relationship between the two could be listed as follows:

(a) An enabling macro-environment to facilitate social development.

(b) Direct efforts for promoting social development as reflected in the expenditure on the social sector.

(c) Composition of social sector expenditure in terms of the provision of hardware and software of infrastructure, quality of services, supervision, evaluation and monitoring, etc.

The above conditions are not adequately satisfied in Gujarat. Enabling macro-environment primarily includes, (i) employment generation during the course of economic growth which improves the access of the population to social services, (ii) favourable natural environment reflected in the decrease in the environmental degradation and reduction in the drudgery in the collection of fuelwood, fodder, water, etc., and (iii) abridged regional disparities and personal inequalities in economic development that lowers seasonal/temporary migration. These factors have not worked very well during the past decades. As seen above, the rate of growth of employment has been lower than the rate of growth of the labour force, considerable depletion and degradation of environmental resources have been experienced during the past decades, and the inequalities of development (as reflected in the development index of the Centre for Monitoring Indian Economy) have increased over time. Studies have shown that seasonal and temporary migration within the state has also risen during the recent decade.

As far as the efforts made by the government for promoting the social sector are concerned, the United Nations Development Programme has measured adequacy of social expenditure in terms of several ratios: (i) Public Expenditure Ratio, (ii) Social Allocation Ratio, (iii) Social Priority Ratio, and (iv) Human Expenditure Ratio. Our study shows that Gujarat has not complied with the norms implicit in these ratios during most of the years of the 1990s except for Social Priority Ratio during the last years for the 1990s.

Environmental Depletion/Degradation and Social Development

A careful examination of the status of social development in Gujarat has shown that environmental changes have affected the health and educational status of Gujarat in several ways (Hirway and Mahadevia 1999) As far as the impact of environmental depletion and degradation on the health status is concerned, the following has been observed by our studies:

Impact on Health

(a) The overall environmental degradation in the state has created/aggravated the shortage of fuelwood, fodder and water in several regions of the state. As a result, the poor and particularly women and children from poor households in the rural areas spend large amounts of time and walk long distances to collect these three necessities (Directorate of Economics and Statistics 2000). This seems to have affected the health and safety of women and children.

(b) Increased shortage of potable water supply and insufficient water supply for cleaning and washing in the state—there has been a continuous increase in the number of *No Source Villages and Partially Covered Villages* over the last two decades—have aggravated health problems in several regions in the state. For instance, the incidence of fluorosis, skin diseases, and stomach-related waterborne diseases has increased in several parts of the State. It has been estimated by us that the annual welfare cost of water-borne diseases in the state comes to around Rs. 2,000 crore (Hirway supported by Pathak, 2002).

(c) Depletion and degradation of forest over the past decades and general environmental degradation have encouraged tribals to migrate to distant areas in search of work. Environmental degradation in other areas also has increased temporary outmigration in several other areas. These migrants face harsh working conditions and low wages, and are forced to live in poor living conditions. A study has shown that as a result, their health is adversely affected; in particular, the nutritional level of tribals has declined over the years.

(d) The incidence of emissions from industries and vehicles has risen considerably in a large number of industrial and urban centres in Gujarat polluting the air. This has led to an increase in the respiratory and other related diseases in the state. The welfare cost of this air pollution has been estimated to be about Rs. 2,900 crore per year.

(e) Inadequate arrangements for the disposal of solid waste (i.e. domestic waste, hospital waste and industrial waste) and liquid waste have created serious health problems in the state.

In short, environmental depletion and degradation have taken their toll in terms of human health in the state.

Impact on Education

(a) The time needed for collection of fuelwood, fodder and water has frequently forced rural households to use children for this work. This has adversely affected the enrolment and retention rates of children in primary and elementary schools.

(b) Increased seasonal or temporary migration, frequently with families, has had a negative impact on the enrolment and retention rates of children in schools.

A recent study on female literacy in the tribal Gujarat has shown that a major cause for the low retention rate of tribal children (6 to 14 years) has been environmental degradation, which works in one of the ways mentioned above.

An interesting observation emerging from our studies is that a reduction in the income poverty in the state is not accompanied by a reduction in the human poverty. Indeed there is a trade-off between the two: *income poverty* has declined in the state to a significant extent by an increased out-migration of people since the migrants are able to have two square meals a day. However, this migration has emerged as an obstacle to the decline in *human poverty*. Surely this is not a favourable condition for human development!

Correlation matrix of all the concerned indicators is quite revealing in this context as shown in Table 3.4.

(a) Per capita income correlates positively and significantly with reduction in income poverty and with most social development indicators.

(b) Agricultural development still helps poverty reduction in the state, but industrial development does not seem to be helping it.

(c) Environmental degradation has affected most social development indicators adversely.

(d) Several indicators of different kinds do not correlate significantly among themselves.

Table 3.4: Correlation between Economic Growth, Human Development and Environment Status

A. Correlation Between Income Poverty and	*Co-efficient*	*Level of Significance*	*B. Correlation Between IMR and*	*Co-efficient*	*Level of Significance*	*C. Correlation Between TFR and*	*Co-efficient*	*Level of Significance*	*D. Correlation Between Literacy Rate*	*Co-efficient*	*Level of Significance*
Per Capita Income	-0.60	S	Per Capita Income	-0.65	S	Per Capita Income	-0.66	S	Per Capita Income	0.61	S
% Area under Irrigation	-0.55	S	% Area under Irrigation	—	NS	% Area under Irrigation	—	NS	% Area under Irrigation	0.60	S
Value of Agri-Production per ha.	-0.54	S	Value of Agri-Production per ha.	—	NS	Value of Agri-Production per ha.	—	NS	Value of Agri-Production per ha.	0.62	S
Value of Agri. Production per capita	-0.65	S	Value of Agri. Production per capita	—	NS	Value of Agri. Production per capita	—	NS	Value of Agri. Production per capita	—	NS
Average Agri. Wage rate	-0.78	S	Average Agri. Wage rate	-0.55	S	Average Agri. Wage rate	—	NS	Average Agri. Wage rate	—	—
Fixed Industrial Investment per capita		NS	Fixed Industrial Investment per capita	—	NS	Fixed Industriai Investment per capita	—	NS	Fixed Industrial Investment per capita	NS	—
No. of Factories per lakh population		NS	No. of Factories per lakh population	—	NS	No. of Factories per lakh population	-0.56	S	No. of Factories per lakh population	0.62	S
No. of Factory Workers per lakh population		NS	No. of Factory Workers per lakh population	—	NS	No. of Factory Workers per lakh population	-0.61	S	No. of Factory Workers per lakh population	0.66	S
Per capita Credit for Industries		NS	Per capita Credit for Industries	—	NS	Per capita Credit for Industries	—	NS	Per capita Credit for Industries	—	NS
% Area Under Wasteland	0.66	S	% Area Under Wasteland	0.57	S	% Area Under Wasteland	0.55	S	% Area Under Wasteland	-0.56	S
% Development of Ground Water	-0.72	S	% No source village	0.61	S	% Area Under DDP/DPAP	0.54	S	% Area Under DDP/DPAP	-0.59	S

Source: Various Official Data

Emerging Issues

Some of the issues emerging from the discussion in this paper are very relevant for understanding sustainable development as well as for designing policies for sustainable development for an economy.

The first major point is that the process of sustainable development is a highly complex process that interlinks economic growth, social development and environmental protection and promotion. There is a need to understand linkages and to formulate a strategy that reinforces the positive linkages. A sound theory of sustainable development is the need of the day.

In the absence of such a theory, one can use the indicators of sustainable development to understand these linkages. And keeping in view the need, these indicators are being presented in a framework that reveals their interrelationships instead of in a descriptive mode.

The sharp focus on economic growth in the established paradigm (i.e. the neo-liberal paradigm) neglects the other dimensions of sustainability: environment comes into the picture only for fighting degradation and depletion; and human development comes into policy-making only as a welfare component. In other words, environmental resources are not treated as natural capital and human resources are not treated as human capital or social capital in the policy framework.

In this context, the discussion on circular causation by Gunnar Myrdal is very relevant. Circular causation is a process in which a certain "variable" impacts another "variable" which, in turn, feeds back on the former one. This feedback can take place directly or through the mediation of intervening variables. There can be multi-causality at various levels and in many forms, but the feedback process is essential for circular causation. This feedback can either counteract the first variable or reinforce it. In the first case, the process tends towards an equilibrium; in the second case, the process is cumulative. If by such a process a state of affairs becomes worse, one speaks of a vicious circle. There are also virtuous circles, in which there is a cumulative process in the desirable direction. Reality is a confusing mixture of a variety of processes including many vicious and virtuous circles. We may use the term "development", then, for a systematic increase in human welfare through virtuous circles of causation between variables positively affecting that welfare. One should note that in this definition, human welfare is not limited to (the availability of) economic goods, nor are the variables affecting welfare only economic variables. Moreover, the "increase in human welfare", implied in the concept of development, does not mean that there are only cumulative processes involved. On the contrary. Beyond a certain point, human welfare is better served by counteracting and restraining feedbacks leading to equilibrium rather than by accumulation. Development by no means excludes "satiation" with respect to certain material components.

Development literature presents both positive experiences of capital accumulation strengthening social development and human development as well as negative experiences of the disruptive nature of capital accumulation, though the disruptive nature of the latter is predominant, particularly in the post-globalisation period. The process of development which becomes non-sustainable as it destroys natural capital without building up substitute capital could be one of the common examples of the disruptive nature of capital accumulation. It feeds on the destruction of the symbolic structures of nature and people on which traditional livelihood is based, including the survival knowledge and cultural capital. Some positive experiences are also documented in the literature by several scholars. These experiments show how manmade capital and natural capital can work together by reinforcing each other.

In short, there is a need to build a sound framework that reinforces the three major aspects of development, namely economically sustainable development, environmentally sustainable development, and socially sustainable development.

Sustainable Development in Gujarat

Our paper shows that the development in Gujarat is far from being sustainable. Though the state economy has achieved a reasonable rate of economic growth—and the rate has accelerated in the 1990s—there is a deceleration in the achievements in education and health, and even reversal in the case of population growth rate and the sex ratio. The state has also experienced severe depletion and degradation of all major environmental resources during the two decades which, in turn, have had an adverse impact on social development. The increasing divergence between economic growth, income poverty, social development and environmental status is not good for the health of the economy. This is bound to hurt even its economic growth sooner or later.

It is clear that there is a need to formulate a new approach for achieving sustainable development in Gujarat. Designing policies and programmes for environmental protection or designing schemes for improving school infrastructure, etc., may not help much because such efforts do not modify the process of economic development adequately. There is a need to take a fresh look at the development of Gujarat and formulate policies that build on the interrelationships among the different components of sustainable development.

APPENDIX

THE APPENDIX: AGENDA 21

Chapters of Agenda 21	*Driving Force Indicators*	*State Indicators*	*Response Indicators*
Category: Social			
Chapter 3: Combating Poverty	-Unemployment rate	-Head count index of Poverty -Poverty gap index -Squared poverty gap Index -Gini index of income -Ratio of average female wage to male wage	
Chapter 5: Demographic Dynamics and Sustainability	-Population growth rate -Net migration rate	-Population density -Total fertility rate	
Chapter 6: Protecting and promoting human health		-Basic sanitation: Percentage of population with adequate excreta disposal facilities -Access to safe drinking water -Life expectancy at birth -Adequate birth weight -Infant mortality rate -Nutritional status of children	-Immunization against infectious childhood diseases -Contraceptive prevalence -Proportion of potentially hazardous chemicals monitored in food -National health expenditure devoted to local health care -Total national health expenditure related to GNP

Chapters of Agenda 21	*Driving Force Indicators*	*State Indicators*	*Response Indicators*
Chapter 7: Promoting sustainable human settlement development	-Rate of growth of urban population -Per capita consumption of fossil fuel by motor vehicle transport -Human and economic loss due to natural disasters	-Percentage of population in urban areas -Area and population of urban formal and informal settlements -Floor area per person -House price to income ratio	-Infrastructure expenditure per capita
Chapter 36: Promoting education, Public awareness and training	-Rate of change of school-age population -Primary school enrolment ratio (gross and net) -Secondary school enrolment ratio (gross and net) -Adult literacy rate	-Children reaching grade 5 of primary education -School life expectancy -Difference between male and female school enrolment ratios -Women per hundred men in the labour force	-GDP spent on education
Category: Economic			
Chapter 2: International cooperation to accelerate sustainable development in countries and related domestic policies	-GDP per capita -Net investment share in GDP -Sum of exports and imports as a percent of GDP	-Environmentally adjusted Net Domestic Product -Share of manufactured goods in total merchandise exports	
Chapter 4: Changing consumption patterns	-Annual energy consumption -Share of natural resources intensive industries in manufacturing value-added	-Proven mineral reserves -Proven fossil fuel energy reserves -Lifetime of proven energy reserves -Intensity of material use -Share of manufacturing value-added in GDP -Share of consumption of renewable energy resources	

Chapters of Agenda 21	*Driving Force Indicators*	*State Indicators*	*Response Indicators*
Chapter 33: Financial resources and mechanisms	-Net resources transfer/GNP -Total ODA given or received as a percentage of GNP	-Dept/GNP -Dept service/export	-Environmental protection expenditures as a per cent of GDP -Amount of new or additional funding for development
Chapter 34: Transfer of environmentally sound technology, cooperation and capacity-building	-Capital goods imports -Foreign direct investments	Share of environmentally sound capital goods imports	-Technical cooperation grants
Category: Environmental			
Chapter 9: Protection of the atmosphere	-Emissions of greenhouse gasses -Emissions of sulphur oxides -Emissions of nitrogen oxides -Consumption of ozone depleting substances	-Ambient concentrations of pollutants in urban areas	-Expenditure on air pollution abatement
Chapter 10: Integrated approach to the planning and management of land resources	-Landuse change	-Changes in land condition	-Decentralized local-level natural resource management
Chapter 11: Combating deforestation	-Wood harvesting intensity	-Forest area change	-Managed forest area ratio -Protected forest area as a percent of total forest area
Chapter 12: Managing fragile ecosystems: combating desertification and drought	-Populations living below poverty line in dryland areas	-National monthly rainfall index -Satellite derived vegetation index -Land affected by desertification	
Chapter 13: Managing fragile ecosystems: sustainable mountain development	-Population change in mountain areas	-Sustainable use of natural resources in mountain areas -Welfare of mountain populations	

Chapters of Agenda 21	*Driving Force Indicators*	*State Indicators*	*Response Indicators*
Chapter 14: Promoting sustainable agriculture and rural development	-Use of agriculture pesticides -Use of fertilizers -Irrigation percent of arable land -Energy use in agriculture	-Arable land per capita -Area affected by salinisation and waterlogging	-Agricultural education
Chapter 15: Conservation of biological diversity		-Threatened species as a per cent of total native species	-Protected area as a per cent of total area
Chapter 16: Environmentally sound management of biotechnology			-R & D expenditure for biotechnology -Existence of national bio- safety regulations of guidelines
Chapter 17: Protection of the oceans, all kinds of seas and coastal areas	-Population growth in coastal areas -Discharges of oil into coastal waters -Releases of nitrogen and phosphorous to coastal waters	-Maximum sustained yield for fisheries -Algae index	
Chapter 18: Protection of the quality and supply of freshwater resources	-Annual withdrawals of ground surface water -Domestic consumption of water per capita	-Groundwater reserves -Concentration of faecal coliform in freshwater Biochemical oxygen demand in water bodies	-Waste-water treatment coverage -Density of hydrological networks
Chapter 19: Environmentally sound management of toxic chemicals		-Chemically induced acute poisonings	-Number of chemicals banned or severely restricted
Chapter 20: Environmentally sound management of hazardous wastes	-Generation of hazardous wastes -Imports and exports of hazardous wastes	-Area of land contaminated by hazardous wastes	-Expenditure on hazardous waste treatment
Chapter 21: Environmentally sound management of solid wastes and sewage-related issues	-Generation of industrial and municipal solid waste -House hold waste disposed per capita		-Expenditure on air pollutions abatement -Waste recycling an reuse-Municipal waste disposal

Chapters of Agenda 21	*Driving Force Indicators*	*State Indicators*	*Response Indicators*
Chapter 22: Safe and environmentally sound management of radioactive wastes	-Generation of radioactive wastes		
Category: Institutional			
Chapter 8: Integrating environment and development in decision-making			-Sustainable development strategies -Programme of integrated environmental and economic accounting -Mandated Environmental Impact Assessment -National councils for sustainable development
Chapter 23-32: Strengthening the role of major groups			-Representation of major groups in national councils for sustainable developments -Representatives of ethnic minorities and indigenous people in national councils for sustainable development -Contribution of NGOs to sustainable development
Chapter 35: Science for sustainable development		-Potential scientists and engineers per million population	-Scientists and engineers engaged in R & D per million population -Expenditure on R&D as a percent of GDP

Chapters of Agenda 21	*Driving Force Indicators*	*State Indicators*	*Response Indicators*
Chapter 37: National mechanisms and international cooperation for capacity-building in developing countries			
Chapter 38: International Institutional arrangements			
Chapter 39: International legal instruments and mechanisms			-Ratification of global agreements -Implementation of ratified global agreements
Chapter 40: Information for decision-making		-Main telephone lines per 100 inhabitants -Access to information	-Programmes for national environmental statistics

NOTES

1. Bellagio Principles were formulated in 1996 by an Expert Group at Bellagio, Italy. These principles included (1) guiding vision and goal of sustainable development, (2) holistic perspective, (3) essential elements (i.e., economic, ecological and values), (4) adequate scope and flexibility, (5) practical focus, (6) openness, (7) effective communication, (8) broad participation, (9) ongoing assessment, and (10) institutional capacity.
2. The incidence of poverty is taken as 19.31 per cent for 1999-00. The incidence of poverty for 1999-00 as per the Planning Commission is 14.70, which implies 7.8 per cent annual rate of decline (much higher than the annual growth rate of the SDP, 5.53 per cent)!
3. The forest sector has shown improvement during the 1990s.

REFERENCES

Atkinson, G, R. Dubourg, *et al.* (1997): *Measuring Sustainable Development: Macroeconomics and the Environment.* U.K.: Edward Elgaz Publishing.

Bartelmus, Peter, (1994): *Environment, Growth and Development.* London: Routledge Publications.

Bartelmus, Peter, (1996): "Whither Economics- From Optimality to Sustainability?" *Environment and Development Economists* 2(3): 323-345.

Bert, J.M. De Vries, (2001): "Perceptions and Risks in Search for a Sustainable World: A Model-based Approach", *International Journal of Sustainable Development* 4(2).

Brown, Lester R. and *et al.*, (1991): *Vision of a Sustainable World: World Watch Reader on Global Environment Issues.* New York: W.W. Norton & Co.

Chambers, Robert, and Conway, Gorden, (1992): *Sustainable Rural Livelihoods: Practical Concepts for the 21st Century.* U.K.: Institute of Development Studies.

Chopra, Kanchan, and Kadekodi, Gopal, (1999): *Operationalising Sustainable Development.* Economic-Ecological Modelling for Developing Countries. New Delhi: Sage Publications.

Daly, H., (1990): "Towards Some Operational Principles of Sustainable Development". *Ecological Economics* 2 (1-6).

Dasgupta, P., and Maeler, K.G., (1993): "Poverty, Institutions and the Environmental-resource base". *The Development Economics Research Programme,* No. 48. London School of Economics.

Dasgupta, Susmita, *et al.*, (2002): "Confronting the Environmental Kuznets Curve". *Journal of Economic Perspectives* 16(1): 147-168.

Directorate of Economics and Statistics, (2000): "Report of the Time Use Survey for Gujarat". Gandhinagar: Directorate of Economics and Statistics.

Dutt, Amitava Krishna, and Rao, Mohan, J., (1996): "Growth, Distribution, and the Environment: Sustainable Development in India". *World Development* 24(2): 287-305.

The Earth Charter Commission, (2000): *The Earth Charter.*

Ellioff, Jennifer, A., (1994): *An Introduction to Sustainable Development.* London: Routledge.

FES, (1998): *Economic Performance, Social Cohesion, Environmental Sustainability, Three Goals: One Path.* Bonn: The Future Commission.

Ghai, D., *et al.*, (1992): *Grassroot Environmental Action: People's Participation in Sustainable Development.*

Glaeser, Bernhard, (1984): *Eco Development.* Berlin: International Institute for Environment and Society, Science Centre, and Oxford: Pergamon Press.

Graaf, H.J. De, *et al.*, (1996): "Sustainable Development: Looking for New Strategies". *Environment Economics* 16(3).

Hirway, Indira (supported by Noopur Pathak), (2002): *Quick Valuation of Depletion and Degradation of Environmental Resources in Gujarat.* Ahmedabad: Centre For Development Alternatives.

Hirway, Indira, and Mahadevia, Darshini, (1999): "Gujarat Human Development Report". Ahmedabad: Mahatma Gandhi Labour Institute.

Hubner, Kurt, and Nill, Jan, (2001): "Greening of the Innovation System- Opportunities and Obstacles for a Path Change towards Sustainability: The Case of Germany". *International Journal of Sustainable Development* 4(1).

Hueting, Roefie, (1996): "Three Persistent Myths in the Environmental Debate". *Environment Economics* 18(2).

Jodha, N.S., (1986): "Common Property Resources and the Rural Poor". *Economic and Political Weekly,* 21.

Lele, S.M., (1991): "Sustainable Development: A Critical Review". *World Development* 19(6): 607-621.

Mazzucato, V., and Niemeijer, D., (2000): "Rethinking Soil and Water Conservation in a Changing Society: A Case Study in Eastern Burkina Faso". Ph.D. Thesis, Wageningen University.

Meadows, D.H. *et al.*, (1972): *The Limits to Growth.* New York: University Books.

Munasinghe, Mohan, and McNeely, Jeffrey, (1995): "Key Concepts and Terminology of Sustainable Development". In *Defining and Measuring Sustainability: The Biogeophysical Foundations,* Washington, D.C.: The United Nations and The World Bank.

Pezzey, John, (1992): "Sustainable Development Concepts: An Economic Analysis". World Bank Environment Paper No. 2, Washington, D.C.: The World Bank.

Rennings K., and Wiggering, H., (1997): "Steps towards Indicators of Sustainable Development: Linking Economic and Ecological Concepts. *Ecological Economics* 20(1).

Rodenburg, Eric, *et al.*, (1995): "Environmental Indicators for Global Cooperation". Global Environmental Facility, Working Paper II, Washington: UNDP-ENEP-WB.

Sachs, Wolfgang, and Agrawal, Herman (eds.), (2002): "The O'Burg Memo: Fairness in a Fragile World". Memorandum for the World Summit on Sustainable Development. Heinrich Boll Foundation.

Stern, David I. *et al.*, (1996): "Economic Growth and Environmental Degradation: The Environmental Kuznets Curve and Sustainable Development". *World Development Report* 24.

Taylor, Lance, (1996): "Sustainable Development: An Introduction". *World Development* 24(2).

Toye, John, (1993): *Dilemmas of Development.* Oxford: Blackwell.

UNESCO, (2001): *Implementing Agenda 21.* Report of the Secretary General, Commission on Sustainable Development, Acting as Preparatory Committee for the World Summit on Sustainable Development, UNESCO.

UNO, (2002): *Implementing Agenda 21.* Report of the Secretary General, Commission on Sustainable Development, UNESCO, Prepared for World Summit on Sustainable Development. New York: UNO.

Weston, Joc, (1986): *A New Politics of the Environment.* London: Red and Green, Pluto Press.

The World Bank, (1997): "Advancing Sustainable Development: The World Bank and Agenda 21". Environmentally Sustainable Development Studies and Monographs Series, No. 18. Washington, D.C.: The World Bank.

World Commission on Environment and Development, (1987): *Our Common Future.* Oxford University Press.

4

Poverty and Natural Resources

Understanding the Dynamics in the Context of Dryland Regions in Western India

AMITA SHAH

INTRODUCTION

Interface between environment and poverty is complex. Poverty reduction needs appropriation of natural capital, such as land, water, forest and minerals in order to produce economic goods and marine resources. In the absence of the natural capital, the poor may continue to remain poor in a resource-rich environment, especially in the rural settings. Population growth, without properly calibrated distribution and use of natural resources, may further aggravate the situation. Out-migration and dependence on the alternative activities outside the primary sector may also have a negative impact on environment, directly through the processes of production and indirectly through the neglect of land and other natural resources (Bilsborrow 1991). It is, therefore, imperative to work out a strategy whereby most people can find adequate sources of employment as well as incomes from a combination of activities that has relatively fewer negative externalities on environment.

Since the poor depend more critically on the activities based on natural resources in agriculture and allied sectors, they are often seen as causes as well as victims of environmental degradation, setting up a vicious circle. This kind of a monolithic view of poverty and resource degradation has been severely contested in the recent literature that seeks empirical evidence on the interface between poverty and environment (Markandya Undated; Duriaappah 1998; Nadal *et al.* 1998). Alternatively, it has been argued that real-life situations are often diverse, indicating a plurality of interfaces between the two (Nadkarni 2000). For instance, there is ample evidence to show that the poor do not always damage environment, and there is a large number of situations where the non-poor cause environmental degradation. A priori, Duriaappah (1998) has created the following typology to depict the multi-patterned relationship between environment and poverty in the Indian context.

- Exogenous poverty causes environmental degradation,
- Power, wealth and greed cause degradation,
- Institutional failure as the primary cause of degradation,
- Market failure causes degradation,
- Environmental degradation causes poverty, and
- Endogenous poverty causes degradation.

It is difficult to discern a dominant pattern of interface between environment and poverty because of the changing nature of the use of natural resources under varying demographic, institutional and technological situations across time and space. Thus, by and large, the view that obtains in the context of developing economies is that "poor do not initially or indirectly degrade environment, the interface is contingent upon the other groups not degrading the environment. and also on the absence of market or institutional failures" (Duriaappah 1998). Unfortunately, the empirical evidence on the actual interface between poverty and environment is fairly sketchy and somewhat inaccurate. Nevertheless, studies from a large number of situations in developing as well as developed countries lend support to two basic propositions: first, poverty *per se* does not damage environment and second, environmental degradation does hurt the poor (Markandya undated).

Given the above perspectives, the burden of environmental degradation is placed on the policies that have been used for promoting agricultural growth in predominantly agrarian economies. The consequences of these policies have been to intensify, through a variety of channels, the degradation that has been caused by rural, poor communities (Lopez 1992). The proximate causes of environmental degradation by the poor in the agrarian societies, as found in the case of Central America, are (De Janvery and Garcia 1998), (i) soil erosion by small holders as a rational strategy for survival; (ii) semi-proletarianisation of the rural population and collapse of local institutions; and (iii) deforestation as migrants seek land.

A similar situation is likely to prevail in other developing economies. It is ironical that agricultural growth, one of the most important strategies for poverty reduction, is found to have contributed (at least partly) to environmental degradation in a number of developing economies, including in India. Consequently, the growth policies of many agrarian economies have faced severe criticism not only on account of their weak record on poverty reduction but also because of their impact on environmental sustainability. In fact, what is being challenged is the nature of agricultural growth on the lines of the “Green Revolution”, and not agricultural growth *per se*. There is voluminous literature critiquing the “Green Revolution” strategy, especially for its impact on equity, and of late, on environmental sustainability. The most important criticism stems from the fact that on the one hand, the strategy has by-passed dryland farming, and, on the other, it has promoted non-sustainable use of resources, especially of water (due to distorted price structure). As a result, dryland regions have lagged behind in terms of agricultural growth and have continued to be vulnerable to weather. In dryland regions, over-exploitation of groundwater resources has become the most handy mechanism for the poor to survive and for the non-poor to maintain the economic *status quo*.

Strangely enough, the pattern of poverty found in the Indian states does not match the expected pattern. For instance, the states with a predominance of dryland areas have lower incidence of poverty than forest-based states. To an extent this is explained by a high rate of out-migration from dryland states. Apart from this, some structural factors also seem to have exerted influence on the pattern of poverty and its interface with agricultural growth across space. These factors are agrarian relations; entitlement to natural resources, especially forests; and economic diversification particularly when the industrial sector takes a lead in the economy of the State. One observes that the three factors are interlocked and work adversely in the major states constituting the “poverty square”—Rajasthan, Madhya Pradesh (undivided), Uttar Pradesh (eastern), Orissa, West Bengal, Assam, and the north-east—in India (Mehta and Shah 2002). These states, except Rajasthan, together make up the major part of forest-based economies in the country.

The varied pattern of poverty in dryland and forest-based regions has been aptly summarised in a recent report on India's rural development. The report notes that the "drier states (in west) harbour lesser poverty proportions than the wetter ones (in east). In general, the states, which were under the *Zamindari* regime of the yesteryears and have experienced relatively ineffective agrarian and land reforms and thereafter green revolution, have been the losers, while those in the west have been gainers. Within these contours if the monsoon fails, all suffer and *vice versa"* (NIRD 2000).

The four States in western India, viz. Gujarat, Maharashtra, Madhya Pradesh and Rajasthan, represent predominantly dryland situations, though Madhya Pradesh (undivided) faces the double disadvantage of having vast tracts of dryland as well as forest-based economies. In fact, a large part of the forest areas, especially in the west and south-west Madhya Pradesh, has suffered such resource degradation that these areas have become like dryland regions, but without the advantage of large landholdings and developed market economies. However, the four states differ significantly in terms of both levels of poverty and economic growth. Broadly speaking, the states in the western region could be grouped in to two categories—Gujarat and Maharashtra with predominantly *ryotwari* agrarian system, with a higher level of industrial growth and a lower incidence of poverty; and Rajasthan and Madhya Pradesh with feudal agrarian relations, and a relatively higher incidence of poverty. But there are significant variations in the incidence of poverty across the regions and districts. What is the extent of poverty and how far does it vary within each of the four states in the western region? What explains the variations in poverty and how far dryland conditions are responsible for it? And, what are the policy implications for amelioration of poverty on a sustained basis? These issues have been examined in the context of the four major states in Western India.

The paper is divided into five sections including the introduction. Section 2 presents a brief overview of the role of agricultural growth in poverty reduction in India. Section 3 examines the incidence of poverty across regions and discusses the dynamics of poverty under dryland conditions in the four states in Western India. Section 4 presents an analysis of the correlates of poverty at two levels, viz., the region and the district, within the states. Section 5 summarises the discussion and draws policy implications.

AGRICULTURE-ENVIRONMENT-POVERTY INTERFACE IN INDIA: SOME EVIDENCE

Empirical studies provide an overwhelming support for the contention that the agricultural sector has played a crucial role in the reduction of poverty (Sen 1996; Ravallion 2000; Bhalla and Singh 1997; Desai and Namboothiri 1997). This is despite the fact that agriculture and the allied activities contribute a relatively small proportion, (30 per cent), to the gross domestic product in India. Nonetheless, the sector is of critical importance insofar as it ensures an aggregate supply of foodgrains, employs a large majority of workers and thereby provides wage-goods (raising demand for consumer goods and services), and supplies raw material for several important industries, including those which are export-oriented. A recent analysis suggests that the primary sector, besides making a direct contribution to the national economy, continues to have a significant association with the overall economic growth in India.

To a large extent the growth in the agricultural sector has been achieved through adoption of bio-chemical inputs, such as seeds and fertilisers and irrigation, known as *the Green Revolution technology*. Of late, use of these external inputs has started to make a negative impact on the environment (Marothia 1997). The impact, at least till now, is neither widespread nor irreversible (Shah 2000). In fact, the dominant view is that on balance, the land saving technological change represented by the Green Revolution was the single most important factor contributing to the (environmental) sustainability (Rao 2000; Dantwala 1996). This is mainly because it has reduced the pressure on marginal lands and thereby increased the area under fallow land (Ray 1992).

But the Green Revolution technology, if used indiscriminately and without taking proper steps to overcome the environmental damage, may prove counter-productive. For, it has been widely observed that "environmental degradation in India has a tremendous human cost. It hits the poor most and directly too" (for instance, Nadkarni 2000). Hence, regeneration and sustainable use of natural resources, rather than conservation *per se*, becomes imperative for poverty alleviation given the fact that over 60 per cent of the country's working population—the main user of these resources—directly depends on the primary sector. This has been amply demonstrated during the period of growth in the nineties when sub-normal rainfall slowed down poverty reduction at macro-level (Ravallion 2000).

Of late, the slowing down of agricultural growth has led to the questioning the future potential of the Green Revolution technology suggesting that the sector has reached a plateau in terms of providing additional income to its workforce, a significant part of which is under-employed in terms of time or income or both (Bhalla 2000). Therefore, it is argued that poverty reduction in future will have to go beyond the primary sector. The recent evidence, however, does not entirely support the view that the agricultural sector in India has reached near saturation in terms of employment generation and poverty reduction. The empirical evidence from the mid-nineties suggests a broad pattern of a negative association between the levels of labour productivity in agriculture and poverty across the major states in India (Table 4.1).

Table 4.1: Agricultural Productivity and Poverty in Major States in India

States with Lower Level of Agricultural Productivity	*Rural Head Count Poverty Ratio*[a]			*Index of Male*[b] *Agricultural Productivity (1992-95)*
	1987-88	*1993-94*	*Per cent change*	
Assam	48.4	57.0	18.0	89
Bihar	66.5	65.6	-1.3	33
Orissa	63.2	56.6	-10.4	70
West Bengal	57.9	52.4	-9.5	87
Uttar Pradesh	49.2	41.3	-16.0	87
Madhya Pradesh	52.0	36.2	-30.4	95
States with Higher Levels of Agricultural Productivity				
Haryana	21.9	28.0	27.8	244
Punjab	22.0	15.4	-30.0	301
Gujarat	42.8	30.7	-28.3	121
Kerala	46.5	33.4	-28.2	188
Rajasthan	44.4	26.2	-41.0	101
Andhra Pradesh	34.4	29.9	13.1	104
Karnataka	44.4	37.0	-16.4	123
Maharashtra	53.3	51.1	-3.9	108
Tamil Nadu	53.4	42.8	-19.8	122
All India	**49.4**	**42.7**	**-13.6**	**100**

Source: [a] Mehta and Shah 2002; [b] Bhalla 2000.

Endorsing this perspective, the policy approach in the Tenth Five Year Plan lays specific emphasis on sustaining a higher rate of growth in agriculture (i.e. 3.5 per cent) that was achieved during the Eighth Five Year Plan period. According to Radhakrishna (2002), attaining a higher rate of growth is not only essential but also feasible if the right kinds of policies are put in place. Thus, the agricultural sector, once again, has come to the centrestage in the strategy for poverty reduction. This is particularly important for the western region where dryland conditions are predominant. The region has suffered a setback in its agricultural growth due to the frequent failure of the monsoon in the recent past (Table 4.2).

Table 4.2: Growth of Agriculture among States in Western India

States	*Growth Rate Value of Net State Domestic Product in Agriculture*	
	1980-81 to 1990-91	*1990-91 to 1995-96*
Gujarat	1.0	0.3
Maharashtra	4.6	1.9
Rajasthan	6.0	2.0
Madhya Pradesh	5.6	1.0
All India	3.5	2.3

Source: Estimates of State Domestic Products, Economic and Political Weekly Research Foundation, Mumbai

POVERTY IN WESTERN INDIA: UNDERSTANDING THE DYNAMICS

This section examines the incidence of poverty in the four major states in western India—Gujarat, Maharashtra, Madhya Pradesh and Rajasthan—with a view to understanding its dynamics with special reference to the dryland regions in these states.

Profile of the NSSO Regions in Western India

An estimate of poverty across regions in the four states of western India is given in Table 4.3. It is observed that the incidence of poverty varies significantly across as well as within the states in the region. Maharashtra, with a very high level of industrialisation, had the highest incidence (44.5 per cent) of poverty in 1993-94. This was followed by Madhya Pradesh, Gujarat and Rajasthan. The higher incidence of

Table 4.3: Incidence of Poverty (HCR)

	1987-88			*1993-94*			*% Change*	
	Rural	*Urban*	*Total*	*Rural*	*Urban*	*Total*	*Rural*	*Urban*
Gujarat	**42.8**	**40.3**	**42.1**	**30.7**	**29.4**	**32.3**	—	—
Dryland	60.5	53.9	59.3	37.4	27	35.6	-38.2	-49.9
Saurashtra	34.8	54.4	40.0	19.4	34.2	24.8	-44.3	-37.1
Plains	37.9	34.7	36.7	30.9	30.1	30.6	-18.5	-13.3
Northern								
Eastern	51.5	39.3	50.8	31.8	34.3	32.1	-38.3	-12.7
Plains	35.1	30.9	33.5	39.5	21	32.0	12.5	-32.0
Southern								
Maharashtra	**53.3**	**37.1**	**47.9**	**51.1**	**33.2**	**44.5**	—	—
Inland	45.3	40.8	44.1	37.5	38.7	37.9	-17.2	-5.1
Western								
Inland	56.6	52.8	55.8	61.8	55.8	60.2	9.2	5.7
Northern								
Inland Central	59.7	62.9	60.3	61.5	59.3	61.0	3.0	-5.7
Eastern	42.8	16.5	55.7	24.5	11.3	62.4	-42.8	-31.5
Inland Eastern	56	53.9	59.5	64.7	48.8	62.8	15.5	-9.5
Inland Coastal	61.9	54.7	26.1	66.1	56.7	15.3	6.8	3.7
Rajasthan	**44.4**	**38.8**	**43.3**	**33.1**	**26.2**	**27.8**	—	—
Western	40.8	39.2	40.5	25.4	25.4	25.4	-37.7	-35.2
Northern	38.7	42.5	39.6	17.8	35.8	22.8	-54.0	-15.8
Eastern								
Southern	73.0	33.4	69.9	46.0	26.8	43.9	-37.0	-19.8
South Eastern	41.4	25.0	38.1	33.0	45.1	35.7	-20.3	80.4
Madhya Pradesh	**52.0**	**47.0**	**51.1**	**36.2**	**46.5**	**38.7**	—	—
Vindhya	47.0	64.6	49.1	32.0	48.6	34.4	-31.9	-24.8
South	59.6	38.7	54.5	42.6	31.1	44.5	-28.5	-19.6
Central	52.7	59.4	54.4	44.5	51.4	46.6	-15.6	-13.5
South Western	61.0	66.5	62.0	64.6	55.5	63.0	5.9	-16.5
Malwa	46.2	45.5	46.1	22.7	44.0	29.8	-50.9	-3.3
Chhatisgarh	58.5	35.4	55.3	38.2	42.2	38.9	-34.7	19.2
Northern	32.5	41.5	34.6	15.0	43.2	22.1	-53.8	4.1

Source: Dubey and Gangopadhyaya 1998.

poverty in relatively more industrially developed states like Maharashtra and Gujarat (than that in Rajasthan) reflects, to an extent, out-migration from the less to the more developed economies. However, Madhya Pradesh remains an outlier in this context with a higher incidence of poverty. Prima facie, this may suggest a lower rate of out-migration in Madhya Pradesh than in Rajasthan. Another striking difference is that whereas rural poverty is higher than urban poverty in Maharashtra, Gujarat and Rajasthan, it is lower in Madhya Pradesh. This might suggest greater intra-state migration than inter-state migration among the poor in Madhya Pradesh, unlike Rajasthan. This issue is examined later.

What is, however, more important is that the incidence of poverty is significantly high, more than 60 per cent in five of the 22 regions in these States. Of these, four belong to Maharashtra and one to Madhya Pradesh. This kind of high incidence of poverty is found only in the rural areas; the poverty levels are somewhat lower—in the range of 50 to 59 per cent—in the urban areas of the same regions. One of the possible reasons for a very high incidence of poverty in these five regions could be that they are forest-based economies. The forests have suffered degradation and the regions have smaller land-holdings on the one hand and on the other, they are physically remote and socially marginalised. Incidentally, the majority of the districts in the four regions in Maharashtra have a high proportion of tribal population. It may be noted here that the poverty ratio has risen in all the five regions, whereas it has declined—at times substantially—in the rest of the regions of the four states. A similar situation is also observed in the forest-based areas in the eastern parts of Gujarat and southern parts of Rajasthan where degraded forests, combined with a higher proportion of tribal population, have resulted in low social capabilities. However, before moving on to ascertain the correlates of poverty, it might be useful to understand its dynamics in the context of dryland economies which dominate all four states. The forest-based areas, as noted earlier, also face similar problems due to severe degradation and frequent droughts.

Incidence of Poverty in Drought Prone Areas: Hidden vs. Explicit

There is no official delineation of dryland regions in India except for the one adopted for identifying districts to be covered under the Drought Prone Area Programme, a major policy intervention in these regions. Nevertheless, attempts have been made to define dryland regions under certain specific situations (ICRISAT-ICAR 1999; Fan and Hazell 2000). Recognising the critical importance of agronomic potential in determining the poverty-outcome, some scholars (Shah *et al.* 1998) have identified drylands by focusing primarily on the moisture deficiency. They have designated areas as drylands (i) if they are located in agro-climatic regions 1 to 12; (ii) if the length of the growing period is less than 180 days; and (iii) if the proportion of gross irrigated area is between 40 and 50 per cent. Accordingly, 42 per cent of the districts covering 56 per cent of the total geographical areas in the country have been identified as dryland. This proportion is significantly higher among the four states in Western India (Table 4.4).

Table 4.4: Dryland Areas in Western India (1989-90)

States	*% of Dryland*	
	Districts	*Area*
Gujarat	74	88
Maharashtra	77	81
Rajasthan	93	92
Madhya Pradesh	89	81
All India	42	56

Source: Shah *et al.* 1998, p. 121

It is difficult to estimate poverty in the dryland regions since official statistics do not provide separate estimates for such areas. However, a recent study, using state-level estimates, has found that the incidence of poverty was lower in drought-prone (DP) states than in non-drought-prone (NDP) states (Conroy *et al.* 2001). In 1993-94, the proportion of the poor in the DP states was 29 per cent as against 37 per cent in the NDP states. These findings are further substantiated by Kelley *et al.* (1995) in their examination of poverty conditions in the Semi Arid Tropics (SAT) in the country. The study noted that there were significantly fewer absolutely poor people residing in the more marginal rural environment, i.e., districts with less than Rs. 500 per hectare productivity. The severity of poverty had no significant association with the marginal lands. This, by and large, implied that the incidence of rural poverty is relatively higher in the areas with a better land productivity within the SAT regions. Prima facie, this may suggest significant out-migration and the resultant low density of population in the relatively low productivity (or marginal) areas within the SAT.

The above observations further substantiate another interesting finding of a study (Conroy *et al.* 2001): the lower incidence of rural poverty in dryland areas is generally accompanied by the higher incidence of poverty in urban areas. To a large extent this is due to the fact that a larger proportion of the rural workforce has to depend on non-farm employment within or outside the rural areas. Moreover, it may be noted that, to a large extent, poverty in the dryland regions is likely to be transitory in nature (Sagar 1997). This is supported by a detailed analysis based on the panel data collected by the ICRISAT. According to a study by Singh and Binswanger (1993) covering three SAT regions, poverty was not a permanent characteristic of the households. It was further noted that out of the 218 households they had studied, 131 (60%) were initially poor. After nine years, 48 (37%) of these households had moved above the poverty line, and another 9 (10%) of the initially 87 non-poor households became poor despite considerable growth in the average income of the sample households. While a large part of the poverty reduction is likely to be due to the increased access to irrigation, a substantial part of the income growth among the poor can be traced to the state intervention in the form of drought relief measures or employment guarantee schemes, especially in Maharashtra. Both these appear to be non-sustainable in the long run.

Low Agronomic Potential: Instability of Yield

An important feature of the dryland region, however, is its low agronomic potential, not so much in terms of yield-levels but more in terms of uncertainty and fluctuations in yield. As a result, land productivity is found to be fairly low and variable. According to the estimates provided by Fan and Hazell (2000), average land productivity during the 1981-1994 period was Rs. 8,485 (in irrigated areas) Rs. 6,464 (in high potential rain-fed areas) and Rs. 3,291 (in low potential areas) in the country. It is important to note that, compared to the previous year, the low-potential regions had registered a decline in land productivity in 6 out of 14 years; irrigated areas saw a decline in 3 out of 14 years, and in high potential rain-fed regions the decline was observed in only 1 out of 14 years.

The above observation is further substantiated by the estimates of instability in the cereal production in some of the dryland states including three out of the four major states in Western India, viz., Gujarat (58%); Rajasthan (39%); and Maharashtra (29%). Incidentally, Madhya Pradesh has a relatively low level of instability, and hence it is treated as a part of the high-potential regions (World Food Programme 2001). The phenomenon of higher uncertainty has been considered the most distinguishing aspect of dryland agriculture in semi-arid tropics (Walker and Ryan 1990). It has been noted that a high degree of uncertainty of the rainfall at the planting stage induces variability in the area sown. It is this, and not the fluctuations in yield, that makes crop income volatile. This is what makes poverty in dryland regions a transitory rather than a long-duration phenomenon, which eventually leads to an overall low incidence of poverty in these regions. The more worrying feature, as observed in the study, is that "rainfall induced uncertainties in the crop income may also have serious ramifications in terms of devising a sustainable crop insurance or credit scheme". A long-standing absence of an effective credit system might deepen the poverty with the result that many of the transient poor might end up being chronic poor in the long run; or else, they might migrate.

Coping Mechanisms

Four sets of coping mechanisms help in overcoming the basic constraints of the low agronomic potential in the region. First, dryland regions have relatively low population density and hence have larger land holdings. But this feature is likely to disappear as population increases. Secondly, the coverage of the drought relief measures undertaken by the state has been increasing. Thirdly, specialisation in high value horticulture and commercial crops like oilseeds and spices has been taking place in these regions. Fourthly and perhaps most importantly, people tend to migrate from these regions. Since the first two are somewhat exogenously determined, the effective strategies are limited to the latter two. These strategies have been discussed below briefly.

Diversified Farming System and Predominance of High Value Crops

According to the estimates prepared by Shah *et al.* (1998), drylands in India constitute 45 per cent of the total area under cereal production; 66 per cent of the area under oilseeds; and 68 per cent of the area under non-food crops. A number of studies have examined the impact of commercialisation on Indian agriculture. A seminal study by Nadkarni (1985) on Andhra Pradesh, Karnataka and Tamil Nadu provides a vivid account of how the strategy works in a dryland areas vis-à-vis wet regions. It finds that to a large extent, commercialisation of agriculture in the dryland regions has helped increase income among cultivating households across different categories of land holdings. It has been noted that commercialisation has been facilitated by a substantial contribution of labour from the landless households which also tend to gain in terms of employment as well as higher wage rates. On the whole, therefore, commercialisation seems to reduce poverty, though it increases inequality within a village. An important feature of commercialisation is that it tends to work more effectively in the area which has adopted commercial crops on a large scale rather than in the isolated and less commercialised regions. Thus remoteness plays an important role in determining the poverty reducing impact.

Areas estimated to be under non-food crops, representing the level of commercialisation in the four states, are given in Table 4.5. It can be seen that Gujarat, Maharashtra and Rajasthan have a larger

Table 4.5: Commercialization of Agriculture and Migration in Four States in Western India

States	*A*		*B*		*C*	
	Per cent area under commercial crops		*No. of Cows and Buffaloes (in '000s)*		*Per cent out-migration*	*Net Inter-state Migrants per 1,000 persons (91-01)*
	1980	*1997-98*	*1982*	*1992*		
Gujarat	50.0	61.6	11437	12072	0.6	19
Maharashtra	27.4	39.4	25134	22894	0.8	44
Rajasthan	22.3	38.4	19548	19371	1.5	07
Madhya Pradesh	13.6	31.5	33552	36660	0.6	10
All India	22.6	35.1	262237	288755	1.2	27

Source: Centre for Monitoring Indian Economy (Agriculture Sector), Various Volumes; Kundu 2002, Tables 3 and 6

proportion of their area under non-food crops than the all-India average; Gujarat has the highest proportion (61.6%), followed by Maharashtra (39.4%) and Rajasthan (38.4%). Madhya Pradesh has a relatively lower level of commercialisation of agriculture, but is catching-up fast—the proportion of area under non-food crops jumped from about 13.6 per cent in 1980 to 31.5 per cent in 1996-97. To a large extent, this is due to the spread of oilseeds, especially soybean, in large parts of central, south and western Madhya Pradesh.

Fortunately, predominance of cash crops like oilseeds is an agronomic feature which can be tapped with the right kind of technology and policy support. But it has been recognised that agricultural research and development (R&D) in India has been so heavily tilted towards irrigated farming (Jodha 1990) that farmers in the dryland regions are pushed to grow more of irrigated crops and varieties. The result is often disastrous. For instance, the choice of such crops leads to over-depletion of groundwater resources, the sustainability of which is being increasingly threatened. Even worse, the need to ensure a certain level of income may lead the farmers to go for a highly risky investment. Given the uncertain rain, the chosen crop may fail leading the farmer to bankruptcy. The increasing number of suicides among the cotton growers in different parts of the dryland regions is partly a manifestation of the lop-sided R&D and price structure that distort the crop choice and hamper long-term sustainability of dryland farming in different parts of the country.

Besides growing high-value crops, dryland regions also have the natural advantage of being able to adopt a more diversified farming system, especially with livestock (producing milk, wool and meat). The recent categorisation of zones in India's SAT takes into consideration this aspect. Accordingly, 5 out of 15 dryland zones (excluding irrigated rice in Zone 1) have livestock as an important activity (ICRISAT and ICAR 1999). Given the fact that livestock economy is losing ground in the majority of dryland regions, and that dairying is increasingly getting tied to availability of irrigation, the sustainability of livestock as a coping mechanism is gradually being eroded. Frequent droughts in large parts of Western India seem to have exerted a significant negative impact on the livestock economy in the region (Table 4.5).

Migration

Given the initially low agronomic potential and limited technological support, migration turns out to be an important coping strategy, especially among the landless and the poor (NIRD 2000; Bilsborrow 1992). The phenomenon, though difficult to establish at macro-level, has been substantiated by a number of micro-level studies from various dryland regions in the country (Haan 1999; Shah 2001; Lipton 1980).

Apart from low and uncertain returns from agriculture the declining size as well as quality of Common Property Resources (CPRs) have also led to deepening of poverty in the dryland regions such as in Rajasthan (Jodha 1986). This, in turn, has led to a significant increase in out-migration, especially among the landless and the poor (Chopra and Gulati 2001). Following the seminal study of Jodha (1986), a number of studies have tried to examine the dependence of the poor on the CPRs. The earlier finding was that the dependence was significant. Strangely enough, the recent studies suggest only limited dependence on the CPRs among the poor (Iyengar and Shukla 1999), possibly because these resources have been severely depleted. The poor from dryland regions, thus, seem to rely increasingly on migration for earning a living. Estimates of out-migration in the four states are given in Table 4.5. It is observed that out-migration is very high in Rajasthan but not so in Madhya Pradesh, even though the latter is a relatively less developed state. Conversely, Maharashtra and Gujarat have a higher incidence of in-migration.

The emerging perspective recognises migration as an integral part of the livelihood strategy rather than as a transitory phenomenon or an aberration. There seems to be some consensus that migration tends to contribute a great deal to the host economy and that it leads to higher rates of labour force participation. For instance, a recent study in south Rajasthan found that nearly two-thirds of the households reported that migration was the most important source of the household income (46%) in the study area (Sudrak 2003). Similarly, a study in two villages in Badwani district in south-west Madhya Pradesh affirms criticality of migration as a coping mechanism, especially for the poor (Shah and Sah 2003). The study also finds that migration is the least preferred option mainly because neither the working conditions nor the living conditions are congenial in the place of destination. There is little evidence that migration reduces inequality between areas of origin or destination (Haan and Rogaly 2002).

A number of studies have inquired into the conditions of migrants at the place of destination. Most of the studies suggest that these migrants especially from the marginalised areas have to face a hostile environment in their place of employment: they work as contract labour which is exploitative, their living conditions are bad, and they suffer a loss of identity. Most of these features are fairly common to all cases of distress migration. However, what may be different in the case of migrants from dryland regions is that their migration is of a long duration (or even permanent) and that a large number of households migrate to the regions with better agronomic conditions or better opportunities for diversification. The long history of out-migration from the dryland regions might have helped build a strong social capital generating a chain of long-duration migrants from the region. This has been amply demonstrated by a recent study on land degradation and migration from the Saurashtra region in Gujarat (Shah 2003).

Another implication of sustained out-migration from the dryland regions could be higher wage rates. This could be further supported by a relatively greater importance of livestock economy absorbing a major part of household labour on the one hand, and high value cash crops on the other. Increasing development of groundwater resources might further push the local wage rate. Since there is no systematic evidence on wage rate differentials between the dryland and other regions, the issue needs detailed probing so that the dynamics of local labour markets and out-migration from the region are understood.

Evidence discussed so far suggests that the hitherto-observed low incidence of poverty in the dryland regions (where the transient poor are predominant) is based on two sets of mechanisms which appear quite fragile at least at this point in time. These are: (i) commercialisation of agriculture without migration, and (ii) out-migration. On the one hand, due to the over-exploitation of ground-water, in future, less water will be available unless requisite measures are taken for recharge. On the other, out-migration cannot be sustained for long since the urban centres are already overcrowded with surplus labourforce pushed out from the rural areas. As a result, a larger proportion of the people may become trapped in long-duration poverty.

Depletion of Groundwater: The Issue of Sustainability

Ironically, development of groundwater is both, a short-term remedy to alleviate poverty and a likely cause for chronic poverty in the long run. The problem of depleting groundwater seems to have worsened since the late eighties, the period which was marked by (i) diffusion of high-yielding varieties, and (ii) frequent occurrence of drought.

Recent evidence on groundwater depletion in the states reveals that the states with very high level of groundwater exploitation like Rajasthan, Gujarat, Maharashtra, Karnataka and Tamil Nadu have exploited more than 30 per cent of the available groundwater resources (World Food Programme 2001). However, what is more worrying is that a large part of the groundwater exploitation is through tube-wells, which are fast becoming the single largest source of irrigation in the country (Shah *et al.* 1998). The growth of tube-wells has been particularly alarming since the eighties. Between 1977-79 and 1988-90, the area irrigated by tube-wells rose by more than 300 per cent. The situation seems to have been aggravated further during the nineties: a large number of areas, especially in the dryland regions, are being classified as dark zones where further depletion of groundwater is banned. Further, the number of wells becoming defunct is also increasing at a rapid rate. Together, these trends suggest non-sustainability of groundwater resources for containing poverty in the dryland areas in the western region.

A part of this phenomenon is reflected by the fact that the impact of droughts, given the level of precipitation, has amplified in the past few decades. Further, more than the availability of foodgrains, the impact of drought is felt in terms of scarcity of drinking water as well as fodder both of which are essential for supporting life systems—human and animal (Shah 2001). A large proportion of the people thus face insecurity of the basic sources of survival, viz. employment and income, asset base (i.e. livestock), food and drinking water. The extent to which this could be recouped through the state-supported relief measures would, to a large extent, determine the poverty outcome. These issues are discussed in the last section.

CORRELATES OF POVERTY: A DISAGGREGATED ANALYSIS

This section examines the correlates of poverty in the four states at regional and district levels. Ideally, the analysis should be carried out at the regional level for which poverty estimates are available. But the regional level data are not available—except for rural areas—on a number of important variables. Hence, we have confined our analysis to rural areas in the 22 regions of the four States (Table 4.3). Subsequently, a district-level analysis has been carried out using estimates of households below poverty line (BPL) as proxy for poverty estimates. It may be noted that the two sets of estimates are not comparable. Also, there are methodological problems with respect to the manner in which BPL surveys have been conducted (Sundaram 2003). Nevertheless, in the absence of a better alternative, we have used the BPL estimate as an indicator of income poverty. The analysis is carried out by estimating correlation coefficient for 14 and 21 variables at the regional and district levels for all the states taken together. The district level exercise is conducted separately for each of the four states as well. The main results from the empirical exercise follow.

Region-Level Analysis

Variables which have a significant association with rural poverty among the 22 regions in western India are given in Table 4.6. It is

Table 4.6: Correlates of Rural Poverty in the Regions of Four Western States (1993-94)

*Variables**	*Value of correlation co-efficient*
Urban poverty 1993-94	.581**
Rural wage	-.460*
Wasteland	-.458*
Labour productivity	-.539*
Household size	-.581**

Source: NIRD 2000; Dubey and Gangopadhyaya 1998.

* The 14 variables used for the correlation exercise are: 1. Rural Head Count Ratio, 1993-94, 2. Urban Head Count Ratio 1993-94, 3. Population Growth Rate, 4. Female Literacy, 5.Land Productivity, 6. Rural Wage, 7. Village Electrified, 8. Rural Non-Farm Workers, 9. Wasteland, 10. Safe Drinking Water, 11. Labour Productivity in Agriculture, 12. Gross Irrigated Areas as a per cent to GCA, 13. Child Mortality, 14. Household Size.

observed that rural poverty is significantly influenced by 5 out of the 14 variables used for the analysis. Of these, four seem to have an impact on poverty reduction as indicated by the negative sign of correlation co-efficient. These include important factors like rural wages, labour productivity, proportion of wasteland to total geographical area and the household size (which, perhaps, reflects the size of the landholding). Similarly, the negative association between poverty and wasteland might indicate permanent out-migration and low population density in the semi-arid regions as noted earlier by the study on the SAT. This is perhaps why rural poverty is found to be positively associated with urban poverty in the same region.

What is surprising is that the extent of irrigation does not turn out to be a significant variable associated with rural poverty. This, of course, does not mean that irrigation does not have a positive impact on poverty alleviation—this has already been amply demonstrated by a number of studies in the past (for instance, Bhattarai and Narayanamoorthy 2003). Instead, what the result suggests is that people move from areas with low irrigation to those with high irrigation *within the region*. This is particularly true of the dryland areas in Madhya Pradesh and Maharashtra where areas around river banks are irrigated, but those farther from river banks in the same districts constitute the core areas of dryland regions in the state. Such movements, however, may not help lift the households out of poverty as noted earlier by Haan and Rogaly (2002). This suggests that poverty across regions with varying levels of irrigation is mediated by "migration plus remittance". This captures two types of migratory movements: (i) people shift permanently to regions with a higher level of irrigation, and those who stay back in the relatively less irrigated regions receive remittances; (ii) people from the forest-based regions migrate seasonally to different rural as well as urban locations. Whereas the former may help reducing poverty in the place of origin, the same may not be true of the latter. In fact, the latter type of migration may lead to a rise in poverty at destination without necessarily reducing that in the place of origin. This phenomenon seems to be taking place in large parts in Maharashtra and Madhya Pradesh which have a very high incidence of rural as well as urban poverty as noted in the previous section. Overall, the regional scenario of poverty appears fairly complex as it is mediated by migration of different types and with different outcomes. It is often difficult to gauge the impact of the various kinds of migratory movements since data are not available on migration and other variables at the regional level. To that extent the analysis should be treated as partial.

District-level Analysis

A more disaggregated analysis at the district level could help overcome some of the limitations of data. The result of a correlation exercise at district level using 21 variables is presented in Table 4.7. It indicates a significant association between the proportion of BPL households and most of the variables (except rural sex ratio, proportion of wasteland and land productivity).

The variables having a significant association with the BPL estimates include demographic and social development indicators such as population growth and infant mortality (having a positive association), and population density and female literacy (having a negative association). Other variables like urbanisation and infrastructural development index also have significant negative association with the BPL estimate.

It is important to note that irrigation turns out to be a significant variable influencing poverty reduction at district level. What is surprising is that neither land productivity nor proportion of wasteland was found to be significant. Data on rural wages were not available.

Forest area and tribal population have a significant positive association with rural poverty. This reinstates our earlier observation about the high incidence of poverty in forest-based regions and tribal communities who live in those regions. Essentially, these observations support the assertion about the double disadvantage of the people in the forest-based region: they have to face dryland like conditions as well as physical remoteness and social marginalisation.

Similarly, rural non-farm employment is found to be negatively associated with the BPL estimates. This is also in close conformity with the pattern observed at the macro-level by several studies in the past (Ravallion 2002).

Inter-State Variations

We tried to examine whether the pattern of poverty and its correlates vary across states in western India. The value of correlation co-efficient for the four states is separately given in Table 4.7. Apparently, the results do not show any dissimilarities between the two sets of states,

Table 4.7: Correlates of Poverty in the Districts of the Four Western States (1995)

Variables	*Value of correlation co-efficient*				
	All four states	*Gujarat*	*Mahara-shtra*	*Madhya Pradesh*	*Rajasthan*
Population growth rate	.185*	—	—	—	—
Population density	-.191*	—	-.393*	-.470**	—
Infant mortality rate	.354**	—	.591*	—	—
Female literacy	-.474**	-.494*	-.647**	—	-.551**
S.T.	.781**	.874**	.685**	.607**	.856**
Urban population	-.573**	-.581**	-.426*	-.607**	-.741**
Forest area	.401**	.713**	—	.461**	.430*
Female work participation	.443**	.774**	.520**	.567**	.566**
Irrigated area	-0.456***	—	—	-.420**	—
Non-farm workers	-.275*	—	—	—	—
Non-farm in emp.	-.582**	-.613**	-.600**	-.564**	-.633**
Composite infrastructure Index	-.352**	—	-.416*	-.301*	—
GCA % to	-.264**	-.569*	-	-.387**	—
Rural sex ratio	—	—	-.470*	.351*	—
Wasteland	—	—	—	-.295*	—

Source: Centre for Monitoring Indian Economy (District Profiles), Various issues

*, **, *** indicate significance at 1 per cent, five per cent and 10 per cent levels respectively.

viz. Gujarat-Maharashtra and Rajasthan-Madhya Pradesh. Nevertheless, the following observations are worth noting:

(a) Population growth is not found to be significantly associated with poverty at the state level.

(b) Variables like the proportion of the Scheduled Tribe population, female workforce participation, and non-farm employment are the common variables having a significant association with poverty in all the four states. Female workforce participation is positively linked with poverty suggesting that the higher female work participation is an outcome of poverty.

(c) A positive association with forest area is found in three states—Gujarat, Rajasthan, Madhya Pradesh. Similarly, female literacy is found to be negatively associated with poverty in three states: Maharashtra, Gujarat, Rajasthan.

(d) Surprisingly, significant association with irrigation is found only in Madhya Pradesh, where the proportion of out-migration is lower, given its low level of development.

(e) Finally, whereas Maharashtra and Madhya Pradesh show a significant association with the rural sex ratio, the direction of association is found to be opposite in the two states. In Maharashtra the correlation is negative, suggesting an impact of male out-migration on poverty reduction. In Madhya Pradesh, however, the association is found to be positive. This might suggest that although large-scale migration takes place among the tribal population in these regions, the outcome in terms of poverty reduction may not be significant unlike what has been found in the relatively more industrialised states like Maharashtra. Strangely, the rural sex ratio does not have any significant relationship with poverty among the districts in Gujarat and Rajasthan.

These differentiated outcomes of migration substantiate the contention that the interface between natural resources and poverty is multi-patterned, especially when it is mediated by the important structural factors like agrarian relations, access to forest resources and the diversification of the state economy. It is, therefore, important to understand the dynamics of these inter-relationships by examining the situations at more disaggregated levels. The analysis presented here provides only a broad pattern of similarities in the association between poverty and the factors that influence it. It is also important to probe further the dissimilarities that obtain across states and regions by looking into the initial situations as well as the processes that bring differential outcomes. This should form the agenda for future research that could inform policy formulation for poverty reduction in the western region.

SUMMARY AND IMPLICATIONS FOR POLICY FORMULATION

(a) The foregoing analysis has presented a multi-patterned interface between natural resources and poverty in the Indian context. Given the critical importance of agricultural growth for poverty reduction, a two-fold categorisation of states and regions, having differential patterns of poverty-natural resource interface, was identified. In doing so, it reinstated the mediating role of the three structural factors, viz. agrarian relations, entitlement to forest resources and economic diversification of the state economy.

It is demonstrated that dryland areas generally have a lower incidence of poverty vis-à-vis forest-based regions, but this situation may not continue. For, a lower incidence of poverty in the dryland areas is achieved largely by over-exploitation the of natural resources (especially the groundwater), which is difficult to sustain for long. Forest-based areas, on the other hand, suffer largely because of resource degradation as well as social marginalisation.

What this implies is that in both the situations poverty reduction (via promoting sustainable use of natural resources) is rooted in the property rights regime. The central issue, therefore, is the rural households' effective access to and control over the critical resources, viz. groundwater and forests. The future policies should, therefore, address these issues in a holistic manner, rather than consider regeneration of groundwater in isolation from the status of forest and/or vegetation in the region. This is particularly important because a large part of the forest-based areas in the western states also faces the problems of resource degradation as do dryland areas.

(b) The disaggregated analysis indicated a positive association between poverty and the proportion of forest areas as well as tribal population. While this only confirms what is already known as macro-reality, the finding has a particular relevance for the western region. For a large part of the forest in the contiguous areas of the four states harbours pockets of hardcore poverty in the western zone. The development of the region, therefore, calls for an area-based approach, and the area would consist of southern Rajasthan, eastern-tribal belt of Gujarat, western and south-west Madhya Pradesh and the hinterland of Maharashtra. The region is not only geographically contiguous, it is also agro-climatically and culturally homogeneous.

Evolving an area-based approach would require a close collaboration between the four states. This necessitates, in turn, exploring avenues for regional co-operation within the overall framework of federal finance in the country. In the absence of these, the poor may keep circulating in the regions and the states with little improvement in their well-being.

(c) An analysis of the correlates of poverty at the regional and district levels has brought out certain additional insights. One of the important observations emerging from the analysis is that whereas agricultural labour productivity is an important factor in reducing poverty at the regional level, irrigation is *not* found to have any significant impact on poverty reduction. On the contrary, a district-level analysis suggested a significant *negative* association between the extent of irrigation and poverty. This suggests that irrigation has a fairly localised impact on poverty reduction perhaps because it tends to be intensive rather than extensive.

One of the important implications of such an approach is planning for a more sustainable use of irrigation so that livelihood support is provided to a large number of households within the region. Ideally, the area- or region-based approach should work towards the goal of providing minimum water for all (Shah *et al.* 1998). This will not only ensure curbing distress migration and thereby reducing the pressure on natural resources at destination, but will also help regenerate land and water resources in the place of origin. Eventually, the strategy will turn out to be environmentally more sustainable.

(d) We also looked into the differentiated pattern of correlates of poverty across the four States. The disaggregated analysis however, did not bring out significant dissimilarities that seem to be obtaining across the two sets of states viz., Gujarat and Maharashtra on the one hand, and Rajasthan and Madhya Pradesh on the other. To an extent, this could be attributed to the non-availability of data as well as improper specification of some of the variables such as migration, extent (rather than intensity) of irrigation, and poverty.

It is likely that the impact of relatively higher economic development, especially of the industrial sector in Gujarat and Maharashtra, is reflected more in terms of *severity* and *duration* of poverty, than its *incidence*. The latter has already been influenced by migration from various places—within and outside the state. Understanding of the intensity as well as chronicness of poverty may help in understanding the dynamics at regional and sub-regional levels. Given data limitations, special efforts will have to be made to understand the dynamics of poverty in high-poverty areas in the region. Such an exercise would have to cover villages and households extensively so as to be representative of the district or sub-region.

Participatory poverty appraisal, carried out recently in Gujarat and Madhya Pradesh, may provide useful lessons. The need, however, is to simultaneously examine the functional aspects of some of the critical factors in poverty reduction such as the status of natural resources, access to these resources among the poor households, nature and impact of migration, scope for improving efficiency in the use of natural resources and institutional mechanisms that could help achieve the goal of "water for all", especially in the dryland areas in the region.

(e) Future policies should be based on a detailed understanding of the different patterns of interface between poverty and natural resources within the region. The poverty analysis thus ought to step out of the existing bi-polar situation of generalisation at macro-level and minute details of a few location-specific situations at micro-level. A detailed inquiry into not only the status of poverty and natural resources but also in the processes leading to poverty should then be carried out as an input for the area-based approach suggested above. While some states like Gujarat have a rich experience of decentralised planning, the need is to move away from administrative boundaries and adopt a new system in which regions are defined by the boundaries of natural resources, i.e. a watershed or a river basin. This, in turn, would help evolve a regional perspective for development and poverty reduction in western India.

REFERENCES

Bhalla, G.S. and Singh, Gurmail, (1997): "Recent Developments in Indian Agriculture: A State Level Analysis". *Economic and Political Weekly* 32 (13).

Bhalla, Sheila, (2000): "Behind Poverty: The Qualitative Deterioration of Employment Prospects for Rural Indians". Paper presented at the Third Asian Conference of Agricultural Economists, October 18-20, 1968, at IDS, Jaipur.

Bhattarai, M. and Narayanamoorthy, A., (2002): "Impact of Irrigation on Agricultural Growth and Poverty Alleviation: Macro Level Analyses in India". IWMI-Tata Water Policy Programme, No. 12, Vallabh Vidyanagar, Gujarat.

Bilsborrow, Richard E., (1992): "Rural Poverty, Migration, and the Environment in Developing Countries: The Case Studies". Policy Research Working Paper 1017. The World Bank.

Chopra, Kanchan, and Gulati, S C., (2001): *Migration, Common Property Resources and Environmental Degradation: Interlinkages in India's Arid and Semi-arid Regions*. New Delhi: Sage Publication.

Conroy, C.; Iyengar, S.; Lobo, V.; and Rao, B., (2001): "Household Livelihood and Coping Strategies in Semi-arid India: Adapting to Long Term Changes". Research Report for SPWD. Ahmedabad: Gujarat Institute of Development Research.

Dantwala, M.L., (1996): "My Academic Dialogues: Agricultural Price Policy and the Green Revolution". *Indian Journal of Agricultural Economics* 51(1).

De Janvry, A., and Gracia, R., (1988): "Rural Poverty and Environmental Degradation in Latin America: Causes, Effects and Alternative Solutions". S 88/1/L3/Rev.2. Rome: IFAD.

Desai, B.M., and Namboothiri, N.V., (1997): "Developing Agriculture in Gujarat: A Strategic Perspective for Ninth Plan". *Economic and Political Weekly* 32(13).

Dubey, A., and Gangopadhyaya, S., (1998): "Counting the Poor: Where are the Poor in India". *Sarvekshna*, Analytical Report, Number 1.

Duriaappah, Anantha, K., (1998): "Poverty and Environmental Degradation: A Review and Analysis of the Nexus". *World Development* 26(12).

Fan, Shenggan, and Hazell, Peter, (2000): "Should Developing Countries Invest More in Less-Favoured Areas? An Empirical Analysis of Rural India". *Economic and Political Weekly* 35(17):1455-64.

Haan, Arjan De, and Rogaly, Ben, (2002): "Introduction: Migrant Workers and Their Role in Rural Change". *Journal of Development Studies* 38(5):1-13.

Haan, Arjan De, (1999): "Livelihoods and Poverty: The Role of Migration: A Critical Review of the Migration Literature". *Journal of Development Studies* 36(2):1-47.

ICRISAT and ICAR, (1999): *Typology Construction and Economic Policy Analysis for Sustainable Rainfed Agriculture*.

Iyengar, S. and Shukla, N., (1999): "Regeneration and Management of Common Property Land Resources CPLRs) in India: A Review". Working Paper No. 110. Ahmedabad: Gujarat Institute of Development Research.

Jodha, N.S., (1986): "Common Property Resources and Rural Poor in Dry Regions of India". *Economic and Political Weekly* 30(27):1169-81.

Jodha, N.S., (1990): "Drought Management: The Farmer's Strategies and Their Policy Implications". International Institute for Environment and Development, Paper No. 21.

Kelley, T.G., and Rao, Parthasharathi P., (1995): "Marginal Environment and the Poor: Evidence from India". *Economic and Political Weekly* 30(40):2429-95.

Kundu, Amitabh, (2003): "Globalisation, Inequality and Mobility of Population in India". Paper presented at the seminar on Labour Mobility in a Globalising World: Conceptual and Empirical Issues.

Lipton, Michael, (1980): "Migration from Rural Areas of Poor Countries: The Impact of Rural Productivity and Income Distribution". *World Development* 8:1-24.

Lopez, R., (1997): "Where Development Can or Cannot Go: The Role of Poverty-Environment Linkages". Proceedings of the Annual Bank Conference on Development Economics. Washington, D.C.: The World Bank.

Markandya, A., undated: "Poverty Alleviation and Sustainable Development: Implications for the Management of Natural Capital". University of Bath, U.K.

Marothia, D., (1997): "Agricultural Technology and Environmental Quality: An Institutional Perspective". *Indian Journal of Agricultural Economics* 52(3).

Mehta A.K., and Shah, Amita, (2002): "Chronic Poverty in India: Incidence, Causes and Policies". CPRC Working Paper.

Nadal, A., (1998): "Maize in Mexico: Some Environmental Implications of the North America Free Trade Agreement (NAFTA)". Montreal: Commission for Environmental Cooperation.

Nadkarni, M.V., (1985): *Socio-Economic Conditions in Drought Prone Areas.* New Delhi: Concept Publishing Company.

Nadkarni, M.V., (2000): "Poverty, Environment, Development: A Many Patterned Nexus". *Economic and Political Weekly* 35 (14).

NIRD, (2000): *India: Rural Development Report: Regional Disparities in Development and Poverty.* Hyderabad: National Institute of Rural Development.

Radhakrishna, R., (2002): "Agricultural Growth, Employment and Poverty: A Policy Perspective". *Economic and Political Weekly* 37(3):243-50.

Ravallion, Martin., (2000): "What Is Needed for a More Pro-Poor Growth Process in India?" *Economic and Political Weekly* 35(13).

Ray, Sumit, (1996): "Development, Environment and Poverty: Some Issues for Discussion" *Economic and Political Weekly* 31(4).

Rao, C. H. Hanumantha (2000): "Declining Demand for Foodgrains in Rural India: Causes and Implications", *Economic and Political Weekly*, 35 (4).

Sagar, V., (1995): "Public Intervention for Poverty Alleviation in Harsh Agro-Climatic Environment: Case of Rajasthan". *Economic and Political Weekly* 30 (41).

Sen, Abhijit, (1996): "Economic Reforms, Employment and Poverty: Trends and Options". *Economic and Political Weekly* 31 (35).

Shah, Amita, (2000): "Food Security and Environment: Issues and Evidences". Working Paper No. 116, Ahmedabad: Gujarat Institute of Development Research.

Shah, Amita, (2001): "Drought-proofing: Exploring Wide Options", in *Towards Hunger Free India: Agenda and Imperatives,* ed. M.D. Asthana, *et al.* World Food Programme. New Delhi: Manohar Publication.

Shah, Amita, (2003): "Land Degradation and Migration in a Dryland Region in India: Understanding the Dynamics". Unpublished Report. Ahmedabad: Gujarat Institute of Development Research.

Shah, Amita, and Sah, D.C., (2003): "Chronic Poverty in South West Madhya Pradesh: A Multi-dimensional Analysis of its Extent and Causes", in *Chronic Poverty in India* (ed) Aasha Kapur Mehta *et al.* New Delhi: IIPA.

Shah, Mihir; Banerji, Debashish; Vijayshankar, P.S; and Ambasta, Pramathesh, (1998): *India's Drylands*. New Delhi: Oxford University Press.

Singh, R.P. and Binswanger, Hans, (1993): "Income Growth in Poor Dryland Areas in India's Semi-arid Tropics". *Indian Journal of Agriculture Economics* 48 (1):51-64.

Sudrak, (2003): "*Ajeevika Study*". Unpublished Study. Udaipur.

Sundaram, K., (2003): "On Identification of Households Below Poverty Line in BPL Census 2002: Some Comments on the Proposed Methodology", *Economic and Political Weekly* 38(9).

Walker, Thomas, S., and Ryan, James G., (1990): *Village and Household Economies in India's Semi-arid Tropics*. Baltimore and London: The Johns Hopkins University Press.

World Food Programme, (2001): "Food Insecurity Atlas of Rural India". Chennai: M.S. Swaminathan Research Foundation.

5

Goa: Been There, Done That, Now What?
Resource Management and Democratic Processes

PRANAB MUKHOPADHYAY

This paper is divided into five parts beginning with an introduction to the State of Goa. The second section discusses Goa's success on some of the development indices. The third part highlights some of the issues of concern in the State. The fourth section examines local-level governance, prospects of natural resource management and issues of institutional design. The fifth section presents the discussion on possible policy interventions in the current scenario.[1]

INTRODUCTION

Goa, a small state on the western coast, is popularly known as a recreation zone, and is not a flag on the academician's map or an agenda point on the social analyst/policy maker's framework.[2] In some circles it has acquired the reputation of being a model state in terms of social development indicators, but it has never entered policy debates of the mainstream (unlike the Kerala model), probably due to its size as well as academic remoteness.

Goa was a Portuguese colony from 1510 to 1961 when it joined the Indian Union. After 16 years of being a Union Territory, along with Daman and Diu which were also Portuguese colonies, it became a state in 1987.[3] Like the rest of the world, this little "paradise" has much to talk about and much to worry about too.

Goa made headlines for the continued opposition to "polluting" industries or projects – ranging from the Thapar-Du Pont Nylon 66

Project to the more recent Meta Strips case to luxury tourism-based projects—both hotels and housing complexes (Alvares 1999). This has reflected in government policy which in its own words now seeks to attract "clean industries".[4]

A PROGRESSIVE STATE

Goa enjoys one of the highest per capita incomes in the country—Rs. 38,000 in 1999-2000 (Government of Goa 2002, p. 173).[5] The primary sector contributed about 13 to 15 per cent, the secondary sector about 27 to 34 per cent and the tertiary sector 51 to 57 per cent of the net state domestic product (NSDP) in the late 1990s. Trade, hotels and restaurants alone contributed about 14-15 per cent of the NSDP. In the occupational structure too the impact of tourism-related activities is evident. The 2001 census indicates a significant drop in the working population in the agricultural sector (cultivators by 26 per cent and agricultural labourers by 19 per cent over the 1990s). Correspondingly, employment rose in the non-agricultural sector, presumably in tourism. Workers in the categories of Household Industry and Other Workers rose by 43.3 and 45 per cent respectively. This corresponds to the growth in the tourist traffic in the state during this period.

In terms of development indicators, Goa has much to write home about. It has a high literacy rate (currently the fourth highest in the country—male 83 per cent and female 67 per cent), a low fertility rate—TFR of 1.8 children per woman as opposed to the national average of 2.9—widespread knowledge about contraception, and a high mean age at marriage for girls—25 years (IIPS 2002). The infant mortality rate is one of the lowest in India—37 deaths between 0-11 months per 1,000 live births. These indicators suggest a progressive state as far as the achievement of developmental goals is concerned. However, this commendable record has generated a sense of complacency not only among the public policy-makers but also among the social commentators.

FLOURISHING TOURISM BUT AT A PRICE!

So where do we go from here? We will briefly try and enumerate some of the concerns.

Goa has an above (national) average (Female-Male Ratio (FMR); however, it has reasons to worry on this front as the FMR for the 0-6 age group is falling (about 933).

Despite the high per capita income, the nutritional status of women and children in Goa is worrisome.[6] The recent National Family Health Survey II, 1998–99 (NFHS II) revealed that anaemia is a critical issue among the women and children in the state. Of all the women surveyed by the NFHS II 1998-9, 36 per cent have some form of anaemia. The proportion of children between 6-35 months suffering from moderate to severe anaemia is 29.8 per cent.

Tourism, one of the major sectors of the Goan economy in terms of both its employment and income contribution to the Net State Domestic Product (NSDP), has its costs. In 1981, Goa had a population of 10 lakh, while the total tourist inflow in that year was 4.4 lakh. In 1991, the resident population was about 11 lakh, and the tourist inflow was 8.7 lakh. In 2001, the resident population was 13.4 lakh, and the tourist inflow rose to 13.8 lakh; the inflows overtook the local population for the first time. Obviously the growth in tourist inflows has outstripped the growth of the local population. This floating population makes demands—some argue disproportionate—on all resources.

Demand for water has risen and untreated waste-water disposal has created ecological problems. Water samples collected in areas surrounding tourist accommodations have revealed a startlingly high incidence of bacteria in the drinking water sources (Gonsalves and de Souza 1998).[7] This must be seen alongside the problem of low sanitary standards—41 per cent of the households in Goa have no toilet facility at all—and the limited access to water supply—only 63 per cent of the households are within 15 minutes of safe water supply (IIPS 2002, p. xvi). Garbage disposal is currently a matter of debate in various urban and semi-urban areas in Goa since much of the current waste is not locally recyclable by natural means.

The beach-based tourism in Goa has led to numerous instances of Coastal Regulatory Zone (CRZ) violations along the coastline. Some cases have been successfully challenged, but the sheer magnitude (number) of violations and the sluggishness or the unwillingness of the state to administer the Act have let many violators "off the hook'".

The other coastal zone problem in the state that has repeatedly come up is the issue of fishing rights. All villages along the coast had traditional fishing communities (*ramponkars*) who used non-mechanised fishing equipment. In the seventies, their livelihoods were threatened by large mechanised boats—trawlers—which were capable of mass fish collection. The number of trawlers grew with the increased global demand for fish.

There is a long history of struggle by the *ramponkars* protesting against the entry of trawlers in their fishing zones, and on occasions they have been successful in regulating the trawler activity. The most recent movement of the *ramponkars* is to oppose the attempts to introduce aquatic sports in some parts of Goa which, they say, affects their fish catch in the coastal zone.

Likewise, the opposition to various industrial and hotel projects by the neighbouring villages has had a similar impact on public policy and the legal system. All these issues bring us to the key question of natural resource management by local communities, institutions, property rights and social norms which govern the articulation of demands as well as the allocation of resources. Does self-governance lead to better utilisation and preservation of resources?

Kerala has been a fore-runner in setting standards of local self-governance and the implementation of the Panchayati Raj in empowering local communities. A large part of this success story is ascribed to the high levels of literacy and political mobilisation achieved in that state. With its high literacy rates (like Kerala) and high per capita income(*un*like Kerala), Goa holds out a hope for establishing an effective participatory decision-making system.

LOCAL INSTITUTIONS

In developing countries, which have various forms of market and state failures, choosing the instrument for resource allocation is often difficult since it is not clear which is relatively more desirable, the market or the state.[8] In such situations, the search for alternative allocation mechanisms leads to the community as a unit of decision-making.[9] The resident communities in Goa have evolved systems of control and regulation, especially in the management of local natural resources. So even in the presence of an over-arching state, it makes sense to use these local community systems since they are likely to be transparent and participatory. This would reduce transaction costs in the administration and supervision of natural resources (Chopra, Kadekodi and Murthy 1990).

In the context of natural resource management, the cases of successful conservation seem to indicate that communities play a crucial role in creating the framework for a long-term resource use and define better bequest motive than either the state or the market (Baland and Platteau 1999; Hayami and Platteau 1997). The literature shows that cooperation emerges not by state decree alone but through historical evolution—interaction of agents—especially in the context of common property (Ostrom 1990 and 1993). For a stable system of resource sharing to arise, there must be an acceptable resolution of conflicting demands on resources. Even though the state may honour the legal rights of private ownership and its use, it is unable to supervise and intervene on a day-to-day basis. This would be best done at the local level and, if possible, by institutions of civil society. The stability of these institutions, however, is contingent on some form of acceptance by agents participating in the economic process[10] of a structure of property rights[11] and the legal framework.

The literature on institutions distinguishes between self-evolved systems, described as "endogenous normative law", and externally-imposed systems, for example, made by the legislature, described as "positive law" (Aoki 2001). In Goa there is evidence of both such local-level institutions.

Goa has a history of traditional land management institutions–the *gaunkaris* or *communidades* as referred to by the Portuguese.[12] These are essentially in the nature of village republics. They were oligarchic in their constitution; only original settler-families had the right to decision-making in the village. All agricultural lands were jointly owned by the *gaunkaris,* and they alone had the right to auction these lands periodically to the highest bidder. The rents from the auction were used for land management (embankment and sluice-gate repairs) and paying land taxes (*foros*) to the king; the remaining amounts were distributed as rents to the *gaunkars*.

After Goa joined the Indian Union in 1961, the Land Tenancy Act of 1964 and its successor Acts reduced the powers of the *communidades* and replaced them with the panchayats in 1963 as they existed in the rest of the country at that time.

The tenants, who became effective owners of the land following the Tenancy Acts, were expected to form Tenants' Associations (TAs). These associations were expected to replace the *communidades* in the maintenance of village lands, sluice gates and embankments which keep saline ingress from affecting cultivation in the *khazan* (recovered) lands in the coastal zone. However, not surprisingly, these TAs did not evolve into the institutions they were supposed to replace (Government of Goa 1992; Mukhopadhyay 2002b).

Currently, there are three local institutions that exist in Goa: panchayats, TAs and *communidades*. The panchayats are constitutional bodies; they are democratic in nature and are at the lowest rung of development. The TAs do not even exist in most villages. In places where they do, the only major activity they undertake seems to be the lucrative auction of sluice gates (which gives the successful bidder the fishing rights at the sluice gate that controls the inflow and outflow of tidal waters). And then, there is the *communidade,* which still has a whole structure of governance present in each village but very little administrative or financial powers. Members of the *communidade* continue to receive dividends if the *communidade* makes a profit.[13]

This multiplicity of local institutions–an endogenous type (*communidade)* which is administratively and financially disenfranchised, and two of exogenous variety, democratic (*panchayats*) and interest-driven (TAs)—has created a peculiar incongruence in the management of natural resources at the local level. The responsibilities of one institution have now been handed over to numerous departments which are either at the district or the state level. For example, the maintenance of the *bunds* is now the responsibility of the Soil Department or the Department of Agriculture. These departments have no direct incentive for the day-to-day maintenance of the *bunds* as their revenues are not dependent on *bunds,* unlike the *communidades*, where land rents (and therefore individual dividends) would fall if the *bunds* were not maintained

The TA is financially not viable as none of the members (tenants) pays its dues. The main reason is that the TA has no administrative powers and, therefore, no enforceable fee structure, which the *communidades* had. However, the TAs are supposed to contribute 50 per cent of the expenses for land upgradation in their individual areas while the state promised to match the TA contribution. What has happened in reality is that the state has paid its share but the TAs have reneged on paying their share; in many cases they have not even submitted accounts of expenses.

The panchayats have no institutional interest in natural resource management. On the contrary, their incentives lie in natural resource destruction (in terms of land conversion). In many parts of Goa, for instance, house tax is the single largest source of panchayat revenue followed by construction and licensing fees (greater than grants from all sources). None of its revenues come from the maintenance of agricultural land infrastructure or forest cover in its area. There is, therefore, a direct incentive for the panchayat to encourage not just construction but even land conversion. In terms of duties and responsibilities, local road maintenance and street lighting are its major infrastructure-related responsibilities. Soil conservation, maintenance of irrigation works, etc., are not on the list of panchayat duties in Goa. Also, they do not have the enabling finances or revenue-raising instruments at their disposal (Fernandes and Mukhopadhyay 1999).

DISCUSSION: POLICY INTERVENTIONS

The post-independence efforts at institutional engineering have not moved in the desired direction essentially because of the lack of appreciation of incentive structures for different agents in the economy. This gives us an opportunity to join some of the contributors who argue that local dependence on a larger authority has often been the cause of decline in the local management and institutions. We presume that they imply that the share of grants forms a disproportionate portion of the revenues of local governments (panchayats). Jodha (1985), for example, has pointed out that panchayats in India are not geared for an effective local empowerment by the structure of their governance. The peculiar nature of financial dependence of these institutions, which rely less on local mobilisation and more on state benevolence for local developmental projects, makes them particularly vulnerable. Individual panchayats refuse to levy appropriate fees anticipating a loss of popularity among its members. This leads to an inefficient allocation–under-allocation at the local level.

We wish to push Jodha's argument a little further. The problem of (lack of) autonomy of the panchayats is not the only problem. In fact, the very search for local financial sustenance forces them to undertake measures which are not conducive to local resource preservation as discussed above. Secondly, the panchayats do not have the administrative and judicial powers that any institution needs to enforce the rule of law. The separation of powers into those that control and those that provide service creates an imbalance in the institution design which needs to be addressed.

What does all this mean for the votaries of the local green brigade and for the democratic agenda? One alternative could be to revert to an earlier institution, which has had a successful history of local resource management such as the *communidade*. The process of reversal to a modified institution like the *communidade* would need to be examined very carefully. Frequent institutional changes could leave undesirable residues.

The other solution lies in further empowering the panchayats now that they have started establishing their legitimacy replacing the communidades as local-level governments. But in that case the institutional design and incentive structure of the panchayats must be changed to provide a direct institutional incentive for natural resource preservation. For example, the maintenance of the green cover, or soil preservation, could be tackled at the *panchayat* level rather than at the district level which impersonalises and slows down decision-making.

NOTES

1. Research support is acknowledged to the South Asian Network for Development and Environment Economics. I am grateful to Sudarshan Iyengar for earlier discussions, which have helped in the framing of some issues in this paper. The usual disclaimer applies.
2. For example, the Human Development Report on West and Central India (National Council for Applied Economic Research 2002) does not even include a section on Goa.
3. There were numerous attempts to incorporate Goa into the existing states in India, notably in Maharashtra. There have also been counter attempts to forge a regional Konkan identity (read statehood like Chhattisgarh, Uttaranchal, etc.) by carving out sections of Maharashtra and Karnataka. This is part of a larger debate on the Goan identity and still makes its appearance in varied forms including the Konkani-Marathi language issue (see, Newman 1999 and 2001).

4. However, mining which is considered by many as a large polluter has almost escaped the opposition's onslaught.
5. Foreign remittances play a big role in the prosperity of the Goan economy, in many ways similar to Kerala. The average per capita deposit mobilised in 1999-2000 was about Rs 45,000 with Tiswadi taluka topping the list with Rs 1, 36, 256 per capita.
6. This also raises suspicions about the distribution of income gains in the state especially when the official poverty line is very low.
7. While this is bad news for the tourist zones (for tourists as well as for local residents), we do not have counter-factual data to indicate that the situation is different in the non-tourist zones.
8. The market is suspect on the equity front and the state is infamous on the efficiency and corruption front.
9. Economic theory rationalises this behaviour as an attempt at risk sharing or risk pooling (Ray 1999).
10. This is contrary to the early view on property rights which argues that establishment of complete rights to private property leads to the internalisation of externalities. The initial distribution (allocation) would not effect the final outcome because the most efficient user would buy the resource by paying the highest price and use it most efficiently, assuming, of course, that there are perfect capital markets.
11. Aoki (2001) describes this as the development of proto-institutions.
12. We will not go into the history of these institutions in this paper as it would detract us from our current focus. The interested reader may look up Mukhopadhyay 2002a.
13. In some cases where the government has acquired lands and paid large sums of money to these institutions as compensation, the interest earned forms the dividends and the constituent members receive an annual bounty. In places where no such acquisition has taken place the *communidades* have no revenues and no dividends accrue to the members.

REFERENCES

Alvares, C., (1999): "Goa: The Politics of Environmental Abuse". In N. Dantas (ed.). *The Transformation of Goa.* Mapusa: Other India Press, pp.114-136.

Aoki, M., (2001): *Towards a Comparative Institutional Analysis.* Cambridge: Massachusetts Institute of Technology Press.

Baland, Jean-Marie, and Platteau, Jean-Philippe, (1999): *Halting Degradation of Natural Resources: Is there a Role for Rural Communities?* Oxford: Oxford University Press.

Chopra, K.; Kadekodi, G.K.; and Murthy, M.N., (1990): *Participatory Development: People and Common Property Resources.* New Delhi: Sage Publications.

Desouza, S., and Mukhopadhyay, P., (2001): "Tourism & Health in Goa". In V. Patel (ed.). *State of Goa's Health.* New Delhi: Voluntary Health Association of India.

Fernandes, A., and P. Mukhopadhyay, P., (1999): "Re-Designing Panchayat Finances and Attitudes: A Case Study of Goa", *Indian Journal of Rural Development* (April-June).

Gonsalves, D.V., de Souza, J., (1998): "Impact of Tourism Industry on Ground Water in Calangute, Goa", *Indian Journal of Environmental Protection* 18(6): 425-430.

Government of Goa, (1992): "Report of the Agricultural Land Commission". Submitted to the Government of Goa, Panaji, Mimeographed.

Government of Goa, (2002): "Economic Survey: 2002-2003". Government of Goa: Directorate of Planning, Statistics and Evaluation.

Hayami, Y., and Platteau, J.P., (1997): "Resource Endowments and Agricultural Development: Africa vs. Asia," CRED, Belgium: University of Namur.

IIPS, (2002): "National Family Health Survey (NFHS-2) 1998-99". Mumbai and Measure DHS+, ORC Macro, Maryland: Indian Institute of Population Studies.

Jodha, N.S., (1985): "Population Growth and Decline of Common Property Resources in Rajasthan, India". *Population and Development Review*, 11(2): 247-64.

Mukhopadhyay, P., (2002a): "Resource Use and Property Rights". Paper presented at the Beijer Institute Research Seminar on Property Rights Structures and Environmental Resource Management, May , Durban..

Mukhopadhyay, P., (2002b): "Institutional Change & Resource Use: A Case Study in Western India". Paper presented at the conference on Environmental History of Asia, Jawaharlal Nehru University, December, New Delhi.

National Council for Applied Economic Research, (2002): *Human Development Report: West and Central India.* New Delhi: Oxford University Press.

Newman, R.S., (1999): "The Struggle for a Goan Identity," in N. Dantas (ed.). *The Transformation of Goa.* Mapusa: Other India Press, pp.17-42.

Newman, R.S., (2001): "Konkani *mai* Ascends the Throne: The Cultural Basis of Goan Statehood". In R.S. Newman (ed.). *Of Umbrellas, Goddesses and Dreams.* Mapusa: Other India Press, pp. 54-80.

Ostrom, E., (1990): *Governing the Commons.* Cambridge: Cambridge University Press.

Ostrom, E., (1993): "The Evolution of Norms, Rules, and Rights". Discussion Paper Series No. 39, Beijer International Institute of Ecological Economics. Stockholm: Royal Swedish Academy of Sciences.

Ray, D., (1999): *Development Economics*, New Delhi: Oxford University Press.

Wadhwa, D.C., (2002): "Guaranteeing Title to Land", *Economic and Political Weekly* 37(47): 4699-722.

PART II

URBANISATION AND INDUSTRIALISATION

6

Urbanisation and Growth Dynamics in India

An Analysis with Special Reference to Western and Central Regions

AMITABH KUNDU and NIRANJAN SARANGI

The impact of economic reforms and liberalisation on the special structure of Indian economy is one of the areas of major policy concern, which has not been investigated with adequate empirical rigour. It is often argued that the trend of reasonably high growth in income and decline in poverty in India during the nineties notwithstanding, the regional inequality has acquired alarming proportions. The inequality across states in terms of both per capita income and percentage of people below the poverty line has gone up significantly. In line with the above it is expected that the process of urbanisation would have got a boost since the early nineties, although the growth in the urban population would be uneven in space.

The proponents of reform have often argued that linking of India with global economy would lead to a massive inflow of capital from outside the country and a rise in indigenous investment. This, in turn, would give impetus to the process of urbanisation since much of the investment and consequent increase in employment would be within or around the existing urban centres. Even if industrial units are located in rural areas, they would, in a few years, also be urbanised. However, critics of globalisation have pointed out that employment generation in the formal urban economy might not be high due to the capital-intensive nature of industrialisation. A low rate of industrial and infrastructural investment in the public sector-necessary for keeping budgetary deficits low–would, however, slow down agricultural growth. Thus, the protagonists as well as the critics of economic reform converged on the proposition that urban growth in the post-liberalisation phase would be high.

The recent data from the Population Census for the year 2001 provide an opportunity in understanding the trends and processes in urbanisation during the first decade of structural adjustment. A preliminary analysis of the Census data suggests that quick generalisations based on macro-overviews and ideological predispositions, as noted above, are likely to be completely misleading. The 2001 Census has recorded a significant decline in the urban growth as compared to the previous decade. The significant fact is that India portrays quite marked regional variations in the urban growth during the nineties as was possibly anticipated. A large majority of the urban population has been concentrated in only six most urbanised states, namely, Maharashtra, Gujarat, Tamil Nadu, Karnataka, Punjab and West Bengal, which together account for about half of the country's urban population. But the urban growth in these states until 1991 used to fall short of that in the less urbanised states, which clearly reveals that there has been a spatial concentration of urban population in the nineties.

Keeping the above overview in mind, the present paper attempts to analyse the dynamics of urbanisation and its interdependency on the dynamics and economic development at the state and district levels. It is pertinent to mention here that Census 2001 has its own importance since it came one decade after the liberalisation measures were undertaken and, therefore, kindles the curiosity of researchers and experts leading them to analyse the spatial-temporal processes of urbanisation in the nineties. The paper also discusses the changing structure of urban hierarchy and differentials in the growth rates of urban centres in different size classes. Further, it looks into the regional trends and patterns of urbanisation focusing on the nineties and examines how it makes a sharp departure from the past pattern. However, the Census data on urbanisation has very often been questioned on the grounds of reliability and spatial-temporal comparability. The Census is the only organisation that classifies settlements into rural and urban categories and provides population figures at the settlement level. Importantly, over the Censuses the application of census definition in identifying urban settlements as well as the state intervention in doing so has raised serious doubts about their longitudinal comparability. Therefore, it will be worthwhile to begin with an overview of the definitional issues relating to the urban data provided by the Population Census in the post-independence period before attempting a temporal and cross-sectional analysis in the subsequent sections.

Section-I deals with the definitional problems relating to the identification of urban settlements and their spatial-temporal comparison. Section-II analyses the trends in urbanisation at macro-level over the past four decades. It also looks into the changing structure of urban hierarchy and differentials in the growth rates of urban centres in different size classes. Section-III examines the trends and patterns at the state level and looks into the interdependency between the indicators of urbanisation and socio-economic development at three points of time, viz. 1981, 1991 and 2001. Section-IV attempts to explain the trends and patterns at the district level in the two selected states of Maharashtra and Rajasthan drawn from within the region under study here, the former being highly urbanised and developed and the latter less urbanised and less developed. A district-level correlation matrix is also prepared for all the three points of time. This enables us to assess whether the pattern observed in the developed state is different from that in the less developed one. Further, a discussion of the state-and district-level analysis gives insights into the dynamics of urbanisation within a macro-micro framework. Section-Final summarises the major findings and puts forward a perspective on urbanisation economic development.

DEFINITIONAL PROBLEMS IN THE CENSUS DATA

The 1951 Census, the first census in independent India, is believed to have overestimated the urban population because the states did not apply uniform criteria to identify urban centres. It reported a high growth rate (annual exponential) of 3.47 per cent per annum during 1941-51, which was attributed, at least partly, to definitional anomalies and partly due to the massive immigration in the wake of the partition of the country. An attempt was made in the Population Census of 1961 to standardise the concept of urban centre and make the data cross- sectionals comparable. The definition has by and large remained unchanged since then, although there have been variations in its application across states and over time.

The 1961 Census, adopted two-fold criteria to identify urban centres. First, the settlements that were given urban civic status like corporation, municipality, cantonment, etc., by the state governments were identified as Statutory Towns. As urban development is a state subject (and so is the responsibility of assigning the civic status), there is a wide variation in the conditionality adopted in assigning the civic status across the states. Keeping these considerations in view, and to make the data on urbanisation spatially comparable, the Census added a category of non-statutory or census towns. Secondly, three demographic criteria were applied to identify these census towns. These were: (i) population size of 5,000 or more, (ii) density of at least 400 persons per sq. km., and (iii) 75 per cent or more of the male workers engaged outside agriculture.

The adoption of such a two-fold categorisation of "statutory" and "census" towns was expected to take care of the differences. But it created problems of temporal comparability since the rather stringent requirements for identifying the census towns resulted in the declassification of a large number of towns, which were identified in 1951 (which was based on a less rigorous definition). The urban growth rate of 2.3 per cent during 1951-61 is, therefore, considered to be on the lower side, largely due to this definitional anomaly.

Similarly, even spatial comparability could not be achieved accurately. Most of the publications of the 1961 Census mention only corporation, cantonment, notified area committee and town committee from the above list. A few of the census documents like the *Provisional Population Totals* and *The Indian Population Bulletin,* 1991, however, take a broader view and include other places "having distinct urban characteristics even if such places did not strictly satisfy all the demographic criteria" as urban units.

The Number of Statutory and Census Towns: Problems of Comparability

The number of statutory towns has increased from 2,758 in 1981 to 2,996 in 1991, and further to 3,798 in 2001 (Table 6.1). The figure had gone up by 238 in 1991, while the increase in 2001 is more than three times that, viz. 802. The number of the Census towns had gone

Table 6.1: Status of Urban Centres in Various Censuses

S. No.	*States/UTs*	*1981*			*1991*			*2001*		
		Statutory Towns	*Census Towns*	*Total Urban Centres*	*Statutory Towns*	*Census Towns*	*Total Urban Centres*	*Statutory Towns*	*Census Towns*	*Total Urban Centres*
1.	Andhra Pradesh	85	167	252	116	148	264	116	94	210
2.	Arunachal Pradesh	—	6	6	—	10	10	—	17	17
3.	Assam	65	15	80	74	19	93	80	45	125
4.	*Bihar*	151	69	220	172	99	271	125	5	130
5.	Chhattisgarh	—	—	—	—	—	—	75	22	97
6.	Delhi	3	27	30	3	29	32	3	59	62
7.	Goa	9	6	15	13	18	31	14	30	44
8.	Gujarat	70	185	255	79	185	264	168	74	242
9.	Haryana	77	4	81	84	10	94	84	22	106
10.	Himachal Pradesh	45	2	47	57	1	58	56	1	57
11.	Jammu & Kashmir	57	1	58	72	2	74	72	3	75
12.	Jharkhand	—	—	—	—	—	—	44	108	152
13.	Karnataka	244	37	281	179	127	306	226	44	270
14.	Kerala	48	58	106	66	131	197	60	99	159
15.	*Madhya Pradesh*	275	52	327	387	78	465	339	55	394
16.	Maharashtra	232	75	307	246	90	336	251	127	378
17.	Manipur	31	1	32	28	3	31	28	5	33
18.	Meghalaya	5	7	12	7	5	12	10	6	16
19.	Mizoram	6	—	6	22	—	22	22	—	22
20.	Nagaland	4	3	7	8	1	9	8	1	9
21.	Orissa	95	13	108	102	22	124	107	31	138
22.	Punjab	132	2	134	112	8	120	139	18	157
23.	Rajasthan	192	9	201	199	23	222	184	38	222
24.	Sikkim	8	—	8	8	—	8	8	1	9
25.	Tamil Nadu	120	314	434	111	358	469	721	111	832
26.	Tripura	10	-	10	12	6	18	13	10	23
27.	*Uttar Pradesh*	678	26	704	710	43	753	638	66	704
28.	Uttaranchal	—	—	—	—	—	—	74	12	86
29.	West Bengal	105	186	291	116	266	382	123	252	375
	Union Territories									
30.	Andaman & Nicobar Islands	1	—	1	1	—	1	1	2	3
31.	Chandigarh	2	2	4	2	3	5	1	—	1
32.	Dadra & Nagar Haveli	—	1	1	—	1	1	—	2	2
33.	Daman & Diu	2	—	2	2	—	2	2	—	2
34.	Lakshadweep	—	3	3	—	4	4	—	3	3
35.	Pondicherry	6	—	6	8	3	11	6	—	6
	All India	**2758**	**1271**	**4029**	**2996**	**1693**	**4689**	**3798**	**1363**	**5161**

Note: (a) The towns including those appearing as constituents of urban agglomerations have been considered as separate units. (b) Estimated numbers of urban centres have been considered for Assam in 1981 and Jammu and Kashmir in 1991. (c) The states whose names are in italics have been bifurcated in the late nineties. The figures for 2001 for Bihar, Madhya Pradesh and Uttar Pradesh are, therefore, not comparable with those of earlier ones.

Source: Census of India, Paper-2, Rural-Urban Distribution, 1991 and 2001 (unpublished)

up from 1,271 in 1981 to 1,693 in 1991 but it declined in 2001 to 1,363.[1] Therefore, the net increase in the total urban centres (counting all the units comprising urban agglomerations individually) work gone up by only 472 in 2001 over the 1991 figure. In fact, this increase is basically due to the increase in the statutory towns (+802), although the number of the Census towns had declined (-330) in 2001. The corresponding increase in the number of urban agglomerations (UAs), however, shows a different trend: the number went down by 63 in 1981 (from 339 in 1971 and 276 in 1981) but increased significantly (by 105) in 1991. The number has once again gone up in 2001, but this time only by 1 (Table 6.2).

It would, therefore, be legitimate to ask the question whether the Census organisation has been more rigorous in applying the demographic criteria in identifying the urban centres in 2001. Or alternatively, can it be attributed to their *not* applying the criteria more rigorously? Further, state governments have used their discretion in different ways in declaring settlements as urban by giving them statutory status, across space as well as over time. Therefore, the massive increase in the statutory towns in 2001 points to the need to look into the role of state activism in influencing urban data.

The failure to provide an unambiguous list of urban areas was partially responsible, besides the discretionary rights being exercised differently at the state level, for the problem of cross-sectional comparability of the data. Uttar Pradesh, for example, reported very few small towns in 1961. This was because the Directorate of Census Operations did not include Town Area Committees (TACs) and Notified Area Committees (NACs) in the list of statutory towns.[2] Similar problems exist due to the exclusion of some other "urban local bodies" at the state level, to a greater or lesser extent, in many other states as well.[3] The problem could be only partially rectified in the Census of 1971 wherein 58 of these towns were treated as urban in the state. In 1981, however, as many as 382 towns were brought under the urban fold; majority of them had town area committee status in 1961 and 1971. It may, therefore, be advisable to re-compute the urban population in the state of Uttar Pradesh in 1961 and 1971 by considering these settlements as towns.

The 2001 Census shows an addition of as many as 397 towns to

Table 6.2: Number of Towns/Urban Agglomerations (UAs), Towns within and outside the UAs

S. No.	*States/UTs*	*1981*			*1991*			*2001*		
		Towns/ UAs	*Towns within UA*	*Towns outside UA*	*Towns/ UAs*	*Towns within UA*	*Towns outside UA*	*Towns/ UAs*	*Towns within UA*	*Towns outside UA*
1.	Andhra Pradesh	234 (4)	22	230	213 (15)	66	198	173 (37)	74	136
2.	Arunachal Pradesh	6	—	6	10	—	10	17	—	17
3.	Assam	77 (4)	7	73	87 (6)	12	81	110 (10)	25	100
4.	Bihar	179 (15)	56	164	211 (21)	81	190	120 (9)	19	111
5.	*Chhattisgarh*	—	—	—	—	—	—	84 (12)	25	72
6.	Delhi	6 (1)	25	5	7 (1)	26	6	4 (1)	59	3
7.	Goa	15 (2)	2	13	26 (3)	8	23	38 (3)	9	35
8.	Gujarat	220 (30)	65	190	225 (46)	85	179	180 (39)	91	141
9.	Haryana	77 (4)	8	73	90 (7)	11	83	97 (11)	20	86
10.	Himachal Pradesh	46 (1)	2	45	55 (2)	5	53	56 (1)	2	55
11.	Jammu & Kashmir	56 (2)	4	54	72 (7)	9	65	69 (7)	13	62
12.	*Jharkhand*	—	—	—	—	—	—	95 (11)	68	84
13.	Karnataka	250 (7)	38	243	254 (22)	74	232	237 (24)	57	213
14.	Kerala	85 (9)	30	76	109 (16)	104	93	98 (17)	78	81
15.	Madhya Pradesh	303 (49)	73	254	433 (60)	92	373	368 (42)	68	326
16.	Maharashtra	276 (14)	45	262	290 (18)	64	272	347 (15)	46	332
17.	Manipur	32	—	32	30 (1)	2	29	29 (1)	5	28
18.	Meghalaya	7 (1)	6	6	7 (1)	6	6	10 (1)	7	9
19.	Mizoram	6	—	6	22	—	22	22	—	22
20.	Nagaland	7	—	7	9	—	9	9	—	9
21.	Orissa	103 (8)	13	95	119 (9)	14	110	132 (10)	16	122
22.	Punjab	134 (19)	19	115	120 (22)	22	98	157 (19)	19	138
23.	Rajasthan	195 (12)	18	183	215 (19)	26	196	216 (23)	29	193
24.	Sikkim	8	—	8	8	—	8	9	—	9
25.	Tamil Nadu	245 (34)	223	211	260 (34)	243	226	668 (27)	191	641

(contd. Table 6.2)

(contd. Table 6.2)

S. No.	*States/UTs*	*1981*			*1991*			*2001*		
		Towns/ UAs	*Towns within UA*	*Towns outside UA*	*Towns/ UAs*	*Towns within UA*	*Towns outside UA*	*Towns/ UAs*	*Towns within UA*	*Towns outside UA*
26.	Tripura	10	—	10	18	—	18	23	—	23
27.	Uttar Pradesh	659 (26)	71	663	702 (31)	82	671	670 (32)	63	638
28.	*Uttaranchal*	—	—	—	—	—	—	76 (8)	18	68
29.	West Bengal	130 (32)	193	98	160 (38)	260	122	239 (21)	157	218
	Union Territories									
30.	Andaman & Nicobar Islands	1	—	1	1	—	1	1	2	3
31.	Chandigarh	1 (1)	4	—	1 (1)	5	—	1	—	1
32.	Dadra & Nagar Haveli	1	—	1	1	—	1	2	—	2
33.	Daman & Diu	2	—	2	2	—	2	2	—	2
34.	Lakshadweep	3	—	3	4	—	4	3	—	3
35.	Pondicherry	4 (1)	3	3	7 (1)	5	6	4 (1)	3	3
	All India	**3378 (276)**	**927**	**3102**	**3768 (381)**	**1302**	**3387**	**4368 (382)**	**1162**	**3986**

Note: (a) The number of UA is shown within brackets where they exist. The total number of towns/UAs obtained by counting UA as a single unit is shown outside the bracket. (b) The towns including those appearing as constituent units of UA have been considered as separate units. (c) The number of towns within and outside UA is shown in separate columns. (d) For 2001, figures for Gujarat and U.P do not include 10 and 3 towns respectively. (e) States shown in italics are the new ones and therefore figures are given only for 2001.

Source: Census of India, Paper-2, Rural-Urban Distribution, 1991 and 2001 (unpublished)

the urban list in Tamil Nadu (Table 6.3). This inclusion has made significant effect in the urban growth rate of the state between 1991 and 2001 and the level of urbanisation in 1991. The urban growth rate of Tamil Nadu is one of the highest (3.6) among the major states of the country. This growth rate in fact has doubled from 1991. The inclusion of such a huge number of towns has been on the merit of statutory notification – a matter of state's discretion. If there was no sudden addition in 2001 or if these towns were included in the previous census (they could have been notified in 1991 on the statutory basis), these striking differences of urban growth and level of urbanisation between 1991 and 2001 would have been reduced. It appears that the state government decided on the inclusion of these towns only because

Table 6.3: Addition, Declassification, and Merger of Towns

S. No.	States/UTs	1981					1991				
		No. of new towns	New town as per cent of urban pop.	No. of declassified towns	Declassified towns as per cent of urban pop.	No. of merged towns	No. of new towns	New town as per cent of urban pop.	No. of declassified towns	Declassified towns as per cent of urban pop.	No. of merged towns
1.	Andhra Pradesh	37 (32)	5.6	13	0.82	12	35 (35)	2	79	7.05	10
2.	Arunachal Pradesh	4 (4)	28.54	—	—	—	7 (7)	25.63	—	—	—
3.	Assam	13 (4)	3.72	—	—	—	37 (31)	7.96	5	—	—
4.	Bihar	57 (41)	5.9	2	0.05	4	3 (2)	0.36	11	2.37	—
5.	Chhattisgarh	NA	NA	NA	NA	NA	19 (18)	5.24	3	—	14
6.	Delhi	10 (10)	1.02	2	0.16	6	35 (35)	9.19	2	—	3
7.	Goa	16 (16)	25.98	—	—	—	17 (16)	20.05	3	—	1
8.	Gujarat	29 (28)	24	—	—	20	43 (23)	3.24	63	1.59	2
9.	Haryana	15 (8)	3.8	2	0.62	—	15 (14)	3.32	4	0.22	—
10.	Himachal Pradesh	11	3.3	—	—	—	2 (1)	4.67	1	0.79	1
11.	Jammu & Kashmir	16 (1)	NA	NA	NA	NA	1 (1)	0.2	—	—	—
12.	Jharkhand	NA	NA	NA	NA	NA	33 (33)	4.17	14	1.86	—
13.	Karnataka	51 (45)	3.4	19	127	7	45 (27)	6.48	39	1.86	—
14.	Kerala	90 (78)	27.5	1	0.27	—	18 (17)	3.71	41	—	15
15.	Madhya Pradesh	143 (45)	7.4	1	0.03	4	39 (26)	2.29	9	—	6
16.	Maharashtra	62 (48)	3.7	11	0.25	22	79 (78)	2.51	23	0.54	14
17.	Manipur	6 (2)	7.37	7	4.77	—	4 (4)	3.82	2	—	—
18.	Meghalaya	—	—	—	—	—	4 (1)	11.86	—	—	—
19.	Mizoram	16	19.56	—	—	—	—	—	—	—	—
20.	Nagaland	2 (1)	8.17	—	—	—	—	—	—	—	—
21.	Orissa	17 (11)	4	1	0.15	—	18 (13)	2.82	3	—	1
22.	Punjab	7 (6)	0.9	21	2.01	—	41 (16)	5.2	3	0.22	1
23.	Rajasthan	26 (18)	2	2	0.19	3	17 (17)	1.02	14	1.4	3
24.	Sikkim	—	—	—	—	—	1 (1)	24.44	—	—	—
25.	Tamil Nadu	38 (38)	1.9	3	0.06	—	456 (59)	21	61	1.05	32
26.	Tripura	8 (6)	36.87	—	—	—	7 (6)	12.08	2	—	—

(contd. Table 6.3)

(contd. Table 6.3)

S. No.	States/UTs	1981					1991				
		No. of new towns	New town as per cent of urban pop.	No. of declassified towns	Declassified towns as per cent of urban pop.	No. of merged towns	No. of new towns	New town as per cent of urban pop.	No. of declassified towns	Declassified towns as per cent of urban pop.	No. of merged towns
27.	Uttar Pradesh	62 (20)	2.3	5	0.12	8	45 (42)	1.36	7	—	4
28.	Uttaranchal	NA	NA	NA	NA	—	9 (8)	3.44	5	—	1
29.	West Bengal	111 (110)	4.6	3	0.08	17	105 (102)	4.75	48	—	64
Union Territories											
1.	Andaman & Nicobar Islands	—	—	—	—	—	2 (2)	13.93	—	—	—
2.	Chandigarh	1 (1)	1.36	—	—	—	—	—	—	—	4
3.	Dadra & Nagar Haveli	—	—	—	—	—	—	56.61	—	—	—
4.	Daman & Diu	—	—	—	—	—	1 (1)	49.83	—	—	—
5.	Lakshadweep	1 (1)	19.48	—	—	—	—	—	1	—	—
6.	Pondicherry	5 (3)	8.22	—	—	—	—	—	2	—	3
	All India	856 (579)	4.38	93	0.32	103	1138 (636)	5.09	445	—	221

Note: (a) NA: Not Available. (b) The towns including those appearing as constituent units of UAs have been considered as separate units. (c) The number of new census towns is shown in the parentheses.

Source: Census of India, Paper-2, Rural-Urban Distribution, 1991, 2001 (unpublished)

of the Seventy-fourth Constitutional Amendment and the state government's perception that all these settlements should be regarded as urban.

There are a few states where a large number of Census towns have been declassified which is likely to affect the level and growth rate of urban population during the nineties. The problem needs an in-depth investigation. In Tamil Nadu, for example, 61 census towns have been declassified and 59 new census towns added, besides the inclusion of 397 statutory towns in the urban list of 2001. Andhra Pradesh and Kerala are the two other states, wherein there are apprehensions of under-enumeration of the urban population and both report declassification of a large number of census towns, 79 and 39 respectively. In the case of Kerala, the 1991 Census had identified as many as 78 new census towns compared to only 17 in 2001. In a few other states like Gujarat, West Bengal and Karnataka too, 63, 48 and 39 Census towns respectively have gone out through declassification. But they have also gained through the inclusion of 23, 102 and 27 new census towns in 2001. Maharashtra is yet another state that has lost more than 23 census towns and has gained as many as 78 new Census towns. It, therefore, would be difficult to argue that the stringency in the application of demographic criteria has adversely affected the urban growth rates, except in the case of Tamil Nadu, Kerala, Gujarat and Andhra Pradesh.

Keeping this in view, it would be important to assess whether the concept of census town was applied rigorously in 1991 or 1981 as it is claimed to have been done in 2001. For doing that, an attempt should be made to see whether the declassified towns of 2001 would satisfy the demographic criteria in 1991, using the data from the Population Census of that year. This exercise has been done in the case of Gujarat as an illustrative example as presented below. It may be seen from Table 6.4 that the population figures and the growth rate for the nineties have also been worked out as presented below:

(i) The large declassification of the census towns in some of the states such as Andhra Pradesh, Gujarat and Tamil Nadu in 2001 is due to the state not applying the demographic criteria rigorously in 1991. Had the criteria been applied properly, there would have been fewer towns and lower urban population in 1991. The revised adjusted (annual exponential) growth rate for 1991-2001, thus, would have gone up. For example, the percentage of urban population is revised downwards from 26.84 to 25.51 in Andhra Pradesh and from 34.40 to 33.65 in Gujarat. Consequently, the growth rate (annual exponential) of urban population during 1991-2001 is revised to 1.9 against the recorded low figure of 1.4 in Andhra Pradesh and 3.1 instead of 2.8 in Gujarat.

Table 6.4: Towns of Gujarat Declassified in 2001

S. No	*Name of Town*	*Percent Male Workforce in Agri-culture*	*Popula-tion in 1991*	*S. No*	*Name of Town*	*Percent Male Workforce in Agri-culture*	*Popula-tion in 1991*
1.	Madhapar VP	21.13	16709	33.	Umrala VP	28.98	9091
2.	Naliya VP	26.86	8102	34.	*Paliyal VP*	*52.06*	*8322*
3.	*Chhapi VP*	*31.51*	*5716*	35.	Vallabhpur NP	19.09	14280
4.	Becharaji VP	28.50	8177	36.	*Dhuvaran VP*	*33.94*	*8784*
5.	Saji VP	28.19	10404	37.	*Sojitra NP*	*32.93*	*14853*
6.	Sola VP	27.95	5717	38.	*Vasa NP*	*30.51*	*12185*
7.	Vinzol VP	10.44	2634	39.	*Kathlal VP*	*34.63*	*14151*
8.	Barwala NP	27.99	13485	40.	Virpur VP	27.36	6785
9.	Ranpar NP	27.56	11765	41.	*Thasra NP*	*35.56*	*14004*
10.	*Mandal NP*	*50.31*	*10990*	42.	Pali NP	28.08	14818
11.	*Sayla NP*	*35.57*	*11772*	43.	*Shivrajpur VP*	*75.99*	*5133*
12.	Chotila VP	27.99	11581	44.	Chhani NP	20.13	14605
13.	Patdi NP	16.58	4092	45.	Vaghoda VP	23.08	11148
14.	*Lakhtar NP*	*40.42*	*11139*	46.	*Sankheda VP*	*30.98*	*91.29*
15.	*Jetalsar VP*	*31.15*	*11309*	47.	*Bahadarpur VP*	*51.01*	*6228*
16.	*Tankara VP*	*41.33*	*7790*	48.	*Sinor VP*	*43.17*	*8625*
17.	*Vinchhiya VP*	*37.92*	*9459*	49.	*Kavant VP*	*36.66*	*6597*
18.	*Lalpur VP*	*38.38*	*11539*	50.	*Jetpur VP*	*30.09*	*6466*
19.	Beyt VP	3.66	4891	51.	*Hansor VP*	*34.92*	*9589*
20.	Jodiya NP	20.40	2083	52.	Amod NP	29.33	14348
21.	Bikha NP	29.93	11041	53.	Amroli VP	2.14	13069
22.	Dungarpur VP	3.32	4674	54.	Olpad VP	24.04	10758
23.	*Mendarda NP*	*45.08*	*13142*	55.	Kathor NP	28.59	11720
24.	Talala NP	26.00	14372	56.	Mandvi NP	23.22	14297
25.	*Malia NP*	*48.08*	*11057*	57.	Kadod NP	26.05	10493
26.	*Shapur NP*	*50.01*	*9850*	58.	Ahwa VP	20.26	10963
27.	*Delwada VP*	*41.29*	*9120*	59.	Waghai VP	14.03	1938
28.	*Dhari NP*	*34.54*	*22460*	60.	Kaliawadi VP	10.26	4438
29.	*Dungar VP*	*46.17*	*6713*	61.	Saribujrang VP	25.85	6733
30.	*Valia NP*	*36.42*	*10714*	62.	Bansda VP	29.96	9728
31.	*Babra NP*	*34.37*	*14539*	63.	Kosamba VP	4.53	11655
32.	*Songadh VP*	*34.08*	*5771*				

Notes: (a) Declassification of 63 towns has been done on the basis of 1991 census. (b) Out of these, 30 (shown in italics) could not fulfil the workforce criteria even after considering 705 per cent (instead of 75 per cent) as the cut-off point for non-agricultural activity. (c) Population of these 30 towns in 1991 was 3,07,46 (d) Deducting this population from 1991's urban population of Gujarat, one obtains:

(i) Adjusted population in 1991=13857155 (as against 14164301)
(ii) Adjusted growth rate in 1991-01 = 3.06 (as against 2.8),
(iii) Adjusted level of urbanisation in 1991 = 33.65 (as against 34.40)

Source: Primary Census Abstract, Part II-B, Gujarat, 1991.

(ii) Applying the above exercise in Tamil Nadu, the revised urban population works out to 33.91 per cent instead of 34.20 per cent. However, a further adjustment has been made for this state. As mentioned earlier, Tamil Nadu has identified a large number of statutory towns in the 2001 Census. To make data temporally comparable, the new statutory towns have been considered as urban centres in 1991 in our revised calculations. Selection of towns on the basis of demographic criteria does not seem to fit here since these are statutory towns. As a result, the revised population figures go up in 1991 and the growth rate of urban population dip to 2.0 per cent as against 3.6 per cent during 1991-2001.

Factors Causing Differentials in the Growth of Number of Towns/Urban Agglomerations

The enormous decline in the number of census towns in 2001 could be attributed to the Directorate of Census Operations being more rigorous or restrictive in applying the demographic criteria to potential urban centres in various states. However, the problem of discretion exercised by the State Directorates or even officials at the district level cannot be totally ruled out, no matter how rigorously we may like to implement the demographic criteria. This can take place because there are practical difficulties in applying the criteria to rural settlements for the identification of census towns before the actual census is undertaken.

A similar explanation may be given for the addition of very few UAs in the Census of 2001. Unlike the flexibility in identifying UAs in the earlier censuses, the present census put forward a few conditions, such as *(i) at least one of the units in the group must be a statutory town and (ii) at least one must have a population of over 20,000 (as per the 1991 Census)*. Application of these conditions understandably knocked out a number of UAs and came in the way of identification of a large number of new units.

How important is the impact of these factors in bringing down the number of census towns in 2001 or deceleration in the urban growth would be anyone's guess. It may nonetheless be pointed out that despite the conscious efforts made to eliminate "towns with rural characteristics", there are as many as 636 new census towns identified in 2001. This is larger than the figure of 1991, which were only 579 (Table 6.3). It is, thus, evident that the main reason for the decline in the number of census towns is not the "laxity" in identifying new towns. Rather, this is due to the declassification and merger (of old census towns) with other towns and their being declared statutory towns. In 2001 as many as 445 towns were declassified compared to 93 in the 1991 Census. Furthermore, as many as 221 towns have been merged with the existing towns compared to 103 in 1991.

URBANISATION TRENDS SINCE INDEPENDENCE

The Pattern at the Macro Level

India experienced a very high growth rate of urban population in 1951, the highest until then, as per the Census of 1951. The annual compound growth rate was as high as 3.47 per cent (Table 5). Scholars have dismissed this high growth rate attributing it to the massive in-migration from across international borders due to the partition of the country and to a rather loose definition of urban centres in the first census conducted after independence. The adoption of a rigorous definition of urban place in the 1961 Census, as discussed in the previous section, resulted in the declassification of as many as 803 towns comprising a population of 4.4 million. Understandably, the growth rate came down to only 2.3 per cent in 1961. But it picked up a bit going up to 3.2 per cent during 1961-71. The increase was largely owed to the increase of population in the existing urban centres rather than any emergence of new towns.

The growth rate of the urban population during the seventies was 3.8 per cent, which is the highest in the last century. A large part of the increase can be attributed to the emergence of new urban centres; the Census of 1981 recorded as many as 1,054 new towns. There is also an apprehension that the definition of a census town may not have been applied rigorously in a few states, with the result that the number of new towns mushroomed. This high growth, however, set many demographers and urban planners speculating about hyper-urbanisation, similar to what had happened after publication of the

1951 Census results. Even government committees and international organisations talked of the spectre of over-urbanisation and predicted massive rural to urban migration and urban growth. Subsequently, the Census of 1991 recorded a significant decline in the urban growth. The growth rate came down to 3.1 per cent, which was much below all official projections. The trend went against not only the popular perception of "urban explosion" but also the projections made by the Expert Groups set up by various government departments.

The story was the same for the nineties. A number of government committees set up during the eighties and the nineties, besides the Indian Infrastructure Report and the Ninth Five Year Plan, had predicted a high urban growth. The Taskforce on Urban Development (Planning Commission 1983) had projected urban population in the country for the years 1991 and 2001, using two alternative variants. The high urban growth rate observed during 1971-81, as mentioned above, constituted the basis for the computation; both the projected figures were very much on the higher side.

The other official agencies in India making projections for urban development in the subsequent years maintained the "optimism" and, in fact, went beyond that. The Expert Committee for Population Projections for the Eighth Plan had predicted an annual growth rate of 4.4 per cent during the eighties and 4.1 per cent during the nineties. The Eighth Plan document (Planning Commission 1992) lowered the estimate of the urban population by the turn of the century since the Census of 1991 had reported a much lower rate of urbanisation in the eighties than was anticipated by the Expert Committee. The projected growth rate of urban population during the nineties, however, was maintained at 4.1 per cent. The Approach Paper to the Ninth Plan (Planning Commission 1997) did not mention any exact figure but anticipated a "higher rate of growth of urban population". The Expert Group on the Commercialisation of Infrastructure Projects of India Infrastructure Reports (1996), too, implicitly assumed a rapid pace of urbanisation as a consequence of the new economic policy.

It may nonetheless be pointed out that each subsequent projection in the nineties revised the growth rate downwards as more recent data on fertility and mortality became available from the Sample Registration System (SRS). The United Nations had projected as late as the mid-nineties the growth rate of urban population to be close to that of the eighties, viz. 3.1 per cent, which was the lowest among all the official projections. However, even this can now be dismissed as an overestimate since the 2001 Census records a significant decline in the urban growth, the annual rate being only 2.73 per cent (Table 6.5). This will be the lowest growth in the post-independence period, if the rate of the fifties is revised upwards to take care of the definitional anomalies discussed above. The Census 2001 thus provides an occasion to have a fresh look at our urban database and re-examine our perspective on urbanisation.

Table 6.5: Number of Towns and Percentage and Growth Rate of Urban Population in India since 1901

Census Year	*No. of Towns/ UAs*	*Percentage of Urban Population to Total Population*	*Annual Exponential Growth Rate*
1901	1827	10.84	—
1911	1815	10.29	0.03
1921	1949	11.18	0.79
1931	2072	11.99	1.75
1941	2250	13.86	2.77
1951	2843	17.29	3.47
1961	2365	17.97	2.34
1971	2590	19.91	3.21
1981	3378	23.34	3.83
1991	3768	25.72	3.09
2001	4368	27.78	2.73

Note: Estimates of population have been taken for Assam in 1981 and Jammu & Kashmir in 1991.

Source: Paper-2, Rural-Urban Distribution, 1981, 1991 and 2001 (unpublished).

The United Nations' (UN) study of World Urbanisation Prospects had placed the annual growth rate of urban population during the nineties at about 3.0 per cent, which is about what was observed during 1981-91. The UN has, however, revised their Prospect Document twice since then; both of these had come out before the 2001 Census results on urbanisation became available. The urban growth rate in the 1996 revision document is 2.72 per cent, and 2.80 per cent for the periods 1990-95 and 1995-2000. The subsequent revision of 1999 places the two figures at a slightly higher level, viz.

2.82 per cent and 2.84 per cent. The figures are much below those projected in 1995, possibly because these take into consideration the decline in the natural increase in population as reported in SRS.

The percentage of urban population projected in the 1995 UN Report was 28.6 in 2000. The two subsequent revisions place this at 28.4 per cent, an increase by of 2.9 percentage points over the figure of 1991. It may be observed that the projected figures are fairly close to the growth rate of 2.7 per cent and the percentage of urban population 27.8 obtained from the Census.

Urbanisation Pattern across Size Class of Urban Centres

It has been mentioned that the process of urbanisation in India is primarily large-city oriented. This is manifested at the national level as well as in a number of states; the share of Class 1 cities is much above that of the others. Importantly, the share has been going up systematically through all the decades in the last century. The present section analyses the changing structure of urban population across the size classes of settlements over the past ten census decades, putting the period since independence in a sharp focus. The growing top heaviness has been examined in the context of the movement of towns across the six census categories and emergence of new urban centres. Explanation of the changing settlement structure has also been sought in terms of the differential demographic growth for towns in different size categories.

It may be observed in Table 6.6 that Class 1 cities dominate India's urban scene in terms of their share of urban population. This share, though very high, was still comparable with that of other lower order size categories in the beginning of the 20th Century. In 1901, the share of Class 1 cities was 26 per cent of the urban population, whereas Class IV and V towns had 20.83 per cent and 20.14 per cent population respectively. The share of Class 1 towns has gradually increased. The gaps between the shares increased significantly during 1931-41, a decade before independence and partition of the country. At the time of independence, however, a large number of displaced populations were absorbed in Class 1 cities. This led to an increase in the share of Class 1 cities by 7 percentage points during 1941-51, similar to what was observed during the preceding decade. The

Table 6.6: Class-wise Number of Towns and Percentage and Growth Rate of Urban Population in India

Census Year	*Class I*	*Class II*	*Class III*	*Class IV*	*Class V*	*Class VI*
			Number of Towns			
1901	24	43	130	391	744	479
1911	23	40	135	364	707	485
1921	29	45	145	370	734	574
1931	35	56	183	434	800	509
1941	49	74	242	498	920	407
1951	76	91	327	608	1124	569
1961	102	129	437	719	711	172
1971	148	173	558	827	623	147
1981	218	270	743	1059	758	253
1991	300	345	947	1167	740	197
2001	393	401	1151	1344	888	191
			Percentage of Urban Population			
1901	26.00	11.29	15.64	20.83	20.14	6.10
1911	27.48	10.51	160.04	19.73	19.31	6.57
1921	29.07	10.39	15.92	18.29	18.67	7.03
1931	31.02	11.65	16.08	18.00	17.14	5.21
1941	38.23	11.42	16.35	15.78	15.08	3.14
1951	44.63	9.96	15.72	13.63	12.97	3.09
1961	51.42	11.23	16.94	12.77	6.87	0.77
1971	57.24	10.92	16.01	10.94	4.45	0.44
1981	60.37	11.63	14.33	9.54	3.58	0.05
1991	65.02	10.95	13.19	7.77	2.06	0.29
2001	68.67.	9.67	12.23	6.84	2.36	0.23
			Annual Exponential Growth Rate			
1901	—	—	—	—	—	—
1911	0.54	-0.73	0.46	-0.55	-0.43	0.72
1921	1.57	0.68	0.50	0.03	0.46	1.47
1931	2.24	2.89	2.28	1.59	0.89	-1.25
1941	4.81	2.59	2.51	1.47	1.50	-2.26
1951	5.02	2.10	3.07	2.01	1.97	3.31
1961	3.72	3.50	3.05	1.65	-4.05	-11.62
1971	4.29	2.93	2.65	1.67	-1.14	-2.32
1981	4.34	4.43	2.69	2.43	1.64	5.05
1991	3.84	2.38	2.26	1.02	-0.13	-2.45
2001	3.42	1.76	2.15	1.64	1.93	0.80

Notes: (a) Size class wise figures exclude Assam in 1981 and Jammu & Kashmir in 1991. (b) All classes exclude six towns in 1941, four each in 1931 and 1921, and two each in 1911 and 1901 of Goa which could not be assigned to any size class as the figures of their population for these years are not available. Total number of towns therefore would not match the figures of Table 6.3.

Source: Paper-2, Rural-Urban Distribution, 1981, 1991, and 2001 (unpublished)

increase was maintained at this level in the following two decades. Since the seventies, however, the increment in the share of these cities has been about 3 percentage points, which was maintained in the nineties as well. The percentage of urban population living in Class 1 cities has gone up from 65.2 to 67.3. The share of Class IV and V towns has been declining over the entire period. The combined share of these two categories of towns went down steeply from 41 per cent to 7.5 per cent during 1901-2001. Importantly, the percentages of urban population in the medium towns, viz. Class II and Class III, remained by and large stable over the entire century; their shares hovered around 11 per cent and 13 per cent respectively.

The massive increase in the share of Class 1 cities has often been attributed to the faster growth of the large cities without taking into consideration the increase in the number of these cities. Indeed, the basic reason for the increasing dominance of these cities is graduation of lower order towns into Class 1 category. In 1901, for example, there were only 24 towns in Class 1 category; the is number went up to 393 in 2001. This can be attributed to the natural growth of population and rural-to-urban migration in the towns below the cut-off point of one hundred thousand, enabling these to go over the point.

The general impression that the larger urban centres in the country grow at a higher rate has persisted not just among the planners and administrators but also among the statisticians and demographers working in this area. The Population Census computes the growth rates of towns in a size class by considering the population belonging to that size class in the initial as well as terminal years without taking note of the generally upward movement of the urban centres. As a consequence, the growth rate of Class 1 cities works out as very high since this size category would, over time, gain in the number of cities. Understandably, the size categories that lose in the number of towns would generally show a low growth rate. Indeed, Class V and Class VI categories often show a negative growth rate not because their towns are experiencing depopulation but because many of them move in to the higher-size categories.

In view of the problems of comparability, scholars have proposed that the base year classification of urban centres should be maintained for both base and terminal years for computing the growth rates. This would imply that the population of only those towns that belong to a category in the base year should be added up in the terminal year as well. This would make the number of towns at both the time points the same for each category in computing the growth rates. Fortunately, the Census itself has given the population of the common towns in 1991 in Appendix 10 of Provisional Population Totals that are extremely useful in comparing the growth rates across the size classes. It may, however, be noted that since the base-year categories constitute the basis for classification of towns, all the new towns are excluded from this calculation. Furthermore, even the towns declassified in the terminal year are excluded. This might be responsible for an upward bias in the growth estimates in Class V and Class VI categories, since these two categories would claim most of the declassified towns.

It has been argued that the Indian urban structure reflects a stable morphology and no distortion as the population growth is more or less uniform across the size classes. It is evident from Table 6 that this is not the case. The urban centres in Class 1 categories show distinctly higher growth rates in 1971 than the lower order towns (except Class VI towns). Indeed, Class VI towns do not fall in line as they exhibit a higher growth rate. One must hasten to add that Class VI towns constitute a special category as many of these towns are industrial townships or pilgrimage centres or have come into existence through establishment of a public sector unit.

The pattern is identical in 1991, although there is a general deceleration in the urban growth in all the size categories. Nonetheless, one can note the Class 1 cities having an edge over the Class II, III, IV and V towns in terms of the growth rate during 1981-91. Recalculation of the growth rates has been attempted based on the data from Census 2001 in an identical manner. It is noted that after the new towns and the towns declassified in the 2001 Census are excluded, there remain 315 common towns in the censuses of 1991 and 2001. The Class VI towns have registered a higher growth rate during the nineties compared to even the Class I cities, the reasons for which have been discussed above. Among the other size class of urban centres, Class I cities maintained a distinctly higher growth rate. One would, therefore, stipulate that the urban structure is becoming more skewed due to the higher demographic growth in larger cities, in addition to the other factors discussed above.

These adjusted growth rates (annual exponential growth rate) for Class I (common) towns during the seventies and eighties are 3.46 per cent and 2.96 per cent respectively. The recent Census has indicated a marginal decrease in the growth rate of Class I towns to 2.76 per cent, computed on the basis of 291 common Class I towns during 1991-01. Small towns (IV-VI together) indicated 3.07 per cent and 2.57 per cent growth during 1981 and 1991. This has gone down to 2.22 during 1991-2001. Onc may, thus, argue that the decline in the growth rate of smaller towns is higher compared to the Class I cities.

A higher demographic growth in the Class I cities is partially due to the natural growth and immigration. It may also be noted that a large number of satellite towns in the vicinity of these cities have emerged. These have become part of the city agglomeration over time. There are also outgrowths that have been treated as parts of the agglomeration by the Census. Further, therc has been expansion in the municipal boundaries of the Class I cities, contributing to urban growth. These are the factors responsible for the higher growth rate of Class I cities.

Metro cities or the cities that have a population of one million or more corroborate further the thesis of concentrated urban development. Between 1981 and 1991 million-plus cities on an average grew at the rate of 3.25 per cent, which is higher than the growth rate of common towns which was 2.83 per cent during this period. During 1991-2001, the growth rate went down across size categories including that of the metro cities. The latter has come down to 2.88 per cent, but the growth rate of the common towns has declined more sharply to 2.6 per cent. It is thus cvident that the demographic growth in the metro cities is higher than that of common towns or Class I cities. The spatial concentration of urban growth can be seen not only in terms of an increase in the share of urban population in Class I cities but also in the million-plus cities. The latter claimed about 26.41 per cent of the urban population in 1981, which rose to 32.54 per cent in 1991 and further to 37.81 per cent in 2001.

It is important to cxamine if the state capitals in the country have grown differently from the Class I cities or the common towns during the past two decades. The demographic growth in the state capitals and the national capital is on a par with that of the million plus cities. During the decades 1981-91 and 1991-2001, these cities have registered growth rates of 3.36 per cent and 2.79 per cent respectively. The share of the urban population living in the capital cities has been 24.8 per cent, 25.7 per cent and 25.9 per cent in these three Census years. This further confirms the proposition of unbalanced urban growth across size categories. It may nonetheless be mentioned that the growth rate of the capital cities declined substantially in the nineties compared to the previous decade. It is to be considered whether the structural adjustment, expenditure control and fall in the infrastructural investments by the Central and State governments have adversely affected the growth of the capital cities.

TRENDS AND PATTERNS OF URBANISATION: AN INTERSTATE ANALYSIS

Levels and Pattern of Urbanisation and Urban Growth

The regional variations in the distribution of urban population are significant. A large proportion of the urban population is concentrated in the six most urbanised states, namely, Maharashtra, Gujarat, Karnataka, Punjab, Tamil Nadu and West Bengal. Together they account for about half of the country's urban population. Looking at the 2001 Census figures of individual states separately, among the major states, Tamil Nadu has claimed to be the most urbanised state with 43.86 per cent urban population, followed by Maharashtra (42.4%), Gujarat (37.35%), Karnataka (33.98%), and Punjab (33.95%). The urban population in these states is much above the national average of 27.78 per cent, whereas the less developed BIMARU states report significantly lower percentage of urban population. Thus, the levels of urbanisation in most of the economically developed states were high in the post-independence period as revealed through the Census data presented for the last four decades in Table 6.7. Maharashtra, Tamil Nadu, and West Bengal had a high per capita income and reported a large percentage of population residing in urban areas. This is due to the concentration of economic activities in the three metropolises of Calcutta (now called Kolkata), Bombay (now called Mumbai), and Madras (now called Chennai) and a few of the towns linked to them. Evidently, there seems to be a direct relationship between economic parameters and urban development indicators that can be explained in terms of the location of agro-processing and

Table 6.7: Pattern and Levels of Urbanisation and Growth of Urban Population across States/UTs

S. No	*States*	*Percentage Urban Population*				*Annual Exponential Growth Rate*		
		1971	1981	1991	2001	1971-81	1981-91	1991-01
1.	Andhra Pradesh	19.31	23.25	26.84	27.08	3.94	3.55	1.37
2.	Arunachal Pradesh	3.70	6.32	12.21	20.41	8.32	9.28	7.00
3.	Assam	—	—	11.08	12.72	0.00	3.27	3.09
4.	Bihar	10	12.46	13.17	10.47	4.34	2.65	2.57
5.	Chhattisgarh	—	—	—	20.08	—	—	3.09
6.	Delhi	89.70	92.84	89.93	93.01	4.56	3.79	4.14
7.	Goa	26.44*	32.46*	41.02	49.77	4.37	3.96	3.32
8.	Gujarat	28.08	31.08	34.4	37.35	3.42	2.90	2.80
9.	Haryana	17.66	21.96	24.79	29.00	4.65	3.58	4.11
10.	Himachal Pradesh	6.99	7.72	8.7	9.79	3.02	3.11	2.81
11.	Jammu & Kashmir	—	—	23.83	24.88	0.00	3.78	6.87
12.	Jharkhand	—	—	—	22.25	—	—	2.55
13.	Karnataka	24.31	28.91	30.91	33.98	4.08	2.55	2.53
14.	Kerala	16.24	18.78	26.44	25.97	3.19	4.76	0.74
15.	Madhya Pradesh	16.29	20.31	23.21	26.67	4.45	3.71	2.71
16.	Maharashtra	31.17	35.03	38.73	42.40	3.35	3.27	2.95
17.	Manipur	13.19	26.44	26.69	23.88	9.70	2.98	1.21
18.	Meghalaya	14.55	18.03	18.69	19.63	4.87	3.10	3.16
19.	Mizoram	11.36	25.17	46.2	49.50	11.79	9.57	3.27
20.	Nagaland	9.95	15.54	17.28	17.74	8.49	5.58	5.27
21.	Orissa	8.41	11.82	13.43	14.97	5.21	3.08	2.61
22.	Punjab	23.73	27.72	29.72	33.95	3.62	2.55	3.19
23.	Rajasthan	17.63	20.93	22.88	23.38	4.52	3.31	2.71
24.	Sikkim	9.37	16.23	9.12	11.10	9.55	-3.23	4.83
25.	Tamil Nadu	30.26	32.98	34.2	43.86	2.45	1.76	3.56
26.	Tripura	10.43	10.98	15.26	17.02	3.26	6.19	2.52
27.	Uttar Pradesh	14.02	18.01	19.89	20.78	4.78	3.29	2.84
28.	Uttaranchal	—	—	—	25.59	—	—	2.84
29.	West Bengal	24.75	26.49	27.39	28.03	2.75	2.54	1.84
	Union Territories							
1.	Andaman & Nicobar Islands	22.77	26.36	26.80	32.67	6.38	4.10	4.40
2.	Chandigarh	90.55	93.60	89.69	89.78	5.92	3.07	3.40
3.	Dadra & Nagar Haveli	0	6.67	8.47	22.89	—	5.28	14.59
4.	Daman & Diu	—	—	46.86	36.26	—	4.93	1.87
5.	Lakshadweep	0	46.31	56.29	44.47	—	4.46	-0.77
6.	Pondicherry	42.04	52.32	64.05	66.57	4.66	4.92	2.26
	All India	**20.22**	**23.73**	**25.72**	**27.78**	**3.79**	**3.09**	**2.73**

Note: * The figures for Goa in 1971 and 1981 correspond to the figures for Goa, Daman, and Diu.

Source: Population Census, Paper 2, 1981, 1991 and 2001.

manufacturing activities in a handful of port cities during the colonial period. Furthermore, the rural population thrown out of the agrarian system due to frequent natural calamities, tottering agriculture and lack of sectoral diversification sought absorption in these cities. As a matter of fact, a rapid increase in the urbanisation in these few urbanised states can be attributed to the available opportunity of manufacturing employment, infrastructural facilities, and level of social development among other things.

The pattern of urban growth across states is significantly different from that of the levels of urbanisation. Between 1949 and 1991, the developed states such as Karnataka, Punjab and Tamil Nadu (with a high percentage of urbanisation) had shown medium or low growth of urban population. In contrast, high urban growth was registered in the relatively backward states, viz. Bihar, Madhya Pradesh, Orissa, Rajasthan and Uttar Pradesh (states having a low parentage of urban population) (Table 6.7). This implies that the relationship between urban growth and economic development was generally negative. However, some of the developed states like Maharashtra and Haryana were exceptions; they had recorded a higher urban growth than that of the country.

The urban scenario in the post-independence period was, thus, characterised by dualism. The developed states attracted population in urban areas due to industrialisation and infrastructural investment. Interestingly, the backward states too – particularly their backward districts and small and medium towns – experienced rapid urban growth. This can partly be attributed to government investment in the district and taluka headquarters, programmes of urban industrial dispersal and transfer of funds from the states to local bodies through a need-based or what is popularly known as "a gap filling approach". A part of the RU migration to smaller towns from the rural hinterland in the backward states could, however, be explained in terms of the push factors, owing to lack of diversification in the agrarian economy.

The nineties, however, made a significant departure from the earlier decades since many of the developed states like Gujarat, Haryana, Maharashtra, Punjab and Tamil Nadu an registered urban growth above the national average (Table 6.7). Karnataka has remained slightly below the national average, and West Bengal is an exception whose growth rate is not particularly impressive. The backward states, on the other hand, have experienced some growth—either below that of the country or, at most, equal to that.

The urbanisation process has, thus, become concentrated in the developed regions and has excluded the backward states. Furthermore, larger cities have recorded a relatively higher growth than smaller towns. This could, at least partly, be attributed to the measures of decentralisation whereby the responsibilities of resource mobilisation and launching of infrastructural projects have been given to the local bodies as noted above. Large municipal bodies that have a strong economic base, particularly those located in the developed states, have an advantage that has clearly been manifested in their high economic and demographic growth.

Levels and Pattern of Urbanisation and Urban Growth across Size Categories of Towns

The size class distributions of urban population and changes therein over the past two decades provide an interesting insight into the development dynamics of the states (Table 6.8). The smaller towns with a population below 20,000 have been clubbed into one category for the purposes of analysing the growth profile and structure of urban population. The share of population in the Class I cities has been going up consistently, as noted in the previous section. The inter-state variation in the share is very high and reveals a regional pattern. Besides the smaller states like Chandigarh, Delhi, Meghalaya and Pondicherry, and those that have a high concentration of urban population in the Class I cities are the economically prosperous states of Maharashtra, Tamil Nadu, and West Bengal. This is clearly a reflection of the impact of the colonial regime during which industrial activities were concentrated in the three metropolitan cities. Three other developed states that had a high concentration in the Class I cities are Andhra Pradesh, Gujarat, and Karnataka. Kerala also falls in this category due to its unique settlement pattern identifying a large number of Class I cities. The less developed states like Madhya Pradesh, Orissa, Rajasthan, and Uttar Pradesh exhibit a low percentage of urban population in Class I cities. The share of Class II and Class III towns, however, has remained stable in most of the states, as at the national level. The only exceptions are the smaller states like Andaman and Nicobar Islands, Goa, Himachal Pradesh, Meghalaya, Mizoram and Nagaland wherein the number of towns in different categories is small and shifting of a few towns makes a significant difference in the percentage shares.

Table 6.8: Pattern and Levels of Urbanisation in Different Size Categories across States

S. No	*States*	*1981*			
		Class I	*Class II*	*Class III*	*Class IV-VII*
1.	Andhra Pradesh	53.69	16.17	20.95	9.19
2.	Arunachal Pradesh	—	—	—	100.00
3.	Assam	NA	NA	NA	37.56
4.	Bihar	54.12	14.38	19.26	12.24
5.	Chhattisgarh	—	—	—	—
6.	Delhi	99.32	—	—	0.68
7.	Goa	—	65.61	8.05	26.34
8.	Gujarat	57.92	14.53	13.37	14.18
9.	Haryana	56.64	10.82	14.8	17.74
10.	Himachal Pradesh	—	21.54	12.49	65.97
11.	Jammu & Kashmir	65.8	—	11.74	22.46
12.	Jharkhand	—	—	—	—
13.	Karnataka	58.6	6.46	17.75	17.19
14.	Kerala	53.13	9.52	31.86	5.49
15.	Madhya Pradesh	46.84	18	12.24	22.92
16.	Maharashtra	75.24	5.95	10.88	7.93
17.	Manipur	41.72	—	11.18	47.1
18.	Meghalaya	72.39	—	14.61	13.00
19.	Mizoram	—	61.15	—	38.85
20.	Nagaland	—	—	55.9	44.1
21.	Orissa	41.63	12.76	21.83	23.78
22.	Punjab	46.4	13.28	21.31	19.01
23.	Rajasthan	46.52	10.05	22.02	21.41
24.	Sikkim	—	—	9.22	32.18
25.	Tamil Nadu	62.19	15.99	12.52	9.03
26.	Tripura	58.6	—	9.22	32.18
27.	Uttar Pradesh	51.49	12.71	12.34	23.46
28.	Uttaranchal	—	—	—	—
29.	West Bengal	76.84	10.78	7.71	4.67
Union Territories					
1.	Andaman & Nicobar Islands	—	—	100	—
2.	Chandigarh	100	—	—	—
3.	Dadra & Nagar Haveli	—	—	—	100.00
4.	Daman & Diu	—	—	72.37	27.63
5.	Lakshadweep	—	—	—	100.00
6.	Pondicherry	79.55	—	13.74	6.71
	All India	**60.37**	**11.63**	**14.33**	**13.62**

Note: (a) NA: Not Available. (b) All India average excludes Assam in 1981 and Jammu & Kashmir in 1991, (c) Bihar, Madhya Pradesh, and Uttar Pradesh represent their undivided status for 1981 and 1991.

(Table 6.8 contd.)

(Table 6.8 contd.)

S. No	*States*	*1991*			
		Class I	*Class II*	*Class III*	*Class IV-VII*
1.	Andhra Pradesh	66.88	12.6	16.53	3.99
2.	Arunachal Pradesh	—	—	—	100
3.	Assam	37.56	11.65	25.61	25.18
4.	Bihar	52.62	17.58	20.8	9.00
5.	Chhattisgarh	—	—	—	—
6.	Delhi	—	—	0.62	99.78
7.	Goa	—	51.84	6.59	41.57
8.	Gujarat	66.43	12.73	10.52	10.32
9.	Haryana	58.54	15.11	11.95	14.40
10.	Himachal Pradesh	24.70	—	19.6	55.70
11.	Jammu & Kashmir	NA	NA	NA	NA
12.	Jharkhand	—	—	—	—
13.	Karnataka	64.60	7.35	17.68	10.37
14.	Kerala	66.34	7.22	19.08	7.36
15.	Madhya Pradesh	50.38	13.94	12.82	22.86
16.	Maharashtra	77.85	6.49	10.39	5.27
17.	Manipur	39.66	—	17.96	42.38
18.	Meghalaya	67.54	—	20.18	12.28
19.	Mizoram	48.68	—	17.79	33.53
20.	Nagaland	—	52.38	21.71	25.91
21.	Orissa	44.43	14.65	19.73	21.19
22.	Punjab	54.36	19.79	12.89	12.96
23.	Rajasthan	50.09	13.67	21.31	14.93
24.	Sikkim	—	—	67.52	32.48
25.	Tamil Nadu	65.96	15.21	11.19	7.64
26.	Tripura	37.62	—	27.59	34.79
27.	Uttar Pradesh	55.99	11.45	13.94	18.62
28.	Uttaranchal	—	—	—	—
29.	West Bengal	81.71	6.58	7.66	4.05
		Union Territories			
1.	Andaman & Nicobar Islands	—	100.00	—	—
2.	Chandigarh	100.00	—	—	—
3.	Dadra & Nagar Haveli	—	—	—	100.00
4.	Daman & Diu	—	—	100.00	—
5.	Lakshadweep	—	—	—	100.00
6.	Pondicherry	77.64	11.97	3.93	6.46
	All India	**65.2**	**10.95**	**13.19**	**10.66**

Note: (a) NA: Not Available. (b) All India average excludes Assam in 1981 and Jammu & Kashmir in 1991. (c) Bihar, Madhya Pradesh, and Uttar Pradesh represent their undivided status for 1981 and 1991.

(Table 6.8 contd.)

(Table 6.8 contd.)

S. No	States	2001			
		Class I	*Class II*	*Class III*	*Class IV-VII*
1.	Andhra Pradesh	75.31	13.95	8.35	2.41
2.	Arunachal Pradesh	—	—	37.66	62.35
3.	Assam	44.34	14.37	18.56	22.72
4.	Bihar	59.31	13.66	23.57	3.46
5.	Chhattisgarh	63.02	8.94	13.17	14.86
6.	Delhi	99.78	—	—	0.22
7.	Goa	15.65	28.90	9.20	46.24
8.	Gujarat	76.50	9.67	9.47	4.36
9.	Haryana	72.57	5.78	11.89	9.75
10.	Himachal Pradesh	24.30	—	25.87	49.82
11.	Jammu & Kashmir	63.03	14.70	3.89	18.38
12.	Jharkhand	71.34	7.09	12.34	9.22
13.	Karnataka	67.20	9.63	17.28	5.88
14.	Kerala	68.82	11.32	14.05	5.80
15.	Madhya Pradesh	55.77	12.00	15.95	16.29
16.	Maharashtra	79.70	6.66	9.42	4.22
17.	Manipur	43.12	—	19.41	37.47
18.	Meghalaya	59.19	12.90	10.39	17.52
19.	Mizoram	52.08	—	16.73	31.18
20.	Nagaland	30.44	22.57	34.40	12.89
21.	Orissa	48.41	17.12	18.20	16.27
22.	Punjab	58.39	16.45	12.50	12.67
23.	Rajasthan	57.23	13.94	20.80	8.03
24.	Sikkim	—	—	48.60	51.40
25.	Tamil Nadu	56.35	11.64	12.21	19.80
26.	Tripura	34.86	—	33.37	31.77
27.	Uttar Pradesh	62.16	9.95	14.40	13.49
28.	Uttaranchal	47.10	12.04	20.47	20.39
29.	West Bengal	83.54	4.34	5.96	6.16
		Union Territories			
1.	Andaman & Nicobar Islands	86.07	—	—	13.93
2.	Chandigarh	100.00	0	0	0
3.	Dadra & Nagar Haveli	—	—	100.00	0
4.	Daman & Diu	—	—	100.00	0
5.	Lakshadweep	—	—	-	100.00
6.	Pondicherry	78.01	11.47	10.52	0
	All India	**68.67**	**9.67**	**12.23**	**9.43**

Notes: (a) NA: Not Available. (b) All India average excludes Assam in 1981 and Jammu & Kashmir in 1991. (c) Bihar, Madhya Pradesh and Uttar Pradesh represent their undivided status for 1981 and 1991.

Source: Computed from the data of Paper 2 "Rural-Urban Distribution, 1981-1991 and 2001" (unpublished).

The share of population in smaller towns (Class IV, V and VI) declined significantly during the eighties, with the exception of Goa, Sikkim, and Tripura. The general trend in most of the states is towards concentration of population in the larger cities, leading to a top-heavy urban structure. The three states contradict the pattern observed in other states.

The pattern has not changed very significantly during the nineties; the concentration in larger cities has gone up in most of the states[4] (Table 6.8). The six states that reported a high share of population in Class I cities in earlier years have generally maintained their position in 2001. Even the less developed state of Kerala has registered an increase in this percentage figure. The only state wherein the share of the cities has declined is Tamil Nadu and this is due to the emergence of a large number of new towns belonging to the lower order size categories. Further, the new states of Chhattisgarh and Jharkhand have reported high figures for the share of Class I cities, much higher than that of their respective parent states of Madhya Pradesh and Bihar. The state of new Uttaranchal, however, has a lower concentration of population in these cities – much below the national average and even below the figure of its parent state of Uttar Pradesh. The population share claimed by Class II and Class III towns has remained stable in most of the states during the nineties (Table 6.8). The exceptions are once again the smaller states, wherein a shift of one or two towns has a significant impact on the size class distribution of urban population. In the case of the smaller states, the percentage share has gone down in almost all the states (with a few exceptions of small north-eastern states), as is for the country as a whole.

The growth rates of urban centres in different size classes have been computed by taking the base year classification for initial as well as the terminal years to take care of the problems of graduation of towns into higher categories during the decade. The rates for the Class I cities work out to be generally higher than the smaller order towns in the developed states during the period 1971-91 as was noted for the country (Table 6.9). In states like Andhra Pradesh, Gujarat, Haryana, Karnataka, Maharashtra, Punjab and Tamil Nadu,[5] the growth rates of these cities are significantly higher than those of all lower order towns except those in Class VI category.[6] West Bengal is the only exception among the developed states wherein the growth

Table 6.9: Pattern of Growth of Urbanisation (Common Town/UAs) in Different Size Categories across States

S. No	*States*	*1971-81*			
		Class I	*Class II*	*Class III*	*Class IV-VII*
1.	Andhra Pradesh	3.80	3.69	3.76	3.55
2.	Arunachal Pradesh	—	—	—	4.57
3.	Assam	NA	NA	NA	NA
4.	Bihar	4.48	2.40	4.34	3.59
5.	Chhattisgarh	—	—	—	—
6.	Delhi	4.52	—	—	—
7.	Goa	-	2.65	3.54	3.80
8.	Gujarat	4.11	2.68	2.79	2.87
9.	Haryana	5.16	4.10	3.39	2.99
10.	Himachal Pradesh	—	2.42	-0.25	1.98
11.	Jammu & Kashmir	NA	NA	NA	NA
12.	Jharkhand	—	—	—	—
13.	Karnataka	4.44	3.59	3.19	2.88
14.	Kerala	2.71	3.46	1.65	3.16
15.	Madhya Pradesh	3.95	3.48	3.95	3.15
16.	Maharashtra	3.48	3.08	2.66	2.34
17.	Manipur	4.45	—	—	8.37
18.	Meghalaya	3.53	—	—	6.80
19.	Mizoram	—	—	8.53	10.51
20.	Nagaland	—	—	4.66	5.34
21.	Orissa	4.80	3.29	3.91	3.86
22.	Punjab	3.32	3.58	2.86	3.11
23.	Rajasthan	4.29	3.38	3.84	3.31
24.	Sikkim	—	—	—	9.54
25.	Tamil Nadu	2.77	2.20	2.06	1.71
26.	Tripura	2.76	-	-	1.59
27.	Uttar Pradesh	2.68	3.24	3.63	3.31
28.	Uttaranchal	—	—	—	—
29.	West Bengal	2.32	2.88	4.12	3.59
Union Territories					
1.	Andaman & Nicobar Islands	—	—	6.38	—
2.	Chandigarh	—	—	—	—
3.	Dadra & Nagar Haveli	—	—	—	—
4.	Daman & Diu	—	—	—	2.09
5.	Lakshadweep	—	—	—	—
6.	Pondicherry	4.84	—	5.09	1.86
	All India	**3.46**	**3.09**	**3.33**	**3.07**

Note: NA: Not Available as Census was not held in Assam in 1981 and Jammu & Kashmir in 1981 and 1991 respectively.

(Table 6.9 contd.)

S. No	States	1981-91			
		Class I	Class II	Class III	Class IV-VII
1.	Andhra Pradesh	4.00	3.35	2.81	2.58
2.	Arunachal Pradesh	—	—	—	5.91
3.	Assam	NA	NA	NA	NA
4.	Bihar	2.14	1.97	2.51	2.84
5.	Chhattisgarh	—	—	—	—
6.	Delhi	3.80	0	0	2.62
7.	Goa	—	1.60	1.95	3.64
8.	Gujarat	3.13	2.66	2.14	2.31
9.	Haryana	3.42	2.77	2.84	3.51
10.	Himachal Pradesh	—	4.09	0.33	2.69
11.	Jammu & Kashmir	NA	NA	NA	NA
12.	Jharkhand	—	—	—	—
13.	Karnataka	2.95	2.99	1.85	1.90
14.	Kerala	3.32	4.86	2.56	2.36
15.	Madhya Pradesh	2.85	3.34	2.75	2.77
16.	Maharashtra	3.28	2.41	2.47	2.62
17.	Manipur	2.48	—	3.26	3.17
18.	Meghalaya	2.41	—	2.59	6.67
19.	Mizoram	—	7.28	—	7.20
20.	Nagaland	—	—	4.93	4.47
21.	Orissa	3.17	2.65	2.40	2.11
22.	Punjab	3.04	2.61	2.65	2.00
23.	Rajasthan	3.28	2.68	3.21	2.63
24.	Sikkim	—	—	-3.80	-1.70
25.	Tamil Nadu	1.88	1.32	1.35	1.52
26.	Tripura	1.76	-	2.19	1.69
27.	Uttar Pradesh	3.14	2.80	3.29	2.87
28.	Uttaranchal	—	—	—	—
29.	West Bengal	2.05	3.37	3.50	3.59
Union Territories					
1.	Andaman & Nicobar Islands	—	—	4.10	—
2.	Chandigarh	3.06	—	—	—
3.	Dadra & Nagar Haveli	—	—	—	100.00
4.	Daman & Diu	—	—	—	5.27
5.	Lakshadweep	—	—	—	4.93
6.	Pondicherry	4.68	—	3.54	3.70
	All India	**2.96**	**2.75**	**2.59**	**2.57**

Note: NA: Not Available as Census was not held in Assam in 1981 and Jammu & Kashmir in 1981 and 1991 respectively.

(Table 6.9 contd.)

(Table 6.9 contd.)

S. No	States	1991-2001					
		I	II	III	IV	V	VI
1.	Andhra Pradesh	2.02	2.14	1.71	1.74	-0.03	—
2.	Arunachal Pradesh	—	—	—	4.46	3.11	—
3.	Assam	3.05	2.70	2.16	2.10	2.07	4.70
4.	Bihar	3.23	2.74	2.60	2.33	2.95	1.47
5.	Chhattisgarh	3.94	2.02	2.00	1.38	1.40	—
6.	Delhi	4.18	—	—	—	—	—
7.	Goa	—	1.82	2.37	1.61	0.75	2.18
8.	Gujarat	3.60	1.98	2.10	1.99	1.87	-1.38
9.	Haryana	4.12	4.80	3.30	2.84	3.84	5.58
10.	Himachal Pradesh	2.70	—	2.41	2.30	1.86	2.69
11.	Jammu & Kashmir	6.44	—	8.30	5.07	6.16	6.75
12.	Jharkhand	2.79	2.48	3.05	1.78	0.98	0.56
13.	Karnataka	2.69	3.03	2.18	2.52	0.98	0.56
14.	Kerala	1.10	1.38	1.12	1.68	2.12	—
15.	Madhya Pradesh	2.67	2.84	2.72	2.27	2.04	-0.25
16.	Maharashtra	2.91	2.72	2.05	2.55	2.41	3.23
17.	Manipur	1.93	—	1.96	1.79	1.97	1.01
18.	Meghalaya	1.82	—	2.24	4.24	3.15	—
19.	Mizoram	3.92	—	2.69	3.29	2.41	1.80
20.	Nagaland	—	5.38	2.84	7.38	5.37	—
21.	Orissa	3.08	1.87	. 213	1.58	1.88	-0.64
22.	Punjab	2.99	2.34	2.23	2.26	2.59	6.45
23.	Rajasthan	3.24	2.82	2.39	2.42	1.65	—
24.	Sikkim	—	—	1.53	—	—	3.00
25.	Tamil Nadu	1.71	0.97	1.31	1.16	1.31	-0.83
26.	Tripura	—	—	1.35	2.39	2.63	1.85
27.	Uttar Pradesh	2.87	2.46	2.83	2.36	2.42	2.83
28.	Uttaranchal	3.19	2.46	2.13	1.87	2.31	2.73
29.	West Bengal	1.99	2.43	2.23	1.60	1.68	0.52
		Union Territories					
1.	Andaman & Nicobar Islands	—	2.90	—	—	—	—
2.	Chandigarh	3.40	—	—	—	—	—
3.	Dadra & Nagar Haveli	—	—	—	6.24	—	—
4.	Daman & Diu	—	—	1.87	—	—	—
5.	Lakshadweep	—	—	—	—	—	—
6.	Pondicherry	2.31	1.85	2.38	—	—	—
	All India	**2.76**	**2.37**	**2.27**	**2.19**	**2.22**	**3.26**

Note: NA: Not Available as Census was not held in Assam in 1981 and Jammu & Kashmir in 1981 and 1991 respectively.

Source: Paper-2 Rural-Urban Distribution, 1991 & 2001 (unpublished).

rate of the Class I cities is below that of the lower order towns. This, however, is the pattern observed for the less developed states like Bihar, Kerala, Madhya Pradesh, Rajasthan and Uttar Pradesh. Here, the smaller towns have grown at the same or higher rate than the Class I cities.

The growth pattern has remained similar during 1991-2001 (Table 6.9). The developed states like Gujarat, Maharashtra, Punjab and Tamil Nadu exhibit a pattern identical to that of the preceding two decades. Importantly, a few other backward states like Assam, Bihar, Himachal Pradesh, Orissa and Rajasthan too, exhibit this pattern, i.e., their Class I cities grew at a faster rate than their lower order towns. The only exceptions, besides a few of the smaller states, are Kerala, Madhya Pradesh and Uttar Pradesh among the backward states and Andhra Pradesh, Haryana, and Karnataka among the developed states. The pattern for West Bengal remains similar to the one in the previous decades.

Disparity in Urban Growth across Size Categories

It would be important to look at the disparity in the growth rates to ascertain the stability of growth in different size categories (Kundu 1983). The coefficient of variation in the growth rates of the urban centres belonging to the different size categories during the eighties and nineties is given in Table 6.10. Significantly, Class I cities show a greater stability and consistency in growth as is reflected in lower coefficients of variation during the eighties. The disparity in their growth rates has been noted to go down during the eighties compared to the seventies. As far as the lower order size categories are concerned, the coefficients of variation in the growth rates have remained stable or gone up during the two decades.

The growth scenario in the nineties, however, makes a significant departure from the earlier trends. The coefficient of variation has gone up significantly for Class I cities. This implies that although Class I cities have maintained an edge in terms of growth rates they are now subject to greater instability. Further, the disparity of growth within the size categories also projects temporal variation in some states. One can attribute this rising instability in the growth of Class I cities to the policies of globalisation and linking of only a few of these cities that have registered a high demographic growth to the national and international market.

Table 6.10: The Disparity of Growth Rates of Towns within Size Class Distribution across States/UTs

S. No	*States*	*As per their Size Class Distribution: 1981*					
		Class I	*Class II*	*Class III*	*Class IV*	*Class V*	*Class VI*
1	Andhra Pradesh	54.32	77.55	51.45	62.23	62.55	—
2	Arunachal Pradesh	—	—	—	—	44.70	—
3	Assam	—	47.31	71.46	101.06	106.95	154.27
4	Bihar	22.29	56.39	47.67	67.23	75.58	—
5	Chhattisgarh	27.54	59.50	30.73	33.30	44.29	—
6	Delhi	—	—	—	—	—	—
7	Goa	—	61.82	—	119.64	142.12	114.27
8	Gujarat	46.27	93.79	58.28	81.03	106.19	109.67
9	Haryana	57.25	44.55	46.59	214.86	65.79	55.11
10	Himachal Pradesh	—	—	215.03	60.66	109.03	90.28
11	Jammu & Kashmir	12.78	—	15.18	67.52	69.66	191.15
12	Jharkhand	45.24	129.78	47.03	75.69	129.91	—
13	Karnataka	43.52	86.19	61.00	69.56	92.38	111.59
14	Kerala	45.31	87.63	166.06	46.55	7.77	—
15	Madhya Pradesh	35.53	56.76	47.11	49.67	64.78	145.61
16	Maharashtra	57.94	45.67	62.36	65.93	82.69	212.12
17	Manipur	—	—	—	39.66	110.61	87.10
18	Meghalaya	—	—	—	—	—	70.49
19	Mizoram	—	—	—	—	47.48	—
20	Nagaland	—	—	27.67	45.08	22.53	—
21	Orissa	70.55	40.25	39.97	52.61	74.87	159.99
22	Punjab	84.06	27.07	93.98	90.91	71.35	78.40
23	Rajasthan	33.21	28.11	33.97	40.81	63.28	—
24	Sikkim	—	—	—	—	—	-260.08
25	Tamil Nadu	65.32	50.99	74.10	87.46	119.59	108.49
26	Tripura	—	—	—	41.78	23.84	62.27
27	Uttar Pradesh	45.28	31.25	39.41	63.27	43.05	47.58
28	Uttaranchal	7.31	39.99	50.45	51.83	79.29	91.45
29	West Bengal	48.10	87.66	138.95	57.43	71.17	80.25
Union Territories							
1	Andaman & Nicobar Islands	—	—	—	—	—	—
2	Chandigarh	—	—	—	—	—	—
3	Dadra & Nagar Haveli	—	—	—	—	—	—
4	Daman & Diu	—	—	—	—	—	—
5	Lakshadweep	—	—	—	—	—	—
6	Pondicherry	—	—	92.10	—	—	—
	All India	63.42	75.93	80.18	90.81	87.08	241.44

(Table 6.10 contd.)

S. No	States	*As per their Size Class Distribution: 1991*					
		Class I	*Class II*	*Class III*	*Class IV*	*Class V*	*Class VI*
1.	Andhra Pradesh	64.60	92.40	62.20	97.30	—	—
2.	Arunachal Pradesh	—	—	—	82.70	32.20	—
3.	Assam	67.80	78.20	70.60	86.70	64.80	94.60
4.	Bihar	35.60	51.10	42.00	54.60	24.80	—
5.	Chhattisgarh	91.10	103.90	54.70	114.00	74.30	—
6.	Delhi	—	—	—	—	—	—
7.	Goa	—	41.10	—	56.50	138.40	51.00
8.	Gujarat	47.10	75.10	83.30	97.30	104.20	428.60
9.	Haryana	46.40	57.70	29.00	52.10	123.00	88.50
10.	Himachal Pradesh	—	—	—	—	—	—
11.	Jammu & Kashmir	68.00	—	37.53	38.22	67.16	77 70
12.	Jharkhand	23.60	38.00	95.20	53.40	190.90	-9.40
13.	Karnataka	41.30	71.20	51.50	150.20	230.30	269.70
14.	Kerala	54.00	151.70	174.00	194.90	57.90	—
15.	Madhya Pradesh	46.50	115.50	55.70	163.00	92.30	—
16.	Maharashtra	50.10	118.20	63.90	127.90	211.00	78.90
17.	Manipur	—	—	23.50	49.60	65.90	82.00
18.	Meghalaya	—	—	15.50	1.90	31.40	—
19.	Mizoram	—	—	14.20	14.80	25.40	96.80
20.	Nagaland	—	35.20	32.30	54.70	33.90	—
21.	Orissa	45.00	48.50	58.40	65.00	151.90	-40.20
22.	Punjab	30.80	44.80	64.70	57.10	110.60	96.50
23.	Rajasthan	34.80	38.90	39.10	54.40	104.30	—
24.	Sikkim	—	—	—	—	—	67.80
25.	Tamil Nadu	112.80	68.70	120.00	122.20	146.40	-104.00
26.	Tripura	—	—	219.10	123.80	32.10	5.00
27.	Uttar Pradesh	60.00	33.40	85.80	52.60	52.10	65.90
28.	Uttaranchal	47.90	49.20	59.70	41.60	58.00	178.70
29.	West Bengal	109.60	47.30	89.30	86.70	85.20	191.90
				Union Territories			
1.	Andaman & Nicobar Islands	—	—	—	—	—	—
2.	Chandigarh	—	—	—	—	—	—
3.	Dadra & Nagar Nicobai Islands	—	—	—	—		—
4.	Daman & Diu	—	—	109.00	—	—	—
5.	Lakshadweep	—	—	—	—	—	—
6.	Pondicherry	—	—	97.20	—	—	—
	All India	**72.12**	**86.16**	**81.30**	**108.13**	**110.52**	**136.19**

Source: Computed from Paper 2, Rural-Urban Distribution, 1991 and 2001 (unpublished)

It may nonetheless be argued that despite the coefficient of variation being high in Class I cities, it is lower than that of all lower order towns. The smaller towns in the country have had high instability in their growth even in the earlier decades and hence it cannot be linked to the policies of structural adjustment and their impact on the process of urbanisation.

Interdependency between Urbanisation and Socio-Economic Development

It has been observed that the patterns and trends of urbanisation in the backward states have been different from those of the relatively developed ones. This arouses curiosity about the factors, which explain the spatial pattern in the trends and processes of urbanisation. Hence, an attempt has been made by constructing a correlation matrix pertaining to the indicators of urbanisation and socio-economic development. The exercise has been carried out for seventeen major states over the period 1981-2001 (see, Sivaramkrishnan, Kundu and Singh 2002).

The per capita income of Delhi, Gujarat, Haryana, Maharashtra and Punjab was much higher than the national average in 1981. Similarly, Karnataka, Tamil Nadu and West Bengal constitute moderately developed states in terms of per capita income. Further, it has been observed that these states are highly urbanised as well. On the other hand, Bihar, Orissa, Rajasthan and Uttar Pradesh reported a much lower per capita income than the national average, and the proportion of urban population in these states is quite below that in the former ones. Therefore, one would infer that the economically better off states tend to have a higher percentage of urban population in the country. This hypothesis is confirmed by the correlation of the level of urbanisation with per capita income, which also turns out to be very high, viz. 0.85 and significant at 1 per cent.

Importantly, the correlations between the level of urbanisation and per capita income are positive and highly significant throughout the periods 1991 and 2001, the values being 0.84 at both the time points. Indeed, the developed states have been maintaining their urban status. Thus, the pattern of urbanisation has not changed across states over the period and the developed states constitute a higher percentage of urban population than the less developed ones. It can be said that urbanisation and economic development have been complementary to each other in the post-independence period.

It must be emphasised that the level of urbanisation expressed usually as percentage of urban population is different from the rates of urban growth. The poorer states like Bihar, Orissa, Madhya Pradesh, Rajasthan and Uttar Pradesh have experienced a high growth of urban population during the seventies. The rates were above 4.5 per cent, which is much higher than the average urban growth rate in the country (3.8%) or that in the developed states such as Gujarat, Maharashtra, Punjab and Tamil Nadu. Some of the developed states such as Delhi, Haryana and Karnataka have also shown a high growth of urban population (4.6%, 4.7%, and 4.1% respectively). Therefore, a clear pattern could not be established between urban growth and per capita income of the states in 1981. Interestingly, the correlation coefficient between the two indicators is 0.03 which is statistically insignificant and does not reveal any pattern. The correlation coefficient is similar for the period 1981-91, which works out to be 0.09. The low correlation has been attributed to the dual pattern existing in the urban economy during the seventies and the eighties. A large number of the poor states in the country have registered high urban growth rates possibly due to rural urban migration linked to the operation of push factors. There are, however, several developed states that attracted rural migrants through the operation of pull factors and recorded a high urban growth.

During the nineties, growth of urbanisation had been concentrated in the developed states, which marks a sharp departure from the past pattern. The correlation coefficient between per capita income and growth of urban population is 0.43, and it is statistically significant at 5 per cent level. In the nineties several of the developed states reported growth of urban population which is on a par with the national average of 2.7 or slightly higher than that. The growth rates of urban population in the backward states, however, have gone down; these are often similar to the national urban growth rate or slightly below it. This could possibly be attributed to the process of liberalisation that has resulted in shifting of the population to the urban centres in the developed states that have received a large part of the industrial and infrastructural investment.

The flow of foreign capital and its association with urbanisation reveals that there exists a strong and positive relationship between the two. Importantly, the correlation between per capita flow of Foreign Direct Investments (FDI) and infrastructure indicators like roads railways and telecom is positive and very strong, suggesting that these investments directly or indirectly became instrumental in the infrastructural development. Alternatively, it may be argued that the states having/providing basic infrastructure facilities have been able to corner a larger flow of foreign direct investment.

Industrial income as a percentage of the aggregate state domestic product shows a positive correlation with the level of urbanisation in all the three periods. The correlation coefficients, however, are negative when we relate industrialisation with the growth of urban population during the seventies and eighties. The pattern changed during the nineties. The correlation coefficient is no longer negative because the capacity of industrially backward states to attract migrants has gone down over the years. Moreover, worker enterprise ratio in the urban areas correlates positively and in a highly statistically significant manner with both the level and the growth of urban population in 2001. This further confirms the proposition that industrialisation became a significant factor in explaining the level and growth of urbanisation across states in the nineties.

There is, nonetheless, no denial of the fact that urbanisation results in the growth of regular jobs. The states with high levels of urbanisation or experiencing a high urban growth have indeed provided job opportunities which are somewhat stable and of a long-term nature. Both the level and the growth of urban population correlates positively with the percentage of regular workers in urban areas at both the time points, 1991 and 2001. Importantly, the correlation has improved over time. One would infer that more regular (urban) jobs were generated in the urbanised states in the nineties. Furthermore, the impact is not restricted only to the urban areas. In the case of rural areas also, the correlation coefficients are much higher than in the urban areas. Further, the correlation of the urban unemployment rate with the growth of urbanisation during the 1990 is significantly negative. The correlation coefficient observed is –0.54 which is significant at 5 per cent level. One would, therefore, infer that high growth of urbanisation occurred in the states where there was growth of regular jobs and urban unemployment rate was low.

In the context of poverty, it is seen that apart from Bihar, Madhya Pradesh, Rajasthan and Uttar Pradesh, the incidence of poverty is high in Assam and Orissa. It has already been mentioned that the level of urbanisation correlates positively with economic development at all the time points under consideration. One would, therefore, expect a negative correlation between urbanisation and rural poverty. This indeed is the case. The value was –0.44 in 1961 which became –0.59 in 2001. The correlations work out as negative even with urban poverty but the values are somewhat lower.

The data have been taken from the Centre for Monitoring Indian Economy (CMIE) report for the three periods. The indicators of physical as well as financial infrastructure, viz. roads, railway lines, telephone connections, village electrification, bank deposits and credit to industry, exhibit highly significant correlations with the urbanisation level at all the three points of time under consideration. Excepting village electrification, all the indicators also show very high correlation values with per capita income and expenditure. Moreover, correlations have remained almost the same suggesting that no substantial alternation has occurred in the ranking of the states. In other words, the poorer states have not been able to improve their position relative to the rich states. The relationship between infrastructural facilities and growth of urban population is also positive and generally significant at the three points. This implies that the process of urbanisation is directly related to the improvement in the infrastructural facilities across the states.

The sex ratio has a negative correlation with urbanisation implying that rural-to-urban migration is generally male-selective resulting in a reduction in the female-male ratio. Its correlation with the urban growth turns out to be highly significant during the nineties suggesting that male-dominant migration streams have backed up the urbanisation process.

The levels of urban basic amenities like access to safe drinking water, sanitation facilities and electricity are positively correlated with urbanisation, although the values are statistically insignificant. It is thus not possible to argue that the more urbanised states provide the basic amenities to a larger percentage of their urban population. On the other hand, the correlation of these indicators with urban growth has become negative over the years. It appears that the growth of urban population over the decades has led to an increased pressure on the basic amenities, which has resulted in deterioration in the standard of living.

PATTERNS OF URBANISATION IN TWO SELECTED STATES: A DISTRICT-LEVEL ANALYSIS

This section analyses the pattern of urbanisation across the districts in the states of Maharashtra and Rajasthan and examines the nature of interdependency between the level and the trend of urbanisation with the socio-economic indicators over three decades—1971-81, 1981-91 and 1991-2001. It is hoped that the analysis will be able to bring forth the significant differences in the nature and pattern of urbanisation and their correlates at the different stages of economic development.

Maharashtra

Levels and Pattern of Urbanisation and Urban Growth

Maharashtra is economically one of the developed states in the country. Availability of a good infrastructure network including ports and widespread industrial enterprises since the colonial period has contributed significantly to the development of the state in recent decades. The level of urbanisation, which by itself is an important indicator of development, has shown a strong positive association with industrialisation. In fact, Maharashtra had the highest percentage of urban population among all the large states in 1991. It has been able to maintain this position over the past several decades. In the 2001 Census, however, Tamil Nadu has reported the highest percentage of urban population as well as the highest growth of urban population.[7]

An analysis of disaggregated figures of the percentage of urban population at the district level indicates high disparity. The data obtained from the past three censuses substantiate this fact. In 1981, for example, the industrially developed districts like Nagpur, Pune and Thane reported a much higher share of urban population than the state average of 35.03 per cent. The rates of the three districts were 56.75 per cent, 47.53 per cent and 44.34 per cent respectively. Greater Bombay, being at the heart of the state's financial-cum-commercial activities, has been an exception since it comprises 100 per cent urban population. On the other hand, out of the total 26 districts, 11 districts reported figures below 20 per cent. The lowest among them were Ratnagiri (8.73), Ahmadnagar (12.95), Satara (13.04) and Bhandara (13.1). Therefore, the coefficient of variation of the level of urbanisation across districts works out to as high as 71.6 per cent reflecting a high degree of dispersion.

The 1991 Census also reveals a similar pattern of urbanisation. Importantly, Nagpur, Pune and Thane which were highly urbanised districts in 1981 exhibited a higher percentage of urban population in 1991 as well, their figures being 61.48 per cent, 50.76 per cent and 64.74 per cent respectively. The figures, in fact, reveal a significant upward revision during the eighties. In comparison, the revision of urban population in the backward districts is small. The respective shares of urban population in 1991 for the districts of Ahmadnagar, Bhandara, Satara, and Ratnagiri were 15.81, 13.15, 12.91 and 8.97; the rates were the same as earlier or lower. Of the four new districts which have come up during 1991 the Census, Sindhudurg and Gadchiroli show very low share of urban population, viz. 7.6 and 8.7 per cent respectively. The process of urbanisation in the state has thus been highly disparate across districts, the coefficient of variation being 70.5 per cent in 1991.

The urbanisation pattern across the districts did not change even in 2001. The highly urbanised districts have shown a very high share of urban population, much above the state average (42.4%). These developed districts have thus been able to maintain their relative positions in all the three censuses. Mumbai and Mumbai (suburb) (the erstwhile Greater Mumbai) comprised 100 per cent urban population in all the censuses. The less urbanised districts of Bhandara (15.44%), Satara (14.24%), Ratnagiri (11.33%), Sindhudurg (9.56%) and Gadchiroli (6.93%) are stagnant in terms of their position in the urban hierarchy. One would thus infer that the highly urbanised districts report higher shares of urban population in subsequent censuses whereas the less urbanised or backward districts have experienced arginal improvements over the time span of three decades, of time span, thereby maintaining the level of disparity. The Coefficient of Variation (CV) in the percentage of urban population works out to be very high across the districts, viz. 67.6 per cent.

The annual growth rate of urban population during the three decades under consideration, however, shows some interesting departures from the existing pattern of urbanisation. The highly urbanised districts of Nagpur, Pune and Thane had experienced a high urban growth during the period 1971-81 – 3.28 per cent, 3.93 per cent and 5.84 per cent respectively. The growth rates of Thane and Pune are much above the state average of 3.39 per cent whereas Nagpur is almost on a par with it. The exceptionally high urban growth in Thane can be attributed to the emergence of new towns. Out of 33 new towns of Maharashtra, Thane alone claims 11 (census towns) and their inclusion reflects a marked increase in the workforce engaged in the non-agricultural activities in the large villages in the neighbourhood of metro cities of Maharashtra.

What is, however, more interesting is that in 1971-81, the growth rates of several backward districts such as Bid (4.32), Osmanabad (3.71) and Kolhapur (3.45) were also above the state average and quite comparable to those of the developed districts. Furthermore, a few other backward districts like Dhule, Parbhani and Sholapur have experienced growth rates around the state average, though their share of urban population is very low.

The developed districts maintained their high urban growth during 1981-91 as well. The backward districts like Aurangabad, Bid and Osmanabad too maintained their growth rates at a level higher than the state average of 3.32 per cent. The new district of Gadchiroli reported an exceptionally high growth rate of urban population—14.85 per cent.

The Census 2001 reports a decline in the overall urban growth rate in the state from 3.32 per cent in 1981-91 to 2.95 per cent in 1991-2001. The district of Thane (5.53) also experienced a reduction in the growth rate compared to the earlier two decades. But the urban population in Pune has grown at a rate of 4.02, which is higher than the growth rate during the eighties. The growth rate of the urban population in relatively backward districts during the nineties has also registered a decline from that of earlier decades. However, the districts like Ahmadnagar, Aurangabad, Latur and Ratnagiri have recorded growth rates higher than the state average.

Size Class Distribution of Towns

The size class distribution of towns in Maharashtra shows a high degree of concentration of urban population in Class I cities in 1981 claiming over 75.24 per cent of the total urban population in the state. This figure has gone up to 77.8 per cent (1991) and 79.7 per cent (2001). With the rising share of urban population in larger towns, the smaller towns (Class IV-VI) have lost their share over time, from 7.9 per cent in 1981 to 5.3 per cent in 1991 and to 4.2 per cent in 2001. This is a figure much lower than the national average of 9.4 per cent in this category. Moreover, the growth rate of Class I towns has also been higher than the growth rates registered by smaller towns in all the three decades under consideration in the state.[8] It may, therefore, be argued that the rate of growth of urban population has been high in the case of larger towns compared to the smaller towns.

The State of Maharashtra reports a large number of towns (23) being declassified in 2001, falling in both backward and developed districts. All the declassified towns are census towns and fulfilled the population criterion in 1991. The declassification of these census towns seems to be due to a decline in the share of non-agricultural workforce. This reflects a process of adjustment of economic forces within a district resulting in spatial reorganisation of economic activities.

Rajasthan

Rajasthan, part of old Rajputana of medieval India, comprised many kingdoms with different administrative and development experiences. Important urban centres of the state can be identified like the historical cities of Ajmer, Jaipur, Jodhpur and Udaipur which were the headquarters of the princely states. A cross-sectional analysis of the urbanisation data at the district-level provides interesting insights into the development dynamics in the state.

Levels and Pattern of Urbanisation and Urban Growth

As per the 1981 Census, Rajasthan had five districts with the percentage share of urban population much above the state average of 20.9 per cent. These were Ajmer (42.8%), Bikaner (39.48%), Jaipur (36.39%), Jodhpur (34.77%) and Kota (32.18%). These places have historical importance and reflect the features of any developed district in the country. At the lowest end of the spectrum were the backward districts of Banswara (6.22%) and Dungarpur (6.46%) in 1981. The disparity in the levels of urbanisation in the state thus works out to be 53.14 per cent.

A few of the developed districts have maintained their relative positions in the 1981-91 decade as well. In fact, the districts of Bikaner (39.72%), Jaipur (39.46%), Jodhpur (35.11%) and Kota (36.44%) had significant increases in their share of urban population in 1991. On the other hand, the increase in the case of the backward districts like Banswara and Dungarpur was meagre. The overall disparity in the level computed through the CV, has, however, came down to 47.3 per cent in 1991. This implies that the districts in the middle level have interchanged their positions with one another resulting in a spatially more balanced urban growth.

The 2001 Census reports certain features that contrast sharply with those observed in 1991. The level of urbanisation increased more rapidly in the urbanised districts than in the backward districts. Ajmer (40.09%), Jaipur (49.38%) and Kota (53.42%) experienced substantial increases in their urban populations, higher than in any other district. Banswara (7.15%) and Dungarpur (7.24%) did not improve their relative positions even during the nineties. Furthermore, one of the backward districts, Barmer, registered a sharp decline in its urban share, from 10.11 per cent in 1991 to 7.4 per cent in 2001. Understandably, the disparity level for the nineties went up from 47.3 per cent in the previous decade to 53.85 per cent.

The growth rates of urban population in most of the backward districts of the state like Chittaurgarh (5.07%), Banswara (5.08%), Pali (7.69%) and Jalore (9.02%) were high during 1971-81. The developed districts of Kota (5.71%) and Jaipur (5.08%) too experienced a high urban growth which can be attributed to the large number of new towns emerging in these districts. The coefficient of variation, thus works out to be a modest 33.06 per cent, which is less than what was observed in the case of the level of urbanisation.

During 1981-91, the traditional growth centres like Jaipur and Jodhpur reported a lower urban growth than in the previous decade. The backward district like Bhilwara and Jhalawar, on the other hand, picked up the tempo registering growth rates above 5 per cent, which was much above the state average of 3.3 per cent. As a result of this spatially balanced urban development, the coefficient of variation declined from 33 per cent during the seventies to 29.23 per cent in the eighties.

During 1991-2001, the pattern of growth once again reported a departure from the previous decade. Growth rates in the less urbanised districts were lower—Jhalawar (1.08), Sirohi (1.67), and Banswara (1.85)—than those reported by the developed districts—Jodhpur (2.4%), Kota (3.06%) and Jaipur (3.8%) as shown by the figures in parentheses. The coefficient of variation across the districts has shown a marginal increase to 31.26 per cent during the nineties, as urban growth has been concentrated in the urbanised districts.

Size Class Distribution of Towns

The share of urban population in the Class I cities in Rajasthan went up from 46 per cent to 50 per cent during 1981-91, but the figures still remain below the national average. The share further went up to 57.2 per cent during the nineties. The percentage of urban population in Class II towns in the state has, however, gone up in the face of a declining trend at the national level. But the smaller towns (Class IV-VI) have reported a substantial decline in their share, from 21.4 per cent in 1981 to 14.9 per cent in 1991 and 8 per cent in 2001.

The growth rates of larger towns have remained above the growth rates of smaller towns during 1971-81. But, the difference narrowed during the eighties, with a general decline in the growth rates. The nineties, however, reported widening of the gap between the growth rates of Class I and smaller towns.

Inter-dependencies between Urbanisation and Developmental Indicators

An attempt has been made to examine the inter-dependency between urbanisation and associated development at the district level in the two select states over the period from 1981 to 2001. The following indicators were included in preparing the correlation matrix (Tables 6.11(a) to 6.11(c) and 6.12(a) to 6.12(c).

Table 6.11(a): Interdependency among Indicators of Urbanisation and Socio-Economic Development at District Level in Maharashtra

	LEVEL -UR	*GROW -UR*	*ROAD*	*RAILWAY*	*TELECOM*
LEVEL-UR	1				
GROW-UR	0.22	1			
ROAD	-0.38	-0.11	1		
RAILWAY	.815 (**)	-0.06	-.406 (*)	1	
TELECOM	.906 (**)	0.11	-0.34	.952 (**)	1
PC-PKD	.882 (**)	0.05	-0.36	.971 (**)	.992 (**)
PC-CRIND	.876 (**)	0.26	-0.30	.862 (**)	.952 (**)
LETTER-U	0.33	-0.34	0.09	0.29	0.38
SEXR-U	-.762 (**)	-.580 (**)	0.18	-6.21 (**)	-.767 (**)
HOSPITAL	.843 (**)	-0.04	-0.14	.663 (**)	.779 (**)
	PC-BKD	*PC- CRIND*	*LITER -U*	*SEXR -U*	*HOSP*
PC-PKD	1				
PC-CRIND	.993 (**)	1			
LETTER-U	0.37	.399 (*)	1		
SEXR-U	-.735 (**)	-.844 (**)	-.20	1	
HOSPITAL	.755 (**)	.719 (**)	.539 (**)	-.546 (**)	1

* Correlation is significant at the 0.05 level (2 tailed)
** Correlation is significant at the 0.01 level (2 tailed)

Table 6.11(b): Interdependency among Indicators of Urbanisation and Socio Economic Development at District level in Maharashtra (1991)

Panel I

	LEVEL-UR	*GROW-UR*	*PCI*	*SR-SEC*	*SR-TERT*
LEVEL-UR	1				
GROW-UR	-0.035	1			
PCI	.709 (**)	0.136	1		
SR-SEC	.449 (8)	0.006	.726 (**)	1	
SR-TERT	.593 (88)	-.430 (*)	-0.034	-0.115	1

Panel II

	LEVEL -UR	GROW -UR	ROAD	RAIL-WAY	TELE-COM
LEVEL-UR	1				
GROW-UR	-0.035	1			
ROAD	-0.181	-0.314	1		
RAIL-WAY	.449 (*)	-0.314	0.176	1	
TELECOM	.775 (**)	-0.118	-0.263	0.245	1
PC-PKD	.765 (**)	-0.096	-0.324	0.232	.990 (**)
PC-CRIND	.780 (**)	-0.052	-0.316	0.254	.979 (**)
LETTER-U	0.175	-0.301	-0.01	0.213	2.247
SEXR-U	-.716 (**)	-.368 (*)	0.258	0.003	-.551 (**)
HOSPITAL	.705 (**)	-.147	0.084	0.341	.720 (**)
SCH-MH	-.473 (**)	-0.167	0.341	0.002	-0.323

	PC-BKD	PC- CRIND	LITER -U	SEXR -U	HOSP	SCH-MH
PC-PKD	1					
PC-CRIND	.989 (**)	1				
LETTER-U	.262	0.265	1			
SEXR-U	-.577 (**)	-.623 (**)	0.194	1		
HOSPITAL	.682 (**)	.684 (**)	0.34	-0.327	1	
SCH-MH	-0.341	-0.312	0.193	.436 (*)	-0.179	1

* Correlation is significant at the 0.05 level (2 tailed)

** Correlation is significant at the 0.01 level (2 tailed)

Table 6.11(c): Interdependency among Indicators of Urbanisation and Socio-Economic Development at District Level in Maharashtra (2001)

Panel I

	LEVEL-UR	GROW-UR	PCI	SR-SEC	SR-TERT
LEVEL-UR	1				
GROW-UR	0.380(*)	1			
PCI	.840(**)	0.36	1		
SR-SEC	.489(**)	.696(**)	.695(**)	1	
SR-TERT	.540(**)	0.098	0.161	0.16	1

Panel II

	LEVEL -UR	*GROW -UR*	*ROAD*	*RAIL-WAY*	*TELE-COM*
LEVEL-UR	1				
GROW-UR	.380 (*)	1			
ROAD	0.19	0.21	1		
RAIL-WAY	0.33	0.14	0.25	1	
TELECOM	.742 (**)	0.06	0.09	0.09	1
PC-PKD	.712 (**)	0.03	0.04	0.05	.989 (**)
PC-CRIND	.702 (**)	0.01	0.04	0.04	.987 (**)
LITTER-R	0.04	-0.04	0.25	0.28	-0.02
LITTER-U	-0.02	-0.18	0.09	0.21	0.14
SEXR-U	-.743 (**)	-.563 (**)	-0.19	-0.14	-.639 (**)
HOSPITAL	.559 (**)	0.08	0.28	0.31	.617 (**)
SCH-MH	-.543 (**)	-0.02	-0.16	-0.20	-.362 (*)

	PC-BKD	*PC-CRIND*	*LITER -R*	*LITER-U*	*SEXR-U*	*HOSP*	*SCH-MH*
PC-PKD	1						
PC-CRIND	.998 (**)	1					
LITTER-R	0.01	0.00	1				
LITTER-U	0.17	0.15		.435 (*)	1		
SEXR-U	-.598 (**)	-.592 (**)	0.18	0.10	1		
HOSPITAL	.607 (**)	.594 (**)	0.27	.367 (*)	-0.30	1	
SCH-MH	-0.31	-0.33	0.07	0.04	.382 (*)	-0.32	1

* Correlation is significant at the 0.05 level (2 tailed)

** Correlation is significant at the 0.01 level (2 tailed)

Table 6.12(a): Interdependency among Indicators of Urbanisation and Socio-Economic Development at District Level in Rajasthan (1981)

	LEVEL -UR	*GROW -UR*	*PCI*	*SR-SR- SEC*	*BANKS TERT*	*PC-*	*PC- BKD*	*GRIND*
LEVEL-UR	1							
GROW-UR	-0.204	1						
PCI	0.257	0.151	1					
SR-SEC	.466(*)	0.091	-0.0191					
SR-TERT	.540(**)	-0.324	-.536(**)	.407(*)	1			
BANKS	.601(**)	0.025	0.126	.574(**)	.545(**)	1		
PC-BKD	.639(**)	0.138	.452 (*)	.563(**)	0.088	.440(*)	1	
PC-CRIND	.588(**)	0.104	0.282	.711(**)	0.158	0.356	.856(**)	1

Table 6.12(b): Interdependency among Indicators of Urbanisation and Socio-Economic Development at District Level in Rajasthan (1991)

	LEVEL-UR	*GROW-UR*	*PCI*	*SR-SEC*	*SR-TERT*
LEVEL-UR	1				
GROW-UR	-0.181	1			
PCI	0.247	-0.13	1		
SR-SEC	0.364	-0.092	0.08	1	
SR-TERT	.510 (**)	-0.114	-.507 (**)	0.0279	1
PC-BKD	.658 (**)	-0.004	.529 (**)	.586 (**)	-0.084
PC-CRIND	.467 (**)	0.153	0.283	.725 (**)	-.113
LITER-U	0.14	0.146	0.226	.536 (**)	-0.102
SEXR-U	0.063	-0.166	-0.05	0.024	-0.179
WATER-U	0.224	-0.269	0.186	0.342	0.232
TOILET-U	.522 (**)	0.03	0.341	0.336	0.202
ELECT-U	0.376	-0.059	0.324	.555 (**)	-0.027

	PC-BKD	*PC-CRIND*	*LITER-R*	*SEXR-U*	*WATER-U*	*TOILET-U*	*ELECT-U*
PC-PKD	1						
PC-CRIND	.897 (**)	1					
LITTER-R	.382 (*)	.411 (*)	1				
SEXR-U	-0.105	-0.077	-0.089	1			
WATER-U	0.191	0.144	0.342	-0.021	1		
TOILET-U	.506 (**)	0.31	.594 (**)	-0.034	.406	1	
ELECT-U	.489 (**)	.411 (*)	.749 (**)	0.228	.420 (*)	.731 (**)	1

* Correlation is significant at the 0.05 level (2 tailed)

** Correlation is significant at the 0.01 level (2 tailed)

Table 6.12(c): Interdependency among Indicators of Urbanisation and Socio-Economic Development at District Level

	LEVEL - UR	*GROW -UR*	*PC-BKD*	*PC-CRIND*	*LITER -R*	*LITER -U*	*SEXR -U*	*HOSP*	*SCH -MH*
LEVEL-UR	1								
GROW-UR	0.259	1							
PC-BKD	.727(**)	0.23	1						
PC-GRIND	.418(*)	0.303	.605(**)	1					
LITER-R	0.316	0.086	0.125	-0.02	1				
LITER-U	0.155	-0.26	.408(*)	.354(*)	-0.117	1			
SEX-U	-0.049	-0.259	-0.074	-0.157	-0.01	0.046	1		
HOSPITAL	-.361(*)	-0.009	-0.305	-0.284	-0.234	-0.26	-.413	1	
SCH-MH	0.004	0.138	-0.041	0.01	0.151	0.101	-0.289	-0.16	1

* Correlation is significant at the 0.05 level (2 tailed)

** Correlation is significant at the 0.01 level (2 tailed)

1. Percentage of urban population (LEVEL-UR)
2. Growth of urban population (GROW-UR)
3. Per capita income (PCI)
4. Share of secondary sector in district income (SR-SEC)
5. Share of tertiary sector in district income (SR-TERT)
6. Road length per 100 sq. km. (ROAD)
7. Railway lines per 100 sq. km. (RAILWAY)
8. Telephone connections per 100 persons (TELECOM)
9. Per capita bank credit (PC-BKD)
10. Per capita industrial credit (PC-CRIND)
11. Females per thousand males in urban areas (SEXR-U)
12. Literacy in rural areas (LITER-R)
13. Literacy in urban areas (LITER-U)
14. Middle and higher secondary schools per thousand persons (SCH-MH)
15. Hospitals and dispensaries per thousand persons (HOSPITAL)

Limitations of Data Availability

Data are not available for all the indicators for the three consecutive time points. Therefore correlation matrices for the states at different time points are of different sizes and vary with the number of indicators. Figures for the per capita income, percentage share of secondary sector, and percentage share of tertiary sector in the total district income are obtained from the human development reports of the respective states. In fact, in the case of Maharashtra all the three figures for 1993-94 are also used for 1991. However, we could not include indicators on the percentage of workers in industrial or commercial activities because the results from the Census of 2001 were yet to become available. The infrastructural indicators and the indicators on hospitals and schools are taken from the CMIE District Profile 2000. The demographic indicators are taken from the Population Census.

Maharashtra

Levels of urbanisation across districts in the state of Maharashtra exhibit a strong positive correlation with the per capita income for both the eighties and the nineties. The relationship has become stronger over the period, from 0.71 in 1991 to 0.84 in 2001 [Tables 6.11(a) to 6.11(c)]. Thus, as observed in the state-level analysis earlier, complementarity exists between economic development and urbanisation at the district level too.

The correlation between the growth of urban population and per capita income became positive and strong in 2001, which was insignificant in 1991. This confirms that urban growth has become increasingly a phenomenon of developed districts and the intra-state disparity increased during the nineties. The district level evidence in Maharashtra, therefore, explains exactly a similar pattern as noticed in the macro-level.

The level of urbanisation has been a significant phenomenon of the districts showing a higher parentage share of secondary and tertiary sector activities. Correlations are very strong and positive at both the points. Importantly, correlation between the urban growth and the percentage share of secondary sector income in the districts has improved sharply and become statistically significant at 1 per cent level, from 0.01 in 1991 to 0.67 in 2001. The improvement in the relationship during 1991-2001 can be taken to suggest an increase in urbanisation due to the increasing industrial activity in the post-liberalisation phase. As has already been mentioned in the earlier section, Maharashtra attracted a large volume of foreign direct investments during this period which explains the shifting of occupational structure over time along with the increasing level of urbanisation in the state of Maharashtra.

Availability of physical infrastructure has played an important role in the process of urbanisation in the state of Maharashtra. This may be inferred from the strong inter-dependency between the level of urbanisation and the infrastructural indicators at all the time points. Particularly, the correlations of the former with railways per 100 sq. km. and telephone connections per 100 persons are very high at all the three points of time. The relationship of road network with the level of urbanisation is negative, –0.38 in 1981 and –0.18 in 1991, but the correlation improved to 0.19 in 2001 suggesting increasing importance of roads as a factor in the urbanisation process. Consequently, the districts having better infrastructural facilities are likely to have a higher share of urban population than those with a poor infrastructure.

Similarly, all the indicators of financial infrastructure have reflected a positive and significant correlation with the urbanisation level. This inter-dependency exists also between economic indicators and urbanisation levels. The infrastructural facilities seem to have accelerated the tempo of urbanisation and economic development of the state.

The number of middle and higher secondary schools (per thousand persons) unfortunately does not rise with the level of urbanisation. This is reflected in the negative correlation between the indicators during the eighties as well as the nineties. However, health facilities tend to go with urbanisation. The number of hospitals per thousand population exhibits a positive correlation with the level of urbanisation.

Socio-demographic indicators like literacy in urban areas have a positive correlation with the level of urbanisation, in both 1981 and 1991. The correlation coefficients, however, are not very high—ranging between 0.17 and 0.33. Urban literacy, however, tends to go down at higher levels of urbanisation, at all the three points of time, though the correlations are not very significant. This can be attributed to inflow of illiterate migrants in the cities and towns in the urbanised districts in search of livelihood.

Another interesting point is that the level of urbanisation relates negatively with the urban sex ratio over the past three decades. This implies that male population increases (relative to female population) as urbanisation increases. This is possibly due to the migration of male population from rural to urban areas in search of jobs. This pushes up the sex ratio in large cities and urbanised districts in the state of Maharashtra.

Rajasthan

The correlation between the level and growth of urbanisation in Rajasthan was negative and insignificant in 1981 as well as in 1991. However, the degree of association weakened over time, and in 2001 the relationship showed positive and relatively stronger coefficient, –0.20,—0.18 and 0.26 respectively [Tables 6.12(a), 6.12(b) and 6.12(c)]. This implies that even in a backward state like Rajasthan high urban growth has occurred mostly in highly urbanised districts during the nineties.

However, unlike Maharashtra, which shows a very strong and positive correlation between per capita income and urbanisation, Rajasthan reports a weaker correlation between the two for 1981 as and 1991.[9] Importantly, the urban growth is negatively correlated with the secondary and tertiary activities at both the time points. The latter also holds a similar relationship with the per capita income for both the time points. This implies that the districts, which contribute a larger share of income from secondary and tertiary activities, are backward. Therefore, one would infer that the state of Rajasthan has witnessed much of the urban growth in the agriculturally developed areas. This is a contrast to the pattern observed in Maharashtra.

The correlation matrix for 1981 shows a positive and significant relationship of per capita bank credit and per capita credit available to industries with the level of urbanisation. This has been noticed throughout the eighties and the nineties. But the per capita bank credit does not show such high correlation with the growth of urban population. Of course, the correlation has improved over time, but it remains statistically insignificant even in 2001. Similarly, credit to industry has been showing a positive correlation with the growth of urban population since 1981, and the value has increased over time. And yet, it is not significant even at 5 per cent level.

The level of urbanisation exhibits a positive relationship with urban literacy, though the values are insignificant at all the three points of time. In the case of the growth rate, however, there is no consistent pattern in the relationship. The high growth of urban population seems to be having a negative impact on the urban literacy at the district level in Rajasthan as is the case in many other states. The reason lies in the fact that most of the rural migrants to urban areas who come to cities and towns in search of jobs are illiterate. A marked differential that exists between the urban and rural literacy rates in the state provides corroborating evidence.

The level of urbanisation exhibits an insignificant positive relation with the urban sex ratio in both 1981 and 1991, whereas in 2001, its value is still lower. The correlation between the growth of urban population and sex ratio is negative and significant. One would, therefore, argue that high urban growth is associated with male-selective migration leading to a low female-male ratio.

Among the other infrastructure indicators like hospitals and middle and higher secondary schools per thousand population, the data are available only for the year 2001. The level of urbanisation has a strong inverse relationship with the availability of medical facilities. The indicator pertaining to the middle and higher secondary schools shows a negligible positive correlation with both the level and growth of urban population. One would conclude that with the rise in the level and growth in urban population, infrastructure facilities come under stress, which is reflected in low per capita values in the urbanised districts.

MAJOR FINDINGS

First, an overview of the results of the 2001 Census urban data suggests that there has been a more judicious and analytical understanding of census criteria than in 1991. The three-fold census criterion appears to have been applied more rigorously, as a result of which there has been a large-scale declassification of towns. Further, the number of merged towns within the big cities is much larger than the previous census. However, the present census has identified more new Census Towns than did the Census 1991. In spite of that, the net addition to the total number of towns is 472, which is much less than that in 1991. This is explained by the larger declassification and merging phenomenon that occurred in the Census 2001.

Second, large city-oriented urbanisation is still evident, although a large number of the UAs were derecognised in the 2001 Census. A number of the UAs have lost their status as a result of certain conditionality put forward by the census for qualifying as an agglomeration. Merger of a large number of towns with the big cities has, on the other hand, expanded the size of already existing UAs. A negligible increase in the number of the UAs, therefore, does not mean that the growth is less centrifugal than before.

Third, urbanisation, as it is stated earlier, has indicated a significant deceleration in its growth rates in recent decades. Excepting the period 1971-81, urban growth as a whole has registered a steady decline in the country. The rate has gone down to 2.73 per cent in the present census (1991-2001) as compared to 3.1 per cent during 1981-91.

Urban growth across size categories presents some interesting features: Class I towns/cities have grown at a faster rate than other categories. Importantly, the share of urban population in Class I towns/cities is markedly higher than the other smaller categories. Consequently, the dominance of Class I towns/cities has been maintained which has not been the case with smaller towns. Indeed, Class I towns/cities are having an edge over the other categories since 1941–the decade before the partition and independence.

Fourth, economic development of a particular region/state has been regarded as a significant factor in increasing urbanisation, which is confirmed from the analysis of the urban scenario in the country since independence. Importantly, the study has demonstrated spatial patterns of the level of urbanisation and urban growth as distinctly different. From independence in 1947 to 1991, the level of urbanisation has generally been high in the case of developed states like Gujarat, Haryana, Maharashtra and Tamil Nadu, although they experienced medium or low urban growth. In contrast, a high urban growth was registered in the relatively backward states such as Bihar, Madhya Pradesh, Orissa, Rajasthan and Uttar Pradesh, which had a low percentage of urban population. The decade of the nineties, however, makes a significant departure from the earlier decades: many of the developed and highly urbanised states registered urban growth above the national average. The backward states, on the other hand, experienced growth rate either below the national average or equal to that. Consequently, the disparity in terms of growth of urban population across the states went up during the nineties.

Fifth, a changing pattern of urbanisation in the size class distribution of towns across the states is observed during the nineties. Until the nineties, in developed states the Class I towns/cities were noted to have recorded higher growth rates than smaller towns, whereas in the less developed states the smaller towns had grown at a similar or higher rate than Class I cities. This pattern witnessed a change in the nineties. Many of the backward states like Assam, Bihar, Himachal Pradesh, Orissa and Rajasthan have reported a high urban growth in their Class I cities. However, the pattern in the developed states has remained similar to that in the eighties. Furthermore, Class I cities (million plus cities) and capital cities are recording a higher growth rate than the smaller categories. This has resulted in raising the coefficient of variation within the Class I towns during 1991-2001. Consequently, cities in Class I category show a significant disparity in their growth rates. One would argue that the international policy of linking a few "fit" cities of the developing countries to the process of globalisation has made the gap somewhat wider.

Sixth, analysing the interdependencies between the indicators of urbanisation and those of socio-economic development, it has been found that the economically better states have a higher percentage of urban population than the relatively backward states. This phenomenon has been noticed throughout the last three decades under the study. Further, the relationships between the indicators of economic development and the growth of urban population have improved significantly over time and become significant in the nineties. This emphasises the fact that the developed states have recorded a high growth of urban population, many registering acceleration in the rate.

Seventh, the levels of basic amenities like access to safe drinking water, sanitation facilities, and electricity are positively correlated with urbanisation, although the values are statistically insignificant. It is, thus, not possible to argue that the more urbanised states provide basic amenities to a larger percentage of urban population. On the other hand, the correlation of these indicators with urban growth has become negative over years. This implies that the growth of urban population over the decades has led to an added pressure on the basic amenities and resulted in deterioration in the standard of living.

It has been argued that urbanisation in the later years has been backed up by industrialisation, the two processes showing a high degree of correspondence in space. But unfortunately, similar relationship does not exist between the indicators of urbanisation, social development and access to basic services. It is indeed alarming that in the case of a few of the amenities such relationships have weakened over time and even turned negative. One would infer that the urban growth in the nineties has neither promoted social development nor provided access to basic amenities to larger sections of the urban population.

Eighth, The patterns of interdependency between urbanisation and socio-economic development—assessed through district level data—are significantly different in the developed state of Maharashtra compared to the less developed state of Rajasthan during the last three decades. The correlations between the level and growth in urbanisation in Maharashtra are high and significant at all the three points of time (1981, 1991, 2001). These suggest that highly urbanised districts register a higher growth in urban population. Further, the levels of urbanisation across districts in the state of Maharashtra show strong correlations with the secondary and tertiary sector activities whereas Rajasthan shows no such significant relationship. This implies that it is industrialisation that has resulted in a higher level of urbanisation in Maharashtra, but not in Rajasthan.

NOTES

1. This is not the first time in the post-independence censuses that the number of census towns has remained constant or gone down. With the application of stringent definition of urban centres adopted in 1961, as noted above, the number had declined by 225 in 1971.
2. Places having town area committees have been tested on the three demographic criteria for being declared as urban which resulted in exclusion of 192 places that have been regarded as urban by the local self-government department of the State.
3. Rural Urban Relationship committee found that in 1961, "the census classified as many as 4197 places with population varying from 5,000 to 20,000 as rural although a number of them had urban local bodies". Report of the Rural Urban Relationship Committee, Ministry of Health and Family Planning 1961, Vol. 1, Government of India.
4. Andaman and Nicobar Islands merit a special mention as their share has gone up from zero to 85 per cent due to the city of Port Blair graduating to a Class I city.
5. In case of Punjab, this holds good for 1981-91 only.
6. It has been mentioned earlier that class VI towns are of special type. Many of them come into existence with the establishment of a large public or private sector unit. Their socio-economic characteristics, including demographic growth, do not follow the pattern observed in case of different size class of urban centres.
7. This has encouraged researchers to examine the definitions of "urban centre" as adopted at the state level in 1991 and 2001. It may indeed be argued that the definition in 1991 was a little more rigorous which would have reduced the growth rate during 1991-2001. This point has been examined at length in the section headed "Definitional Problems in the Census Data".
8. The Class VI category, however, has a number of townships set-up by public enterprise, military establishments, etc., and therefore do not fall in the size class pattern in terms of the growth rate. In most states, these towns have a much higher growth rate than the state average, as is the case in Maharashtra.
9. The information on per capita income is not available for 2001.

REFERENCES

Government of Gujarat, (1991): Primary Census Abstract, Part II-B, Gujarat.

Government of India, (1981): Census of India. Rural-Urban Distribution, Paper-2 (unpublished).

Government of India, (1991): Census of India. Rural-Urban Distribution, Paper-2 (unpublished).

Government of India, (2001): Census of India. Rural-Urban Distribution, Paper-2 (unpublished).

India Infrastructure Reports (1996): *Export Group on the Commercialisation of Infrastructure Projects: Policy Imperatives for Growth and Welfare*. New Delhi: National Council of Applied Economic Research.

Kundu, A. (1983): "Theories of City Size Distribution and Indian Urban Structure: A Reappraisal", *Economic and Political Weekly,* 18: 31, pp. 1361-68.

Ministry of Health and Family Planning, (1961): "Report of the Rural Urban Relationship Committee" Vol. 1. Government of India.

Planning Commission, (1992): Eighth Five-Year Plan (1992-97). Government of India.

Planning Commission, (1997): Mid-Term Appraisal of Ninth Five Year Plan (1997-2000). Government of India.

Sivaramkrishnan, K.; Kundu, Amitabh and Singh, B.N. (2002): "The Census 2001-Urbanisation and Growth Dynamics in India: An Analysis of Trends and Processes". Study commissioned by the Ford Foundation, Delhi.

7

Gujarat: Urban Development Dynamics

H.M. SHIVANAND SWAMY and K. MUKUNDAN

Cities play a critical role in the economic development process. They are now seen as the engines of national development and a source of employment and offer a higher quality of life. They are places of high productivity and contribute significantly towards a region's income. At the national level, 30 per cent of urban population contributes to 60 per cent of the national income.[1] The city of Ahmedabad, in 1977, with 7 per cent of the total population, contributed 14.3 per cent of the total income of the State and, in 1995, accounted for 8.02 per cent of the urban population of the state and contributed 17.40 per cent of the state's income. Considering the importance of cities in the national economy, there has been a shift in the urban policies from a desire to control the growth of cities by curbing rural-to-urban migration, to acceptance of urbanization as a desirable process. This paper traces the pattern of urban development in Gujarat, identifies the emerging issues and attempts to suggest broad strategies.

Levels, Patterns and Determinants of Urbanization in Gujarat

Gujarat's steady transformation into a predominantly urban society is now a demographic, economic and political reality. At the beginning of the 20th century, Gujarat's population was 9.09 million with an urbanization level of 22 per cent. The last four decades saw an almost three-fold increase in the urban population of the state with the present level of urbanization at 37 per cent. Over the decades a slowdown in the rate of growth in population, in both rural and urban areas, has been observed in the case of Gujarat Urban Primacy (Fig.7.1 and Tables 7.1 and 7.2).

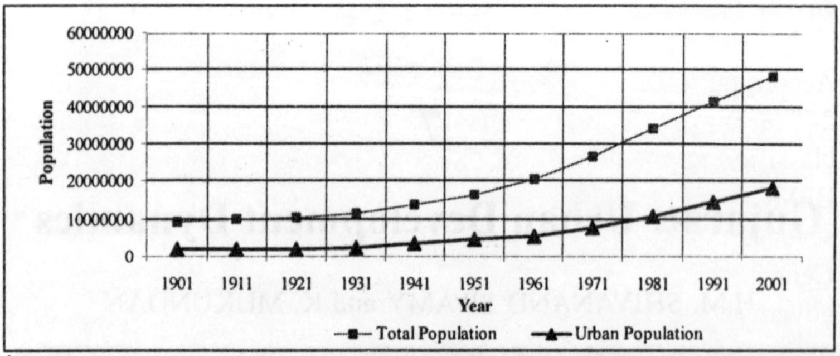

Fig. 7.1: Growth of the State's Population and Urban Population (1901–2001)

Table 7.1: Urbanization Levels and Growth Trends

Year	*Gujarat*			*India*		
	Urban Population Million	*Urbanization Level %*	*Growth Rates %*	*Urban Population Million*	*Urbanization Level %*	*Growth Rates %*
1961	5.31	25.74	—	78.9	18.0	—
1971	7.49	28.06	41.05	109.1	19.91	38.22
1981	10.60	31.10	41.52	159.5	23.70	46.23
1991	14.24	34.47	34.34	217.2	25.71	36.09
2001	18.93	37.36	32.94	285.4	27.78	21.35

Source: Census of India

Table 7.2: Urban Population Growth in Gujarat, 1901-2001

Census Year	*Towns Numbers*	*Population in Millions*		*Level of Urbanization %*
		Total	*Urban*	
1961	181	20.6	5.3	25.77
1971	216	26.7	7.5	28.08
1981	255	34.1	10.6	31.10
1991	264	41.3	14.2	34.49
2001	242	50.7	18.9	37.34

Source: Census of India, 2001.

Urban Primacy

According to the 2001 Census of India, Gujarat now has a total of 242 urban areas.[1,2] For administrative purposes, these areas are classified as municipalities and municipal corporations under the BPMC Act and Gujarat Nagarpalika Act (1963). At present, there are seven municipal corporations and 142 municipalities. The remaining Census towns having a population less than 15,000 people are governed under the rural administrative set-up as per the provisions of the Gujarat Panchayat Act (1993). About 80 per cent of the urban population resides in just 63 of the 242 cities and towns of the state and the seven municipal corporations—Ahmedabad, Surat, Vadodara, Rajkot, Bhavnagar, Jamnagar and Junagadh (hereinafter referred to as "corporation cities") – accommodate more than half of the state's urban population, indicating their primacy (Table 7.3). Of these, Ahmedabad, Surat and Vadodara are "million-plus" cities. The process of urbanisation is expected to intensify over the next two decades. The city of Ahmedabad is likely to grow into a mega-city with the inclusion of Gandhinagar, Sanand, Kalol and many other surrounding urban areas into its fold. Similar trends are anticipated for the other corporation cities also.

Table 7.3: Index of Primacy (2001)

City	*Population within Municipal Limits*	*Share in State's Urban Population*	*Population of Urban Agglomerations*	*Share in State's Urban Population*
	In Millions	*%*		*%*
Ahmedabad	3.5	18.58	4.5	23.89
Surat	2.4	12.86	2.8	14.85
Vadodara	1.3	6.90	1.5	7.89
Rajkot	0.96	5.10	1.0	5.30
Bhavnagar	0.4	2.37	0.5	2.95
Jamnagar	0.5	2.70	0.5	2.73
Junagadh	0.2	1.33	0.2	1.00
Total	9.26	49.41	11.00	58.95

Source: Census reports.

Size-Class Distribution

In 1991, Gujarat had 21 large cities (Class I cities with a population of more than 100,000); 27 medium towns (Class II towns with 50,001-100,000 population); and 177 small towns (Class III-VI towns with a population of less than 50,000). By 2001 the number of Class I and Class II towns had gone up to 26 and 37 respectively. In 2001, there were 77 and 55 of Class III and Class IV towns in Gujarat. Of the total urban population, over 50 per cent resides in seven municipal corporation areas and 26 per cent in Class I and II towns (Annex Table 7.1).

Spatial Patterns of Urbanization and Industrial Development

Industrial Location Policy: Determinant of Urbanisation Pattern

The rapid pace of industrialisation during the past five decades in Gujarat is one of the prime factors contributing to its urban growth. In terms of spatial pattern of urbanisation (talukas were ranked as per their share of urban population in the state) 31 talukas (inclusive of top 25 urbanised talukas in 1981, 1991 and 2001) account for 72 per cent of the state urban population and 40 per cent of the state total population. (Refer Annex Tables 7.2, 7.3 and 7.4)

Since its formation in 1961, Gujarat has emerged as a leading industrial state in the country. From its traditional textile base, it has diversified into fields like chemicals, petrochemicals, dyes and dye intermediates, pharmaceuticals, engineering, food processing, agro-based industries, dairy, edible oils and a host of other sectors. A five-fold increase in the number of working factories and a two-and-a-half-times increase in factory employment have occurred in the past 25 years. There are around 2,000 medium-and large-scale units, around 2.3 lakh small-scale units and 257 industrial estates in the state of Gujarat. The growth of small-scale industries is phenomenal and large-scale investments are on the anvil. The economy of Gujarat had a moderate growth of 5.83 percent per annum during 1980-98. However, most of this growth has been between 1990-91 and 1997-98 when the economy marked a high growth rate of 8.61 per cent.

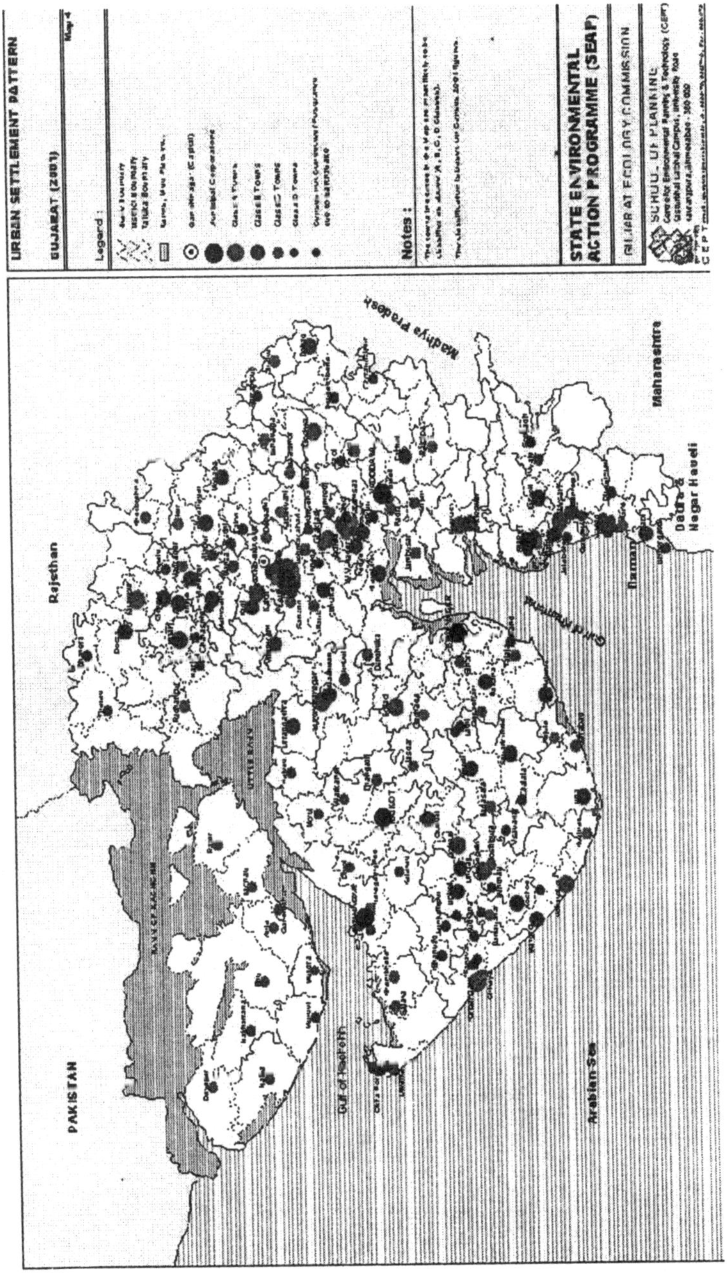

Fig. 7.2: Distribution of Urban Centres

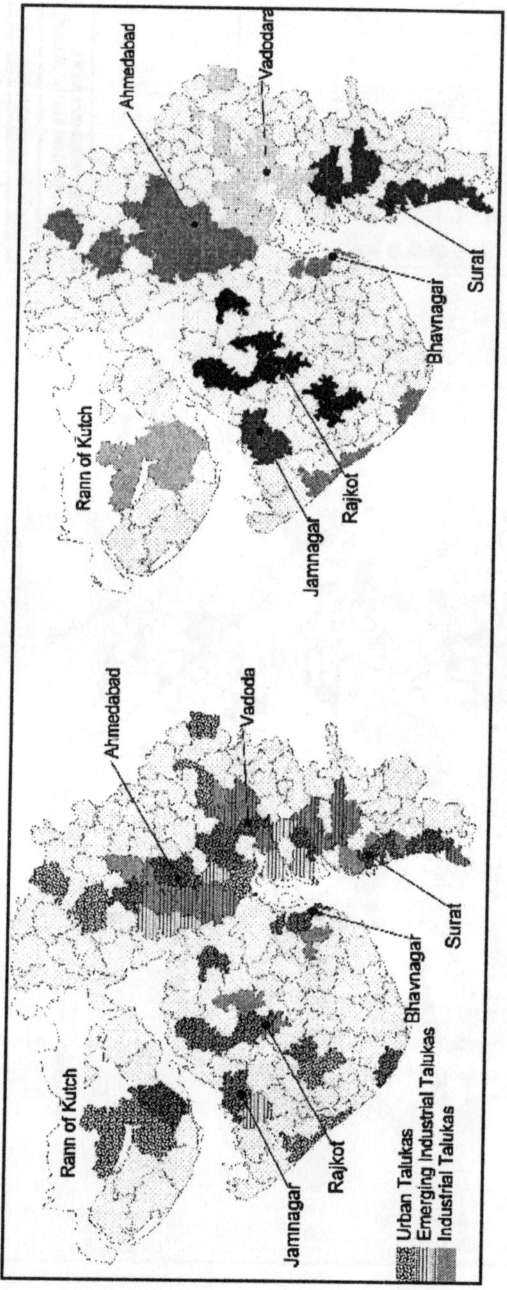

Fig. 7.3: Distribution of Urban and Industrial Talukas

An analysis of the industrial development in Gujarat based on the following indicators[3] :

(a) Employment in the manufacturing units in the year 1986, 1991 and 1996;
(b) Employment and investments in commissioned industrial projects (1991-1999);
(c) Employment and investments in industrial projects under implementation (1991-1999).

A composite map combining the industrial and emerging industrial talukas indicates the emergence of 48 talukas and these constitute 82.5 per cent of 1996 employment, 94 per cent of commissioned investments, 72 per cent of investment under implementation. In order to ensure a balanced growth in the region, industrial incentives for the backward regions have been part of the state's industrial policy. An overview of the incentive zones in the three successive industrial policies of 1985-1990, 1990-95, 1995-2000 indicates limited correlation between the actual industrial growth. (Fig. 7.3). However, a composite map (Fig. 7.4) shows concentration of industrial development in certain areas of the state, particularly

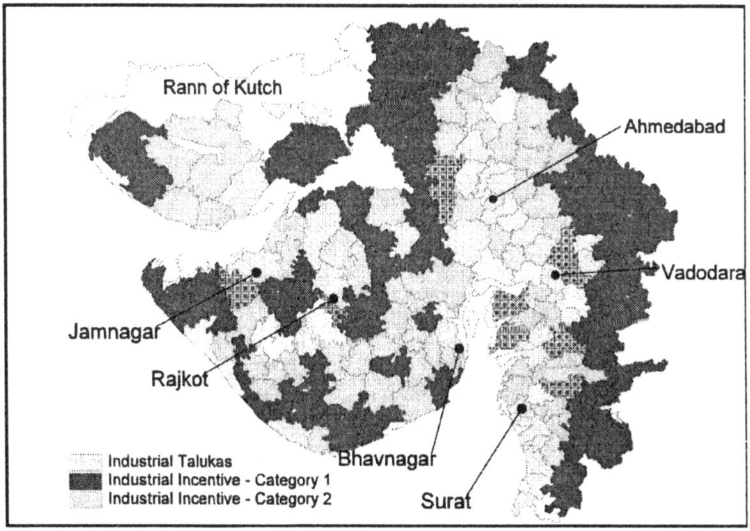

Fig. 7.4: Composite Map

around the corporation cities of Ahmedabad, Surat, Vadodara, Bhavnagar, Rajkot and Jamnagar. In effect, industrial growth is dependent on incentives; the drivers seem to be proximity to larger urban centres and quality of infrastructure. Another reason for the growth around large centres is the restrictive industrial growth policies within certain distance from cities and most industries have located themselves outside the prescribed limits. The reason for such development is the availability of a good infrastructure and an analysis of inter-relation between the urbanized talukas[4] and industrial talukas substantiates this assessment.

The emerging pattern has two distinct characteristics of concentration of activities around these urbanized talukas. An overview of the industrial development in the state depicts concentration of industrial development and urbanisation in 48 talukas, which account for 82.5 per cent of the 1996 employment, 94 per cent of commercial investments and 72 per cent of the investments in projects under implementation. These form investments in 82 talukas that form 8 linked clusters, six of which are around the municipal corporations and two are coastal areas of Kuchchh and Veraval-Porbandar. The second character is of Urban Sprawl (Fig. 7.5, 7.6 and 7.7). The urban growth in Gujarat is shifting from the urban core (within the urban local authority areas) to the periphery. Such developments are often found to be scattered, leap-frogging and/or strip development. The expanding share of population living on the fringes of corporation cities and other large and medium towns during the past decade has been remarkable (Table 7.4). Presently, almost 15 per cent of the urban population resides outside the municipal limits in the agglomeration areas. These agglomeration areas fall under several urban and rural local bodies. Owing to the large population in these areas, the scale of services required is huge and addressing them in their entirety is a daunting task for the various local bodies, especially when there is lack of adequate coordination between them.

The role of the urban development authorities is also restricted mostly to the real estate development and physical planning aspects. In the absence of a coordinated and planned effort to address the growing needs of the increasing population, the quality of development and life is of concern. Development beyond the municipal area in open lands often has fewer upfront costs owing to limited land-use

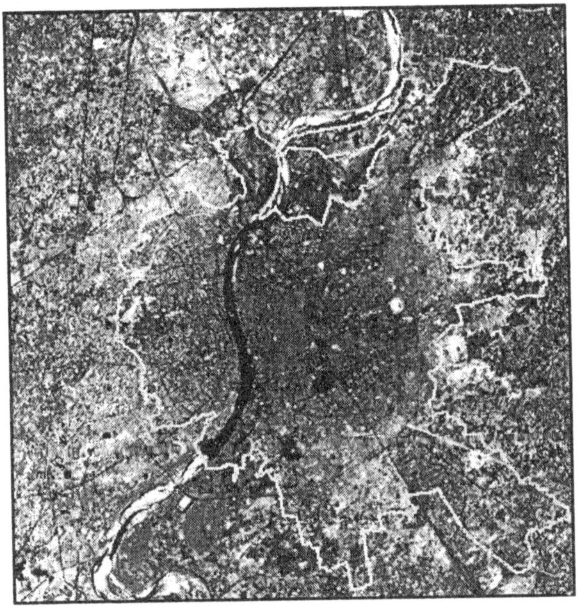

Fig. 7.5: IRS-1C/1D: LISS-III Imagery, 1999, Ahmedabad Urban Sprawl

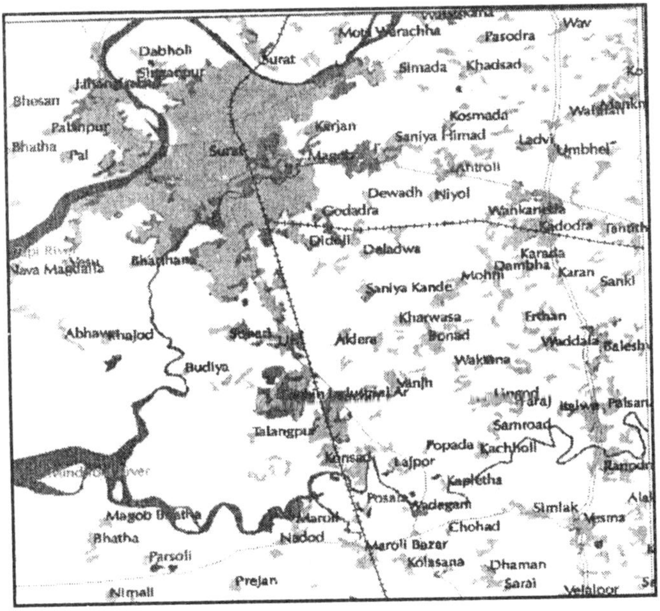

Fig. 7.6: IRS-1C, L2A1, Year 1999, Surat Urban Sprawl

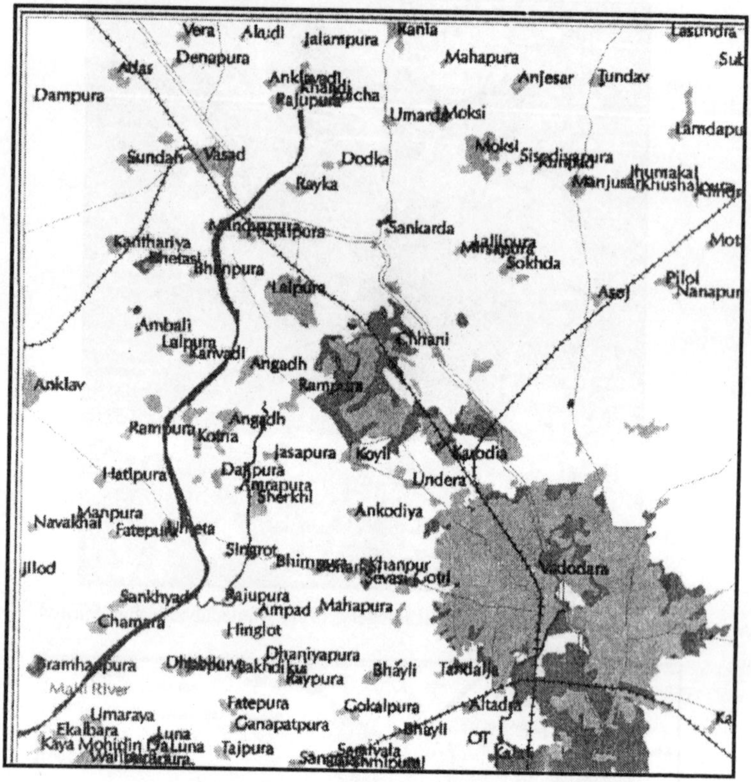

Fig. 7.7: IRS-1C L2A1, 1999, Vadodara Urban Sprawl

regulations and development requirements, and are thus more profitable for the developer. Such urbanisation patterns are quite a cause of concern because of high consumption of land resource and higher infrastructure costs.

Industrial and urban development along with growth and prosperity also lead to resource degradation. Water required for industrial uses, residential areas etc. is returned to the lakes/rivers in a far lower quality than originally supplied. Also, the over-exploitation of water resources to meet the ever-increasing demand of population results in a rapidly diminishing ground-water level. Similarly, solid waste from the households in the city is dumped in an open area outside the city polluting the environment. Faced with low resource mobilisation sources and subsidised provision of services, the urban local bodies are finding it difficult to cater to the increased demand for services.

Table 7.4: Urban Areas with Population Spillover beyond Municipal Limits

Urban Area	*Population-2001*		*% Spill-over*	*Urban Area*	*Population 2001*		*% Spill-over*
	Agglo-meration	*Muni-cipal Area*			*Agglo-meration*	*Muni-cipal Area*	
1. Ahmedabad	4.52	3.52	22.21	21. Dohad	0.11	0.08	29.35
2. Surat	2.81	2.43	13.43	22. Kalol	0.11	0.10	10.72
3. Vadodara	1.49	1.31	12.49	23. Gondal	0.10	0.10	1.53
4. Rajkot	1.00	0.97	3.54	24. Amreli	0.10	0.09	5.33
5. Jamnagar .	0.56	0.45	19.83	25. Khambhat	0.09	0.08	13.67
6. Bhavnagar	0.52	0.51	1.28	26. Mahuva	0.08	0.07	12.36
7. Junagadh	0.25	0.17	33.10	27. Visnagar	0.07	0.07	10.43
8. Navsari	0.23	0.13	42.34	28. Kadi	0.06	0.06	6.31
9. Wadhwan	0.22	0.16	28.85	29. Sidhpur	0.06	0.05	7.55
10. Anand	0.22	0.13	40.17	30. Bilimora	0.06	0.05	11.05
11. Porbandar	0.20	0.13	32.59	31. Mangrol	0.06	0.06	2.18
12. Nadiad	0.20	0.19	1.97	32. Dholka	0.06	0.05	3.76
13. Bharuch	0.18	0.15	15.94	33. Halol	0.04	0.04	7.55
14. Veraval	0.16	0.14	10.55	34. Padra	0.04	0.04	8.37
15. Valsad	0.15	0.07	52.75	35. Idar	0.03	0.03	9.91
16. Mahesana	0.14	0.10	29.98	36. Vijapur	0.03	0.02	19.88
17. Godhra	0.13	0.12	7.09	37. Ranavav	0.03	0.02	18.37
18. Palanpur	0.12	0.11	9.73	38. Kalol	0.03	0.02	11.55
19. Patan	0.11	0.11	1.35	39. Dakor	0.03	0.02	5.60
20. Anklesvar	0.11	0.07	39.68				

Status of Urban Services

With the cities playing a major role in promoting growth, owing to the rapid pace of urbanisation, there is a widening gap between the demand and supply of services.

Water Sources

While all corporation cities have their own organised water supply systems which cater to the water needs in their respective jurisdictions, water is supplied either through a pipeline distribution system with house connections and/or public standposts. With the rapid growth in these cities as well as the vagaries of rainfall most corporation cities draw water from additional sources, i.e. groundwater and lakes. Among most non-corporation cities (88%), groundwater is the most frequently used source of freshwater supply. With the depletion of groundwater sources due to high exploitation, the cities have little option than resorting to extension of the existing piped network to more distant water sources, usually at a considerable cost. Ahmedabad is a typical case in point. First, the corporation city sunk tube-wells in the bed of the Sabarmati river to meet its water supply requirements. And as demand increased, it constructed a dam in Dharoi across the Sabarmati river, with state government assistance, to augment supply. Because the water level in the Dharoi Dam falls to dead storage during the dry summer months, the city embarked upon yet another project to bring water from the Mahi river through an underground pipeline. In Jamnagar, the construction of a 100-km-long pipeline is underway to bring water from the Sani Dam. A completed pipeline project (Sardar Sarovar Project)[5] has provided relief to Rajkot and other towns in Saurashtra in June, 2002. Currently, Reliance Industries in the vicinity is also providing desalinated water to the city during the summer months.

Coverage

There is a wide disparity in the levels and population coverage of water supply among the six corporation cities and the different classes of towns in Gujarat. Except in Surat and Bhavnagar, the per capita supply of water in the corporation cities is below the water supply standards as set by The Central Public Health Environmental Engineering Organisation. The per capita availability in the small and medium towns is also much lower than the stipulated norms. Except in Surat where only 67 per cent of urban households are covered by piped water systems, the proportion of households served in other corporation cities is relatively high, ranging from 76 per cent in Ahmedabad to 98 per cent in Vadodara. However, small and medium towns fall far short of full coverage, i.e., only about 60 per cent of urban households. Other households not covered by piped distribution systems obtain water from public standposts and/or from shallow wells. Those with no access even to these sources obtain water from water vendors who supply it from nearby water bodies through tankers. This water is untreated, and is often contaminated. Towns and cities in Kachchh and Saurashtra remain poorly served.

Disparities in supply

Likewise, there are many intra-urban disparities in the levels of water supply. For example, for the Ahmedabad Municipal Corporation where data is available, different areas, covered under different projects (or phases of a project), receive water at varying levels. Majority of the households living in slum areas are largely dependent on public standposts and receive water at very low rates (70 per cent receive less than 20 LPCD) (Suhane 2000)[6].

Supply levels

Although a large proportion of the urban population especially in the corporations are reported to be covered by the public water supply systems, there are severe deficiencies with regard to the quantity of water made available. In Gujarat, all cities experience water shortage, with only a few hours' supply on average per day. For instance, the corporation cities of Ahmedabad, Vadodara and Surat supply water twice a day. The duration of the supply varies from half-an-hour to two hours. In the corporation cities of Saurashtra, households get water only once in two or three days over a four to six-month period. In several other towns in the same region, water is often supplied every alternate day. In summers, the supply is restricted to once a day in many cities of Gujarat. To meet the shortfall, private water vendors operate and supply water through tankers for which they charge hefty amounts. In Rajkot, private vendors charge Rs. 50/kl under normal conditions and Rs. 100/kl during the summers. Similarly in Jamnagar, the price varies from Rs. 25 to Rs. 60/kl. Trading in water has become a booming business in Ahmedabad, Rajkot, Jamnagar, Bhavnagar, Amreli and Junagadh.

Sewerage

In most cities in Gujarat, the Underground Drainage System (UGD) comprises sewer pipes that collect household wastewater but are also connected to storm-water drains. Thus, storm-water and untreated wastewater together are discharged directly into the rivers, streams, lakes, and/or coastal waters. This is in addition to the untreated or partially treated effluent discharges by industrial units located mainly in the urban areas. Direct discharges of domestic sewage and wastewater into the surface water bodies are the main source of surface-water and groundwater pollution in the state. In the six corporation cities, the combined wastewater generated is estimated at 1069 mld (1998). Of this about half (538 mld) is trerted before disposal. In terms of population coverage, the top four cities of Ahmedabad, Surat, Vadodara and Rajkot fare better. In Jamnagar and Bhavnagar cities, the service is only through open drainage. The situation is much worse in Gujarat's 143 non-corporation cities. Only six Class A towns have some level of underground drainage network, of which only three towns (Nadiad, Navsari and Anand) have systems in operation. Treatment plants exist only in eight towns. The situation in the lower order towns is not different. With very limited coverage, much of the wastewater generated (1,350 mld) in these towns is dumped untreated into nearby surface water sources. Most areas not served with sewerage network depend on onsite sanitation facilities such as septic tanks with soakaways, pit latrines or soak pits. Where these are used, the pits in many cases get saturated, resulting in sewage overflows into open drains or on to roadsides, spreading polluted water and creating health risks. The problem becomes worse during the monsoon season when flooding occurs.

Solid Waste Management

The six corporation cities, particularly Ahmedabad and Surat, are the largest generators of solid wastes in Gujarat. Compared to these larger and richer cities, medium and small cities generate much less amount, i.e. ranging from 5 tonnes of solid wastes per day in Class D cities to 40 tonnes per day in Class A cities. Solid waste collection particularly in Surat has now vastly improved following the outbreak of plague that hit the city in 1994. While collection rates in the corporation cities of Ahmedabad and Bhavnagar are also relatively high, roughly 30 to 40 per cent of the wastes still go uncollected in Jamnagar, Rajkot and Vadodara. Moreover, collection services are often not extended to the slum areas. With more than 20 per cent of the population in Jamnagar, Rajkot, Ahmedabad and Surat being slum-dwellers, this presents a significant problem. In some areas, household waste is burnt, causing localised air pollution. Often, however, uncollected waste is left either on the roadside, on vacant plots, or dumped into rivers or the sea. Even where collection bins are provided, they are inadequate in terms of the number and storage capacity. Often wastes are left to accumulate near or around them. The amount left uncollected usually finds its way into municipal sewers or open drains, causing blockages and flooding. Since a system of collecting garbage at the household level is almost non-existent (informal neighbourhood organised system of garbage collection is practised in some areas), street cleaning has become a mode of waste collection. *Safai kamdars* or street sweepers are employed by urban local bodies to clean roads, and take the garbage to municipal bins. At present, the range of population served per *safai kamdar* varies from 273 to 2,337. Based on the Public Health Department's prescribed norm of 400 to 600 m road length per sweeper depending on the class of town and population density, Gujarat currently requires an additional 50,150 cleaners for more efficient street-cleaning. In most cities solid waste is disposed of in small, uncontrolled dumping sites. These are generally open pits or landfill sites in low-lying areas to which unsegregated wastes are dumped and left to decay. Because these are unsanitary landfills with no provision for leachate collection, they pose serious groundwater and surface water pollution risks. Moreover, along with the municipal wastes, toxic and hazardous wastes from industries are also indiscriminately dumped in these sites, compounding the risks to human health. Composting is being practised in 21 cities. In Valsad, this process helped in generating revenue and also helped in solving the problem of solid waste disposal as the clean and segregated refuse requires lesser area. One town, Limbdi in Surendranagar district, is operating a biogas plant. Vyara town in Surat district has achieved 100 per cent efficiency in Solid Waste Management. Several other towns as Rajkot and Surat have achieved better service performance with the privatisation of solid waste management.

Sanitation

While there has been better progress in the sanitation coverage than in the water supply coverage in Class A and B cities, this is not the case in Class C and D towns where half of the total number of households do not have individual toilets. The percentage of households with no latrine had declined considerably from 36.8 per cent to 31.1 per cent during the period 1983 to 1988-89, but this figure went down only marginally to 30.6 per cent in 1993 (NSSO 1988). One-third of the urban population (comprising mostly slum-dwellers) still has to do without basic sanitation facilities. With no access even to public toilets, they resort to defecating in open lands, nearby railway lines, banks of streams and nallahs, and/or on roadsides.

Urban Transport

The public transport facilities in the cities and towns of Gujarat are limited. In Ahmedabad, the facility is being provided by the AMC owned Ahmedabad Municipal Transport System (AMTS). In the cities of Surat, Vadodara and Rajkot, the Gujarat State Transport Corporation (GSRTC) is providing the service. In Jamnagar and Bhavnagar private operators provide transport services with arrangement from municipal corporations. Until a recent decision to discontinue bus services, transport services were provided by the GSRTC. While there have been discussions on privatisation of the services, an appropriate framework to involve the private sector is yet to be in place. The Urban Transport Plan and the Development Plan continue to be developed at different points of time and the tendency is to support major investments than focusing on low-cost management solutions.

Stress on Environment

Air pollution

The two major sources of air pollution in Gujarat are industries and vehicular emissions. However, the contribution of each source to the ambient pollution levels is difficult to determine given the current data and in the absence of an emissions inventory. The common air pollutants are sulphur dioxide (SO_2), nitrogen dioxide (NO_2), suspended particulate matter (SPM), carbon monoxide (CO) and lead (Pb). In the six corporation cities, most of the monitoring stations recorded values for SPM the (1997-98) which are above the standard limits prescribed by the GPCB for residential and industrial areas. In most industrial locations, the SPM levels are generally above the residential norms but below the limits prescribed for industrial areas. The ambient concentrations of the SPM are particularly high in Rajkot and Surat where the recorded values (589 to 1200 ug/m^3) are way above the standards for both industrial and residential areas. SPM levels in Rajkot are consistently high for four out of five years. NO_x appears to be a less significant problem although the levels exceed standards in a few industrial locations in Vadodara and other non-corporation cities. However, SO_2 levels exceed the prescribed standards in a number of industrial and residential locations in Ahmedabad, Surat and Vadodara, probably due to the concentration of industries in these areas. In the other 47 small and medium towns where GPCB monitoring data are available, air pollution is largely attributable to emissions from industries as most are industrial towns. As in the corporation cities, the SPM levels generally exceed the acceptable limit in the industrial zones. In certain areas like Sayajigunj of Vadodara, railway station area of Surat, Kandla, Sikka and Morbi, the levels are two to three times higher than the prescribed standard.

While air pollution from industries has become a serious problem in urban Gujarat and in the state as a whole, the problem of vehicular emissions is also assuming serious proportions in several cities. The rate of growth of vehicles in Gujarat (11.4 per cent per annum) is the highest in the country. Every year, about 400,000 vehicles are added to the roads of the state. Of these, about 278,000 are two-wheelers, 30,000 are cars, and 16,000 are vehicles for transporting goods. The number of vehicles per 1,000 persons has increased from 3.82 in 1971 to 34.19 in 1991. On the other hand, growth in the road infrastructure in the state has been slower. The number of vehicles per km of road has increased from 3.06 in 1971 to 21.05 in 1991 and 43.45 in 1998. The share of public transport in the vehicle composition has decreased from 5 per cent in 1971 to less than 1 per cent in 1997. Almost 93 per cent of the total motor vehicles registered in Gujarat in 1995-96 were in the municipal corporation areas. Of these, Ahmedabad (56%), Surat (25%) and Vadodara (16%) together accounted for 97 per cent of the total vehicles registered. The problem of vehicular pollution is, therefore, particularly severe and is worsening in the corporation cities where motor vehicle use has risen and where most vehicles use leaded fuel. Fuel adulteration has also become a critical issue, particularly the mixing of kerosene with petrol in three-wheelers (in a 70:30 ratio) resulting in excessive emission levels that further degrade the air quality.

Deteriorating Water Quality

Water scarcity in Gujarat's cities is aggravated by the worsening quality of the available water as a result of pollution of the water sources. Water monitoring results from the Gujarat Pollution Control Board (GPCB) indicate prevalence of organic and bacterial pollution in Gujarat's rivers and lakes, coastal waters and groundwater resources. Among the rivers which are a major source of urban water supply for six cities and are found to be highly polluted are Sabarmati, Viswamitri, Par, Aji and Khari rivers.[7] It is important to note that river water is often drawn through infiltration wells. While Ahmedabad, Vadodara, Surat and Rajkot municipal corporations have drinking water treatment facilities, most small and medium towns have disinfection facilities only. Given the fact that the polluted rivers of Gujarat are the major sources of municipal water for most towns and cities along their courses, it is believed that every consumer has, over the years, been exposed to an unknown quantity and quality of pollutants in the water they have consumed. Nine towns use lakes and ponds as drinking water sources. However, of the 21 major lakes for which information is available, only Ajwa, Saputara and Pratap Sarovar have Class A water; Habhoi has Class B water. For drinking water, Bhuj, Dahod, Halol, Kadi and Dholka depend on lakes and ponds with a poor quality water. These towns have no water treatment facilities. Of the 20 reservoirs, 8 have Class A water and 5 have Class B water. The rest have Class C and D water, indicating their poor quality. The quality of water in Aji Dam-2 and Par is of concern. The Shetrunji Dam, Bhavnagar's major source of water, is contaminated with faecal coliform (total coliform: 150 to 1,100).

A GPCB survey of well water quality in 49 small and medium towns shows that the well water is unfit for drinking due to high bacteriological contamination. The continuing presence of faecal coliform and the decreasing levels of dissolved oxygen are indicative of its increasing contamination. The health risks to those who use well water for consumption have become a matter of grave concern, considering that it is the main source of drinking water for most of the 49 towns surveyed. As mentioned earlier, the extent of the sewerage system in the corporation is not complete and the situation is much worse in Gujarat's 143 non-corporation cities. With very limited coverage, much of the wastewater generated (1,350 mld) in these towns is dumped untreated in the nearby surface water sources. Most areas not served with any sewerage network depend on onsite sanitation facilities such as septic tanks with soaka-ways, pit latrines or soak pits. Where these are used, the pits in many cases get saturated, resulting in sewage overflows into open drains or on to roadsides, spreading polluted water and creating health risks. The problem becomes worse during the monsoon season when flooding occurs.

Depletion of Water Resources

To address the inadequacy in water supply and meet the continuously increasing demand, the most common response is to dig more and more wells. In Ahmedabad Municipal Corporation, for example, because of the rapid growth in urban population and the unreliability of rainfall affecting the availability of water in the Sabarmati River, groundwater use has been on the rise. This has resulted in a continuing depletion of the groundwater table at an annual rate of two to three metres due to over-drawal. The situation in its immediate periphery is equally alarming. Of the four peripheral Municipal towns (Memnagar, Ghatlodiya, Ranip and Chandkheda) under the jurisdiction of the Ahmedabad Urban Development Authority (AUDA) for which information is available, less than 20 per cent of the population is covered by the piped water system. Most households depend on housing society bore wells. In the Memnagar Municipal area, there are 180 tube- wells in just two-hectare area, one of the highest densities of wells in India.

Land Resource

The urban areas occupy a very small share of the total available land. In Gujarat, urban areas occupy 2.5 per cent of the state's land. A look at the peripheral areas shows the increasing conversion of land in to non-agricultural uses. The rate of conversion is 4,000 ha per year and is bound to accentuate with increasing urbanisation. Access to land in the cities is becoming increasingly difficult due to the competing demands of housing, industries, commerce, transport, open areas etc. This leads to speculation, higher land prices and development in vulnerable areas, lack of access to the urban poor and uneconomic utilisation of scarce land. Failure to provide serviced land in line with the increasing demand adds to the problem of land shortage. Owing to critical shortages haphazard exploitation of land in the peripheral areas takes place and unauthorised development continues, only to worsen the situation further.

Slums

Unabated growth of the urban population owing to an increase in the economic activities and job opportunities is aggrava-ting the problem of housing shortage, resulting in proliferation of slums. About 18.1 per cent of Gujarat's population is estimated to be living in slum areas(TCPO,1996)[8]. The largest population of slum dwellers is found in Ahmedabad and Surat, Gujarat's two largest cities (Table 7.5).

Table 7.5: Slum Population in Major Cities

City/Town	*Slum as % of Total Population*
Ahmedabad	41.00
Surat	30.70
Vadodara	20.70
Rajkot	21.00
Bhavnagar	25.00
Jamnagar	8.57
Anand	8.57
Bharuch	6.15
Gandhidham	15.50
Navsari	13.37

Source: UIPM Report, CMAG, 2001.

Urban Poverty

The performance of Gujarat with respect to poverty alleviation has been fair. During the year 1983, 41 per cent and 30 per cent of the urban and rural populations was below the poverty line against the national average of 42 and 46 per cent respectively. The recent round of NSS (1999-2000) puts the level of urban and rural population below the poverty line at 16 and 13 per cent respectively. However, poverty defined on the lines of Millennium Development Goals (MDG) would increase this proportion by at least 3 times (Table 7.6).

Table 7.6: Percentage of Population Below Poverty Line

Year	*Gujarat*			*All India*		
	Urban	*Rural*	*Total*	*Urban*	*Rural*	*Total*
1983	40.6	29.8	33.3	42.2	45.6	44.8
1987-1988	39.6	28.7	32.3	40.1	39.1	39.3
1993-1994	29.3	19.7	29.3	33.8	33.4	33.5
1999-2000	15.6	13.2	14.1	23.6	27.1	26.1

Source: NSS various Rounds, Planning Commission, Government of India, March 2002.

The physical environment, in terms of housing conditions and availability of basic services determines the productivity and consequently the quality of life in urban areas. In the corporation cities an estimated 15 to 30 per cent of the population resides in low-income settlements termed "Slums". In smaller towns, the estimates vary enormously depending on the "slum" definition. However, the evidence suggests that the proportion is large and has been growing rapidly. Further, these places continue to be devoid of many amenities and facilities. A Draft State Slum Policy has recently been prepared.

Vulnerability Issues

Concentration of population in certain areas which fall in the risk zones of cyclone and earthquake has increased the vulnerability of a larger part of the population to the disasters. Around 15 per cent of the state urban population is within the cyclonic high risk zone and

28 per cent is in the moderate zone. Ten talukas of the urban-industrial cluster constituting 8 per cent of the states urban population falls under the high risk zone. Around 7.38 per cent of the states urban population is prone to earthquake and 92 per cent is in the moderate risk zone of the earthquake zones. Around 40 per cent of the states population is in the high water scarcity zone. Eighteen of the urban industrial talukas lie in the high scarcity zone affecting 15 per cent of the states urban population (Fig 7.8).

Institutional issues

Weak regulatory and legal environment

Despite its acute water scarcity problem, Gujarat does not have a policy nor any legal instrument to control groundwater overexploitation. Neither does it have an appropriate pricing mechanism that discourages wasteful use and that reflects the cost of providing water. Attempts at water metering had been made but these were rarely taken seriously. However, in Surat water metering for bulk consumers continues to be in operation. In many cases, meters malfunctioned soon after installation because of the high particulate matter in the mains. Affordability studies indicate that consumers are willing to pay for water supply services yet cost recovery is hardly considered. This contributes to the weakening of the revenue base of the cities.

The problem of urban water and air pollution is becoming particularly serious with urbanisation and industrialisation proceeding rapidly in the state and pollution regulation remaining ineffective or poorly enforced. The absence of measures to control indiscriminate dumping of solid waste, including hazardous and toxic wastes, by the industries, exacerbates the problem. Worsening water scarcity in the urban areas is due to the inability of the municipal to control water pollution and domestic wastewater discharges.

Similarly, lack of public transport, inadequate travel demand management and non-existence of an economic instrument to curb the growth of privately owned vehicles contribute to vehicular pollution in the state. While initial steps such as the issuance of Pollution Under Control certificates (PUCs) have been taken, this measure is grossly inadequate to address the problem. Enforcement is also lacking as the

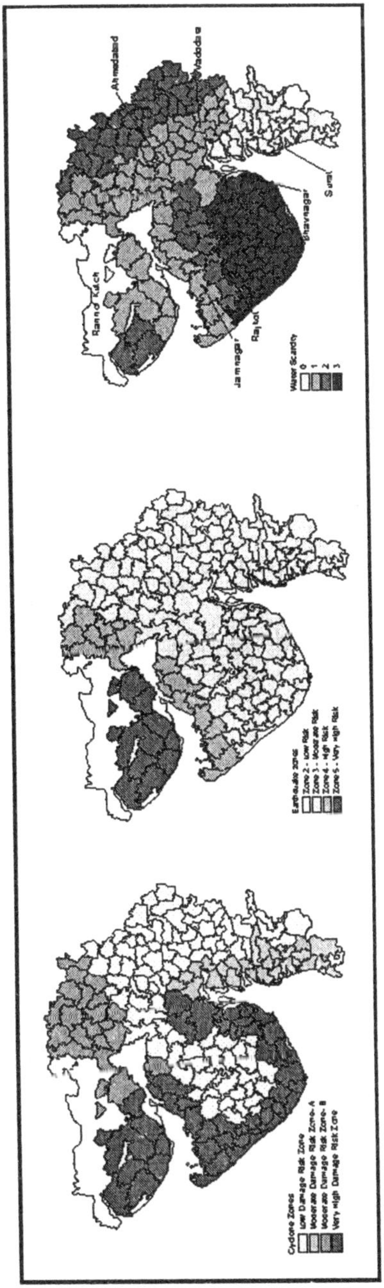

Fig. 7.8: Vulnerable Talukas

PUCs have so far been issued to less than 15 per cent of the total number of vehicles on the road

Poor management of assets and inefficient service

Even as the cities in Gujarat intensify their efforts to augment their water supply, large volumes of water are lost through leakages. There is no reliable information on the quantity lost in the supply system but city governments estimate that 25 to 50 per cent of the total water supply goes as "unaccounted" water. Underground water pipelines have been left in poor condition over the years because operations and maintenance generally receive lower priority than does the system expansion. Compounding the problem is the lack of trained personnel and equipment to monitor, detect and repair the broken and leaking connections.

The underground drainage sewerage systems in most cities face similar problems. Aging and /or corroded pipelines lead to leakages and eventually to contamination of water, due to the proximity of water and sewer lines to each other. Contamination also occurs at cross-over points between the water distribution mains and open street drains. Cholera outbreaks that sporadically occur in cities like Ahmedabad, Surat and other cities are attributed to this problem.

Weak financial and institutional capacity

Urban local bodies (ULBs), comprising municipal corporations and municipalities, are responsible for the provision and maintenance of the basic services like water supply, sewerage and drainage, solid waste management, public transport, etc. However, most ULBs in Gujarat lack the institutional and financial resources needed to operate and maintain the existing services, leave alone expand them to address the inadequacies or meet new demands. Except for a few corporation cities like Ahmedabad, the capacity of most municipalities to generate revenues is limited. Moreover, many local bodies, particularly smaller municipalities, lack technical expertise, are poorly staffed, and unable to deal with increasingly complex urban needs. Saddled with numerous functions and lacking financial resources, most local bodies continue to depend on the state government for their operational requirements.

The problem is more pronounced in the urban areas in the immediate periphery of the corporation cities which are experiencing the pressure from a rapid urban and industrial growth. These peripheral areas do not have effective local bodies to take care of urban planning and management, and the provision of basic services. Environmental conditions and the quality of infrastructure in these areas are very poor.

Limited Coordination

Responsibilities for providing urban environmental services are fragmented among the different agencies and jurisdictions. As such, the current planning and management practices are not-conducive to strong links between and among the related services, such as water, sanitation, solid waste, pollution control, etc. Municipal authorities in charge of solid waste management, for example, pay little attention to the urban drainage systems even though the uncollected garbage is most often the cause of blockages. Industrial estates are being planned and developed by state-level authorities (i.e. Gujarat Industrial Development Corporation, Department of Industry) without close coordination with the urban local bodies responsible for providing the support infrastructure, such as drainage network, public transport, etc. In addition, municipal corporations tend to focus only on the needs within their respective jurisdictions, such as expansion of urban water supply, with little regard for its effects on the urban areas in their periphery or cities located downstream.

Moreover, the delineation of responsibility and authority is sometimes blurred among many urban entities. For example, administrative and jurisdictional conflicts arise between the elected local bodies and Urban Development Authorities (UDAs). The Urban/ Area Development Authorities (UDA/ADA) were established as per the provisions of the Town Planning and Urban Development Act (1976) as apex planning agencies. Although the jurisdictional limits of these development authorities include municipal corporation areas and the outer areas, in practice the planning for municipal areas is prepared by the municipal corporation and for the outer area by the development authorities. Subsequently, attempts are made to integrate them as one plan. In the absence of adequate coordinating mechanisms, most cities lack the foundation for a more comprehensive planning process which integrates environmental concerns in the rban planning and management decisions. What is worse, in Gujarat's rush to industrialise, urban environmental issues are all too frequently considered less important except when occasional critical situations occur, e.g, the Surat plague.

Information Gap

Lack of information hampers the local bodies' capability to effectively plan and manage Gujarat's cities. Even if data are available with the concerned agencies, they are either not readily useable and/or accessible for planning and management purposes, or there are serious problems with them. For example, current data on the coverage of water supply and sanitation may overstate urban access to these services, depending on the definition and standards of "access" used. A large town may be considered as fully covered by a piped water supply system even if the supply is limited only to a few hours a day. Of all the urban environmental services, drainage and solid waste management are the most ignored and the least studied. As a result, the extent and severity of problems related to wastewater and solid waste disposal are not fully understood. Moreover, most local bodies and other responsible urban authorities do not have adequate expertise for undertaking an urban environmental assessment.

Strategies

It is expected that Gujarat will continue to witness rapid industrialization and consequently urbanisation. Forecasts suggest that by 2021, 35 million people constituting nearly 46 per cent of the urban population would be residing in urban Gujarat. By 2050, with population growth achieving stabilisation, the state is likely to accommodate 80 to 90 million people. The urban share is likely to be in the range of 70 per cent. The city regions of Surat and Ahmedabad are likely to reach a size of 10 to12 million.

Spatial planning and landuse

Inability to address the increasing demand for infrastructure in the cities is resulting in an urban sprawl. Such development of cities into city-regions put undue pressure on land and municipal services with no contribution to the city's revenue. The challenge, therefore, is to restrict such unplanned growth by properly planning for such developments in advance so that the resultant growth takes place in the guided direction. The city regions include the municipal corporation and other local bodies. The development of such a region would need metropolitan-wide perspective, planning and action. The 74th Constitutional Amendment mandatorily prescribes constitution of Metropolitan Planning Committee (MPC). The MPC is conceived in order to address and integrate issues of the metropolitan area comprehensively and draw up a plan for the same. But the Committee has not yet been set up, probably owing to the "ambivalence on the future role of the Development Authorities".[9]

Integration of urban and rural areas

The urban areas are dependent on its hinterland for food, water, raw materials for economic activities and skilled manpower. In the context when the conversion of agricultural areas in the peripheral areas is occurring at a rapid pace, an integrated approach for planning of urban and rural areas is imperative. This approach should deal with landuse, resource allocation and institutional mechanism of urban and surrounding regional area. The 74th Constitutional Amendment suggests setting up of District Planning Committees having two major objectives–consolidation of plans of municipalities/MCs and preparation of a development plan for the entire district. The plan would also address the common concerns of the urban and rural local bodies of spatial planning, sharing of resources like water, environmental conservation and hence draw up a integrated development plan.

Land Management Reforms

For the sustainable development of urban areas, judicious landuse patterns to ensure optimal land utilisation would need to be promoted. Urban growth should not be incrementally agglomerative consuming agricultural land, lakes, etc. Rather it should be directed to contiguous settlement areas leaving the intervening vacant land stretches unencumbered. In order to cope with the rapid urban growth, better land management practices especially in the larger towns of the state would need to be evolved.

Focus on energy efficiency in cities

The urban areas are increasingly becoming more energy intensive. This not only puts stress on this non-renewable resource but also contributes to the pollution and is expensive for the economy. An efficient public transport would need to be put in place to reduce the high energy demand due to the manifold increase in personalised modes.

Focus on housing for the urban poor

In the urban informal sector, slums are places of both residence and work. They contribute significantly to the creation of wealth in the urban economy. The urban poor have capably demonstrated their ability to invest in and improve on shelter given even a notional security of land tenure. Official policy must encourage this process, intervening only to the extent of making it orderly, integrating it with the overall urban development, and focusing on the provision, with people's participation, of infrastructural services—which lie beyond the capacity of individuals and small groups—in the areas of investment, technical inputs and management. Shelter at minimum acceptable standards of habitability, guided by economically realistic building and planning codes (especially for the urban poor) is crucial to the urban infrastructure. Those living in self-created substandard shelters should be given help and guidance in progressively improving them according to their capacity for investment in a convenient time-frame. At least a notional security of land tenure must be granted to the inhabitants of unorganized sector housing, in order to encourage them to invest in the improvement of their own shelter and to facilitate the provision of infrastructure by the local bodies.

Infrastructure Development

The quality and efficiency of infrastructure play a major role in determining the quality of urban environment, and consequently the quality of life of citizens. An appropriate physical, economic, social and environmental infrastructure is integral to sustainable urbanization.

Water scarcity in the urban areas has emerged as a key issue. Large quantities of water are lost during transmission. Efforts to reduce the transmission losses, harvest rainwater, recharge aquifers, recycle water from industrial areas/sewerage would need to be taken. The existence of a number of coastal urban settlements also calls for exploration of viable desalination technologies to augment water supply.

In public health services, the focus would need to be changed to the preventive rather than the curative. Emphasis has to be on providing education and awareness to the population and empowering them to participate in managing preventive health care related to environmental sanitation and hygiene.

The focus of urban transport must shift from private to public modes, and the shift made viable with effective incentives and disincentives (including investment in public transport reinforced by cross-subsidization from private transport, modification of land-use and building density regulations, Floor Space Index, vehicular access restriction and other regulations). According to some estimates, the urban poor spend as much as 25 per cent of their income on essential transport. It is necessary for an urban policy and planning to provide them access to affordable transport.

Travel reduction strategies must be explored and encouraged through the urban planning process. Intermediary public transport (e.g. taxis and autorickshaws) must be regulated to make it complementary to and not a substitute for public transport. While progressively stringent emission standards for new motor vehicles entering the market will fulfil part of the objective of reducing pollution, this achievement must be reinforced and sustained by evolving and enforcing similarly progressive standards for the maintenance of vehicles in use, and the creation of appropriate monitoring, training and certification mechanisms towards this end.

New and emerging information and communication technologies are leading to a gradual decrease in the premium on location in the urban areas, making the distinction between "place of work" and "place of residence" less critical to urban dynamics and form. They have the potential to effect changes in landuse and traffic patterns. Transport and landuse planning must harness this potential to influence the course of sustainable urbanization.

Environmental Management

An unpolluted, healthy and aesthetically satisfying environment, natural as well as built, conducive to overall well-being, is a fundamental right of every citizen. In urban areas, health, to a great extent, is dependent on the access of the citizen to environmental assets. Clean air and water, and places for recreation and relaxation in the public domain (such as waterfronts, parks, lakes, wooded areas, hills, etc.) are necessary components of a sustainable urban environment, and must be provided for in the planning for that environment, in terms of both conserving existing assets and developing new ones.

Buoyant financing mechanisms for Urban Infrastructure

The two major finance mechanisms currently available at the local government level to Indian cities are property tax and octroi. The former is not buoyant enough to meet the increasing investment and administrative demands. The latter, while buoyant, is not viewed favourably because it impedes the smooth flow of goods and commodities across the country (Rakesh Mohan, 1996).

In the case of Gujarat, octroi has been phased out in all the municipalities. In such a scenario the urban local bodies have little options of raising finances and are mainly dependent on state grants. A viable and buoyant substitute, under autonomous control of the Urban Local Body, is yet to emerge.

Private participation in the provision and maintenance of many services traditionally perceived as local government responsibilities can free some financial resources for diverting them to sectors which must be addressed by local governments. There have been quite a few cases of privatisation of municipal services like the Waste Processing Plant at Ahmedabad, Solid Waste Collection of Surat which transformed it into one of the cleanest city in the country, development of parks/gardens/traffic islands through public-private partnerships in corporation cities. One of the pioneering efforts in raising finances through municipal bonds was undertaken by the Ahmedabad

Municipal Corporation. A total amount of Rs 100 crores was raised through this which was used in the infrastructure projects of the city.

In order to make cities financially sustainable, local government bodies must exercise every possible option to raise finances. Those who derive the maximum profits from cities must be willing to pay for the privilege of living in them and using them. With the degree of autonomy now available to Indian cities due to the 74th Constitutional Amendment, they must aggressively explore and exploit innovative ways of raising finances and becoming economically and environmentally sustainable.

Governance

The Constitution 74th Amendment has opened up opportunities for the devolution of governance to the lowest political strata of society. These have been successfully and positively used in some cases. More should be done to make devolution effective across a broader spectrum of citizens. There is a potential role for partnerships involving citizen groups, social workers, NGOs, academics and professionals, and the lower levels of the legislative, judicial and executive wings.

The role of awareness generation and education must extend across a wide spectrum of the legislative, judicial and executive wings. It has been found that in many instances well-meant judicial directives pertaining to environment have not been successful because they were not backed with adequate information about the administrative, technical and financial preconditions for implementing them. Similarly the bureaucracy, which is usually well-informed about the nature (if not always the structural causes) of various issues, must learn to anticipate problems and have alternative options ready to solve the problems.

It is imperative to decentralize and devolve environmental management to the lowest levels of governance and to capacity-built local government and citizen groups to participate in and take charge of such management as partners. The establishment of ward committees, with appropriate awareness, education and skill development inputs, needs to be encouraged and strengthened towards this end. The emphasis in urban governance must shift from excessive regulation to an enhanced use of essentially economic instruments in the form of levies, tariffs and a range of other incentives and disincentives.

The key lies in the ability of the State to respond to the demands of urban centers in managing growth and conversion of local demands into operational programmes. The larger centres such as Surat and Ahmedabad have positioned themselves as global cities and have articulated their demands and strengthened the response mechanisms. In a state where there is an element of balanced growth and the uniqueness of the economic base of most cities, there is a need to focus on the basic strengths of these centres for Gujarat to remain as the engine of growth.

Gujarat has declared 2005 as the "Urban Year" and the immediate priorities as inputs required for growth are sustainable management of water and wastewater resources, improvement of transport systems and of the quality of life of the urban poor.

NOTES

1. Ministry of Urban Affairs and Employment
2. Census of India defines all Towns, Cities and Urban Agglomerations as below: **Town :** The following are treated as towns: (i) Statutory Towns, i.e. municipal corporation, municipal board, cantonment board, notified area, etc. (ii) Census towns which are non-statutory towns and are actually rural areas but satisfy following criteria: —Minimum Population of 5000, —Density of population of at least 400 per sq.km, —75 per cent of the male working population engaged in non-agricultural activity—**City:** Class I Town – Population of 100000 and above, Class II Town – Population of 50000 – 99999, Class III Town –Population of 20000–49999, Class IV Town –Population of 10000 – 19999, Class V Town – Population of 5000 – 9999, Class VI Town –Population below 5000, **Urban Agglomerations:** Sometimes two or more towns may be contiguous to each other, making it necessary to consider them together for studies on urbanisation in the area. In some other cases there are large railway colonies, university campuses, port areas, military camps, etc., just outside the statutory limits of a town, but adjoining it. Though these areas may not themselves qualify to be treated as towns, it would be realistic to treat them as urban. Such areas are termed as "outgrowths" (O.G.) and may cover whole or part of a village. The above two types of contiguous urban areas are called "Urban Agglomerations". An urban agglomeration may comprise: (a) A town and contiguous outgrowths; or (b) Two or more towns and their outgrowths, if any; all of them forming a contiguous spread of urban area.
3. The talukas were ranked on the basis of their share in the industrial employment and investments in the state and a composite industrial employment map for the years 1986, 1991 and 1996 has been prepared taking the top 25 talukas in the three years. The industrial talukas have been identified taking into account the employment in manufacturing units in the years 1986, 1991 and 1996 and employment and investments in commissioned industrial projects (1991-1999).

4. The talukas where the industrial projects are under implementation have been taken as "Emerging Industrial Talukas". There are 29 such talukas and seem to be concentrated in and around the industrial talukas.
5. Sardar Sarovar Project envisages supplying Narmada water to the water scarce regions of Gujarat via a network of canals and pipelines. A total of 3525 MLD drinking water is to be supplied to 8215 villages and 135 urban areas of Saurashtra, Kuchchh, North Gujarat and Panchmahal District. Of 3525 MLD of water allocated for drinking and other non-agricultural purposes from Sardar Sarovar, 2925 MLD will be used for drinking water purpose while 600 MLD would be for industrial purpose. As per the recent estimates (2002), the total cost of Sardar Sarovar Canal based Drinking Water Supply Project is around 7400 Crores. The entire drinking water project has been divided into three phases of implementation: (a) Immediate Phase which covers Saurashtra and Kuchchh areas, (b) Phase I which covers Panchmahal, Sabarkantha, Banaskantha and Surendranagar districts, and (c) Final Phase covers rest of the areas. Of the four modules –B, C, D, K to be completed in the immediate phase, Modules B and D (covering Amreli and Bhavnagar districts) have already been completed. The work for Modules C and K covering Jamnagar and Rajkot districts and Kuchchh area is in progress. Last year during the summer months, to the cater to demand of Saurashtra, an arrangement was made to supply water from Narmada through Narmada and Mahi canal up to Pariyej. Also, surplus water from Kadana and Panam reservoir was pumped onto Pariyej and Kaneval reservoir which is supplying water to the Bhavnagar, Amreli and Ahmedabad (Bhal area) areas. Two bypass tunnels at the Narmada Dam site are under construction. It is expected that in the current year, approximately 10,000 cusecs of water would be available in the Narmada main canal by gravity and from this the remaining areas of Kuchchh and Saurashtra would be covered.
6. Suhane Rajesh (2000), *Dynamics of Water Supply Management System,* School of Planning, Unpublished Dissertation, Ahmedabad.
7. Criteria for classification of inland surface water: (A) Drinking water without conventional treatment but after disinfection, (B) Outdoor bathing, organised, (C) Drinking water with conventional treatment followed by disinfection, (D) For propagation of wildlife and fisheries, (E) For irrigation, industrial cooling etc.
8. A compendium on Indian Slums, Town and Country Planning Organisation, Ministry of Urban Development, Government of India, New Delhi, 1996.
9. Centre for Policy Research (2001), The Future of Urbanisation.

REFERENCES

Census of India, (1991 and 2001): Census of India, Government of India, New Delhi

CEPT, (2003). Sectoral Social Environmental Assessment (SSEA) and preparation of Social & Environmental Management Framework (SEMF), Ahmedabad.

CEPT, (1998-02): "State Environmental Action Programme: Urbanisation Processes", A World Bank-aided project undertaken by GEC, Ahmedabad

Centre for Policy Research, (2001): *The Future of Urbanisation,* New Delhi

Suhane, Rajesh, (2000): Dynamics of Water Supply Management System, School of Planning, Unpublished Dissertation, Ahmedabad.

Annex Table 7.1: Number of Towns according to size-class

Size Class	*1971*			*1981*			*1991*			*2001*		
(Population ranges)	*No*	*Popn. Lakhs*	*%*	*No.*	*Popn. Lakhs*	*%*	*No.*	*Popn. Lakhs*	*%*	*No*	*Popn. Lakhs*	*%*
Class-I (> 1,00,000)	7	33.8	45.1	11	53.2	50.1	19	85.4	59.9	26	119.15	66.8
Municipal Corporations	6	32.5	43.4	6	46.0	43.4	6	67.1	47.1	7	93.49	53.5
Other Class-I towns	1	1.3	1.75	5	7.2	6.75	13	18.3	12.8	19	25.66	13.2
Class-II Towns (50000-99999)	18	11.7	15.7	27	18.2	17.0	33	22.1	15.5	37	24.07	13.5
Class-III Towns (20000-49999)	42	13.3	17.7	57	17.8	16.8	58	17.2	12.1	81	24.12	13.5
Class-IV (10000-19999)	73	10.5	14.0	86	12.2	11.5	92	13.4	9.4	57	8.71	4.9
Class- V Towns (5000-9999)	71	5.4	7.2	61	4.5	4.3	51	4.01	2.8	23	1.89	1.1
Class- VI Towns (<5000)	5	0.2	0.3	13	0.3	0.3	11	0.4	0.2	18	0.436	0.24
Total	216	75.0	100.05	255	106	100	264	142.5	100	242	178.39*	100

Note: *The difference in total urban population as given in Census and as shown in this table is due to the outgrowth population which has not been included here.

Annex Table 7.2: Urbanisation shares

Rank of Talukas	*Urban population Share*			*Change*
Top	*1981*	*1991*	*2001*	*1971-2001*
5	47.22	48.98	55.47	11.80
6-10	8.26	9.00	8.78	-0.14
11-25	13.57	13.58	13.50	-0.90
26-50	13.10	12.42	10.75	-3.13
51-75	8.07	7.54	5.85	-2.90
Rest urban talukas	9.78	9.25	5.66	-4.72
Rural talukas(no.)	41.00	37.00	53.00	
Rank of Talukas	*Urban population Share*			*Change*
Top	*1981*	*1991*	*2001*	*1971-2001*
5	47.22	48.98	55.47	11.80
6-10	55.48	57.21	64.25	11.66
11-25	69.05	70.79	77.75	10.76
26-50	82.15	83.21	88.50	7.63
51-75	90.22	90.75	94.34	4.72

Annex Table 7.3: Employment and Investment Shares

Rank Top	*Share of Employment*					*Investment*	
	1986	*1991*	*1996*	*1991-99 commi-ssioned*	*1999 under imple-mentation*	*1991-99 commi-ssioned*	*1999 under imple-mentation*
5	44.72	41.05	38.86	42.86	47.31	64.71	59.97
6-10	16.23	14.71	13.48	18.54	21.07	10.71	12.84
11-25	19.58	20.42	19.99	21.70	25.89	14.55	16.86
26-50	9.84	11.47	13.92	12.42	5.73	7.91	8.44
51-75	4.85	6.03	6.48	3.70	0.00	1.84	1.72
Rest Indl.Talukas	4.78	6.32	7.27	0.78	0.00	0.29	0.17
Non-Indl. Talukas (nos)	12.00	3.00	2.00	78.00	87.00	78.00	87.00
Rank	Cumulative of Employment						
5	44.72	41.05	38.86	42.86	47.31	64.71	59.97
10	60.95	55.76	52.34	61.40	68.38	75.42	72.81
25	80.53	76.18	72.33	83.10	94.27	89.96	89.66
50	90.37	87.65	86.25	95.52	100.00	97.87	98.11
75	95.22	93.68	92.73	99.22	100.00	99.71	99.83

Annex Table 7.4: Cyclone Vulnerability

Risk zones	*Indicators*	*Urban-Industrial*	*% share*	*Gujarat State*
Low damage (39m/s)	No. of talukas	27		90
	Urban Population	8372924	44.26	10777958.5
	Total Population	13155024	25.67	26448324
Moderate damage (44m/s)	No. of talukas	18		28
	Urban Population	4459089	23.57	4645886.5
	Total Population	7836558	15.29	9832344.5
Moderate damage (47m/s)	No. of talukas	3		20
	Urban Population	293918	1.55	658182
	Total Population	1101613	2.15	5116797
Very high damage (50m/s)	No. of talukas	10		16
	Urban Population	1551393	8.20	2834476
	Total Population	3428976	6.69	9850622.5

Annex Table 7.5: Earthquake Vulnerability

Risk zones	*Indicators*	*Urban-Industrial*	*% share*	*Gujarat State*	*% share*
Low	No. of talukas	1		3	
	Urban Population	26751	0.14	42532	0.22
	Total Population	175627	0.34	877630	1.71
Moderate	No. of talukas	53		155	
	Urban Population	14062551	74.34	17477891	92.39
	Total Population	23652711	46.15	44068007.5	85.99
High Risk	No. of talukas	2		17	
	Urban Population	217189	1.15	921524	4.87
	Total Population	987486	1.93	4719691.5	9.21
Very High risk	No. of talukas	2		9	
	Urban Population	370833	1.96	474556	2.51
	Total Population	706347	1.38	1582759	3.09

Annex Table 7.6: Water Scarcity

Water Scarcity	*Data*	*Urban-Indl. Talukas*	*% share*	*Gujarat State*	*% share*
No scarcity zone	No. of talukas	15		33	
	Total Population	7051206	13.76	10339133	20.17
	Urban Population	4126221	21.81	4466347.5	23.61
Scarcity	No. of talukas	25		61	
	Total Population	12608038	24.60	20413290	39.83
	Urban Population	7727164	40.85	9112543	48.17
Acute scarcity	No. of talukas	10		46	
	Total Population	3430325	6.69	11329610	22.11
	Urban Population	1632689	8.63	2429299	12.84
Severe Scarcity	No. of talukas	8		44	
	Total Population	2432602	4.75	9166055	17.89
	Urban Population	1191250	6.30	2908313.5	15.37

8

Municipal Finances and Development in Small and Medium Towns: Gujarat

DARSHINI MAHADEVIA

Interest in research on Small and Intermediate Urban Centres (SIUC), or what we call in India Small and Medium Towns (SMT) has been to seek alternatives to the processes of concentration of productivity, high-income jobs and economic and social development in a few large or metropolitan cities in a country. These urban centres invite interest also for improving the performance of the regional economies and for a balanced regional development so that there is some amount of equity in the urban system. The national and international policies on the SIUC/SMT have always carried such economic and social objectives (Hardoy and Satterthwaite 1986). Further, there was, and still is, a consensus among the urban planners and policy-makers on slowing down the growth of the metropolitan cities which are expanding in size beyond their means. The outcomes of such a growth are poor environmental conditions, high rates of crime, breakdown of social systems, traffic jams and delays, high cost of urban infrastructure and, in general, poor quality of life.

Some researchers believe that the developing countries have not been successful in their attempts to divert the urban growth and development to "growth poles", "growth centres", "growth axes" and "new towns" (Hardoy and Satterthwaite 1986, 5), and the fate of the SMTs in India has been the same. The report of the National Commission on Urbanisation (NCU) has been highly critical of the Integrated Development of Small and Medium Towns (IDSMT) scheme launched in 1979 to divert urban growth away from the large/ metropolitan cities. The NCU calls it an example of "ad-hocism" in spatial planning dominated by the geographers and urban planners while resource allocation was being left to the economic planners (Government of India 1988a). Under the IDSMT, it was decided to select 236 towns with populations ranging from 20,000 to 100,000 and gives each town financial back up of Rs. 1.07 crore (in which the centre's share was 55 lakh), for strengthening its infrastructure (Ministry of Works and Housing 1977). Subsequently, the definition of the SMTs has been changed, and now urban centres with populations of up to 3 lakh are considered under the scheme.

Further, the NCU had proposed that the few very large cities and metropolitan cities be treated separately. To decongest them and spread growth to other cities and thereby bring in an overall economic development, the concept of cities Generating Economic Momentum (GEM) was evolved. The cities that had a high demographic or economic momentum, or both, or had a potential for development if the right kind of investment was made, were listed as GEMs. The idea was to move away from the colonial to a more broad-based system of wealth accumulation. It was not necessary for these cities and towns to be located in the backward regions, argued the NCU report because "equity of development would still be ensured if, instead of 100 wilderness areas being developed at great cost, the existing towns which have a potential receive a threshold level of investment" (Government of India 1988a, p. 32). The cities in the GEM's list were classified into two, National Priority Cities and State Priority Cities.

The United Nations (UN) Conference on Human Settlements (Habitat Conference) held in Vancouver in 1976 had suggested recommendations, which were unanimously approved by the 132 member governments. The conference pointed to the urgent need for every government to establish a national policy on human settlements embodying the distribution of population and related economic and social activities over the national territory (Recommendation A.1) as an integral part of any national economic and social development policy (A.2) with the aim of improving the conditions of human settlements, particularly promoting a more equitable distribution of benefits of development among the regions and by making such benefits and public services equally accessible to all groups (A.4) (Hardoy and Satterthwaite 1986).

In most developing countries, after their independence, there was a major thrust on decentralised development and promotion of small and medium towns. The thrust was to induce development in the rural areas. Over time, however, instead of depending on settlement hierarchy and regional development approach, the government began to intervene directly in the rural development and for rural poverty alleviation through programmes like the Integrated Rural Development Programme in India. The other reason why the developing countries wanted to develop small and medium towns was because the large cities—now the metropolitan cities—were a colonial legacy and had played a major role in supporting colonial appropriation in these countries.

In a seminar on Urban Development Strategies held by the UN Centre for Regional Development, Nagoya (Japan), in 1974, development of the SIUC was emphasised because (i) of a viewpoint that these towns have maximum employment multiplier, and (ii) these towns provide the possibility of amenity-based strategy of decentralising social services in rural areas (in Minocha and Yadav 1989, p. 11). Besides, these towns can counter primacy by facilitating multiple growth areas via decentralisation, offering rural areas accessibility to higher urban services, providing linkages to rural and urban areas and promoting spatial integration via more dispersed population (Minocha and Yadav 1989).

There are several reasons why the Third World governments would (should) consider the current and potential role of these centres in their national social and economic development plans and give emphasis to these centres in their urban policies (Hardoy and Satterthwaite 1986).

1. The SIUCs are the places where the rural people and the rural enterprises interact, and hence, these centres can play a very important role in the development of rural areas by providing social and economic facilities.
2. These settlements have local political importance since the sub-national and sub-regional levels of government are located there. It is through these centres that the needs and priorities of the sub-national and sub-regional populations get represented at the national levels. In the current context of India, it is through these centres that the democratic

decentralisation, enshrined in the Indian Constitution through the Seventy-third and Seventy-fourth Amendments, can be achieved. The national governments have not been able to stimulate urban development away from the large cities because of the poor understanding of the local circumstances, needs and possibilities in the urban centres that are meant to serve as growth centres.

3. In the developing countries, some of these centres can play an important role in the national goals. For example, if a country has a national goal of raising agricultural productivity or reducing food imports, some centres can be provided with infrastructure to meet the goal. In the current context of India, where the drought and spectre of hunger looms over a number of states and disasters occur repeatedly, these centres can be of importance in food distribution and disaster management away from the state headquarters.
4. Long-term policies for the development of the SIUCs can lessen the tendency towards undesirable concentrations of industries, services and government officials.
5. Support can be extended to small and intermediate urban settlements to enhance the economic and social development of the nearby large cities and metropolitan centres.

Even though the SIUCs (or the SMTs) are important in India, there is no adequate information about these centres. Now it has become necessary to have the information, especially because in the current environment of urban reforms in many states, the Urban Local Bodies (ULBs) have been mandated to take the full responsibility of taking up development projects at the city level. Under the reforms, it is envisaged that the urban areas would improve their infrastructure to attract investments. And, the onus of raising the finances for the infrastructure development has been left to the ULB itself. The Seventy-fourth Constitutional Amendment (74th CA) in a way supports the idea of decentralisation of the responsibility of urban infrastructure development. The Rakesh Mohan Committee Report or the India Infrastructure Report (Expert Group on the Commercialisation of Infrastructure 1996) has strongly recommended commercialisation and privatisation of the urban infrastructure. In the

2002-03 Central budget, the government provided for the setting up of a City Challenge Fund (CCE) to support the infrastructure efforts of the urban centres. However, it is not clear what type of urban centres would be able to make this transition.

The SMTs are also expected to follow the above model of urban development. But would they be able to do so? What is the current state of affairs with regard to municipal financing in the SMTs? These are some of the questions that this paper attempts to answer taking the example of Gujarat. Unlike the states in South India, the ULBs in Gujarat support a large number of activities. The parastatals supported by the state government take care of two very important city-level functions: water supply and sanitation systems. Urban public transport is also a responsibility taken up by the parastatals. In Gujarat, provision of water supply and sanitation is the mandatory responsibility of the ULB under the Municipal Act. Would the ULBs of the SMTs be able to discharge these responsibilities if they have to manage their own finances? To be able to answer this and other questions posed above, it is necessary to look at the status of municipal finances in the SMTs—their incomes, expenditures and level of facilities. Such an analysis would be more interesting when it is compared with the situation in the large and metropolitan cities. This is what this paper attempts to do.

Before we move on, we need to discuss briefly the problem in defining the SMTs. All definitions are based on population size. But for different purposes, different definitions (classifications) of the urban centres have been adopted. The Census of India classifies urban centres in the following six groups: (i) Class I, population 100,000 and above, (ii) Class II, population 50,000 to 99,999, (iii) Class III, population 20,000 to 49,999, (iv) Class IV, population 10,000 to 19,999, (v) Class V, population 5,000 to 9,999, and (vi) Class VI, population below 5,000. The NCU proposed a different system of classification of cities and towns. It classified the cities into six classes and towns into two classes. It proposed the following classification of cities: (i) C1, population 1 lakh to 5 lakh, (ii) C2, population 5 to 10 lakh, (iii) C3, population 10 to 20 lakh, (iv) C4, population 20 to 50 lakh, (v) C5, population 50 to 100 lakh, and (vi) C6, population 100 lakh and above. The towns are classified into: (i) T1, population 20,000 to 50,000, and (ii) T2, population 50,000 to 100,000.

Under the 74th CA, the urban centres are classified into four classes—M, A, B and C—for the purpose of urban governance and financial allocations. The Class M cities are the cities with municipal corporations (population 3 lakh and above); Class A cities are the cities with municipalities (population 1 to 3 lakh); Class B towns are the towns with Nagar Panchayats (population 50,000 to 1 lakh); and Class C towns are the towns with a population less than 50,000. The classification used in the sub-division of urban data in the National Sample Survey (NSS)[1] is as follows: (i) C1, population < 50,000; (ii) C2, population 50,000 to 2 lakh; (iii) C3, population 2 lakh to 4 lakh; (iv) C4, population 4 lakh to 10 lakh; and (v) C5, population > 10 lakh. Straightaway, we have a problem of classification and data availability. We have used the following classification of urban centres: (i) Class 1, population < 50,000; (ii) Class 2, population 50,000 to 2 lakh; (iii) Class 3, population 2 lakh to 10 lakh; (iv) Class 4, population > 10 lakh[2]. In this context then, the paper

- looks at the urbanisation structure in the state,
- examines the level of facilities across different size classes of the urban centres, and
- studies the municipal income and expenditure pattern in different size classes of urban centres in the state.

The responsibility of providing basic urban services lies with the state governments. But every state government makes its own institutional arrangements for this purpose. For example, for the provision of basic services like water supply, sewerage, sanitation and solid waste disposal, state governments have (i) their own departments, (ii) state-level boards and corporations, like Water Supply Boards, (iii) statutory and non-statutory bodies at the city level, or (iv) local bodies. There are separate institutional arrangements for capital works and maintenance of the assets created (Kundu 1993, p. 67).

With regards to water supply, sanitation and sewerage facilities, the capital assets can be created by any one of the above-stated institutions and the maintenance can be carried out by the asset creating institution or could be handed over to the ULB. Thus, two types of arrangements are possible: (i) the capital asset creating body maintains the assets created and (ii) the capital asset creating body hands over the asset created to the ULB for maintenance. When the ULB itself creates the assets and maintains them, it is the first type of arrangement.

The following different options for carrying out capital works in the water supply and sewerage sector have been found in the literature.

1. State government departments such as the Public Health Engineering Department (PHED), Public Works Departments (PWD), Urban Development Department, Department of Local Self-Government and its district offices may directly take up capital works in the ULBs.
2. The state-level or city-level parastatals such as the Water Supply and Sewerage Boards which take up the capital works on behalf of the state governments in the urban area. Finance for the capital projects comes from the state government budgets in the form of grants, soft loans, or state government guaranteed loans from financial institutions. Many states have set up such boards. This arrangement is found in all the states of South India (including Andhra Pradesh, our case study), Punjab (our case study), and other states. These parastatals also maintain the capital assets on behalf of the ULB if the latter is not in a position to do so. In some states such a board carries out the capital works on behalf of the smaller ULBs which are not in a position to take up this task for instance, in Gujarat the Gujarat Water Supply and Sewerage Board (GWSSB) performs this function. The GWSSB then recovers the money from the ULB and hands over the asset to the ULB for operations and maintenance. Same is the case with the Punjab Water Supply and Sewerage Board (PWSSB). But such is not the case with the Bangalore Water Supply and Sewerage Board, which continues to maintain the asset created.
3. Special state-level development agencies such as Housing Boards and Slum Clearance Boards also create capital assets on the sites they develop and hand over the assets to the ULB under whose jurisdiction the project is located.
4. There are some private and public sector undertakings and agencies, which take up the responsibility for construction

of water supply and drainage systems within their townships or localities, for instance, in Rourkela and Bhillai.

5. In the states in Western India, as per the Municipal Act, water supply and sanitation are the mandatory responsibilities of the ULBs, which are expected to incur even capital expenses for the same. The ULBs of the small towns in these states are not in a position to do so and hence the parastatals created for the same step in. But in the metropolitan cities like Ahmedabad, Vadodara, Surat, Mumbai, Pune and Nagpur, the local bodies themselves design and implement the capital projects. Such local bodies are financially strong and hence they can undertake the responsibility of construction.
6. Along with the local bodies, in some states, the Urban Development Authorities also invest in water supply and sanitation projects. In some cities both the local bodies and the urban development authorities undertake capital projects.

In some cities, a number of agencies undertake capital works for water supply and sanitation. For example in Calcutta (now Kolkata), there is a host of agencies that take up capital projects related to water supply and sanitation. There is the Calcutta Metropolitan Development Authority (CMDA), Calcutta Metropolitan Water and Sanitation Authority (CMWSA) and Calcutta Improvement Trust (CIT), besides the municipal bodies, housing boards, state government departments, irrigation departments and the waterways departments. This holds true for the cities. However, in the smaller towns in most states it is the PHEDs or the water supply boards which are responsible for capital works.

The financial arrangement for the capital works also differs depending upon the agencies involved in the process. In states where capital investment is the responsibility of the state government, funds are made available for capital works in the state budget. When the boards on behalf of the state government undertake projects, grants are routed to the boards, which are reflected in the state budgets. If the boards take up construction on behalf of the local bodies, then the responsibility of arranging funds rests with the local bodies. Most of these cases are mostiy funded through a mixture of grants and loans.

Where as the grants are routed from the state government through the boards, the local bodies are expected to repay the loans themselves.

The responsibility for maintenance of the assets lies mostly with the local bodies. But when the local bodies lack the financial and technical capability to do so, the state boards or the state government departments continue to look after maintenance of the assets for a certain period of time even after the construction is complete. In Punjab, for example, either the local bodies themselves or the PWSSB carries out the capital works in water supply and sanitation. The PWSSB undertakes construction work on behalf of the local governments, and takes advance deposit from the local government body before starting capital works. After the construction is completed, PWSSB does the test-running of the system and then hands over the scheme to the local body for maintenance and operation. However, the PWSSB might continue to look after operation and maintenance if the local government does not have the technical or administrative capabilities to do so. Further, if the state government feels that the local body is neglecting the operation and maintenance of the assets, then that function might be handed over to the PWSSB. In the case of Andhra Pradesh also, there is a water supply and sewerage board, which undertakes the capital works in small and medium towns.

The GWSSB is the nodal agency in Gujarat, which is responsible for the design and construction of water supply schemes in the urban centres. After the construction is completed, the assets are handed over to the local bodies for maintenance. But the GWSSB is responsible only for smaller towns; the larger urban local bodies, that is, corporations, undertake construction work themselves and maintain it also thereafter. For sewerage systems, too, it is the GWSSB that is responsible for construction of sewerage schemes for the smaller urban centres. The schemes are funded either by grants from the state government through the Gujarat Municipal Finance Board (GMFB) or borrowings from the HUDCO or other agencies or a mix of the two (Sharma 1996).

Construction and maintenance of roads in all the states is the function of the ULB, whether small or big. In recent times, in some metropolitan cities, talks are going on about constructing toll-roads through the setting up of a Special Purpose Vehicle. Such an arrangement has come into existence for a few state and national highways. Small and medium towns located on such stretches may benefit from the new system of road financing.

Provision of streetlights is the sole responsibility of the ULB. Similarly, the ULB has the responsibility of solid waste collection and disposal.

Methodological Issues[3]

According to Census 2001, there are 242 urban centres in Gujarat, but the census could not be conducted in the 10 urban centres because of the earthquake. In mid-2002, the census for the *talukas* that were not covered by Census 2001 has been conducted, but the data are not available as yet. So census information is available only for 232 urban centres (Table 8.1). Out of these, 173 are in the first size class, which constitutes 74.57 per cent of the total urban centres and around 20 per cent of the total urban population. The second size class has the next highest share in urban centres (22.84%) and also second highest share in population. There were no urban centres in 200,000 to 400,000 size class. It was then decided to merge this size class with 400,000 to 1 million-size group that is quite appropriate. The largest proportion of population is in the metropolitan cities, population above 1 million; there are only three such cities in the state.

Table 8.1: Distribution of Census Towns, 2001

Urban Size Class	*No of Urban Centres*	*Total Population*	*% Share in Urban Centres*	*% Share in Population*
< 50,000	173	3,358,090	74.57	19.59
50000 - 2 00,000	53	4,607,435	22.84	26.87
200,000 - 1 million	3	1,925,334	1.29	11.23
> 1 million	3	7,255,183	1.29	42.31
All Urban	232*	17,146,042	100.00	100.00

Source: Population Census 2001.

The urban population distribution in Gujarat is quite skewed. The last two size classes, consisting of only six urban centres, account for nearly 54 per cent of the total urban population in the state. So the first two size classes have roughly 46 per cent of the total urban population. Thus Gujarat has a concentration of urban population in the cities and metropolises and not in the small and medium towns.

Table 8.1 excludes the urban centres for which census could not be carried out in 2001 because of the earthquake. These were Anjar, Bhachau, Bhuj, Gandhidham, Kandla, Mandvi, Mundra and Rapar in Kachchh district and Morvi and Wankaner in Rajkot district.

Data on facilities are available for 139 towns. Financial data are also available for nearly the same number of towns except that for every year, there were some towns for which data were not available. A gap exists between the number of settlements declared as urban in the census and the urban settlements for which the municipal data is available because the latter depends on the declaration of a settlement as urban by the Department of Urban Development of the state government. As per the 74th CA implemented in the state, all the ULBs have been given the designation of municipality or Municipal Corporation depending on their size. But a settlement has to be declared a ULB or a local self-government by the state government. In Gujarat, 149 urban settlements are declared local self-governments, of which 143 are municipalities and 6 are municipal corporations.[4] In general, urban centres with a population above 15,000 are declared a ULB. A state government body, the Gujarat Municipal Finance Board (GMFB), which has the responsibility of allocating grants to the ULBs, collects data on finance and facilities from them for the purpose of devolution of funds. The GMFB, therefore, is expected to have data of only 149 ULBs. The procedure for collecting data is as follows:

The GMFB sends a form to all the ULBs to fill in the financial data as per a common format, which most ULBs fill out and return to the GMFB. Some do not or are not in a position to fill in the information if their accounts are not finalised. Hence, there is a fluctuation in the number of urban centres for which the financial data are available. Since in most years the names of the urban centres for which data are missing do not match, we have included them for our analysis. Financial data were available for the years 1994-95, 1995-96, 1996-97, 1997-98 and 1998-99. But every year the number of urban centres for which data are available is different. Information on the number of urban centres in each year for which data are available and the names of the urban centres for which data are not available are given in Table 8.2.

Table 8.2: List of Missing Towns in Financial Data

Year	*No. of urban centres included*	*Urban centres for which data are not available*	
1994-95	138	Size Class I	: Dhandhuka
1995-96	137	Size Class I	: Thangadh, Kaalol
1996-97	132	Size Class I	: Tharad, Chaklasi, Jasdan, Navagam Ghed
		Size Class II	: Botad, Mangrol
		Size Class III	: Jamnagar
1997-98	126	Size Class I	: Tharad, Kheda, Ranavav, Kaalol, Idar, Thangadh, Navagam Ghed, Boriavi
		Size Class II	: Palanpur, Petlad
		Size Class III	: Bhavnagar, Jamnagar, Rajkot
		Size Class IV	: Vadodara
1998-99	100	Size Class I	: Bhayavadar, Boriavi, Chaklasi, Chhaya, Chhota Udaipur Dhandhuka, Dharampur Dwarka, Gariadhar Harij, Jasdan, Joshipura Karamsad, Kheda, Kheralu Navagam Ghed Manavadar, Radhanpur, Rajpipla, Rajula Ramol, Sihor, Thangadh, Tharad Vijapur, Visavadar
		Size Class II	: Botad, Dholka, Godhra Kaalol, Palanpur, Ranip, Viramgam, Visnagar
		Size Class III	: Bhavnagar, Jamnagar, Rajkot.
		Size Class IV	: Ahmedabad, Surat

For all the years, per-town and per-capita calculations have been done by taking the total number of urban centres as mentioned in Table 8.3. For example, for the year 1998-99 finance data are available only for 100 urban centres, so for 1998-99 we have only 100 urban centres for analysis (Table 8.3).

Among the urban centres whose data on finance and facilities we have used, the largest proportion, about 58 per cent, is in the smallest size class (Table 8.3). But the population that this size class accommodates is just 14 per cent. This was expected. But it is important to note that in our analysis, representation of the smallest size urban centres is much lower than their representation in the total urban system. This is because municipal and facilities data are not kept properly for very small urban centres. In that sense, the data on the facilities and finance are not truly representative. In all probability, the urban centres left out of the data set are the Nagar Panchayats with very small urban populations and those that are completely dependent on the state government grants or grants from the Members of Parliament or Members of the Legislative Assembly for development expenditure.

Table 8.3: Distribution of Selected Towns and Their Population by Size Class

Urban Size Classes	*No of Urban Centres*	*Total Population*	*% Share in Urban Centres*	*% Share in Population*
1994-95 to 1997-98				
< 50,000	81	2,261,293	58.27	14.25
50,000-200,000	52	4,428,223	37.41	27.90
200,000-1 million	3	1,925,334	2.16	12.13
> 1 million	3	7,255,183	2.16	45.72
All Urban	139	15,870,033	100.00	100.00
1998-99				
< 50,000	54	1,486,554	54.00	22.43
50,000-200,000	45	3,835,643	45.00	57.87
200,000-1 million	NA	NA	NA	NA
> 1 million	1	1,306,035	1.00	19.70
All urban	100	6,628,232	100.00	100.00

Source: Census 2001; data from GMFB

Finances of Small and Medium Towns

While looking at the finances of the SMTs, we have looked at the finances of the other cities and also of the metropolises. Similarly, we have also observed the situation in other urban centres along with the SMTs with regard to poverty, employment and levels of living. Financial data cover the following aspects: (i) overall budget size, (ii) income and its composition, and (iii) expenditure and its composition. For all, per capita figures have been worked out for making comparisons.

Budget Size

Overall

First, we will discuss the average budget size across different size classes of the urban areas. The average size of a ULB's budget indicates its capability to take up development projects and to handle municipal finances. Secondly, the budget will be broken up into revenue and capital accounts to assess the capability of a ULB to take up capital projects and its efficiency from the point of view of administration, whether the taxes are collected efficiently or not, whether the expenditure on personnel is too high, and so on. Thirdly, we will examine the nature of budget, whether it is deficit or surplus.

The average size of the budget of an urban centre in each size class in the state is given in Table 8.4. The budget size is defined by the income/receipts of a ULB and not by its expenditure. The per capita budget size, that is, the per capita receipts in each of the size class, is given in Table 8.5. The average budget size of a ULB grows with the rise in its size. There is nothing unexpected in this situation.

We have budget data for four years. The average budget size in the towns with a population below 50,000 varied between Rs. 73 lakh to Rs. 173 lakh at current prices and Rs. 67 lakh to Rs 116 lakh at constant (1993-94) prices. The average budget size over the four years was Rs. 90 lakh at constant prices. In the next size class of urban centres, the average budget size varied between Rs. 389 lakh and Rs. 659 lakh at current prices and Rs. 356 lakh and Rs. 442 lakh at 1993-94 prices. The average budget size in the second-class size of towns is four times that in the first size class. As we move to the cities with a population between 200,000 and 10,00,000 the average budget size increases by 9 times that of the second size class and 37 times that of the first size class. Finally, the average budget size of the municipal corporations is 367 times that of the smallest size class of towns and 10 times that of the cities in the third size class.

As far as the composition of the budget is concerned, the share of both revenue account and capital account tends to fluctuate in the total budget over time. This is true for all the size classes of urban centres and is generally observed in individual city studies as well. This is because the capital projects depend on the availability of funds. Generally, funds for capital projects come from the transfer of surplus from the revenue account or state government grants. The large cities have the capability to access soft loans or borrow from financial institutions at commercial rates. Sources of soft loans nearly dried up in India in the 1990s decade, especially in the second half of the 1990s. Therefore, this may not be the source of capital funds any more. In

Table 8.4: Average Budget Size

Size Class	1994-95			1995-96			1997-98			1998-99		
	Revenue	*Capital*	*Total*	*Revenue*	*Capital*	*Total*	*Revenue*	*Capital*	*Total*	*Revenue*	*Capital*	*Total*
Current Prices (Rs lakh)												
< 50,000	63	10	73	76	16	92	110	29	139	118	55	173
50,000-200,000	319	70	389	381	72	453	449	104	553	521	138	659
200,000 – 1 million	3495	300	3796	4619	323	4942	N.A	N.A	N.A	N.A	N.A	N.A
> 1 million	39073	3896	42969	46061	1117	47178	51846	9544	61390	20583	2706	23289
All Urban	1082	123	1206	1298	68	1366	1081	213	1294	500	118	618
Constant Prices (Rs lakh)												
< 50,000	58	9	67	64	13	77	80	21	101	79	37	116
50,000-200,000	292	64	356	320	61	380	329	76	405	350	92	442
200,000 – 1 million	3196	275	3470	3882	271	4153	N.A	N.A	N.A	N.A	N.A	N.A
> 1 million	35725	3562	39287	38714	939	39653	37929	6982	44911	13810	1816	15626
All Urban	990	113	1103	1091	57	1148	791	155	946	336	79	415
Per cent share												
< 50,000	86.08	13.92	100.00	83.03	16.97	100.00	79.23	20.77	100.00	68.28	31.72	100.00
50,000-200,000	82.09	17.91	100.00	84.09	15.91	100.00	81.22	18.78	100.00	79.10	20.90	100.00
200,000 – 1 million	92.09	7.91	100.00	93.47	6.53	100.00	N.A	N.A	N.A	N.A	N.A	N.A
> 1 million	90.93	9.07	100.00	97.63	2.37	100.00	84.45	15.55	100.00	88.38	11.62	100.00
All Urban	89.76	10.24	100.00	95.03	4.97	100.00	83.57	16.43	100.00	80.93	19.07	100.00
Per cent Growth Rate (constant prices)												
< 50,000	—	—	—	10.34	44.44	14.93	25.00	61.54	31.17	-1.25	76.19	14.85
50,000-200,000	—	—	—	9.59	-4.69	6.74	2.81	24.59	6.58	6.38	21.05	9.14
200,000 – 1 million	—	—	—	21.46	-1.45	19.68	—	—	—	—	—	—
> 1 million	—	—	—	8.37	-73.64	0.93	-2.03	643.56	13.26	-63.59	-73.99	-65.21
All Urban	—	—	—	10.20	-49.56	4.08	-27.50	171.93	-17.60	-57.52	-49.03	-56.13

Note: 1. If population figures of Census 2001 are considered, there are no urban centres in the third stratum in Gujarat.
2. Financial data for urban centres in the fourth stratum were not available for the years 1997-98 and 1998-99.

Source: GMFB data

any case, the SMTs are not likely to take loans to fund capital projects. In fact, in most urban centres, except metropolitan cities, loans are not likely to be a source of capital funds. Thus, by and large, the capital projects depend on the grants coming from the state government, which have been fluctuating. Further, the urban centres, especially the small and medium ones, may not have the capability to complete quickly the capital projects, and hence they may ask for grants in some years and not in others. This could also be the reason for fluctuations in the share of the capital account in the total budget since the grant is released only in response to the demand from the ULB.

The average budget size in the state has increased for the SMTs but not for the metropolitan cities. In the latter, the average budget size decreased in 1998-99 compared to the previous year in real terms. A negative sign in the all-urban increase in the average budget size is because of the non-availability of data in the third size-class for the last two years of our analysis. The revenue as well as capital account budgets have fluctuated a great deal. In fact, the municipal finances in the state do not live up to the expectation of the state in terms of either growth rates or stability in the composition of the budgets.

Per Capita Budget Size

The per capita budget size which, in fact is the per capita income is more telling than the average budget size. On an average, the per capita budget size becomes larger as we move to the larger size class category of urban centre in the four years (for which we have data). That is, the larger the urban centre, the greater its per capita income (revenue collection and grant disbursement from the state government). At constant prices, the average per capita income during the four-year period was: Rs. 367 (< 50,000), Rs. 507 (50,000 to 200,000), Rs. 742 (200,000 to 1,000,000), and Rs. 1,720 (> 1,000,000) (Table 8.5). Compared to the smallest size class of towns, metropolitan cities in the state had nearly four-and-a-half times per capita income. As compared to the second size class of towns, metropolitan cities had three-and-a-half times per capita income. Not only on the revenue side, but also on the capital side, the per capita income in the small and medium towns is much smaller than in the other and metropolitan cities. Thus, the per capita development expenditure is much higher

Table 8.5: Per Capita Income

Size Class	*1994-95*			*1995-96*			*1997-98*			*1998-99*		
	Revenue	*Capital*	*Total*	*Revenue*	*Capital*	*Total*	*Revenue*	*Capital*	*Total*	*Revenue*	*Capital*	*Total*
Current Prices (in Rs)												
< 50,000	271.82	43.95	315.77	319.97	65.41	385.38	425.67	111.57	537.24	471.42	219.01	690.43
50,000-200,000	427.67	93.32	520.99	501.42	94.88	596.30	571.20	132.05	703.25	636.13	168.12	804.25
200,000 – 1 million	692.61	59.50	752.11	884.64	61.83	946.47	N.A	N.A	N.A	N.A	N.A	N.A
> 1 million	1959.68	195.41	2155.10	2248.60	54.54	2303.13	1960.95	360.99	2321.93	1677.05	220.52	1897.56
All Urban	1128.19	128.64	1256.83	1313.48	68.65	1382.13	1212.66	238.39	1451.05	805.34	189.75	995.09
Constant Prices (in Rs)												
< 50,000	248.53	40.18	288.72	268.93	54.98	323.91	311.40	81.62	393.03	316.30	146.94	463.25
50,000-200,000	391.03	85.32	476.35	421.44	79.75	501.19	417.87	96.60	514.48	426.81	112.80	539.61
200,000 – 1 million	633.27	54.40	687.67	743.53	51.97	795.50	N.A	N.A	N.A	N.A	N.A	N.A
> 1 million	1791.77	178.67	1970.44	1889.93	45.84	1935.77	1434.57	264.09	1698.65	1125.22	147.96	1273.18
All Urban	1031.53	117.62	1149.14	1103.97	57.70	1161.67	887.14	174.40	1061.54	540.34	127.32	667.66

Note: 1. If population figures of Census 2001 are considered, there are no urban centres in the third stratum in Gujarat.
2. Financial data for urban centres in the fourth stratum were not available for the years 1997-98 and 1998-99.

Source: GMFB data

in the larger cities than in the smaller ones. Whether this is the impact of the size or the result of greater attention being paid to the larger cities is not clear. It can be argued that in the larger cities, there would be an advantage in costs because of the economies of scale in infrastructure. But at present we do not have any evidence in this matter. We may, however, state the fact that the income receipts for recurring costs and development expenditures are higher in the larger cities in the state than in the small and medium towns. What types of receipts are higher in the larger cities and metropolitan cities would be clear when we look at the break-up of the receipts.

What is true on an average during the four years is also true for all the four individual years of the study. This is clear from Chart 8.1 where the total per capita receipt line goes up with the increase in the

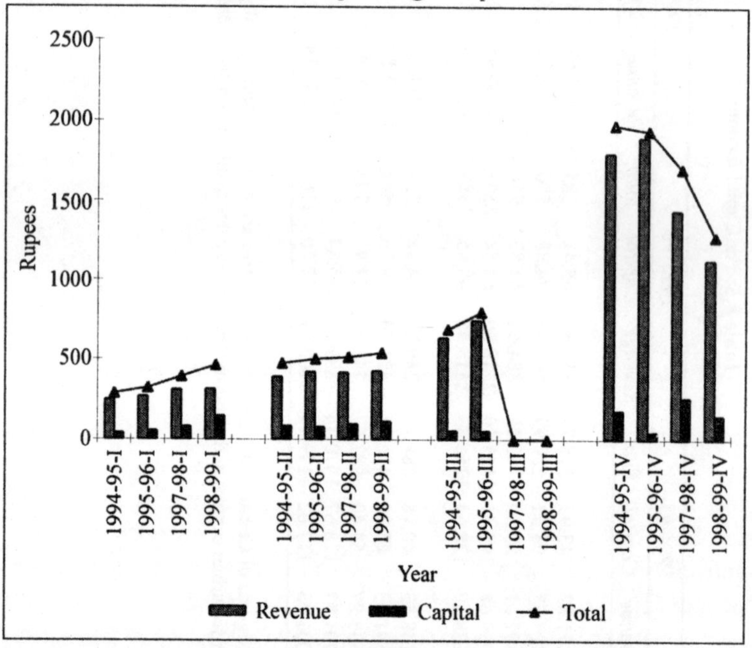

Chart 8.1: Per Capita Income (Constant Prices)

size class and so do the bars of per capita revenue receipts and per capita capital receipts. The chart also shows that there is a noticeable increase in the length of the bar, especially on the revenue side, as one moves from size class 2 to size class 3 and a significant jump when one moves to the size class of metropolitan cities Chart 8.2.

The jump is more pronounced in the revenue account income than in the capital account income Chart 8.3. Why is this the case would be clear when we examine the break-up of the revenue income.

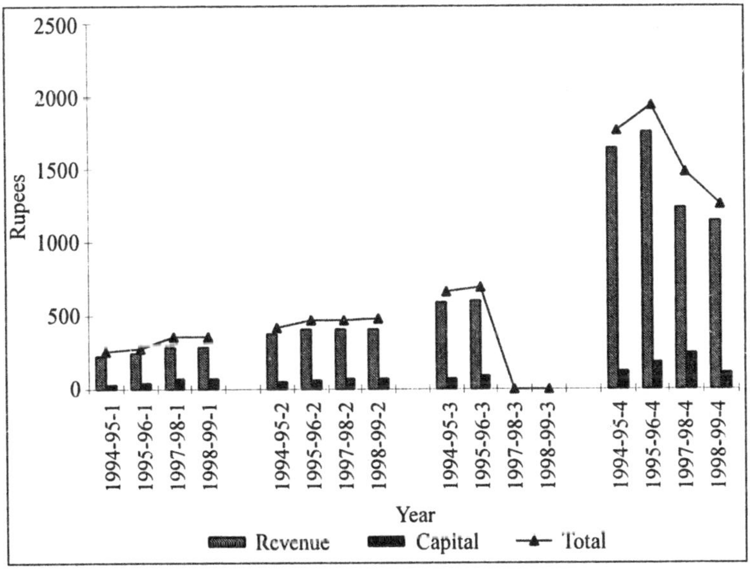

Chart 8.2: Per Capita Expenditure, Gujarat (Constant Prices)

Over time, the per capita receipts have been increasing at constant prices in all the size classes of towns except the metropolitan cities, where one finds a decline in the last two years. This is because of the decline in the revenue income. While in the other size classes, there is a general increase over time in the per capita income on the capital side, in the metropolitan cities, the per capita income on the capital side has fluctuated. This is what we have observed in individual metropolitan studies in the state (Kundu 2002; Mukherjee and Mahadevia 2002).

What we observe here is that in all the years, the inter-class difference in the state is quite high. This implies inequity in terms of income levels of the urban centres. In 1994-95, the per capita total income (at current prices) of the fourth stratum was 7.26 times that of the first size class and 4.36 times that of the second size class. However, the difference is seen to have decreased over time. In 1998-99, the per capita total income of the fourth size class was 3 times that of the first

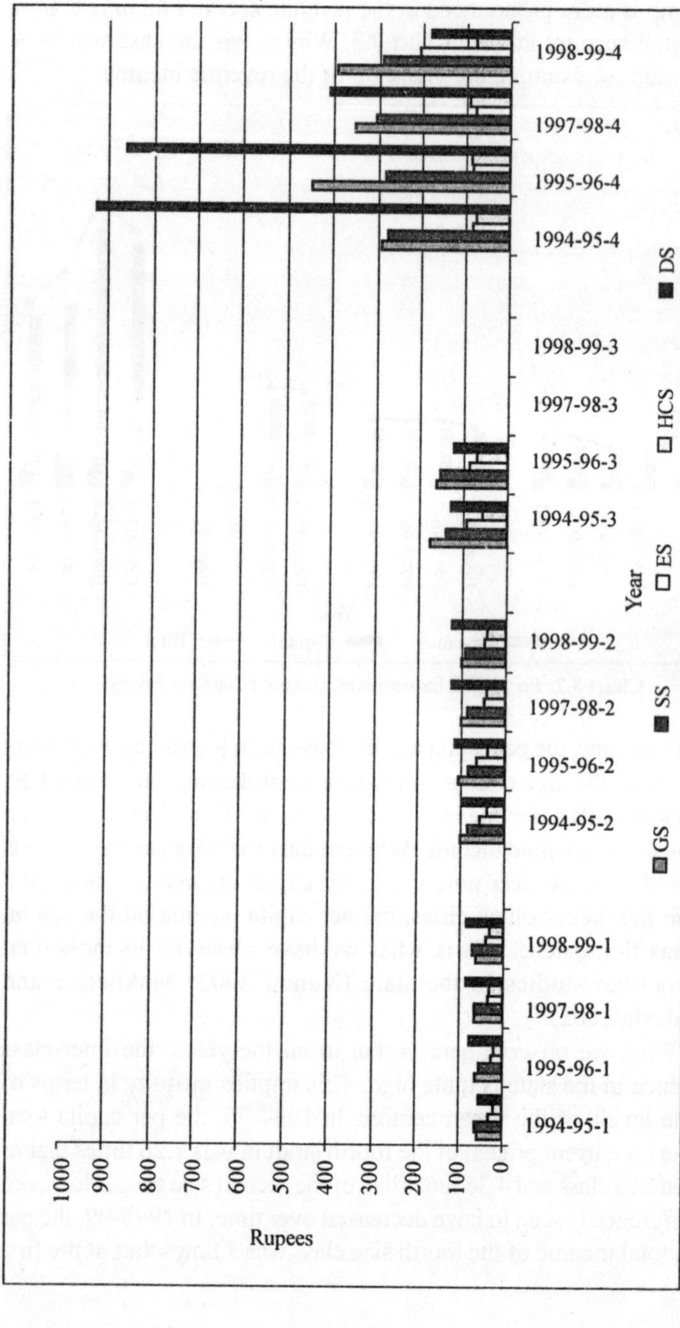

Chart 8.3: Per Capita Expenditure, Gujarat (Constant Prices)

and 2.45 times that of the second size class. But this may be because of the reduction in the income of the fourth size class as already seen. If this is the case, the question is how the SMTs are going to acquire capital for their infrastructural development.

Budgets: Surplus or Deficit?

Information on budgets, whether they are deficit or surplus, is given in Table 8.6. We find that the ULB budgets in each size class have been surplus except for two years in the metropolises. Secondly, the revenue account surplus for most size classes and for most of the years has been more or less equal to the capital account budget. Thus, even if there is capital account deficit, the overall budget remains in surplus, with the exceptions mentioned above.

Income

The subject of local government in India falls under the State List, and hence the powers and functions of local governments in each state are derived from the powers devolved upon the ULB by the respective state governments through legislative action. The resource-raising powers of the local governments thus depend on the taxation powers delegated to them by the state governments. Prior to the 74th CA, in some states, especially those in South India, where the parastatals play a large role in performing the essential functions at the local level, the ULBs were not very powerful. In some instances, the state governments superseded the ULBs. Then, there was no question of the ULBs' powers to raise resources. But given the 74th CA and the policy inclination towards decentralisation, the state governments began to recognise the need to devolve taxation powers to the ULBs. That, however, would require significant changes in the existing municipal laws, which some state governments have begun to amend. Currently, there is a wide disparity in terms of the taxation powers of local bodies in India, which is reflected in the financial health and functions of the local bodies.

Municipalities in India have been classified into three groups depending on their functional and fiscal domain:

(i) Those which have a comparatively larger functional and fiscal domains, for example, Gujarat and Maharashtra;

Table 8.6: Average Income and Expenditure (Current prices)

Size Class	*1994-95*			*1995-96*			*1997-98*			*1998-99*		
	Income	*Expend.*	*Surplus/ Deficit*	*Income*	*Expend.*	*Surplus/ Deficit*	*Income*	*Expend.*	*Surplus/ Deficit*	*Income*	*Expend.*	*Surplus/ Deficit*
Revenue Account												
< 50,000	63.21	56.98	6.23	76.22	68.16	8.06	109.81	99.71	10.10	118.00	106.38	11.62
50,000-200,000	319.46	304.66	14.80	380.63	365.92	14.71	449.36	436.34	13.02	521.36	498.31	23.06
200,000 – 1 million	3495.33	3263.96	231.37	4618.67	3728.12	890.54	N.A	N.A	N.A	N.A	N.A	N.A
> 1 million	39072.67	35864.55	3208.11	46060.67	42758.50	3302.11	51846.00	44486.61	7359.40	20583.00	32363.00	11780.00
All Urban	1082.41	998.45	83.96	1298.19	1282.87	15.32	1081.18	951.36	129.81	500.12	487.56	12.56
Capital Account												
< 50,000	10.23	7.71	2.50	15.58	10.32	5.27	28.78	24.96	3.83	54.82	26.15	28.67
50,000-200,000	69.71	39.50	30.19	72.02	55.44	16.58	103.88	73.48	30.40	137.77	89.91	47.89
200,000 – 1 million	300.33	372.00	-71.67	323.00	576.67	-254.00	N.A	N.A	N.A	N.A	N.A	N.A
> 1 million	3896.33	2740.00	1156.33	1117.00	4434.00	-3317.00	9544.00	8871.50	672.50	2706.00	2019.00	688.00
All Urban	123.42	87.01	36.41	67.85	136.72	-68.86	212.54	187.21	25.33	117.84	74.12	43.72
Total Budget												
< 50,000	73.44	64.69	8.74	91.80	78.47	13.33	138.58	124.66	13.92	172.82	132.52	40.30
50,000-200,000	389.15	344.17	44.99	452.65	421.36	31.30	553.24	509.82	43.42	659.14	588.21	70.93
200,000 – 1 million	3795.67	3636.01	159.66	4941.67	4304.91	636.75	N.A	N.A	N.A	N.A	N.A	N.A
> 1 million	42969.00	38604.59	4364.41	47178.00	47192.62	-14.62	61390.00	53358.31	8031.69	23289.00	34382.00	-11093.00
All Urban	1205.83	1085.46	120.37	1366.04	1419.59	-53.55	1293.71	1138.57	155.14	617.96	561.68	56.28

Source: GMFB data

(ii) Those which have a larger fiscal domain but a narrower functional domain, for example, Rajasthan and Manipur.

(iii) Those that have a comparatively larger functional jurisdiction but a narrower fiscal base. (Mathur 2000, p. 10)

On account of their strong financial position, the local bodies in Gujarat and Maharashtra are able to perform more functions compared to those in other states. The level of municipal income is thus an important determinant of the level of services provided by the local bodies. Therefore, to understand the ability of the local bodies to provide services, it is necessary to study the trends in the municipal income of the different size of towns.

Composition of Income

Not only the level of income, but also the composition of income is important. Municipal income can be divided into two, own-source income and external-source income. Own-source income consists of tax and non-tax revenues of the municipal bodies and external revenue includes grants and loans from the state government and other agencies. The share of each of these components varies across states depending on the taxation powers of the local governments, state of finances of the respective state governments and the financial health of the local body itself.

Own vs. External Sources

The mainstay of the revenues of the ULBs has been taxation, mainly octroi. It has been shown time and again that the inclusion or exclusion of octroi as a source of revenue influences the finances of the local bodies (Mathur 2000, p. 39). Own-source revenue would constitute a larger part of the total income of the local bodies. The octroi was abolished in all the ULBs except the municipal corporations in the state in the year 2000. But our analysis pertains to the period when the octroi was in place.

Analysis of own-source income and its share in the total income is important as it indicates the financial strength and flexibility of the local body. After the 74th CA, more emphasis is placed on the local bodies improving their own-source income since it would decrease the dependence on higher-level governments for development funds. The extent of own-source income also determines the level of flexibility in taking decisions and undertaking developmental activities. Recent studies in municipal finance also point out that "...mobilization of internal sources of revenue should be considered one of the primary objectives of municipalities in order to bring some level of fiscal robustness to local finances" (NIPFP 1995).

The extent of external-source revenue in the total income of a local body determines the degree to which it has to depend on funds from other agencies such as state governments or other financial institutions. Sources of external income are grants and loans. If the local body is financially strong, then it is possible for it to take loans on the basis of its own creditworthiness and repay them. But local bodies, which do not have a strong resource base, are not able to do so, and hence they have to depend on grants from the higher-level governments. Thus, to understand the level of financial flexibility and strength, we look into the extent of internal and external sources of revenue in the total income of local bodies.

The percentage share of own-source revenue is quite high in the municipalities of all classes in Gujarat (Table 8.7). With the increase in the size of the ULB, this share in the total income rises. This is true for all the years of our study. This may be because the smaller municipalities do not have a strong resource base. The extent of own-source revenue depends on the ability of the ULB to collect local taxes (in Gujarat they are octroi and property tax) and generate income from its own properties. Collection of the octroi is very much dependent on the economic base of the ULB and the income levels of the population in the urban centre. On both counts smaller urban centres are at a disadvantage compared to the larger urban centres. Further, a smaller ULB would not be in a position to generate income from its own properties given its low economic base. Thus, the smaller towns depend much more on the external sources for their revenues, mainly on the state government grants. While in the smaller towns, the external source of revenue would mainly be grants, for larger towns that would be loans. Composition of each source of revenue would be looked at later on. Over time, the proportionate share of own-source revenue of all the size classes of town has marginally gone down

Table 8.7: Composition of Per Capita Income

Size Class	1994-95			1995-96			1997-98			1998-99		
	Own	*External*	*Total*	*Own*	*External*	*Total*	*Own*	*External*	*Total*	*Own*	*External*	*Total*
Current Prices (in Rs)												
< 50,000	252.02	63.76	315.77	304.27	81.11	385.38	392.18	145.06	537.24	427.03	263.40	690.43
50,000-200,000	380.91	140.08	520.99	451.25	145.05	596.30	516.98	186.27	703.25	567.80	236.45	804.25
200,000 – 1 million	668.88	83.23	752.11	805.76	140.71	946.47	N.A	N.A	N.A	N.A	N.A	N.A
> 1 million	1859.92	295.18	2155.10	2126.93	176.21	2303.13	1840.48	481.45	2321.93	1471.41	426.16	1897.56
All Urban	1063.91	192.92	1256.83	1232.32	149.80	1382.13	1130.13	320.92	1451.05	715.18	279.92	995.09
Constant Prices (in Rs)												
< 50,000	230.42	58.29	288.72	255.73	68.17	323.91	286.91	106.12	393.03	286.52	176.73	463.25
50,000-200,000	348.27	128.08	476.35	379.27	121.92	501.19	378.21	136.27	514.48	380.97	158.65	539.61
200,000 – 1 million	611.57	76.10	687.67	677.24	118.27	795.50	N.A	N.A	N.A	N.A	N.A	N.A
> 1 million	1700.56	269.89	1970.44	1787.66	148.10	1935.77	1346.44	352.21	1698.65	987.25	285.93	1273.18
All Urban	972.75	176.39	1149.14	1035.76	125.91	1161.67	826.76	234.78	1061.54	479.85	187.81	667.66
Per cent Share												
< 50,000	79.81	20.19	100.00	78.95	21.05	100.00	73.00	27.00	100.00	61.85	38.15	100.00
50,000-200,000	73.11	26.89	100.00	75.67	24.33	100.00	73.51	26.49	100.00	70.60	29.40	100.00
200,000 – 1 million	88.93	11.07	100.00	85.13	14.87	100.00	N.A	N.A	N.A	N.A	N.A	N.A
> 1 million	86.30	13.70	100.00	92.35	7.65	100.00	79.27	20.73	100.00	77.54	22.46	100.00
All Urban	84.65	15.35	100.00	89.16	10.84	100.00	77.88	22.12	100.00	71.87	28.13	100.00

Source: GMFB data

from around 80 per cent to around 70 per cent, and the decline is sharper in the smaller size class of towns than the larger ones.

Per capita own-source revenue was higher in the larger urban centres, which have higher per capita own-source revenue, and the difference between the smaller and larger urban centres in their per capita own-source revenues was very high in all the years examined. One disturbing observation is that the all-urban figures for per capita own-source revenues are decreasing, which may be due to a decrease in the per capita own-source income of the last size class.

Tax vs. Non-tax Revenue

Tax and non-tax incomes are own-sources of revenue for local bodies. The income would depend on the taxation powers available with the local bodies, their tax efforts, and the local economic base and incomes. Property tax is the most common local source of tax income of the ULBs. It is considered the most dependable source of local revenues; it is also the most progressive source of local revenues. Many state governments have introduced a value-based property tax system in place of the rent-based system now, which is expected to bring in equity in the property tax regime.

Octroi, which was levied in many states, has now been abolished in most of them except in Maharashtra and municipal corporations in Gujarat. Entry tax is charged by some ULBs, especially the tourist towns. In lieu of octroi, many state governments have also introduced entry tax, which is imposed on all vehicles entering the state that is shared with the ULBs.

Some states have a formula to share the sales tax collected by the state government and entertainment tax and other cesses collected by the ULB on behalf of the state government.

A number of international funding agencies have been advocating sharing of income tax generated at the city level, a tax that is collected by the central government. No action has been initiated on this issue in the country, not even at the policy level.

Introducing user charges for the facilities provided by the ULBs is being advocated in the sphere of urban policies, post-reforms. The measure will allow the ULBs to recover the capital costs incurred for these facilities and maintain them. If the principle of cost recovery from the urban facilities is implemented to the fullest extent then the share of this source, which would form part of the non-tax revenues, would grow. Other sources of non-tax internal revenues are incomes from the municipal properties, either in the form of rent or sale of the properties. The latter would be one-time income, which is parallel to the income from divestment by the state/central government and is best utilised for long-term expenditures such as creation of capital assets. The rental income would be recurring income and has been found to have a very small share in the total income of the ULBs in most cases.

In all the size classes, there was a decline in per the capita tax income in the last year of our analysis (1998-99). The share of tax income in total own-source revenue fluctuates. The fluctuation is much more in the large cities and metropolises than in the small and medium towns where the ratio of tax to non-tax remains 55:45 (Table 8.8). The SMTs in the state thus have quite a large share of non-tax income, that is, grants. However, per capita grants increase with the increase in the size class of urban centres. This means that the gap between the large and small cities in terms of per capita tax income is quite high in the state. This can be seen from the fact that the per capita tax income increases quite a lot with the increase in the size class. The difference between the per capita collection of the smallest size class and metropolises has remained nearly constant (at five times) with regards to tax collection but has varied (from double to ten times) as far as non-tax collection is concerned. This variation is due to the fluctuations in the non-tax collection in the metropolitan cities. In terms of per capita non-tax income, the figures are very low for all size classes (Table 8.8).

External-Source Income

Grants and contributions from higher levels of government and loans from government or other agencies are the sources of external income for a local body. If the share of grants is large, then the financial health of the local body is contingent on the finances available from the state government, in essence, on the financial condition of the state government. If the share of loans is high in the finances of a local body, it is usually considered that it has the creditworthiness to borrow

Table 8.8: Composition of Own Revenue Sources (Per Capita)

Size Class	*1994-95*			*1995-96*			*1997-98*			*1998-99*		
	Tax	*Non-tax*	*Total*	*Tax*	*Non-tax*	*Total*	*Tax*	*Non-tax*	*Total*	*Tax*	*Non-tax*	*Total*
Current prices (in Rs.)												
< 50,000	159.69	92.33	252.02	180.30	123.97	304.27	231.49	160.69	392.18	241.24	185.79	427.03
50,000-200,000	199.81	181.10	380.91	235.06	216.19	451.25	286.86	230.12	516.98	309.34	258.45	567.80
200,000 – 1 million	491.82	177.06	668.88	599.78	205.99	805.76	N.A	N.A	N.A	N.A	N.A	N.A
> 1 million	757.92	1102.00	1859.92	921.30	1205.62	2126.93	1122.21	718.27	1840.48	1070.22	401.19	1471.41
All Urban	479.70	584.20	1063.91	581.09	651.24	1232.32	677.71	452.42	1130.13	444.62	270.55	715.18
Per cent share												
< 50,000	63.36	36.64	100.00	59.26	40.74	100.00	59.03	40.97	100.00	56.49	43.51	100.00
50,000-200,000	52.46	47.54	100.00	52.09	47.91	100.00	55.49	44.51	100.00	54.48	45.52	100.00
200,000 – 1 million	73.53	26.47	100.00	74.44	25.56	100.00	N.A	N.A	N.A	N.A	N.A	N.A
> 1 million	40.75	59.25	100.00	43.32	56.68	100.00	60.97	39.03	100.00	72.73	27.27	100.00
All Urban	45.09	54.91	100.00	47.15	52.85	100.00	59.97	40.03	100.00	62.17	37.83	100.00

Note: Non-tax income includes extraordinary income, education cess and provident and pension fund income, and income other than fees and charges.

Source: GMFB data

from the market on its own. This is a good sign as it indicates financial independence of the local body from state/central government.

Per capita external-source revenue in the state is the lowest in the small size class of urban centres and the highest in the metropolitan cities. This is quite surprising, as one would expect the SMTs to have a higher per capita external source of income, which would have been equitable as the SMTs are not in a position to generate their own revenues because of the restricted economic base.

State Government's Contribution

State government's contribution comes in the form of grants. These grants have a special role in the finances of a local body and particularly in the case of smaller municipalities, which do not have a broad revenue base like the larger local bodies. The system of giving grants-in-aid to municipalities has evolved out of necessity (NIPFP 1995, p. 51). The purpose of giving grants is to equalise either income levels or service levels (NIPFP 1995, p. 58). In the first case, the aim is to reduce the inter-municipality disparities in per capita revenues raised from internal sources. The share of grants in the total revenue is greater in smaller municipalities than in larger municipalities (NIPFP 1995, p 57). The smaller municipalities do not usually have a strong resource base and hence are unable to raise sufficient revenues from their own sources. The purpose of such grants is to mitigate inter-class disparities in the income levels. In some cases grants are given to equalise the expenditure levels on services.

The system of grants is considered to be a step towards decentralisation since it provides finances for local government services (Bahl and Linn 1992, p. 428). But the degree of autonomy that it gives to the local body depends on how the local body is structured.

Dependence on grants makes the local bodies vulnerable since the amount of the grant depends on the financial health of the state government, political considerations and priorities of the state government. Thus there is uncertainty about allocations. Moreover, some grants, mainly the programme grants, carry an expenditure mandate, which restricts the choices of the local bodies (Bahl and Linn 1992, p. 429). Often such grants are made to pursue the national goals of development, but the larger goals might come into conflict with the local objectives.

However, it is found that the municipalities with below-average per capita own-source revenues receive smaller amounts of grants (NIPFP 1995, p. 65), which shows that most states do not follow the basic principles of designing grants and the current system of grants fails to address the problem of the horizontal imbalance in the income levels. The smaller municipalities with low incomes get smaller grants. In Gujarat, the state government's contribution to the local bodies is the highest in the case of the fourth size class (Table 8.9), which means that the local bodies having a population of more than one million benefit more from grants.

Grants can be of two kinds: revenue grant and capital grant. Revenue grants are supposed to fill in the revenue gap of the local bodies and are ad hoc in nature. In some cases, revenue grants are transfers from the state government to compensate for taxes abolished or imposed. It is, therefore, subject to the whims and financial condition of the state government. But on the positive side, these funds can be put to general use and do not come with any conditionality.

Capital grants are usually tied to some programme or project implemented by the central or state government, and hence there is no possibility of putting them to other uses; there is no flexibility in the capital grants. So while analysing the grants the share of the revenue grants as well as of the capital grants should be kept in view to get an idea about the flexibility the local bodies have in the use of the funds they get from the state government.

The per capita revenue grant is the highest for the last stratum in Gujarat, meaning the cities with a population of more than one million (Table 8.9). It is very small for the small and medium towns, whereas what is desirable is that the smaller towns be given more grants rather than the larger cities.

The per capita capital grants given to the smaller municipalities in Gujarat are higher than those given to the larger local bodies. This is because the smaller towns are more in need of grants for capital works than the bigger towns, which can borrow on their own creditworthiness from the market or from financial institutions. For the first and second size classes, the figures show a rising trend, which

Table 8.9: Per Capita Grant Receipts

Size Class	*1994-95*			*1995-96*			*1997-98*			*1998-99*		
	Revenue	*Capital*	*Total*	*Revenue*	*Capital*	*Total*	*Revenue*	*Capital*	*Total*	*Revenue*	*Capital*	*Total*
Current Prices (in Rs.)												
< 50,000	19.81	13.75	33.55	15.70	27.05	42.75	33.49	39.70	73.19	44.39	94.93	139.33
50,000-200,000	46.76	28.84	75.61	50.17	32.75	82.92	54.22	37.84	92.06	68.33	58.68	127.01
200,000 – 1 million	23.73	7.61	31.34	78.87	12.02	90.89	N.A	N.A	N.A	N.A	N.A	N.A
> 1 million	99.76	4.79	104.55	121.67	18.46	140.14	120.46	37.27	157.73	205.64	71.87	277.50
All Urban	64.29	13.43	77.71	81.15	23.07	104.23	82.54	37.96	120.49	90.16	69.32	159.49
Constant Prices (in Rs.)												
< 50,000	18.11	12.57	30.68	13.19	22.74	35.93	24.50	29.05	53.54	29.79	63.70	93.48
50,000-200,000	42.76	26.37	69.13	42.17	27.52	69.69	39.67	27.68	67.35	45.85	39.37	85.22
200,000 – 1 million	21.70	6.96	28.66	66.29	10.10	76.39	N.A	N.A	N.A	N.A	N.A	N.A
> 1 million	91.22	4.38	95.59	102.26	15.52	117.78	88.13	27.26	115.39	137.97	48.22	186.19
All Urban	58.78	12.28	71.05	68.21	19.39	87.60	60.38	27.77	88.15	60.49	46.51	107.01
Per cent Share												
< 50,000	59.03	40.97	100.00	36.72	63.28	100.00	45.75	54.25	100.00	31.86	68.14	100.00
50,000-200,000	61.85	38.15	100.00	60.51	39.49	100.00	58.90	41.10	100.00	53.80	46.20	100.00
200,000 – 1 million	75.71	24.29	100.00	86.78	13.22	100.00	N.A	N.A	N.A	N.A	N.A	N.A
> 1 million	95.42	4.58	100.00	86.82	13.18	100.00	76.37	23.63	100.00	74.10	25.90	100.00
All Urban	82.72	17.28	100.00	77.86	22.14	100.00	68.50	31.50	100.00	56.53	43.47	100.00

Source: GMFB

means larger grants are being given to the local bodies in Gujarat for capital works.

Loan Income

The other source of external income for the local bodies is loans. Per capita loan income increases, by and large, with the increase in the size class of the urban centres. But there are many fluctuations. For example, in 1994-95, the per capita loan in the metropolitan cities was 25 times of the small towns (< 50,000 population) (Table 8.10). In 1997-98, this ratio was 11 times and in 1998-99, it was reduced to 4 times. But in all the size classes, the per capita loans form a very small proportion of the total per capita receipts. This implies that local bodies lack consistency in borrowing.

Table 8.10: Per Capita Loan Income

Size Class	*Per Capita Loan Income at Current Prices (Rs.)*				
	1994-95	*1995-96*	*1996-97*	*1997-98*	*1998-99*
< 50,000	7.19	8.44	103.48	21.72	11.76
50,000-200,000	18.31	6.53	14.18	29.05	10.52
200,000 – 1 million	29.33	3.88	4.74	N.A	N.A
> 1 million	179.17	0.24	5.11	249.98	43.05
All Urban	90.50	3.66	21.53	117.78	17.22

Expenditure

Expenditure level

In general, the budgets in all the size classes of the urban centres have been in surplus. Hence, the total per capita expenditure has been nearly equal to the total per capita income or less than the latter. Two patterns can be discerned easily:

1. With the increase in the size of the urban centre, total per capita expenditure also rises. On an average, during the study period, the per capita expenditure in each of the size class of urban centres (at 1993-94 prices) has been Rs. 310 (< 50,000), Rs. 461 (50,000 to 200,000), Rs. 676 (200,000 to 1,000,000), and Rs. 1,610 (> 1,000,000) (Table 8.11). This means that

Table 8.11: Per Capita Expenditure

Size Class	*1994-95*			*1995-96*			*1997-98*			*1998-99*		
	Revenue	*Capital*	*Total*	*Revenue*	*Capital*	*Total*	*Revenue*	*Capital*	*Total*	*Revenue*	*Capital*	*Total*
Current Prices (in Rs.)												
< 50,000	245.02	33.18	278.20	286.16	43.30	329.46	386.53	96.73	483.27	425.01	104.44	529.45
50,000-200,000	407.87	52.89	460.76	482.04	73.03	555.07	554.65	93.40	648.05	608.01	109.69	717.69
200,000 – 1 million	646.77	73.72	720.49	714.06	110.47	824.53	N.A	N.A	N.A	N.A	N.A	N.A
> 1 million	1798.77	137.43	1936.20	2087.39	216.46	2303.85	1682.60	335.55	2018.16	1709.41	164.48	1873.89
All Urban	1040.68	90.69	1131.37	1297.98	138.33	1436.31	1067.06	209.98	1277.04	785.11	119.35	904.47
Constant Prices (in Rs)												
< 50,000	224.02	30.34	254.35	240.52	36.39	276.91	282.77	70.77	353.54	285.16	70.07	355.23
50,000-200,000	372.92	48.36	421.28	405.15	61.38	466.53	405.76	68.33	474.09	407.94	73.60	481.54
200,000 – 1 million	591.35	67.41	658.75	600.16	92.85	693.01	N.A	N.A	N.A	N.A	N.A	N.A
> 1 million	1644.65	125.65	1770.30	1754.44	181.94	1936.38	1230.94	245.48	1476.42	1146.93	110.36	1257.29
All Urban	951.51	82.92	1034.43	1090.94	116.25	1207.20	780.63	153.61	934.24	526.77	80.08	606.86
Percentage Share												
< 50,000	88.07	11.93	100.00	86.86	13.14	100.00	79.98	20.02	100.00	80.27	19.73	100.00
50,000-200,000	88.52	11.48	100.00	86.84	13.16	100.00	85.59	14.41	100.00	84.72	15.28	100.00
200,000 – 1 million	89.77	10.23	100.00	86.60	13.40	100.00	N.A	N.A	N.A	N.A	N.A	N.A
> 1 million	92.90	7.10	100.00	90.60	9.40	100.00	83.37	16.63	100.00	91.22	8.78	100.00
All Urban	91.98	8.02	100.00	90.37	9.63	100.00	83.56	16.44	100.00	86.80	13.20	100.00

Source: Based on GMFB

the per capita expenditure in the metropolitan cities was 5.2 times that in the small towns (< 50,000 population), in the medium towns (population 50,000 to 200,000) it was 1.5 times that in the small towns, and in the cities (population 200,000 to 1,000,000) it was 2.4 times that in the small towns. As compared to the per capita income, the disparity in the per capita expenditure is higher across different size classes of the urban centres in the state.

2. Over time, the per capita total expenditure (at constant prices), both revenue and capital, has increased in all the sizes of the urban centres. The exceptions are the metropolitan cities, where, in the last two years, the total per capita expenditure like per capita income has declined in real terms. The decline in the per capita expenditure in the metropolitan cities is evidently due to the decrease in the per capita income in the last two years of the study period. But irrespective of the size, the increase is higher on the capital expenditure side than on the revenue expenditure side. In other words, the increase in the total per capita expenditure over time is due to the increase in the per capita capital expenditure. And this is tied to the increase in the per capita capital income in all the size classes of urban centres in the state over time.

In the metropolitan cities, the per capita capital expenditure was higher in 1997-98 than in the previous year in spite of the decrease in the total per capita expenditure that resulted in a decline in the per capita total expenditure. Since a large proportion of the revenue expenditure is on the incomes, this might be a welcome development. By reducing the expenditure in 1997-98, the metropolitan cities in the state were able to keep their budgets in surplus in that year which was not the case in 1998-99. When the per capita revenue income dipped steeply and affected the revenue and capital expenditure of the year. There is no apparent reason for the dip.

In terms of the composition of the expenditure, the share of the capital expenditure has never exceeded 20 per cent of the total expenditure in Gujarat (Table 8.12). In fact, in most years, for all the size classes of towns, it has remained between 10 per cent and 15 per cent. Further, the share of the capital expenditure in the total expenditure has been much lower than the share of the capital income in the total income. This suggests that the income received on the capital account side in the state is being utilised for revenue expenditure in the urban centres that tends to happen much more in the small towns than in the metropolitan cities. This is a situation that needs to be corrected. At the same time, there was a real increase in the per capita capital expenditure in the small and medium towns, whereas the same went down in the metropolitan cities in the last two years of our analysis.

Table 8.12: Expenditure on Services (% Share)

Size Class	*1994-95*	*1995-96*	*1997-98*	*1998-99*
General Services				
< 50,000	25.99	24.76	22.88	22.04
50,000-200,000	26.90	25.50	25.36	24.51
200,000 – 1 million	29.93	26.94	N.A	N.A
> 1 million	17.52	25.44	28.61	34.14
All Urban	19.76	25.53	27.66	28.36
Social Services				
< 50,000	27.33	22.43	23.36	24.54
50,000-200,000	21.82	20.88	21.43	22.14
200,000 – 1 million	23.61	25.84	N.A	N.A
> 1 million	16.67	15.95	24.45	25.22
All Urban	18.11	17.41	23.83	23.75
Economic Services				
< 50,000	14.23	11.56	12.70	13.10
50,000-200,000	15.15	15.72	12.39	11.63
200,000 – 1 million	15.39	14.52	N.A	N.A
> 1 million	5.03	4.72	6.45	17.97
All Urban	7.23	6.89	7.93	14.54
Housing and Community Services Expenditure				
< 50,000	9.26	9.40	11.55	11.43
50,000-200,000	10.07	10.12	10.46	11.29
200,000 – 1 million	9.40	12.05	N.A	N.A
> 1 million	4.58	4.88	7.43	6.99
All Urban	5.71	6.13	8.24	9.46
Debt Services				
< 50,000	23.19	31.84	29.51	28.89
50,000-200,000	26.05	27.79	30.37	30.43
200,000 – 1 million	21.66	20.64	N.A	N.A
> 1 million	56.20	49.00	33.05	15.68
All Urban	49.19	44.04	32.34	23.90

Source: GMFB data

There is, thus, a very high disparity in the expenditure across the size classes in the state due to the differences in the per capita income receipts. On the income side, there is a large difference in the per capita tax income—tax income is quite high in the large cities as compared to the small towns which have a low tax base. The large cities in Gujarat also have higher per capita grants and per capita loan receipts than the smaller towns, which explains the much higher per capita expenditures in the former.

Composition of Expenditure

The composition of expenditure reveals the importance each state gives to different urban activities. It also gives an idea about the distribution of responsibilities between the ULB and the state government. If the state government takes the responsibility for certain urban level activities, then the share of that activity in the ULB's expenditure would be lower. Further, the expenditure composition also shows how the ULBs raise their finances for undertaking their activities. If debt servicing, one of the items under the expenditure, is high, then that would indicate that the ULBs are borrowing money for undertaking development expenditure.

There is no standardised format of maintaining the municipal data in India. The accounting classification of expenditure and income varies across states and even within states. This problem was faced during this exercise, particularly regarding the expenditure data. The data was, therefore, reclassified to make inter-state comparison possible[5]. The expenditure of the local bodies is classified according to the following heads:

1. *General services expenditure:* All items of expenditure meant for administrative purposes.
2. *Social services expenditure:* Expenditure on health, education, social security and welfare services.
3. *Economic services expenditure:* Expenditure on water supply, transport and electricity services.
4. *Housing and community services expenditure:* Expenditure on housing and cultural, religious and recreational services.
5. *Debt services expenditure:* Repayment of principal and interest.

From among the five heads of expenditure, Debt Services (DS) has the highest percentage share in general, irrespective of size class, followed by General Services (GS) (Table 8.12). In some years and in some size classes, however, the percentage share of the GS has been higher than that of the DS in the total expenditure. For example, in 1994-95, in small towns, and in 1994-95 and 1995-96 in cities, this was the case. In the metropolitan cities, the share of the DS in the total expenditure in the first two years of our analysis was quite high. But what is surprising is a high share of the DS in the total expenditure in the small and medium towns. We have already mentioned that even the small and medium towns have received loans, mainly for capital works.

In the third position is the Social Services (SS), with the an exception of cities where the DS is in the third position and the SS in the second position. At the bottom in the expenditure share is the Housing and Community Services (HCS), across all the size classes of towns. This is because the ULBs have not taken up housing and shelter-related activities, with the exception of the Ahmedabad Municipal Corporation which in the recent years has taken up a Slum Networking Programme for slum development in a few pockets and has been incurring expenditures on the same.

Further, noticeably high expenditure, about 50 per cent, is on the GS and DS in the ULBs in Gujarat. The larger the urban centre, the higher the proportion of total expenditure on these two items. And over time, the combined share of the SS and HCS has remained nearly constant, at around one-third of the total expenditure in the small and medium towns. However, the same has increased to one-third from one-fifth in the metropolitan cities because of the decline in the share of DS in the total expenditure.

There is some movement in the share of different expenditure items in the total expenditure. For example, in small towns, the share of the GS, SS and Economic Services (ES) has gone down during the study period, whereas the share of the HCS and DS has gone up. In the medium towns, the share of the GS and ES has gone down, whereas the share of the HCS and DS has gone up and that of SS has remained nearly constant.

Another trend observed in the per capita expenditure on each of the five items is even more important (Table 8.13). In small and medium towns, because the *overall* per capita expenditure has gone up in real terms over the study period in all the five items of expenditure, the per capita expenditure has gone up in real terms, although only marginally. The increases have been small and the medium towns are an exception. There has been a decrease in the real per capita expenditure on economic services. In the metropolitan cities, the overall per capita expenditure has gone down in real terms, as seen before. This is due to the decline in the per capita expenditure in the DS in real terms.

Table 8.13: Per Capita Expenditure on Services (in Rs. at Current Prices)

Size Class	*1994-95*	*1995-96*	*1997-98*	*1998-99*
General Services				
< 50,000	63.67	70.86	88.43	93.68
50,000-200,000	109.74	122.90	140.66	149.02
200,000 – 1 million	193.60	192.37	N.A	N.A
> 1 million	315.20	531.10	481.39	583.63
All Urban	205.68	308.96	295.15	222.64
Social Services				
< 50,000	66.97	64.19	90.30	104.29
50,000-200,000	89.00	100.65	118.85	134.63
200,000 – 1 million	152.72	184.54	N.A	N.A
> 1 million	299.89	332.95	411.41	431.04
All Urban	188.47	210.72	254.23	186.48
Economic Services				
< 50,000	34.87	33.09	49.08	55.69
50,000-200,000	61.81	75.76	68.71	70.73
200,000 – 1 million	99.55	103.69	N.A	N.A
> 1 million	90.40	98.55	108.54	307.18
All Urban	75.26	83.40	84.61	114.12
Housing and Community Services Expenditure				
< 50,000	22.69	26.91	44.64	48.57
50,000-200,000	41.06	48.78	58.01	68.64
200,000 – 1 million	60.81	86.06	N.A	N.A
> 1 million	82.35	101.95	125.10	119.49
All Urban	59.39	74.19	87.97	74.24
Debt Services				
< 50,000	56.81	91.11	114.08	122.77
50,000-200,000	106.26	133.95	168.43	184.99
200,000 – 1 million	140.08	147.40	N.A	N.A
> 1 million	1010.93	1022.84	556.17	268.07
All Urban	511.89	532.97	345.11	187.62

Source: GMFB.

Finally, what is quite noticeable is rise in the per capita expenditure on all the five items with the increase in the size class. And this holds good for all the study years. Thus, large urban centres, in contrast to small and medium towns, have an advantage in terms of higher per capita expenditure under all heads. At the same time, if we look at the per capita expenditure data more closely, we find that the gap between small towns and metropolitan cities under each expenditure head (per capita) varies; the gap is the highest in the DS (metropolitan cities have it eight times of the small towns), followed by the GS (six times), Social Services (four-and-a-half times), then the Economic Services (four times) and the Housing and Community Services (three times). Thus, administering the metropolitan cities is more costly than administering small urban centres, contrary to our understanding of the economies of scale. Further, large cities are able to raise more debt than small urban centres, which many researchers time and again have argued would happen if urban development is left entirely to the market and the urban centres are asked to raise development expenditure through debt.

Availability of Town-level Facilities

Town-level data on facilities were available for only a few facilities. In this section, we have described the availability of town-level facilities across different size classes of urban centres. The data on facilities are of the late 1990s period. It needs to be kept in mind that the level of facilities in any town is an outcome of not only the current investments and expenditures which the data on finances capture, but also of historic achievements. It is assumed that not only in the recent times but in the past (post-independence period), small and medium towns have been handicapped with regard to the availability of basic facilities such as water supply, sewerage, and roads, which are the responsibility of the ULBs.

We have data on two facilities, percentage *pucca* roads and percentage *population* covered by sewerage facility. It is interesting to note that the percentage of roads that are *pucca* increases as the town size increases (Table 8.14). Only 65 per cent roads in the small towns were *pucca* as against 92 per cent in the metropolitan cities. It can also be seen that 35 per cent roads in the small towns and 30 per cent roads in the medium towns are still *kutcha* and require investments for upgradation.

Table 8.14: Levels of Service

Size Class	*% Pucca Road*	*% Pop. Covered by Sewerage*
< 50,000	65.13	20.72
50,000-200,000	69.18	27.22
200,000 – 1 million	75.56	68.97
> 1 million	92.10	64.44

We have data on other facilities obtained from the 54th Round of the National Sample Survey on Housing and Basic Amenities. The information on the level of different facilities in the state across different size classes of urban centres is given in Table 8.15.

Table 8.15: Level of Basic Facilities (NSS, 54th Round)

Per cent Households	*Size Class*				
	< 50,000	*50,000 to 2 lakh*	*2 lakh to 1 million*	*> 1 million*	*All urban*
Having access to tap water supply	91.5	83.1	94.8	97.0	91.1
Having drinking water access within premises	78.5	72.8	86.1	82.3	78.7
Not sharing source of drinking water	65.7	44.1	54.3	68.6	59.2
Having access to bathroom facility	78.0	61.9	77.8	71.8	70.8
Having individual access to bathroom facility	87.2	83.9	68.8	93.9	87.2
Having no drainage facility	27.5	29.8	7.30	1.90	17.4
Having access to *pucca* covered or underground drainage	37.6	37.6	71.0	87.3	58.1
Not having access to latrine	19.6	33.9	16.8	12.1	21.1
Having latrines connected to sewerage system	25.5	11.3	14.2	68.8	35.8
Having individual access to latrines	82.0	71.5	66.5	71.6	73.8
Having latrines inside the premises	92.3	92.3	99.5	84.2	89.6
Reported garbage collection by local authority	12.8	22.0	36.2	44.3	28.8

With regard to access to other basic household level facilities, metropolitan cities have a better performance than smaller urban centres. But like finance, the metropolitan cities do not have an outright supremacy. Nor is there improvement in the level of services with the increase in the size class of urban centres. This is because access to the household level facilities is much more a function of the household income, density of urban living and the structure of the settlement rather than the outcome of the performance of the local bodies. Even then, a higher level of household facilities indicates higher income levels, more strongly in the metropolitan cities than in the smaller towns. But crowding (or higher densities) in the metropolitan cities results in having latrines inside the premises and having individual access to latrines. Sharing of latrines is much more of a metropolitan phenomenon than that of the small towns.

Where the local authority is involved, for example, in garbage collection, the performance is better for metropolitan cities than for small and medium towns. In fact, with the increase in the size class of towns, a larger proportion of the households reported garbage collection by the local authorities (Table 8.15). Only 13 per cent of the households in the small towns reported garbage collection by the local authorities as compared to 44 per cent in the metropolitan cities.

Another area where the local authority has a major role to play and where the local authority finances matter is the availability and type of sewerage system. In small towns, 28 per cent of households the did not have access to drainage, when this figure for the metropolitan cities was 2 per cent. With respect to this facility, we find improvement in the figures with the increase in the size class of towns. Similarly, with respect to the percentage latrines connected to the sewerage system, only 26 per cent households reported it in size class I as compared to 69 per cent in the metropolitan cities. But the size classes in between have a much lower achievement. In short, Table 8.15 shows that the level of facilities at the household level improves with the increase in the size class of urban centres in the state due to better capability of the local authority and higher incomes at the household level.

Conclusions

In short, the financing and level of facilities in the state studied by us reflect the development philosophy of the state. Gujarat's development has been highly iniquitous and quite discriminatory (Hirway and Mahadevia 1999) and this gets reflected in the disadvantage of and discrimination against small and medium towns.

Gujarat state, a fairly urbanised state, has clearly discriminated against the small and medium towns. In fact, the state's urbanisation pattern is highly skewed with the urban population concentrated in metropolitan cities and large cities. Its urban settlement pattern, level of incomes and expenditures and level of facilities portray a picture of the way a market would function. Large cities having a better economic base than small cities would be able to attract more incomes and, therefore, would have higher expenditures and thus better level of facilities. But the state policy discriminates against the weak as would the market. The state government has also been giving higher per capita grant to large cities than to small towns. The large cities have also been able to get higher per capita loans.

How come those urban centres that get larger grants are also able to raise more loans? Is it that the grants flow towards the urban centres that are able to attract more loans? In other words, it seems that grants are given to only those entities that are creditworthy! Although this sounds like absurd, it is true that in many of the current urban development programmes a grant component is attached to the loan component, and those urban entities which are able to attract loans would also be able to access state government grants! In such programmes, the loan comes from either the central government or a multilateral/bilateral agency. Along with some grants, the state government gives a guarantee and it also chips in to provide either some loan or grant or both for the programme. This is going to be the likely scenario of urban development in the near future, under the urban reform programmes that are being implemented in many states. We might, therefore, see a situation like Gujarat wherein market and state discriminate against the weak, small, urban bodies.

Given the existing inequalities in the urban settlement system, differences in the levels of development across size classes of urban centres, and variations in their capabilities—financial and even managerial— to pursue development, how would the SMTs be able to fulfil expectations? The policies of balanced regional development have remained more of a wishful thinking than a concrete achievement. Even a developed state such as Gujarat has not been able to redistribute resources in favour of the weaker urban bodies. Or, may be, such dichotomies can exist only in a developed state like Gujarat whose development path is characterised by many dichotomies. In an environment where urban reforms mean market-based solutions to urban development, the SMTs would lose out much more than now. Not only that, the links between the urban and rural systems and between the SMTs and metropolitan cities would become weak or may even crumble. The question is, how long would we be able to continue with these dichotomies and neglect of the SMTs in our urban system.

NOTES

1. The NSS rounds till the 50th quinquennial round used this classification.
2. We have used this classification because this paper is a part of a larger study where we are comparing the municipal finance situation with poverty, employment, unemployment, and basic facilities data of the NSS rounds.
3. This paper is carved out of an ongoing research titled *Poverty and Levels of Living in Small and Medium Towns in India* at the Institute of Human Development, New Delhi. The research is funded by the Central Statistical Organisation. Author acknowledges the assistance of Anurima Mukherjee for the analysis.
4. As per the discussion with the officials of the Gujarat Municipal Finance Board.
5. As mentioned before, this paper is from a much larger study, where municipal finances in three states Gujarat, Punjab, and Andhra Pradesh have been compared. For making this comparison possible, we have adopted the classification of expenditure mentioned in the main text.

REFERENCES

Bahl, Roy W. and Johannes F. Linn (1992): *Urban Public Finance in Developing Countries*, World Bank, Washington D.C.

Expert Group on the Commercialisation of Infrastructure (1996): *The India Infrastructure Report: Policy Imperatives for Growth and Welfare*, Ministry of Finance, Government of India, New Delhi.

Government of India (1988a): *Report of the National Commission on Urbanisation, Volume II*, Government of India, New Delhi.

Hardoy, Jorge, E. and David Satterthwaite (1986): "Why Small and Intermediate Urban Centres?" in Jorge E. Hardoy and David Satterthwaite (eds.) *Small and Intermediate Urban Centres : Their Role in Regional and National Development in the Third World*, Hodder and Stoughton, London. Sydney, Auckland, Toronto, pp. 1-17.

Hirway, Indira and Darshini Mahadevia (1999): The *Gujarat Human Development Report, 1999 (Draft)*, Mahatma Gandhi Labour Institute, Ahmedabad.

Kundu, A. (1993): *In the Name of the Urban Poor: Access to Basic Amenities*, Sage, New Delhi.

Ministry of Works and Housing (1977): *Report of the Task Force on Planning and Development of Small & Medium Towns & Cities* (Volume I and II), Government of India, New Delhi.

Minocha, A. C. and H. S. Yadav (1989): *Small and Medium Towns and their Role in Regional Development*, Gian Publishing House, New Delhi.

NIPFP (1995): 'Redefining State- Municipal Fiscal Relations: Options and Perspectives for the State Finance Commissions', Volume I, Main Report, New Delhi.

Sharma, N. (1996): *Urban Infrastructure Financing in India: Towards an Alternative*, (unpublished post-graduate thesis), School of Planning, Centre for Environmental Planning and Technology, Ahmedabad.

9

Institutional Finance in Rajasthan

The Recent Trends

SURJIT SINGH

The state of Rajasthan was formed by the integration of 19 princely states and 3 principalities soon after independence in 1947 but the process of full integration was completed only in 1956. Thus, for almost a decade after independence, the state remained engrossed in solving the problems of integration of various regions. Besides it had inherited a legacy of backwardness in more tham one respect. This led to a slow start in the economic development and, in consequence, a rather long delay in raising the levels of living of its people.

Agriculture was, and still remains, the main economic activity in Rajasthan. But some changes have taken place: the farm size has declined, there is a shift in the livestock pattern, and dependence on rain has increased. The service sector is becoming important, but the manufacturing sector is sluggish. Around 1956, the infrastructure and industrial base in Rajasthan was at a low level of development. The pace of economic transformation has been slow because social transformation did not pick up (Singh 1996). The per capita income in the state has risen slowly from Rs.1,373 in 1980-81 to Rs.11,282 in 1998-99 (Acharya and Singh 1999).

In the past, the informal financial sector was the mainstay of the people for economic activities, though today concerted efforts by the state over a period have widened the participation of the formal sector institutions. It is well known that credit plays a vital role in facilitating economic growth. This paper examines in the above context, with the performance of institutional finance in Rajasthan.

Bank Coverage

When social banking began in 1969, Rajasthan had 364 bank offices constituting 4.41 per cent of all the bank offices in India (Table 9.1). In 1975, this number rose to 792 in Rajasthan and 18,575 at all-India level. The population covered by one bank office was 36,119 in Rajasthan compared to 32,488 at the national level. Though the state's share in the all-India offices increased marginally over the period and stood at 5.06 per cent in 2000, the spread of offices in Rajasthan has been significant but declining over time. Between 1969 and 1975, the number of offices jumped by 117.58 per cent, while the next five years saw a reduced growth of 86.52 per cent. The growth in the bank offices further fell to 78.89 per cent during the 1980-85 period, and went further down to 16.15 per cent between 1985 and 1990. The reform period has seen the slowest growth of 4.82 per cent (1990-95) in the spread of bank offices in Rajasthan which fell further to 2.70 per cent during 1995-2000. At the all-India level, the growth in the spread of offices has been even slower than in Rajasthan. It is interesting to note that prior to the onset of reforms, the population coverage in Rajasthan by a bank office had been improving and touched 12,976 persons per office in 1991, while at all-India level it the was 13,667 persons. One observes deterioration in the coverage in the nineties. By 2000, each office covered 16,578 persons in Rajasthan against 15,337 at the all-India level. This is due to the new licensing policy that allows banks to merge rural branches within the service area and closure of unviable offices.

Table 9.1: Scheduled Commercial Banks: Number of Offices and Population Coverage (Rajasthan's Share)

	1969	*1975*	*1980*	*1985*	*1990*	*1995*	*2000*
Rajasthan	364	792	1478	2644	3071	3219	3306
India	8262	18575	32412	52638	60515	63817	65340
Rajasthan's Share	4.41	4.26	4.56	5.02	5.07	5.04	5.06
% change in Office							
Rajasthan	—	117.58	86.52	78.89	16.15	4.82	2.70
India	—	124.82	74.49	62.40	14.96	5.46	2.39
Population Coverage							
Rajasthan	—	36119	21769	13517	12976	15109	16578
India	—	32488	20830	14555	13667	14447	15337

Deposits and Credit Deployed

The credit cycle has three major segments: first, to mop up resources from society through deposit mobilisation and other means; second, to lend the funds so mobilised to worthwhile borrowers for their viable projects; third, to recover fully and promptly whatever has been lent so that the recovered amounts can be put back into the credit cycle. To the recovered amount are added freshly mobilised resources alongside some refinancing from higher institutions. In this section we will look at some of these aspects as they unfolded in the nineties.

In 1992, there were 3,077 scheduled commercial bank offices (SCBs) in Rajasthan. This number continuously rose and reached 3,313 by 1999 (Table 9.2). There was significant deposit mobilisation by these bank offices. In 1992, the total deposits mobilised were Rs.6,341.74 crore with each office mobilising Rs.2.06 crore on an average. In 1999, the deposits totalled 20,647.03 crore, or Rs.6.23 crore per office. On the other hand, credit disbursed increased from Rs.3472.02 crore in 1992 to Rs.9,187.05 crore in 1999. Credit disbursed per office more than doubled during this period. Credit deposit ratio of the SCBs has declined since 1992 when it was 54.75; by 1999 it was 44.50. However, these ratios saw an increase till the mid-eighties.

Table 9.2: Credits and Deposits in SCBs in Rajasthan (June end)

(in Rs.lakhs)

Years	*No.*	*All SCBs*		*Per Office*		*CD*
		Deposits	*Credit*	*Deposits*	*Credit*	*ratio*
1992	3077	634174	347202	206.10	112.84	54.75
1993	3108	744127	396148	239.42	127.46	53.24
1994	3143	875222	416804	278.47	132.61	47.62
1995	3177	1056566	481957	332.57	151.70	45.62
1996	3208	1250975	555867	389.95	173.28	44.63
1997	3256	1436961	629284	441.33	193.27	43.79
1998	3273	1743150	788373	532.58	240.87	45.23
1999	3313	2064703	918705	623.21	277.30	44.50

The number of offices of Public Sector Commercial Banks (PSCBs) continuously increased from 1,784 in 1992 to 1,993 in 1999, growing by 11.7 per cent (Table 9.3). Deposit mobilisation by the

PSCB offices has trebled between 1992 and 1999. In 1992 the total deposits mobilised were 5,360.17 crore, with each office mobilising Rs.3.00 crore on an average. In 1999, the deposits totalled Rs.16,582.72 crore, or Rs.8.32 crore per office. On the other hand, credit disbursed increased from Rs.2,994.47 crore in 1992 to Rs.7, 505.71 crore in 1999. Credit disbursed per office increased by 2.5 times during this period. However, credit deposit ratio declined from 55.87 in 1992 to 45.26 in 1999.

Table 9.3: Credits and Deposits in PSCBs in Rajasthan (June end)

(in Rs.lakhs)

Years		*Public Sector CBs*		*Per Office*		*CD*
	No	*Deposits*	*Credit*	*Deposits*	*Credit*	*ratio*
1992	1784	536017	299447	300.46	167.85	55.87
1993	1813	631338	344614	348.23	190.08	54.58
1994	1847	736418	356620	398.71	193.08	48.43
1995	1880	878591	408171	467.34	217.11	46.46
1996	1905	1025051	465005	538.08	244.10	45.36
1997	1940	1160074	521837	597.98	268.99	44.98
1998	1963	1389352	643652	707.77	327.89	46.33
1999	1993	1658272	750571	832.05	376.60	45.26

In 1975, Regional Rural Banks (RRBs) were set up to cater to the weaker sections in rural India. By 1992, there were 1,071 RRB offices in Rajasthan but this number marginally fell to 1,065 in 1999 (Table 9.4). Deposit mobilisation by these bank offices has been

Table 9.4: Regional Rural Banks in Rajasthan – Deposits and Credits (in Rs. lakhs)

(June end)

Years		*Regional Rural Banks*		*Per Office*		*CD*
	No.	*Deposits*	*Credit*	*Deposits*	*Credit*	*ratio*
1992	1071	33424	16714	31.21	15.61	50.01
1993	1073	42013	19272	39.15	17.96	45.87
1994	1070	52464	22887	49.03	21.39	43.62
1995	1068	67273	28232	62.99	26.43	41.97
1996	1070	86759	34258	81.08	32.02	39.49
1997	1071	107468	42686	100.34	39.86	39.72
1998	1061	137832	53296	129.91	50.23	38.67
1999	1065	167668	64101	157.43	60.19	38.23

significant. In 1992 the total deposits mobilised amounted to Rs.334.24 crore with each office mobilising Rs.0.312 crore on an average. In 1999, the deposits totalled Rs.1, 676.68 crore (Rs.1.574 crore per office). On the other hand, credit disbursed increased from Rs.167.14 crore in 1992 to Rs.641.01 crore in 1999. Credit disbursed per office almost quadrupled during this period. However, credit deposit (CD) ratio of RRBs has been declining significantly since 1992. It was 50.01 in 1992 and by 1999 it went down to 38.23. Thus while deposits mobilised and funds deployed have risen over the years, the CD ratio has declined which is a cause for concern. This means that despite the improvement in the infrastructure and investment climate in Rajasthan and enhanced capacity to absorb credit, resources flowed out of the state from the banking sector. The state with no law and order problem and a significant base of natural and mineral resources has not been able to attract projects that can utilise funds available with the banking sector. It could also mean that banks adhere to prudential norms and lend cautiously. The third reason could be that the informal sector resources are being put to use.

It is worth noting that while the number of commercial bank offices in Rajasthan went up by 274 between 1990-91 and 2000-01, the number of rural offices fell by 148 (Table 9.5). The share of rural offices in the total bank offices thus saw a decline from 65.6 per cent in 1990-1 to 55.9 per cent in 2000-01. This has affected the population coverage adversely. In 1990-91, a bank office served 12,833 persons. The number suddenly fell to 14,104 in 1991-92. In the same year, a rural bank office served 16,678 persons. In 1995-96, in rural Rajasthan 19,155 persons were being served by one office and 14,851 persons at the aggregate level. The situation had deteriorated by 2000-01 when these figures changed to 21,695 and 16,216 respectively.

The amount of deposit mobilised by commercial banks in 1994-5 was Rs. 2,184 per capita, which has continuously increased to touch Rs.4,876 in 2000-01. On the other hand, per capita credit disbursed has improved from Rs.1,115 to Rs.2,419 during the same period. In the case of rural deposits, it is surprising that deposit mobilisation picked up from Rs.1.15 crore per rural office in 1994-95 to Rs. 3.02 crore in 2000-01 despite the fact that several intervening years were drought years. One can ascribe these positive changes to the rising per capita incomes in rural Rajasthan. Finally, the deposits mobilised by commercial banks in Rajasthan constituted 2.78 per cent of the all-India deposits in 1990-91, and this share marginally improved to 2.90 in 2000-01.

Table 9.5: SCB Offices—Deposits

(in Rs. crore)

Years	*Deposits*		*Offices Rural*	*Per Capita*		*Deposits*	*Population*	
	Share	*Total*	*Offices*	*Credit Rs.*	*Deposits*	*Per Rural Office*	*Served Total*	*Rural*
1990-91	2.78	3105	2036 (65.6)				12833	
1991-92	2.68	3120	2035 (65.2)				14104	16678
1992-93	2.67	3160	2044 (64.9)				14297	16949
1993-94	2.72	3202	2046 (63.9)				14463	17300
1994-95	2.80	3219	1928 (59.9)	1115	2184	1.15	14745	18754
1995-96	2.86	3275	1928 (58.9)	1107	2446	1.33	14851	19155
1996-97	2.89	3306	1925 (58.2)	1418	2826	1.62	15072	19592
1997-98	2.89	3329	1914 (57.5)	1700	3286	1.93	15332	20120
1998-99	2.93	3362	1915 (57.0)	1879	3814	2.29	15448	20530
1999-00	2.90	3365	1894 (56.3)	2168	4328	2.63	15906	21189
2000-01	2.90	3379	1888 (55.9)	2419	4876	3.02	16216	21695

Note: In brackets shows is share in total.
Source: CMIE (1999 and 2002).

District Level Situation

When data are disaggregated, we find that the number of scheduled commercial bank offices was greater in 1999 than in 1993 in all the districts excepting Barmer, Bundi, Dungarpur, Jhalawar, Swai Madhopur and Baran (Appendix 1). But deposit mobilisation improved significantly across districts. So is the case with the credit deployed by these banks. Deposits and credit per bank office too saw an increase during the period. However, the credit-deposit ratio witnessed an increase in 1999 over 1993 only in Bhilwara and Jaipur. This means that credit absorption enhanced in these two districts only. The funds are being attracted only to these districts. In 1993 the credit-deposit ratio ranged between a low of 24.91 in Dungarpur and a high of 99.39 in Bhilwara, while in 1999, it ranged between 17.58 in Dungarpur and 113.59 in Bhilwara.

When one looks at the performance of the public sector commercial banks in Rajasthan, one finds that the number of bank offices declined in Barmer and Bundi districts (Appendix 2). Deposit mobilisation and credit deployment has witnessed an increase across districts during 1993-99. But the credit-deposit ratio has witnessed an increase in 1999 over 1993 only in Bhilwara and Jaipur. This means that credit absorption enhanced only in these two districts to which funds were going. In 1993 the credit-deposit ratio ranged between a low of 23.70 in Dungarpur and a high of 104.40 in Bhilwara, whereas in 1999, it ranged between 15.89 in Dungarpur and 118.99 in Bhilwara.

The RRBs performed reasonably well at the district level. The number of RRB offices has gone down in Barmer, Bundi, Jalore, Jhalawar, Kota, Swai Madhopur, Udaipur and Baran and has gone up in Bhilwara, Chittorgarh, Churu, Jaisalmer, Jodhpur, Pali, Sikar and Rajsamand (Appendix 3). The latter are mainly arid and semi-arid districts. In the remaining districts the number did not change. But the change in the number of offices is not reflected in deposit mobilisation or credit deployment, which rose in all the districts. The per office deposit mobilisation has improved significantly in most of the districts, though the credit deployed has not kept pace with deposit mobilisation. The credit-deposit ratio in 1993 was as high as 114.87 in Banswara and as low as 22.03 in Pali. In 1999, the ratio fell in the all districts except Bikaner, Bundi, Chittorgarh, Jalore, Kota, Pali, Sirohi and Tonk. Besides, the CD ratio ranged from 19.35 in Jaipur to 71.18 in Bundi. Credit-deposit ratios of the RRBs were higher than those of the commercial banks since the former have to support government schemes under the mandate to lend to the weaker sections. RRBs also appear to be more relevant in the tribal districts.

Competing Sectors

In India, traditionally agriculture and industry have been the two major clients—competitors for the credit—but now other sectors like housing and trade have also begun to seek their share in credit. Not many studies have tried to examine this issue. The policy directions over a period of time have favoured a few sectors like agriculture, small industries and the weaker sections of society. One of the principal objects of the nationalisation of commercial banks was to bring about certain structural changes in the credit deployment. Data given in Tables 9.6 and 9.7 show that:

Table 9.6: Distribution of SCBs Credit: Agriculture and Industry (Value in Rs. crores and number in lakhs)

Year	*Total % Share*			*Agriculture Credit*				*Industry*	
	Credit	*In Credit in India*	*Acco-unts Lakhs*	*Total*	*Acc-ount*	*Direct*	*Acc-ount*	*Credit*	*Acc-ount*
1990-91	3372.86	2.72	22.42	867.56	10.50	744.90	10.38	1267.17	2.37
1991-92	3767.78	2.76	22.75	1013.29	10.57	887.28	10.48	1412.56	2.31
1992-93	4432.47	2.73	22.58	1145.25	10.39	991.50	10.29	1718.37	2.22
1993-94	4583.15	2.61	22.07	1106.87	10.16	954.26	10.06	1661.82	2.17
1994-95	5419.88	2.57	21.59	1264.89	10.09	1088.59	9.98	2059.65	2.02
1995-96	5519.92	2.17	20.16	1147.21	9.57	1036.17	9.43	2276.29	1.86
1996-97	7248.95	2.55	21.79	1518.94	9.59	1355.94	9.45	3028.81	1.89
1997-98	8908.20	2.07	20.57	1773.60	9.14	1591.60	8.98	3535.50	1.77
1998-99	10096.50	2.64	20.06	2143.80	8.72	1822.20	8.61	3853.60	1.89
1999-00	11944.00	2.06	20.99	2705.50	8.93	2098.10	8.84	4227.10	1.91
2000-01	13662.10	2.54	21.09	3173.70	9.66	2451.40	9.53	4596.30	1.68

Source: CMIE (1999 and 2002).

Table 9.7: Share in Credit Flow by Sectors

Years	*Share in Credit*			*Per Account Credit (Rs.)*	
	Agriculture	*Industry*	*Agriculture*	*Agriculture*	*Industry*
	Total	*Direct*			
1990-91	25.72	22.09	37.57	7176	53467
1991-92	26.89	23.55	37.49	8466	61150
1992-93	25.84	22.37	38.77	9636	77404
1993-94	24.15	20.82	36.26	9486	76582
1994-95	23.34	20.09	00.38	10908	101963
1995-96	20.78	18.77	41.24	10988	122381
1996-97	20.95	18.71	41.78	14349	160255
1997-98	19.91	17.87	39.69	17724	199746
1998-99	21.23	18.05	38.17	21164	203894
1999-00	22.65	17.57	35.39	23734	221314
2000-01	23.23	17.94	33.64	25723	273589

Source: CMIE (1999 and 2002).

1. The total credit disbursed has grown since 1990-91 by almost four times;
2. Agricultural credit has trebled during the reforms (from 1991-92);
3. Direct credit to agriculture has also trebled during the same period;
4. The share of direct agricultural credit continuously declined from 25.72 per cent in 1990-91 to 19.91 per cent in 1997-98 and rose again to touch 23.23 per cent mark in 2000-01;
5. Credit to industry has grown continuously from Rs.1,267.17 crore to Rs.4,596.30 crore in 2000-01 though the share in the total credit disbursed has declined significantly since 1996-7 to touch 33.64 per cent and the share of direct credit to the agricultural sector has increased by 2 percentage points during the same period. The share had peaked at 41.78 per cent in 1996-97;
6. Since 1991-92, the number of accounts in the agricultural sector has been going down, but in 1998-99 it recovered and touched 9.66 lakh in 2000-01. A similar pattern is observed in the number of accounts of direct credit to agriculture;
7. The number of accounts in the industry has been declining, though with minor fluctuations;
8. The per account direct credit flow to agriculture has been continuously rising since 1990-91 (Rs.7,176.30 to Rs.25,722.98; 3.5 times rise) and;
9. The per account credit flow to industry has also seen a similar pattern (Rs.53467.09 to Rs.273589.29; a five-fold rise).

The same data can also be viewed from the angle of per capita delivery of credit to agriculture and industry. We find that since 1980, per capita credit delivered to both the sectors, agriculture and industry, has gone up in all the districts (Appendix 4). It is noteworthy that in 1980, the per capita credit to agriculture was higher in Alwar, Bharatpur, Bundi, Chittorgarh, Churu, Dungarpur, Ganganagar, Jaisalmer, Jalore, Nagaur, Sikar, Sirohi and Tonk (48.1 per cent districts). But by 1990, Bharatpur, Bikaner, Bundi, Chittorgarh, Churu, Ganganagar, Jaisalmer, Jalore, Jhalawar, Jhunjhunu, Nagaur, Swai Madhopur, Sikar, Sirohi and Tonk (51.9 per cent districts) had a higher agricultural credit per capita. The number of districts with higher per capita credit rose in 1995 (55.6 per cent districts). This shows that in a majority of the districts agriculture was given preferential treatment. No doubt there is a wide variation in the credit delivered to the two sectors across the istricts.

Looking from another angle, we find that in 1990-91, agriculture contributed 43.4 per cent to the state income but had only 22.1 per cent of total credit deployed; whereas industry contributed 11.9 per cent to the state income if cornered 37.6 per cent of the credit. In 1995-96, the contribution of agriculture to the state income fell to 37.9 per cent, and its share in the credit deployed went down to 18.8 per cent as against the industry's contribution of 10.7 per cent to the State Domestic Product (SDP) and 41.8 per cent share in credit. In 2000-01, agriculture received still smaller share in credit at 17.9 per cent (contribution to the SDP 30.2 per cent) compared to 33.6 per cent (contribution to the SDP 12.3 per cent) going to industry. The industrial sector has all a long obtained a higher share of credit despite the fact that its contribution to the state income has not been significant.

The correlation between the infrastructure development index and per capita credit delivered is 0.47 for agriculture and 0.39 for industry. Thus a structural change has occurred in the credit deployment due to policy directives. The recommendations of the Ghosh and Krishnaswamy working groups on priority sector lending were largely instrumental in this shift. Further, it has been argued that the credit requirements of agriculture are necessarily different from those in the commodity industry. The latter has a relatively smooth flow of purchases of inputs and sales of outputs over the year. The agriculturists, on the other hand, systematically require to buy inputs and to commit themselves to payments several months before their products are harvested. This feature of agriculture renders it inappropriate to view the ratio of inputs to outputs in the commodity industry than in agriculture as justifying a larger ratio of credit to net product. Besides, even the criterion of the same ratio of credit to net product in each sector is too kind to the commodity industry. In addition, the commodity industry needs less credit per unit of output than agriculture because both input and output flows are smoother over the year. It is also organised in the larger units with more access to internal savings and to the private capital market. Production credit given to the commodity industry is also less liable to be diverted towards family consumption in the slack season. Unlike agriculture, commodity industry seldom turns credit-financed inputs into *subsistence* products which are consumed by the family that owns the firm and which do little to help repay the trade credit even when they are efficiently produced.

Cooperative Institutions

Promotion of credit cooperatives in their present-day corporate form was the first-ever effort in the country at institutionalising credit for the rural areas. It marked the culmination of a series of measures initiated by the government in the last quarter of the 19th century. The measures were taken to combat usury and the resultant indebtedness and alienation of land, all of which were eating into the vitals of an already stagnant rural economy. But the enhanced role of the state in cooperatives over the years has made these institutions perform poorly. The reform process has touched the cooperatives late. Re-capitalisation is slow and so is the modification of cooperative laws.

The cooperative movement has played an important role in the rural economy of Rajasthan. The 1990s, however, witnessed some set-backs to the movement. The number of societies in Rajasthan decreased from 20,101 in 1990-91 to 19,860 in 1998-99, though the membership did not decline (Table 9.8.) There were 70.99 lakh members in 1990-91 and the number grew to 85.61 lakh in 1998-99. As the membership expanded, the advances increased over the period, especially after 1993-94. Advances per member have risen from Rs. 919.81 in 1990-91 to Rs. 1,936.96 in 1998-99; the rise has been sharp after 1993-94. The same is the case with the recovery per member. It is surprising that the number of outstanding loans per member have fluctuated but remained high throughout. The recovery has been reasonably good. As a proportion of advances it was 98.49 per cent in 1990-91. But it has fallen (with the exception of 1991-92). However, it has remained above 80 per cent except in 1993-94 and 1998-99. Recovery as a proportion of loans outstanding has fluctuated over the years between 50.80 (1990-91) and 108.31 (1995-96).

There are various types of societies in operation in Rajasthan, viz., central non-credit societies, agricultural non-credit and credit

Table 9.8: Cooperative Movement in Rajasthan

Year	*No. of Societies*	*Member-Ship No. lakh*	*Loans: Rs. Crore*			*Per Member*			*Recovery as % of*	
			Advanced	*Recovered*	*Outstanding*	*Advances*	*Recovery*	*Outstanding*	*Advances*	*Outstanding*
1990-91	20101	70.99	652.96	643.13	1265.98	919.81	905.96	1783.35	98.49	50.8
1991-92	20247	76.78	626.59	1014.82	2227.1	816.12	1321.79	2900.76	161.96	45.57
1992-93	20255	78.12	437.15	400.51	590.84	559.58	512.68	756.31	91.62	67.79
1993-94	20263	76.09	1504.91	1081.83	1909.44	1997.86	1421.82	2509.52	71.89	56.66
1994-95	20184	78.73	1317.21	1249.73	1400.91	1672.98	1587.27	1779.29	94.88	89.21
1995-96	20155	81.48	1327.49	1155.58	1066.89	1629.27	1418.28	1309.42	87.05	108.31
1996-97	19928	82.6	1544.63	1311.49	1301.42	1869.96	1587.72	1575.53	84.91	100.77
1997-98	19885	83.64	1277.22	1022.99	1553.64	1527.03	1223.08	1857.52	80.1	65.84
1998-99	19860	85.61	1658.26	1286.67	1927.26	1936.96	1502.92	2251.17	77.59	66.76

Source: Statistical Abstract of Rajasthan, various years.

societies and non-agricultural credit and non-credit societies. The number of central non-credit societies and non-agricultural credit societies is not large. From our point of view, agricultural credit societies are important. In 1990-91, there were 5,280 such societies with 47.51 lakh members (Table 9.9). This number rose to 5,502 in 1992-93 but with reforms, the number went down and stood at 5,240 with 54.18 lakh members in 1998-99. The membership has gone up by 6.67 lakh over the years. The fluctuations in these numbers are not so alarming as the number of societies which go into liquidation every year. However, their proportion has been declining over the years: in 1990 11.30 per cent societies faced liquidation, in 1998-99 it came down to 5.20 per cent. In 1998-99, liquidation affected 1.24 lakh members.

The district-level situation is presented in Appendices 5 through 7. The salient points are:

- Out of the 30, in eight districts—Bhilwara, Bundi, Chittorgarh, Ganganagar, Jalore, Jodhpur, Kota and Rajsamand—the number of societies went up between 1994-5 and 1998-99.
- Jaipur has the largest number of societies and Sirohi the smallest.
- Membership has increased in all the districts despite a reduction in the number of societies.
- Non-agricultural non-credit societies are most numerous followed by agricultural credit societies.
- Agricultural credit societies have gained in number in Bikaner, Ganganagar and Jaisalmer. The number fell in Alwar, Bharatpur, Bhilwara, Chittorgarh, Bundi, Dholpur, Jalore, Jhalawar, Jodhpur, Kota, Nagaur, Pali, Swai Madhopur and Tonk. In other districts there was no change.
- Membership has increased in the agricultural credit societies across districts.
- The number of societies under liquidation went down in all the districts between 1994-95 and 1998-99. In 1994-95, the highest proportion of societies under liquidation was in Jaisalmer (21.46%), and the lowest in Barmer (0.96%). In eleven districts more than 10 per cent societies went into

Table 9.9: Co-operative Societies in Rajasthan (membership in lakhs)

Year	Central Non-Credit Societies		Agricultural Societies: Credit Societies		Agricultural Societies: Non-Credit Societies		Non-Agricultural Societies: Credit Societies		Non-Agricultural Societies: Non-Credit Societies		Societies Under Liquidation		All Societies	
	No.	Member	No.	Member	No.	Member*	No.	Member	No.	Member	No.	Member	No.	Member
1990-91	84	1.27	5280	47.51	158	5938	740	0.88	11279	11.03	2234	0.92 (11.30)	19775	61.68
1991-92	87	1.27	5348	46.12	202	5634	739	0.95	11602	19.27	2159	0.66 (10.72)	20137	68.33
1992-93	94	1.27	5502	00.47	227	17146	701	0.90	12011	19.66	2255	1.11 (10.85)	20790	70.11
1993-94	49	1.35	5312	49.19	1518	307122	795	3.20	10474	8.77	2038	1.48 (10.10)	20186	67.06
1994-95	45	1.37	5319	50.04	NA	NA	803	3.50	12149	12.90	1809	1.43 (8.99)	20125	69.60
1995-96	52	1.54	5324	51.85	1132	167190	799	3.83	11130	11.30	1611	1.38 (8.04)	20048	71.58
1996-97	77	1.64	5290	52.71	1404	338233	798	3.71	10942	19.82	1417	1.34 (7.11)	19928	82.60
1997-98	88	1.73	5251	53.16	1391	329520	817	4.32	11077	19.72	1261	1.42 (6.34)	19885	83.64
1998-99	85	1.75	5240	54.18	1439	376299	806	4.36	11258	20.11	1032	1.24 (5.20)	19860	85.41

Note: * numbers. The numbers in parentheses are percentage of total.
Source: *Statistical Abstract of Rajasthan*, various years.

liquidation. In 1998-99 in only four districts more than 10 per cent of societies had gone into liquidation. The range of societies under liquidation in 1998-99 was 14.84 per cent (Jhunjhunu) and 0.35 per cent (Dungarpur).

- Loans advanced by the cooperative societies in 1998-99 fell over 1994-95 in Bharatpur, Alwar, Bundi, Chittorgarh, Dungarpur, Ganganagar, Jaisalmer, Kota and Pali.
- The number of loans outstanding went down only in Alwar and Jaisalmer.
- In this sense, there is a relationship between loans advanced and loans outstanding. The mounting number of outstanding loans has not restricted lending.
- Recovery as a proportion of the outstanding loans rose only in a few districts: Dholpur, Jalore, Sikar, Sirohi, Udaipur, Baran and Rajsamand. On the other hand, recovery as a proportion of the advances improved in Alwar, Bhilwara, Jaisalmer, Jalore, Sirohi and Baran.

Thus we find that though the cooperatives are performing reasonably well, a universal ailment has affected their performance. There are inter-district variations in the cooperative movement in terms of societies, loans disbursed and recovery of overdues. But is heartening that the tribal districts are doing reasonably well. Singh (1999a) has conducted a field survey in ten villages across all agro-climatic regions of Rajasthan and found that 43 per cent of all the farmers borrow money; 38 per cent of the small farmers and 48 per cent of the semi-medium farmers borrow money. The share of the banks in short-term borrowings is 13.34 per cent; that of PACS, 50.58 per cent; that of professional moneylenders 27.31 per cent; and than of the commission agents 8.76 per cent. On the other hand, the share of the banks in long-term borrowings is 29.27 per cent, of the development banks 39.73 per cent, of the relatives 12 per cent, professional moneylenders 12.98 per cent, and the commission agents the 6.02 per cent. This clearly shows that though the informal sector contributes a higher proportion to short-term crop production credit (36.1%) than the long-term productive credit (31%), its role is very important in Rajasthan's agricultural sector.

Priority Sector Lending

The Gadgil Committee (1969) had identified credit gaps in the key sectors of the economy, including in agriculture, and had found that commercial bank finance was skewed; the agricultural sector was neglected. The finding alerted the Reserve Bank of India and led it to take steps to bring the agricultural sector into the mainstream of institutional credit. Further, after the nationalisation of commercial banks, hitherto neglected sectors were given a priority status: banks were asked to provide credit to these sectors in a more concerted way. These sectors included agriculture (direct and indirect), small-scale industry, small road and water transport operators, retail trade and small businesses, education, self-employed persons, etc. Commercial banks are required to achieve the following targets and sub-targets under priority sector lending.

1. The share of commercial banks in the identified priority sectors should reach 33.3 per cent of the outstanding credit by March, 1979 and 40 per cent by March, 1985 and it was expected to be maintained thereafter.
2. Direct finance to agriculture and allied activities was expected to be 17 per cent of the total credit by March, 1989. In February, 1989 this target was further raised to 18 per cent.
3. A target of 10 per cent of the net bank credit for weaker sections, *i.e.* small and marginal farmers, share croppers, tenant farmers, landless labourers, artisans village and cottage industries, Integrated Rural Development Programme (IRDP) beneficiaries and Scheduled Caste and Scheduled Tribe (SC/ST) borrowers, should be maintained.
4. Advances granted under the differential rate of interest scheme (DRI) should form 1 per cent of the total advances outstanding as at the end of the previous year; at least 40 per cent of such advances should go to the SC/ST borrowers and at least two-thirds of the DRI advances should be provided through rural and semi-urban branches.

Priority sector lending is the main instrument of social banking in India. In 1969, the priority sector share in the net bank credit was

16.8 per cent which jumped to 58.6 per cent in 1990, far exceeding the target of 40 per cent (Table 9.10). It stood at 50.8 per cent in 1996. The reform period has thus seen a declining trend in the priority sector lending but still it remains far above the target. Rajasthan's performance has been far better than the all-India level performance. This can be ascribed to the widening of the priority sector. In Rajasthan, central and state schemes corner a bigger share.

Table 9.10: Priority Sector Lending

(In percentage)

	1969	*1990*	*1992*	*1993*	*1994*	*1995*	*1996*
Rajasthan	16.8	58.6	54.6	51.1	52.5	48.7	50.8
India	14.9	40.4	39.3	35.9	37.8	36.6	31.5

Source: Economic Survey

Performance of Rural Financial Institutions

Lending business of any institution depends on (i) mobilisation of deposits, (ii) available resources for disbursement, and (iii) the amount of loan that is recovered for further recycling. Poor recovery of loans results in overdue loans. In the banking parlance *an overdue loan is defined as a loan and interest thereon not paid on due dates.* The recovery of loans is, therefore, central to the smooth functioning of the credit business of financial institutions. Of the total amount that is due at any time period, some is recoverable and some is irrecoverable; the latter often results in bad debts or defaults.

The loans outstanding of all the RFIs have risen steadily since 1980. Their amount rose from Rs.280.64 crore in 1980 to Rs.1,093.59 crore in 1991, i.e. 290 per cent growth, while during the reform period, i.e. between 1991 and 1997, it was only 95 per cent (Table 9.11). The corresponding all-India figures reveal that though the loans outstanding grew by 457 per cent in the first period, the increase was only 57 per cent during the second period. The overdue loans of RFIs in Rajasthan have grown from Rs.72.75 crore in 1980 to Rs.402.66 in 1997. There was a fluctuating trend in the overdue loans in Rajasthan over the period, but the period of the 1990s had relatively higher overdue loans. At the all-India level, the situation was more or less

Table 9.11: Loans Outstanding in all RFIs

(In Rs. crore)

Years	Loan Outstanding		Total Overdues#		Overdues As % of		Bad Debts in Agriculture			
	Rajasthan	India	Rajasthan	India	Loans	Outstanding	Rajasthan	India	As % of Loans	
					Rajasthan	India			Rajasthan	India
1980	280.64	6035.94	72.75	1898.25	25.92	31.45	7.97 (3.69)	215.94	2.84	3.58
1981	351.38	7030.73	86.99	2124.12	24.76	30.71	10.77 (4.38)	245.74	3.07	3.50
1982	457.15	8912.42	112.84	2451.47	24.68	27.51	13.19 (4.86)	271.64	2.88	3.05
1983	558.25	9177.29	134.56	2907.07	24.10	28.56	16.51 (4.98)	331.28	2.96	3.26
1984	640.02	12260.26	171.10	3348.16	26.73	27.31	20.57 (5.43)	379.10	3.21	3.09
1985	726.14	14439.40	206.45	4012.63	28.43	27.79	24.81 (5.36)	463.09	3.42	3.21
1986	850.83	16820.82	242.30	4301.16	28.48	25.57	29.95 (6.00)	499.38	3.52	2.97
1987	976.94	19463.47	269.26	4891.92	27.56	25.13	37.25 (6.41)	581.20	3.81	2.99
1988	1134.97	22607.26	169.45	5435.80	14.93	24.04	25.02 (4.01)	623.99	2.20	2.76
1989	1279.08	25801.33	370.26	6146.69	28.95	23.82	54.41 (7.76)	701.38	4.25	2.72
1990	1469.86	29412.28	518.12	8555.70	35.25	29.09	76.47 (7.72)	990.57	5.20	3.37
1991	1093.59	33620.75	287.73	8661.56	26.11	25.76	53.91 (4.90)	1100.78	4.93	3.27
1992	1490.19	33208.01	491.63	9583.16	32.99	28.86	64.43 (4.56)	1411.45	4.32	4.25
1993	1661.44	36080.99	528.38	10009.95	31.80	27.74	71.10 (5.49)	1294.66	4.28	3.59
1994	872.95	20535.25	269.65	5694.16	30.89	27.73	33.02 (4.52)	730.51	3.78	3.56
1995	1035.32	23067.02	263.82	6084.65	25.48	26.38	31.26 (3.72)	840.41	3.02	3.64
1996	1170.08	27936.19	264.48	8037.33	22.60	28.77	12.98 (1.64)	790.81	1.11	2.83
1997	2149.04	52735.55	402.66	12614.71	18.73	23.92	56.59 (3.69)	1532.81	2.63	2.91

Note: #from direct advances, *loans outstanding. Numbers in parentheses are percentages of India.
Source: Gulati and Bathla 2002

similar. During the eighties, the share of overdue loans in the loans outstanding fluctuated between 14.93 per cent (1988) and 35.25 per cent (1990), while during the nineties, it ranged from 18.73 per cent (1997) to 31.80 per cent (1993). If we look at the period prior to the reforms, we find that during 1980-91, the range of the share of overdue loans in loans outstanding varied between 14.93 per cent (1988) and 35.25 per cent (1990), while since 1991, it has ranged from 18.73 per cent (1997) to 32.99 per cent (1993). This shows that Rajasthan improved its position in the nineties. For instance, in 1980 and 1989, the Rajasthan figures were in the range of 25-30 per cent, while in 1997 it improved its position to below 20 per cent.

Agricultural sector has always been the whipping boy of the financial sector's bad performance. It can be seen from Table 9.11 that in Rajasthan, bad debts in agriculture stood at Rs.7.97 crore which steadily increased till 1987 and, at the beginning of the reforms, stood at Rs.76.47 crore. There was a significant improvement during the reform period, for instance, in 1996 the bad debts amounted to only Rs.12.98 crore. The year 1997 witnessed a sudden surge in bad debts because of the drought. Rajasthan's share in the all-India bad debts was 3.69 per cent in 1980 and it went up to 7.76 per cent in 1989 which has never been surpassed. It fell steadily till 1996 when it was at its lowest, 1.64 per cent but rose again the following year. This shows that the discipline introduced through reforms in the financial sector was instrumental in this decline. The sudden fall since 1994 can also be ascribed to the reforms initiated in the cooperative sector in the state. In the 1980s bad debts as a proportion of loans outstanding have been fluctuating: they have ranged from 3.58 per cent in 1980 to 2.72 per cent in 1989 and from 4.25 per cent in 1992 to 2.83 per cent in 1996. This corroborates the declining credit deposit ratios that suggest that the banks avoid risky loans and concentrate on viable ventures. Fear of increasing NPAs also appears to influence it.

There are various factors affecting the default rate, some are internal, others external to the system. The external factors are essentially related to the non-viability of agriculture. These can further be classified as natural calamities (droughts in Rajasthan, 1987 and 1997), inadequate income generation and factors contributed by other agencies. For instance, most of the commodities produced in Rajasthan do not have a price support and the traders exploit the situation. This is reinforced by the lack of infrastructure facilities (in adequate number of regulated markets) and hence absence of forward and backward linkages within the existing markets. Puhazhendhi and Jayaraman (1999) believe that the introduction of prudential norms and aging of overdue loans have aggravated the problem of mounting overdue loans. The transaction cost of a rural loan is high which augments the non-viability of a loan. ACRC (1989) worked out the transaction cost for commercial banks as 6 per cent and for regional rural banks as 6.99 per cent of the agricultural loans disbursed.

Debt Issues

Extensive studies have been carried out on the indebtedness, borrowings and terms regarding money lending, capital formation and assets. Financial resources of farmers, their utilisation, the need for borrowing and the utilisation of loans have also been investigated. These studies are broad in character and hence permit only broad inferences. These inferences suggest that the bulk of the borrowed funds have been used for current production purposes, and that farmers have relied on their own funds for investment. Along with the rise in incomes, debts too have tended to grow. No definite conclusion seems to emerge as to whether the interest rate is usurious, whether it has declined or risen, and whether the increased activity of the credit institutions has made any favourable impact on the general conditions regarding financing of agriculture. These and other related problems have not been studied in sufficient depth to permit firm inferences. However, all-India indebtedness surveys do lead to some conclusions.

In 1971, in rural Rajasthan, 55.9 per cent of households reported debt and this proportion went down to 24.2 per cent in 1981 to rise again to 35.2 per cent in 1991 (Table 9.12). In comparison, at the

Table 9.12: Rural Debt and Liabilities

Items	*Rajasthan*	*India*	*Rajasthan*	*India*	*Rajasthan*	*India*
% of household reporting debt	55.9	41.3	24.2	19.4	35.2	32.0
Average debt per household Rs.	893	487	1157	653	3891	2116

Note: Debt includes cash loans and current liabilities.
Source: Reserve Bank of India 2001.

national level, the corresponding percentages have been 41.3 (1971), 19.4 (1981) and 32.0 (1979). So the situation in Rajasthan has always been worse than the national situation. Average debt per household in Rajasthan, on the other hand, has risen from Rs.893 in 1971 to Rs.1,157 in 1981, and then to Rs.3,891 in 1991. The corresponding all India figures were Rs. 487, Rs. 653 and Rs. 2,116 respectively. This shows that people are willing to borrow and the social stigma attached to debt is disappearing.

Rural Infrastructure Development Fund

The Rural Infrastructure Development Fund (RIDF) was set up by the Central Government in 1995-96 to facilitate quicker completion of on-going rural infrastructure projects, mainly incomplete irrigation projects. The initial amount allocated for the purpose was Rs.2,000 crore. The Central Government makes a budgetary contribution to teh RIDF it every year. The scope of the Fund has been extended to cover Gram Panchayats, Self-Help Groups and certain other institutions to develop rural infrastructure. Since the setting up of the second RIDF, the states are given loans for new infrastructures also. The repayment period is now seven years. Besides, the rate of interest on the loans to state a government has been reduced from the initial 13 per cent under the RIDF I to 10.5 per cent under RIDF VII. Priority is given to both ongoing and new projects with a short gestation period, say, of two to three years. Irrigation was the main area of thrust initially, but now rural roads and bridges, a means of improving rural connectivity, are being given preference since RIDF II. The loans cover other purposes such as soil conservation, watershed development, drainage improvement, energisation of state-owned tube-wells and setting up of rural market yards. Efforts are also made to cater to the specific requirements of some states like Jammu & Kashmir for inland waterways and rural market yards. Improving other infrastructural needs such as construction of fish jetties, godowns and cold storages are the new additions to the list of eligible candidates.

RIDF in Rajasthan

Under six tranches of RIDF loans, 6,749 projects have been sanctioned constituting 3.55 per cent of all the projects in the country. The tranche-wise distribution of projects is as follows: 38 (RIFD 1), 247 (RIFD 2), 264 (RIFD 3), 47 (RIFD 4), 513 (RIFD 5), and 5,640 (RIFD 6). As on March 31, 2001, Rs.1,044.25 crore were sanctioned for various projects of which 56.1 per cent were disbursed. Rajasthan's share in the total sanctioned was 5.6 per cent and 6.3 per cent of the disbursement. The major component of the projects is rural roads in Rajasthan. (For the impact of roads and bridges under the RIDF in Rajasthan, see Singh 2002).

Micro Finance

The information, resources, skills and technology base of the poor in India is very weak and consequently the scale of their operations is small, irrespective of the economic activity pursued. It is well known that the poor need credit to take care of their expanding families, to obtain medical treatment, and for social obligations on the occasions such as a marriage or a death. The family income is in fact just sufficient to meet the routine production and consumption demands, which are very modest. So when the poor have to face market and climatic uncertainties, their subsistence income comes under tremendous strain and they need to expand or diversify operations. In times of such emergencies, there are no credit institutions to fall back on, and the poor have no option but to seek credit from bigger landlords, traders and moneylenders at high rates of interest (Singh 1999a).

As a single individual, a poor person tends to be rather tentative and hesitant, but as a member of a group, he becomes a more reliable borrower. Group membership makes it easy for him to seek guidance and advice from the people he knows and trusts; a group credit programme provides him protection. Since the individual effort is too inadequate to improve the lot of the poor, it is necessary to organise them in groups so that they get the benefit of collective perception, decision-making, and implementation of programmes for common benefits.

The organisation has power and provides its members strength; it can be an antidote to the helplessness of the poor. Group savings serve a wider range of objectives other than immediate investment, for instance, it imposes discipline on the members to develop savings habit. Savings provide protection to the individual against normal business risks, variations in income, natural calamities and illness and enhance the self-confidence of the individual as it is a sign of encouragement by the group. The individual may even consider making more risky investments because of the cushion provided by savings. Group savings can demonstrate the strength of the unity of members. Savings plus credit can then be a good starting point for group formation; this is how Self-Help Groups (SHGs) are initiated. The approach towards poverty alleviation should be based on self-help; others should help the poor to help themselves.

Micro-finance is thus becoming a source of credit delivery for the poor and especially for women. Till March, 2000, there were 1,14,775 credit-linked SHGs in India and Rajasthan had 1,941 SHGs (1.69 per cent). The SHGs are provided refinance facility. As many as 94,645 SHGs benefited from refinance and the share of Rajasthan in it was 1.31 per cent (Table 9.13). At the all-India level, women's groups which were provided refinance constituted 85.08 per cent of the total, compared to 75.24 per cent in Rajasthan. A total bank loan of Rs. 192.98 crore was delivered to SHGs at the all-India level; Rs.4.56 crore in Rajasthan. This is 2.36 per cent bank loan. By December, 2002, 18,801 SHGs had been credit linked and Rs.37.77 crore have been disbursed in bank loans. The NABARD provided Rs.23.19 crore in refinance. The share of regional rural banks in credit linkage was 52 per cent, followed by commercial banks (37%) and cooperative banks (11%). The Government of Rajasthan has promoted 60 per cent of all SHGs through its various departments, while non-governmental organisations (NGOs) and others have assisted the formation of another 33 per cent. The contribution of regional rural banks is 7 per cent.

Table 9.13: SHGs (up to March 2000)

	No. of SHGs	*No. of SHGs Refinanced*		*Bank*	*NABARD*
	Credit Linked	*Total*	*Women*	*Loans*	*Refinance*
Rajasthan	1941	1236	930	45.57	22.66
India	114775	94645	80521	1929.82	1501.26
% share of Rajasthan	1.69	1.31	1.15	2.36	1.51

Source: NABARD

The field-level experiences exhibit wide disparities. An NGO in south Rajasthan (PEDO) has promoted 628 groups with 12,484 members in the three blocks of Bichhiwara, Simalwara, and Asper. As many as 85 per cent members have taken loans. Savings of Rs. 88.27 lakh have accrued to 628 groups and Rs.114.75 lakh outstanding loans exist giving a loan to saving ratio of 1.29. By 2002, loans worth Rs. 382.24 lakh had been disbursed with 93.54 per cent recovery rate. The break-up of loans is as follows: 25.7 per cent loans are used for purchase of animals like buffalo, cattle, goat and sheep; 19.4 per cent for opening a retail shop in the village or near a bus stand; 16.8 per cent of the loans are used to purchase foodgrains, cattle feed and for construction of a house; and 10.5 per cent for discharging social obligations like weddings and death ceremony (Singh 2000a). Together, these categories account for 72.24 per cent of all the loans. The remaining 20.4 per cent are used for a variety of non-farm activities like purchase of camel-carts, sewing machines, spray-painting guns, embroidery machines, and tent houses and for setting up vegetable shops or flour mills, seeds and fertilisers consumed 2.6 per cent of the loans, 3.1 per cent of the loans were used for medical purposes, and 1.6 per cent for clearing debts with moneylenders. The recovery rates are high, but the members are already borrowing from other sources to repay the loans taken from the groups (Saxena and Bhadu 2002).

Several issues regarding the SHGs need to be examined. For instance, if the SHGs have taken roots in a village, what is the contribution of micro-financing to reducing poverty in that village as a whole and what role does it play in the village economy? In this scheme of things NGOs are central and occupy the *third space* in the development process. Therefore in the areas where NGOs are absent, can then the massive task of development initiatives be left to SHGs alone? (Shetty 2001)

Conclusions

The avowed objective of the nationalisation of major commercial banks was to make credit easily available to those regions and groups of farmers who had been inadequately served earlier (Singh 1990). But in reality, bank branches opened in areas which already had a well-developed banking infrastructure. This led to a skewed distribution of bank credit between districts. This is a supply-led phenomenon, and adequate adjustment has not been made to the emerging demand for credit, and especially for rural credit from different areas of the state. Besides the coverage of population by banks has deteriorated in Rajasthan, and again, more so in the the rural areas. The deposit mobilisation has improved, especially since the reforms initiated. Rural deposits with commercial banks have gone up too. The credit deployed has also gone up, but the credit-deposit ratios for all types of banks have shown a downward trend. This is not a good sign for Rajasthan's economic development. It could mean that there is enhanced dependence on the informal sector for funds which entails a higher cost of investment. This also has serious implications for the agricultural sector's growth in Rajasthan.

The evidence then suggests need for a shift in the development strategy of the state: the service sector that contributes significantly to the state income needs to be supported. A trade-off may have to be made between promotion of the industrial sector and the service sector. This requires attention. Regional differences in the credit disbursement too require serious consideration, if the backward districts have to be developed. The performance of the cooperative bank sector calls for added attention. The performance of other micro-finance institutions like the SHGs too is not as rosy as it is in South India. One may not worry about the rising indebtedness in rural Rajasthan as long as debt servicing takes place. However, in the face of continuing droughts, the problem can become serious and would affect investment in agriculture. Private capital formation in the state is already going down (Acharya and Singh 1999). Overall, the institutional financial scenario does not present a comfortable state of affairs. It must be understood that banking is sound only if it provides credit for growth, not otherwise. Thus a serious effort has to be made to change the situation lest Rajasthan's economy slides down to a lower growth trajectory.

APPENDIX 1

Districtwise All Scheduled Commercial Banks

(in Rs. lakhs)

Districts	All SCBs						Per Office				Credit Deposit Ratio	
	Number		Deposits		Credit		Deposits		Credit			
	1993	1999	1993	1999	1993	1999	1993	1999	1993	1999	1993	1999
Ajmer	141	152	47907	126076	19144	33728	339.77	829.45	135.77	221.89	39.96	26.75
Alwar	152	165	32015	86129	17525	33815	210.63	521.99	115.30	204.94	54.74	39.26
Banswara	86	88	13512	39718	6333	10891	157.12	451.34	73.64	123.76	46.87	27.42
Barmer	78	74	9285	24644	3354	6472	119.04	333.03	00.43	87.46	36.12	26.26
Bharatpur	109	111	17991	48255	14574	22072	165.06	434.73	133.71	198.85	81.01	45.74
Bhilwara	113	120	19431	53706	19312	61004	171.96	447.55	170.90	508.37	99.39	113.59
Bikaner	123	132	28157	77552	11264	23243	228.92	587.52	91.58	176.08	00.40	29.97
Bundi	68	66	7813	19534	6631	10789	114.9	295.97	97.51	163.47	84.87	55.23
Chittorgarh	104	112	18467	53801	8073	18916	177.57	480.37	77.63	168.89	43.72	35.16
Churu	112	116	20477	52476	6038	13663	182.83	452.38	53.91	117.78	29.49	26.04
Dholpur	36	38	5032	14137	2853	5931	139.78	372.03	79.25	156.08	56.70	41.95
Dungarpur	62	63	11337	33005	2824	5802	182.85	523.89	45.55	92.10	24.91	17.58
Ganganagar	202	222	43518	112103	31546	57941	215.44	504.97	156.17	261.00	72.49	51.69
Jaipur	303	373	175287	499790	108767	328530	578.50	1337.24	358.97	880.78	62.05	65.87
Jaisalmer	35	38	3650	11438	1242	3012	104.29	301	35.49	79.26	34.03	26.33
Jalore	67	66	6768	20730	1939	5330	101.01	314.09	28.94	80.76	28.65	25.71
Jhalawar	80	70	6015	17052	4684	8297	75.19	243.60	58.55	118.53	77.87	48.66
Jhunjhunu	87	91	23153	61912	7434	13781	266.13	680.35	85.45	151.44	32.11	22.26

(contd.)

Appendix 1 (contd.)

Districts	*All SCBs*						*Per Office*				*Credit Deposit Ratio*	
	Number		*Deposits*		*Credit*		*Deposits*		*Credit*			
	1993	*1999*	*1993*	*1999*	*1993*	*1999*	*1993*	*1999*	*1993*	*1999*	*1993*	*1999*
Jodhpur	145	157	51067	170094	21478	51950	352.19	1083.40	148.12	330.89	42.06	30.54
Kota	113	122	35695	92862	25949	45769	315.88	761.16	229.64	375.16	72.70	49.29
Nagaur	130	131	18948	48864	6387	12306	145.75	373.01	49.13	93.94	33.71	25.18
Pali	110	115	18685	50910	6409	15696	169.86	442.7	58.26	136.49	34.30	30.83
S.Madhopur	112	69	16830	42436	9057	18043	150.27	615.01	80.87	261.49	53.81	42.52
Sikar	102	111	24014	67008	7949	14442	235.43	424.10	77.93	91.41	33.10	21.55
Sirohi	54	59	11326	34676	3311	9826	209.74	587.73	61.31	166.54	29.23	28.34
Tonk	68	69	8203	23546	4799	9354	120.63	341.25	70.57	135.57	58.50	39.73
Udaipur	151	158	46015	104596	26096	51437	304.74	662	172.82	325.55	56.71	49.18
Baran	62	61	6184	13256	5508	10299	99.74	299.28	88.84	168.84	89.07	56.41
Dausa	48	58	6817	23375	2772	7342	142.02	403.02	57.75	126.59	40.66	31.41
Rajsamand	55	59	10527	37022	2896	9023	191.40	627.49	52.65	152.93	27.51	24.37

APPENDIX 2

Public Sector Commercial Banks—Districtwise

(in Rs. lakhs)

Districts	Public Sector CBs						Per Office				Credit Deposit Ratio	
	Number		Deposits		Credit		Deposits		Credit			
	1993	1999	1993	1999	1993	1999	1993	1999	1993	1999	1993	1999
Ajmer	104	114	42864	116581	17336	29023	412.15	1022.64	166.69	254.59	40.44	24.90
Alwar	100	113	28843	75397	16147	30603	288.43	667.23	161.47	270.82	55.98	40.59
Banswara	49	51	11395	32986	5447	8876	232.55	646.78	111.16	174.04	47.8	26.91
Barmer	44	42	7852	20660	2781	5082	178.45	491.09	63.20	1.21	35.42	24.60
Bharatpur	75	77	16038	41466	13804	20265	213.84	538.52	184.05	263.18	86.07	48.87
Bhilwara	65	69	15124	39894	15789	47469	232.68	578.17	242.91	687.96	104.40	118.99
Bikaner	89	97	25575	67725	10665	20607	287.36	698.20	119.83	212.44	41.70	30.43
Bunḍi	26	27	5567	12927	5623	7371	214.12	478.78	216.27	2.73	101.01	57.02
Chittorgarh	61	66	14984	43435	6687	15168	245.64	658.11	109.62	229.82	44.63	34.92
Churu	50	53	18635	45219	5312	11142	372.07	853.19	106.24	210.23	28.51	24.64
Dholpur	22	24	4720	12974	2576	5330	214.55	540.58	117.09	222.08	54.58	41.08
Dungarpur	36	37	9956	27327	2360	4343	276.56	738.57	65.56	117.38	23.7	15.89
Ganganagar	145	162	38557	91856	29378	50216	265.91	567.01	202.61	309.98	76.19	54.67
Jaipur	204	255	150739	390139	93179	267091	738.92	1529.96	456.76	1047.42	61.81	68.46
Jaisalmer	20	22	2838	8994	895	2168	141.09	408.82	44.75	98.55	31.54	24.10
Jalore	25	25	4579	12592	1357	2633	183.16	503.68	54.28	105.32	29.64	20.91
Jhalawar	35	35	4160	11031	3919	6003	118.86	315.17	111.97	171.51	94.21	54.42

(contd.)

Appendix 2 (contd.)

Districts	Public Sector CBs						Per Office				Credit Deposit Ratio	
	Number		Deposits		Credit		Deposits		Credit			
	1993	1999	1993	1999	1993	1999	1993	1999	1993	1999	1993	1999
Jhunjhunu	35	40	19310	50158	5280	9001	536.39	1253.95	146.67	225.03	27.34	17.95
Jodhpur	112	121	47472	128394	19723	46818	423.86	1061.11	176.10	386.93	41.55	36.46
Kota	65	73	28647	68811	23176	38783	440.72	942.62	356.55	531.27	80.90	56.36
Nagaur	66	67	15537	38972	5277	9395	235.41	581.67	79.95	140.22	33.96	24.11
Pali	36	37	12308	27558	4882	8935	341.89	744.81	135.61	241.49	39.67	32.42
S.Madhopur	71	76	14469	33826	7786	15143	203.79	445.08	109.66	199.51	53.81	44.83
Sikar	48	56	20308	55720	5690	10197	423.08	9.95	118.54	182.09	28.02	18.30
Sirohi	25	29	9417	27412	2811	7119	376.68	945.24	112.44	245.48	29.85	25.97
Tonk	35	36	6493	17986	4154	7068	185.51	499.61	118.69	196.33	63.98	39.30
Udaipur	85	91	36598	103814	23341	43331	430.56	1140.81	274.06	476.16	63.78	41.74
Baran	29	32	4631	12548	4644	7995	159.69	392.13	160.14	249.84	100.28	63.72
Dausa	32	40	5736	19235	2452	6290	179.25	480.88	76.63	157.25	42.75	32.70
Rajsamand	23	26	7985	22635	2143	7086	347.17	870.58	93.17	272.54	26.84	31.31

APPENDIX 3

Regional Rural Banks—Districtwise

(in Rs. lakhs)

Districts	*Regional Rural Banks*						*Per Office*				*Credit Deposit Ratio*	
	Number		*Deposits*		*Credit*		*Deposits*		*Credit*			
	1993	*1999*	*1993*	*1999*	*1993*	*1999*	*1993*	*1999*	*1993*	*1999*	*1993*	*1999*
Ajmer	20	20	754	3071	603	1953	37.70	153.55	30.15	97.65	79.97	63.59
Alwar	46	46	1866	7061	956	2453	40.57	153.50	20.78	53.33	51.23	34.74
Banswara	23	23	343	2054	394	1052	14.91	89.30	17.13	45.74	114.87	51.22
Barmer	32	30	642	2191	329	697	20.06	73.03	10.28	23.23	51.25	31.81
Bharatpur	30	30	1027	4127	569	1799	34.23	137.57	18.97	59.97	55.40	43.59
Bhilwara	33	34	1591	5756	1031	3246	48.21	169.29	31.24	95.47	64.80	56.39
Bikaner	28	28	443	2184	225	1245	15.82	00.78	8.04	44.46	50.79	57.01
Bundi	36	33	999	3911	581	2784	27.75	118.52	16.14	84.36	58.16	71.18
Chittorgarh	34	36	1207	4605	675	2793	35.5	127.92	19.85	77.58	55.92	60.65
Churu	60	61	1549	6413	634	2305	25.82	105.13	10.57	37.79	40.93	35.94
Dholpur	14	14	312	1163	277	601	22.29	83.07	19.79	42.93	88.78	51.68
Dungarpur	22	22	506	3195	336	1176	00.23	145.23	15.27	53.45	66.40	36.81
Ganganagar	44	44	1278	5490	743	2956	29.05	124.77	16.89	67.18	58.14	53.84
Jaipur	72	72	4364	16565	1025	3205	60.61	230.77	14.24	44.51	23.49	19.35
Jaisalmer	14	15	353	1393	222	592	25.21	92.87	15.86	39.47	62.89	42.05
Jalore	41	40	1904	7587	497	2595	46.44	189.68	12.12	64.88	26.10	34.20
Jhalawar	40	31	846	3506	475	1719	21.15	113.10	11.88	55.45	56.15	49.03

(contd.)

Appendix 3 (contd.)

Districts	*Regional Rural Banks*						*Per Office*				*Credit Deposit Ratio*	
	Number		*Deposits*		*Credit*		*Deposits*		*Credit*			
	1993	*1999*	*1993*	*1999*	*1993*	*1999*	*1993*	*1999*	*1993*	*1999*	*1993*	*1999*
Jhunjhunu	48	48	3020	9450	1950	4078	62.92	196.88	40.63	84.96	64.57	43.15
Jodhpur	25	26	548	2519	399	1271	21.92	96.88	15.96	48.88	72.81	50.46
Kota	37	36	1669	7965	635	3274	45.11	221.25	17.16	90.94	38.05	41.10
Nagaur	58	58	2196	6848	785	2403	37.86	118.07	13.53	41.43	35.75	35.09
Pali	68	72	4622	18994	1018	5332	67.97	263.81	14.97	74.06	22.03	28.07
S.Madhopur	34	33	1006	4668	682	2014	29.59	141.45	20.06	61.03	67.79	43.14
Sikar	52	53	3074	9757	1955	3824	59.12	184.09	37.60	72.15	63.60	39.19
Sirohi	27	27	1253	5468	291	1839	46.41	202.52	10.78	68.11	23.22	33.63
Tonk	30	30	1135	3909	406	1904	37.83	130.30	13.53	63.47	35.77	48.71
Udaipur	41	40	1257	7210	548	1851	30.66	180.25	13.37	46.28	43.60	25.67
Baran	31	27	902	3760	603	1839	29.10	139.26	19.45	68.11	66.85	48.91
Dausa	13	15	853	3570	197	805	65.62	2.38	15.15	53.67	23.09	22.55
Rajsamand	20	21	495	3277	232	1094	24.75	156.05	11.60	52.10	46.87	33.38

APPENDIX 4

Infrastructure Index and Credit to Agriculture and Industry

Districts	*Index*	*Per Capita Credit*							
		1980	*1985*	*1990*	*1995*	*1980*	*1985*	*1990*	*1995*
Ajmer	90.89	28	89	178	252	109	210	285	420
Aiwar	92.50	53	118	263	308	46	255	497	683
Banswara	84.86	15		89	131	23		217	386
Barmer	75.47	5		61	91	10		81	88
Bharatpur	91.63	49		355	557	43		242	250
Bhilwara	101.11	36		173	295	94		622	984
Bikaner	92.11	40		270	239	53		150	167
Bundi	107.96	62		360	632	22		84	122
Chittorgarh	99.23	25		184	272	10		63	116
Churu	71.13	15		165	171	12		38	52
Dungarpur	85.35	8	28	93	2	22	35	103	
Ganganagar	95.29	130	309	463	662	21	49	80	145
Jaipur	94.45	50	108	196	263	169	291	601	1232
Jaisalmer	73.60	8	25	84	139	1	11	32	41
Jalore	91.83	22	144	149	115	1	22	22	19
Jhalawar	87.90	12	29	113	223	29	66	76	179
Jhunjhunu	82.73	30	67	116	181	88	88	90	70
Jodhpur	79.56	17	45	98	123	78	177	362	535
Kota	98.23	32	150	275	453	160	378	630	1096
Nagaur	78.74	29	106	174	133	6	34	56	88
Pali	91.74	31	139	175	127	42	115	196	251
S.Madhopur	77.14	14	49	176	373	56	11	53	47
Sikar	84.47	23	68	114	166	4	23	59	85
Sirohi	105.55	25	89	136	110	6	124	282	421
Tonk	86.59	17	45	148	316	6	31	43	48
Udaipur	90.63	15	44	94	90	118	199	306	709
Rajasmand	87.27	35	101	191	260	62	133	249	423

Source: CMIE 2000.

APPENDIX 5

District Level Co-operative Movement in Rajasthan

(in Rs.crores)

District	*No. of Societies*		*Membership*		*Share Capital*		*Working Capital*	
	1994-95	*1998-99*	*1994-95*	*1998-99*	*1994-95*	*1998-99*	*1994-95*	*1998-99*
Ajmer	1011	991	337506	357696	10.12	12.37	93.47	137.14
Alwar	1276	1167	365635	378592	13.63	16.30	118.14	132.02
Banswara	339	356	204549	211863	5.12	6.46	40.62	50.52
Barmer	525	518	228348	258330	10.73	13.46	87.80	98.93
Bharatpur	871	812	256423	268141	12.95	12.32	91.02	106.06
Bhilwara	773	815	314501	335596	10.51	14.28	132.63	138.77
Bikaner	1072	1068	264681	302845	9.74	12.61	67.89	121.75
Bundi	310	346	135423	152170	13.77	15.26	62.35	74.60
Chittorgarh	712	729	290661	311687	10.48	14.08	100.35	103.60
Churu	746	728	244440	259642	7.51	8.43	51.30	68.87
Dholpur	294	280	97138	100169	1.81	3.35	12.91	25.54
Dungarpur	297	287	171503	184956	3.53	4.68	31.50	31.35
Ganganagar	1241	1305	539791	689216	30.86	35.37	257.91	235.67
Jaipur	2420	2408	750322	787550	19.52	31.42	326.43	481.49
Jaisalmer	262	261	56608	57338	3.15	2.10	27.61	17.22
Jalore	493	499	250454	269157	8.68	12.98	92.57	122.77
Jhalawar	357	342	198028	205543	7.08	11.66	90.62	110.60
Jhunjhunu	484	465	315318	348002	8.02	11.36	80.10	84.47
Jodhpur	1268	1318	343878	362592	12.47	17.40	112.72	168.98
Kota	479	506	227016	254012	18.04	22.27	164.06	195.43
Nagaur	757	668	313381	333973	10.45	13.23	77.13	106.92
Pali	841	788	300484	317582	11.73	14.42	123.11	132.74
S.Madhopur	649	631	281127	291031	11.29	15.64	94.54	120.01
Sikar	557	451	338817	352471	11.45	13.11	100.99	108.60
Sirohi	198	183	124465	139368	4.60	7.93	53.01	99.32
Tonk	432	409	191742	201386	7.28	9.94	59.93	74.53
Udaipur	619	605	323465	388348	10.61	13.93	121.58	194.73
Baran	316	301	174542	191850	5.07	9.59	43.54	97.37
Dausa	330	317	119026	126653	1.94	3.49	10.90	23.29
Rajsamand	255	256	114167	123378	2.53	3.97	16.68	41.02

Source: Government of Rajasthan, various years.

APPENDIX 6

District Level Co-operative Movement in Rajasthan

(Rs. crore)

District	*Loans*						*Recovery as % of*			
	Advanced		*Recovered*		*Outstanding*		*Advance*		*Outstanding*	
	94-95	*98-99*	*94-95*	*98-99*	*94-95*	*98-99*	*94-95*	*98-99*	*94-95*	*98-99*
Ajmer	44.01	66.64	47.78	45.45	52.55	80.43	108.58	68.20	90.93	56.51
Alwar	77.79	52.52	00.64	42.27	80.23	74.16	82.27	80.48	79.77	00.57
Banswara	15.82	19.65	16.57	15.90	18.73	25.96	104.73	80.92	88.44	61.25
Barmer	36.72	45.72	00.38	35.77	40.76	58.73	103.50	78.24	93.23	60.91
Bharatpur	42.71	37.11	29.71	25.64	48.06	63.78	69.56	69.09	61.13	40.02
Bhilwara	16.27	42.96	82.10	31.68	74.42	77.59	70.61	73.74	110.32	40.83
Bikaner	22.96	39.91	20.40	28.47	32.35	58.33	88.82	71.34	63.05	48.81
Bundi	35.44	21.40	27.11	14.92	30.50	40.04	76.49	69.72	88.87	37.26
Chittorgarh	51.03	44.19	55.71	34.52	51.62	63.89	109.18	78.12	107.93	54.03
Churu	22.75	27.55	23.09	19.33	27.27	41.73	105.05	70.16	87.65	46.32
Dholpur	4.54	10.48	3.39	7.27	8.88	18.48	74.80	69.37	38.22	39.34
Dungarpur	12.09	9.57	19.01	6.69	12.52	18.23	157.23	69.91	151.87	36.70
Ganganagar	160.03	140.65	156.46	115.28	124.98	132.53	97.60	81.96	125.19	86.98
Jaipur	53.25	132.06	58.78	78.58	89.93	175.44	110.39	59.50	65.37	44.79
Jaisalmer	9.09	2.62	7.77	2.32	15.58	7.03	85.50	88.55	49.87	00.33
Jalore	37.77	95.34	29.86	83.33	50.74	71.53	79.05	87.40	58.84	116.50
Jhalawar	51.11	58.71	51.42	48.55	56.62	73.53	100.61	82.69	90.82	66.03
Jhunjhunu	28.60	33.14	28.92	25.08	53.86	58.89	101.12	75.68	53.69	42.59
Jodhpur	49.69	89.05	63.11	61.99	47.64	93.46	127.01	69.61	132.49	66.33
Kota	62.09	54.88	66.92	32.62	85.67	103.79	107.77	59.44	78.11	31.43
Nagaur	44.62	47.14	38.23	00.34	48.56	72.04	85.68	72.13	78.74	47.20
Pali	49.47	45.64	44.77	41.54	54.99	63.16	90.51	91.02	81.43	65.77
S.Madhopur	34.63	56.66	33.43	29.03	59.72	83.21	96.53	51.24	55.98	34.89
Sikar	37.32	64.50	33.05	49.55	63.71	75.52	89.77	76.82	52.58	65.61
Sirohi	25.75	41.71	19.65	35.90	30.97	56.22	76.32	86.07	63.47	63.86
Tonk	22.20	27.74	27.74	22.78	37.21	48.41	124.96	82.12	74.53	47.06
Udaipur	128.20	243.62	124.08	230.42	61.80	101.34	96.79	94.58	200.79	227.37
Baran	30.74	77.26	28.49	65.97	25.95	57.21	92.68	85.39	109.80	115.31
Dausa	3.53	12.16	3.26	7.54	5.58	13.10	92.35	62.01	58.46	57.56
Rajsamand	6.72	17.69	5.64	14.28	8.99	19.51	83.92	80.72	62.75	73.19

APPENDIX 7

Co-operative Societies

Districts	Central Non-Credit Societies				Agricultural Credit Societies				Non-Agricultural Credit Societies				Non-Agricultural Non-Credit Societies			
	Number		Member*		Number		Member*		Number		Member*		Number		Member*	
	94-5	98-9	94-5	98-9	94-5	98-9	94-5	98-9	94-5	98-9	94-5	98-9	94-5	98-9	94-5	98-9
Ajmer	3	4	188	209	158	150	1666	1765	111	108	51824	58639	643	683	675	970
Alwar	2	4	22	43	309	293	2270	2302	20	23	6460	8039	693	618	761	1198
Banswara	2	3	21	30	88	88	1559	1593	8	7	1594	1678	225	240	225	444
Barmer	1	3	17	29	224	224	1881	2094	5	5	3935	4413	288	277	183	401
Bharatpur	2	6	46	62	265	254	1803	1848	64	57	3736	1826	452	365	287	594
Bhilwara	2	3	58	72	204	200	2137	2146	26	29	10684	15919	476	548	443	860
Bikaner	2	3	136	199	166	171	1341	1580	16	17	22725	23982	772	709	652	659
Bundi		1		2	122	121	927	967	12	12	4645	6149	160	150	259	313
Chittorgarh	1	2	41	49	202	199	1845	1952	14	13	3326	3314	450	356	423	775
Churu	2	3	68	76	176	176	1907	2022	29	29	4099	4958	488	504	271	404
Dholpur	1	2	7	9	92	90	527	510	8	4	1955	2248	156	153	68	429
Dungarpur	1	2	11	17	51	51	1374	1438	20	20	1145	1225	216	207	88	367
Ganganagar	3	5	182	235	485	486	3817	5105	25	28	16881	18901	711	530	987	640
Jaipur	3	11	29	37	279	268	2758	3028	157	174	76879	113042	1759	1742	2663	3117
Jaisalmer	1	2	28	30	80	84	455	462	1	1	30	30	123	141	63	63
Jalore	2	3	7	8	157	156	1568	1641	4	5	2500	5003	267	190	361	709
Jhalawar	1	2	13	20	151	150	1298	1279	20	21	2445	3390	135	91	177	560

(contd.)

Appendix 7 (contd.)

Districts	*Central Non-Credit Societies*				*Agricultural Credit Societies*				*Non-Agricultural Credit Societies*				*Non-Agricultural Non-Credit Societies*			
	Number		*Member**		*Number*		*Member**		*Number*		*Member**		*Number*		*Member**	
	94-5	*98-9*	*94-5*	*98-9*	*94-5*	*98-9*	*94-5*	*98-9*	*94-5*	*98-9*	*94-5*	*98-9*	*94-5*	*98-9*	*94-5*	*98-9*
Jhunjhunu	1	2	50	56	161	161	2199	2366	8	8	1944	2299	215	148	336	868
Jodhpur	2	2	93	7	209	208	2005	2040	44	43	23357	21386	947	1031	909	1238
Kota	2	3	29	41	137	132	1009	1063	46	48	48197	61282	276	253	471	581
Nagaur	1	2	30	31	286	281	2496	2580	15	13	3053	3501	395	256	267	523
Pali	1	3	3	47	217	213	2072	2277	20	19	8217	9779	538	468	620	649
S.Madhopur	2	3	5	11	245	242	1746	1753	14	14	2696	3065	304	245	310	764
Sikar	2	3	81	116	171	171	2588	2716	10	6	5085	5456	289	229	230	581
Sirohi	1	2	28	31	63	63	751	805	11	12	11989	14488	110	97	75	387
Tonk		1		4	165	155	1351	1351	12	12	767	1135	206	213	159	432
Udaipur	2	3	144	242	123	123	1862	2120	54	52	19391	22818	400	433	442	999
Baran	1	1	10	15	145	145	1251	1361	15	10	7300	10728	139	74	185	288
Dausa					107	104	1025	1057	4	5	262	2061	170	174	153	144
Rajsamand	1	1	25	28	81	81	913	954	10	11	3320	5517	146	133	158	153

Note: * - in 00'.

Co-operative Societies

Appendix 9.7: (Contd.)

Districts	*Societies Under Liquidation*				*All Societies*				*% of Liquidation Societies under Liquidation*	
	Number		*Member*		*Number*		*Member*			
	94-5	*98-9*	*94-5*	*98-9*	*94-5*	*98-9*	*94-5*	*98-9*	*94-5*	*98-9*
Ajmer	93	33	3378	1448	1008	991	308144	357696	9.23	3.33
Alwar	250	168	7021	5778	1274	1167	318881	378592	19.62	14.40
Banswara	14	6	998	300	337	356	183172	211863	4.15	1.69
Barmer	5	3	107	60	523	518	212059	258330	0.96	0.58
Bharatpur	86	61	1905	6557	869	812	219299	268141	9.90	7.51
Bhilwara	63	12	2807	2659	771	815	277250	335596	8.17	1.47
Bikaner	114	89	20415	19577	1070	1068	256055	302845	10.65	8.33
Bundi	14	11		1678	308	346	123246	152170	4.55	3.18
Chittorgarh	42	21	4880	3102	709	729	239067	311687	5.92	2.88
Churu	49	12	2880	1354	744	728	231514	259642	6.59	1.65
Dholpur	36	16	1615	565	293	280	63703	100169	12.29	5.71
Dungarpur	7	1	92	18	295	287	148514	184956	2.37	0.35
Ganganagar	13	8	1314	1205	1237	1305	516707	539445	1.05	0.61
Jaipur	220	179	69438	45824	2418	2408	691424	140065	9.10	7.43
Jaisalmer	56	29	1035	420	261	261	55602	787550	21.46	11.11
Jalore	61	25	738	323	491	499	196827	57338	12.42	5.01
Jhalawar	48	39	5903	5421	355	342	157058	269157	13.52	11.40
Jhunjhunu	97	69	1226	747	482	465	261649	205543	20.12	14.84
Jodhpur	63	17	1890	678	1265	1318	325994	348002	4.98	1.29
Kota	16	5		982	477	506	199105	362592	3.35	0.99
Nagaur	58	11		300	755	668	282266	254012	7.68	1.65
Pali	63	38		438	839	788	277624	333973	7.51	4.82
S.Madhopur	81	47	2495	1477	646	631	211318	590731	12.54	7.45
Sikar	83	38	2585	1837	555	451	297616	130966	14.95	8.43
Sirohi	11	2	270	332	196	183	97783	352471	5.61	1.09
Tonk	47	21	4975	16386	430	409	156724	139368	10.93	5.13
Udaipur	38	27	1955	1780	617	655	266106	201386	6.16	4.12
Baran	15	7	398	216	315	301	152250	388348	4.76	2.33
Dausa	49	22	922	1816	330	317	119026	191850	14.85	6.94
Rajsamand	17	15	1295	1118	255	256	114167	126653	6.67	5.86

REFERENCES

Acharya, S.S., and Singh, Surjit (1999): *Economic Performance of Rajasthan*. Background paper prepared for the World Bank.

ACRC (1989): *A Review of the Agricultural Credit System in India*. Report of the Agricultural Credit Review Committee, Reserve Bank of India, Mumbai.

Centre for Monitoring Indian Economy (CMIE) (1999): *Money and Banking*. Bombay, October.

CMIE (2000): Profiles of Districts. Bombay, October.

CMIE (2002): *Money and Banking*. Bombay, September.

Government of Rajasthan. *Statistical Abstract*. Various years.

Gulati, Ashok, and Bathla, Seema (2002): *Institutional Credit to Indian Agriculture: Defaults and Policy Options*. Occasional Papers 23. Mumbai: NABARD.

Puhazhendhi, V. and Jayaraman, B. (1995): "Rural Credit Delivery: Performance and Challenges before Banks". *Economic and Political Weekly* (January 16-23).

Reserve Bank of India (2001): *Reserve Bank of India Bulletin*.

Saxena, R.K., and Bhadu, Rajaram (2002): *Self-Help Groups: Vision, Role and Ideology*. Report of the seminar organised by IDS, Jaipur, SVS, Jaipur and CASA, Delhi.

Shetty, S.L. (2001): "Rapporteur's Report on Working and Impact of Rural Self-help Groups and Other Forms of Microfinancing". *Indian Journal of Agricultural Economics* 56(3):580-604.

Singh, Surjit (ed.) (1991): *Rural Credit: Issues for the Nineties*. New Delhi: Oxford & IBH.

Singh, Surjit (1996): "Rural Social Transformation in India: Some Thoughts" *Anvesak* (January- June).

Singh, Surjit (1998): *Institutional Finance to the Rural Sector: Reforms, Trends and Issues*. Mumbai: Bank of India.

Singh, Surjit (1999a): *Financial Sector Reforms in India: Are They Moving*. Paper presented in the Twelfth World Congress of International Economic Association, August 23-30, 1999, at Buenos Aires.

Singh, Surjit, (1999b): *Institutional Credit in Rural Rajasthan: Grassroots Level Experiences*. Mumbai: Bank of India.

Singh, Surjit (2002): *Impact of Rural Infrastructure Development on Poverty Reduction with Special Reference to Roads and Bridges*. A project report prepared for NABARD, Mumbai.

Singh, Surjit, and Sagar, Vidya (2003): *Agriculture Credit in India*. A draft report submitted to Ministry of Agriculture, Government of India.

PART III

SOCIAL SECTORS

10

Expenditure Allocation and Welfare Returns to Government Efforts

A Suggested Model and its Application

ARCHANA R. DHOLAKIA and RAVINDRA H. DHOLAKIA

Government expenditure is a relatively less researched field than taxation. Most of the studies in this field concentrate on post-hoc evaluation or expenditure incidence or aggregate impact on the economy (see Aaron and McGuire 1970; Musgrave *et al.* 1974; Wulf 1975 and 1981; A. Dholakia 1993; Fan *et al.* 2000, etc). Allocation of government expenditure among the different sectors is generally considered to reflect the political priorities and hence to emanate from the political process. Those familiar with the budget-making exercise in the government usually argue that spending proposals are first invited from different departments under various heads and then are aggregated and pruned by the finance department to ultimately emerge with the budget allocations. Thus, the practice apparently supports the view that budget allocations are exclusively the result of a political process. However, when the finance department "prunes" the expenditure proposals from different departments, other considerations and factors do come into play. The political party in power does take a position on the development strategy and determines the expenditure priorities in the budget. Thus, the budget allocations do not reflect only the shopping list approach, but also do show the finance ministers and the Cabinet's perceptions about the efficiency and efficacy of different expenditures in terms of the ultimate objective of the government. However, very few studies have attempted to answer the practical question such as: How much should a government allocate to different sectors? (See, Mishra, 1982; A. Dholakia 1993; Fan *et al.* 2000).

Mishra (1982) attempted to derive the budget allocation in nominal terms by estimating a simultaneous equation model through the 2 Stage Least Squares (2SLS) method. He considered different annual government expenditures as the dependent variables and various socio-economic-demographic indicators as the independent variables in the model to obtain the allocation of expenditures based on the targeted values of the indicators. It was more of a statistical approach to the problem than any economic theory-based model. As a result, the postulated relationship as well as the measurement of variables could hardly be logically convincing. On the other hand, A. Dholakia (1993) and Fan *et al.* (2000) have the simultaneous equations models to examine the impact of the government expenditures on the specified target variables. Only the direction of the changes in the expenditure allocation can be obtained indirectly from their models once the desired targets are considered. However, the model of Fan *et al.* (2000) is not entirely based on economic logic and has clear elements of a statistical approach. It considers both the target variables and various government expenditures as the endogenous variables in the model. As a result, the allocation of government expenditures among sectors cannot be addressed seriously. Yet the authors have still recommended the direction of changes in the expenditure allocation based on the magnitude of marginal impacts (returns) of different expenditures. Archana Dholakia's (1993) model based entirely on the economic logic is capable of being extended to consider the question of changes in the budget allocation by considering the nature of returns to the government effort in different directions. It can also provide interesting insights which may contradict the conventional recommendation of changes in budget allocations based on the magnitude of the marginal returns (impacts) of different expenditures.

In this paper, we attempt to extend Archana Dholakia's (1993) basic model to consider budget allocations explicitly and illustrate its application by considering the case of Indian states over the period 1971-91. In Section I, we discuss the model in detail and in Section II we consider the measurement of independent variables as implied by the model. Section III discusses measurement of basic welfare as the dependent variable in our model. The illustrative econometric exercise with the data on 14 major Indian, states over the period 1971-91 implied by the model is carried out and the results thereof are discussed in Section IV. Section V, presents the summary and conclusion.

THE MODEL

In order to examine the question of budget allocation among the different sectors, we have to consider the objective of the government in preparing the budget. A list of the basic objectives and targets to be achieved is quite often explicitly spelt out in the beginning of the Finance Minister's budget speech. We may compress the entire list into one broadly defined objective of the government to focus on the essential elements involved in the budget allocation among sectors. This would require either carefully worked out trade-off weights among the competing objectives, if any, or appropriate measurement of the broadly defined objective to take care of various specific concerns of the government. Such a simplification is more realistically applicable in the case of state governments than the central government. Under the Indian Constitution, states are given the principal responsibility to look after various welfare dimensions of the population like education, health, sanitation, nutrition, crime, family welfare–particularly child and women welfare, etc. Thus, states' objectives are more likely to focus around ensuring basic welfare and improving the quality of life of the population.

In order to translate such a broad objective into implementable targets and relate them to government schemes and projects representing the government efforts, it is necessary to distinguish between the general welfare and the basic welfare of the population (see A. Dholakia 1990 and 1993). It is the basic welfare that is the target of the government efforts particularly at the state level, and not the "Total Welfare" or "Maximum Achievable Welfare" in the economy. The latter concepts is somewhat vague and its measurement in varied types of economies has given rise to a lot of controversy. (See Chaudhary 1978; A. Dholakia 1990). Economists are almost unanimous on the point that the concept of welfare has different connotations in regard to time, place and people whose welfare we want to measure, hence a unique measure of welfare cannot be designed. (See Gothaskar 1978; A. Dholakia, 1990). We would, therefore, like to follow an approach that can measure the basic minimum welfare in non-monetary terms and that might be considered more appropriate for capturing the welfare achievements of the LDCs, where the primary objectives of the government are: (i) alleviation of mass poverty, and (ii) meeting the basic needs of the populace in terms of primary education, health, drinking water, etc. To develop a framework for this purpose the whole economy is divided into two groups of individuals: the poor (A) and the non-poor (B). Similarly, all commodities are divided into two groups: the basic commodity (X) and the non-basic commodity (Y). Moreover, we assume a well-defined and well-behaved social welfare function (W) with a lexicographic preference of the government for the poor. It is shown earlier (See A. Dholakia 1990; 1993) that under such conditions, changes in the basic welfare (dW) and changes in the consumption of basic commodities (dX) are directly and proportionately related. Thus, whatever would measure dX would also measure dW'. In order to ensure this, we have to define the basic commodity X, as the ones (i) directly affected by the government expenditure, and (ii) with *marginal utility* higher for the poor and lower (almost zero) for the rich. (A. Dholakia ibid.). As discussed later, the basic commodity X can be decomposed broadly into three components, viz. Health, Education and Nutrition and others.

The next step is to consider the determinants of the production of the basic commodity X. It is clear that the level of X at a given point of time (t) depends on the cumulative efforts put in by the government in the past up to t, geo-physical environment, socio-cultural, demographic and attitudinal factors. This is because the three aspects included in our definition of X (health, education, nutrition and others) are largely the matters of social consumption affected by government efforts besides various other factors mentioned above. The latter category of factors primarily determines the level of the relationship between the stock of government effort and the quantity of basic commodity X. We might say that factors like physical – locational and socio-cultural environment—define the nature and level of technology, while government efforts can be considered as equivalent to inputs for the production function of the basic commodity X. Thus, the postulated functional relationship is:

$$X_t = F(G_{1t}, G_{2t}, Z_{1t}, Z_{2t}, \ldots\ldots\ldots Z_{nt}) \ldots\ldots\ldots\ldots\ldots (1)$$

where X_t is the level of basic commodity X at time t; G_{1t} and G_{2t} are the cumulative stock of government effort up to time t in direction 1 and 2 respectively; and Z_{1t}, Z_{2t}, ... Z_{nt} are various geographic-locational, physical environmental and socio-cultural-attitudinal factors at time t which are treated as exogenous factors here. Holding all these exogenous factors constant, we get the following simple production function in the basic welfare level (X) and government efforts in different directions (G_1 and G_2) :

$$X = f(G_1, G_2) \ldots\ldots\ldots\ldots\ldots\ldots\ldots (2)$$

At any given point of time on the above function, the values would exactly correspond. In other words, if we consider Diagram 1 on the $G_2O\,G_1$ plane the situation at any given point of time would be represented by a point like A. Since the point A is lying within the positive quadrant of $G_2O\,G_1$ plane, it must necessarily lie on some insoquant like X_o. The planner would face a target to achieve a higher level of basic welfare like X_1 over a given period of time.*[1] The basic question is how to achieve X_1 with the help of G_1 and G_2. That G_1 and/or G_2 have to be increased is well recognised. Various options to achieve X_1 if we are on the initial point like A are given by different combinations of increases in G_1 and G_2 from their respective initial values of G_1 and G_2 at A. Usually cumulative government effort from its existing level would not absolutely decline over a period of time, given the way we have defined the term. Thus the range of choice is given by the arc DBC where AC is a vertical line and AD the horizontal line through the point A intersecting the new insoquant X_1*[2] in point C and Point D respectively.

The whole issue about choosing different expenditures could then be considered with a specific reference to the point B, which is taken to represent the continuation of past trends. Thus, it is assumed that the present rate of annual government expenditures in the two directions given by G1 and G2 are remaining the same at point B. Any point on the arc BD would represent higher annual government expenditure in the Direction 1 and lower annual expenditure in the direction 2 as compared to the present level. Similarly, any point on the arc BC would represent higher expenditure in the direction 2 and lower expenditure in the direction 1 as compared to the present level.*3

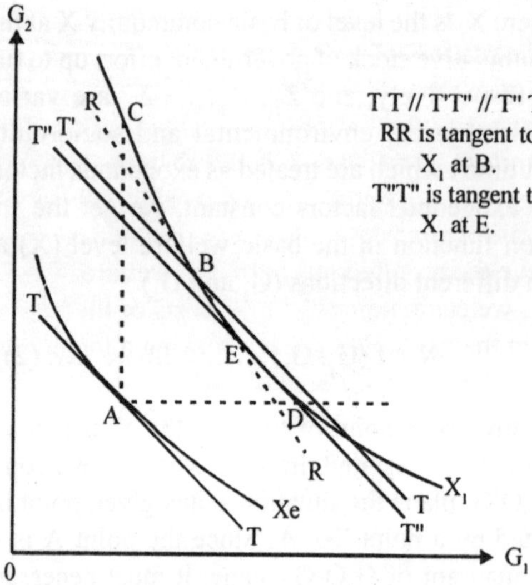

Diagram 1 (a)

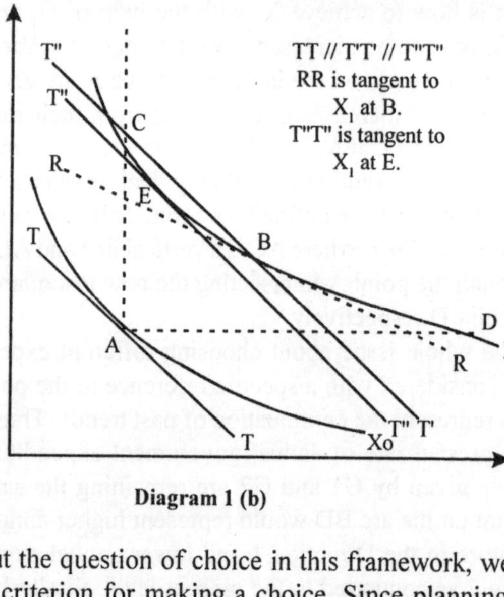

Diagram 1 (b)

Having put the question of choice in this framework, we need to consider the criterion for making a choice. Since planning is by definition an activity involving optimization, it would not be unjustified to assume that the planner would like to avoid all the excess costs which are unintentional in nature.

The concept of excess cost may be thought of as closely akin to the one of excess burden of taxation. The excess cost on the society or the economic system are avoided if the basic relative marginal costs of government efforts are left unaltered by the planned action to achieve the targeted basic welfare level (X_1). This would also imply minimization of social costs at base period (constant) shadow prices to achieve the required level of basic welfare. Considering the initial point A, we can obtain the social costs of the government efforts G_1 and G_2 in the two directions by drawing a tangent to the isoquant X_o at point A. The slope of this tangent, as is well known, is represented by the ratio of the marginal products of G_1 and G_2, viz. r_1 and r_2 respectively. The shadow prices of accumulated government efforts in the two directions—G_1 and G_2 are then considered to be given by the same ratio between r_1 and r_2 in relative terms. In the absence of any explicit target about such relative social costs, the planner may aim to maintain the given parity between the social marginal costs undisturbed while planning to achieve the target X_1 for basic welfare. Therefore, the criterion of maintaining the marginal rate of substitution between the accumulated government efforts G_1 and G_2 existing at point A also at the new point on the arc DBC requires us to examine the behaviour of the marginal products of accumulated government efforts G_1 and G_2 over time.

In order to make a policy choice, the planner should be in a position to assess the ratio of marginal products of G_1 and G_2 at point B on a new isoquant X_1. It is important to note that the planner is not interested in the absolute estimate of the ratio r_1/r_2 at point B nor at point A. For the choice under consideration we need to know only the behaviour of this ratio between points A and B.*[4] Thus, for instance, as shown in Diagram 1 (a), if the ratio r_1/r_2 at B is greater than the one at A, given the convexity of the isoquants, it is obvious that the point where the ratio r_1/r_2 remains constant would lie on the arc BD, implying higher expenditure in direction 1 and lower expenditure in direction 2 than before. We can similarly infer from Diagram 1(b) that the planner should increase expenditure in direction 2 and reduce the expenditure in direction 1 if the ratio r_1/r_2 at B is less than the one at A.

The crucial question to be investigated in making a policy choice in our framework thus boils down to examining the behaviour of the ratio r_1/r_2, i.e. the ratio of marginal products of accumulated government efforts in directions 1 and 2. Thus, if the returns are increasing in direction 1 and if the returns are either diminishing or constant in direction 2, the ratio of marginal products—r_1/r_2 will have a tendency to increase. In such a case it is most likely that the ratio r_1/r_2 would be higher at B than at A so that the planner is best advised to go in for higher expenditure in direction 1 and lower expenditure in direction 2 than before. Such a policy under the circumstances is likely to leave the ratio of shadow prices of accumulated government efforts in the two directions more or less unaffected so as to ensure achievement of the targeted basic welfare level X_1 at minimum social cost calculated at the base period shadow prices.

When we consider a case where the total rate of annual per capita real expenditure by the government increases over time, the reference point B indicating the same level of expenditure as before would lie below the isoquant for the achievable target X_2. Diagram 2 represents such a case. Several real-life situations are most likely to resemble this case. The discussion of Diagram 1 (a) totally applies to the point B in Diagram 2 as well. However, the achievable welfare level (X_1) at point B is lower than the target X_2. The implication of this particular condition is to reduce the sharpness of the conclusions regarding the nature of returns to government efforts and the direction of government expenditure. To illustrate the difference it would make in such a case, let us consider a situation where at point B, the ratio of the marginal products -r1/r2 is higher than at point A. In the earlier case, this would imply increasing the rate of expenditure in direction 1 and reducing it in direction 2. If, however, we consider the latter case when the total rate of government expenditure is higher than before, although it is necessary that the rate of expenditure in direction 1 should increase, it is not necessary that the rate of expenditure in direction 2 should decrease. This happens because even if we move from point B to point E on the isoquant X_1 to ensure the same ratio - r_1/r_2 as at point A, it is quite conceivable that a point like F on the higher isoquant X_2 representing the target level of basic welfare may represent the same ratio - r_1/r_2. At point F, then, we cannot rule out constancy or even an increase in the rate of government expenditure in direction 2 as compared to point B. On the other hand, point F would invariably represent a higher rate of expenditure in direction 1 as compared to point B.

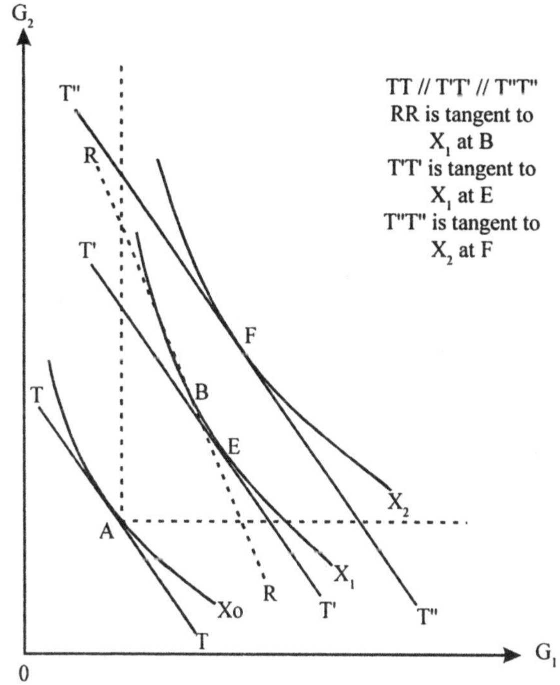

Diagram 2

The message from this discussion is clear. If the ratio of marginal products of the government effort in any two directions is increasing, the rate of government expenditure in the direction of the numerator should increase.

Whether the rate of expenditure in the direction of the denominator should increase, decrease or remain the same depends on the extent of increase in the total rate of government expenditure.

MODEL SPECIFICATION AND MEASUREMENT

From the above discussion, it is clear that the approach of production function for basic welfare with the arguments of the stocks of accumulated government efforts in different directions does provide useful guidelines for effecting changes in the budget allocations when we know the nature of marginal returns to the government efforts in different directions. It is very difficult if not impossible to measure satisfactorily the stock of accumulated government efforts in different directions up to a point in time. This is because it is not only the stock of the physical assets built by the government so far but also the way the government services are provided, their geographic spread and the maintenance and use of the government assets have a definite influence on the stock of basic welfare of the population. Thus, the government's developmental efforts are reflected in its capital and revenue expenditures over time. It is not intended to deny the existence of the qualitative aspects of the government efforts. In fact, very often the extent of the presence of government determines the culture, expectations and mindset of the people. We, therefore, postulate that the quality of the government effort varies directly with the quantity of the accumulated government expenditure.

Like most measurements in general and the ones in social sciences in particular, the measurement of stocks or the level of variables is far less satisfactory or feasible than the flows or the rates of change in those variables. The variable of the accumulated government efforts is no exception to this. Similarly, basic welfare and basic commodity, X in our model, are also the variables whose rates of change are more reliable than their levels. Moreover, from the point of view of effective government intervention through well-defined policy changes based on the right choice of strategies, the crucial variables are necessarily defined in terms of the flow aggregates rather than the stock of government effort. In other words, from the point of view of policy, the government would be controlling the flow of the annual expenditure to effect changes in its cumulative stocks over time. The current annual expenditure by the government can be viewed as the time derivative of the accumulated stock aggregate G. All this requires us to consider our model in terms of the first derivative of eq. (1) with respect to time (t).

$$X^{o}_{t} = F'_{G1} \cdot G^{o}_{1t} + F'_{G2} \cdot G^{o}_{2t} + F'_{Z1} \cdot Z^{o}_{1t} + F'_{Z2} \cdot Z^{o}_{2t} + \dots + F'_{Zn} \cdot Z^{o}_{nt} \quad \dots..(3)$$

where F' with a different suffix represents the partial derivative of the function F(...) with respect to the letter denoted by the suffix;

and a superscript '°' to the letter represents the time derivative of the variable. If we assume only the annual changes in different variables, we are not likely to find considerable or significant changes in the physical, locational, and socio-cultural environmental factors $Z_{1t},...Z_{nt}$

We may, therefore, be justified in ignoring these values and simplifying eq. (3) to

$$X^o_t = F'_{G1} \cdot G^o_{1t} + F'_{G2} \cdot G^o_{2t} = f(G^o_{1t} \cdot G^o_{2t}) \ldots\ldots (4)$$

It should be noted here that such a simplification is valid only when we are studying the changes in aggregates over a relatively shorter period of time when we can justifiably ignore the changes in $Z_{1t},\ldots,Z_{nt}$. Over relatively longer periods of time, however, the changes in environmental factors $Z_{1t},\ldots,Z_{nt}$ are likely to be significant and eq. (4) would need to be modified. A careful examination of eq. (3) clearly indicates the type of modification required in eq. (4) if a relatively longer period of time is considered . Thus , when $Z^o_{1t},\ldots,Z^o_{nt}$ are significant, the level of relationship between X^o_t and G^o_t as described by eq. (4) is likely to shift over time depending on the net effects of changes in the environmental factors. The level of the relationship can change because the intercept changes or the slope parameter changes. The levels of environmental factors $Z_{1t},\ldots,Z_{nt}$ enter as the determinants of not only the intercept of the relationship but also the slope of the relationship between X^o_t and G^o_t as described by eq. (4). Thus, it is an empirically testable proposition whether environmental factors have played any role to significantly affect the level of the relationship as described in eq. (4) over time. The intercept in the functional relationship like eq. (4) would represent the autonomous rate of change in the quantity of basic commodity X, reflecting the direction and magnitude of interplay of various factors in the private economy. The intercept, in other words, represents the annual change in X_t independent of the changes in government efforts in different directions.

It is also possible to interpret the slope coefficients of the functional relationship in eq. (4) if the independent variables are appropriately measured. Taking time derivative of eq. (4), we get

$$dX^o_t/dt = (f_{11} \times G^o_{1t} + f_{12} \times G^o_{2t}) \times G^o_{1t} + f_1\, dG^o_{1t}/dt$$
$$+ (f_{21} \times G^o_{1t} + f_{22} \times G^o_{2t}) \times G^o_{2t} + f_2\, dG^o_{2t}/dt \ldots\ldots\ldots (5)$$

If we assume that G^o_{1t} and G^o_{2t} remain constant over time, i.e. $dG^o_{1t}/dt = dG^o_{2t}/dt = 0$, we get

$$d^2X_t/dt^2 = (f_{11} \times G^o_{1t} + f_{12} \times G^o_{2t}) \times G^o_{1t} + (f_{21} \times G^o_{1t} + f_{22} \times G^o_{2t}) \times G^o_{2t} \quad \ldots\ldots (6)$$

This gets simplified further when we take $G^o_{2t} = 0$ as
$d^2X_t/dt^2 = f_{11} \times (G^o_{1t})^2 = f_{11} \times (dG^o_{2t}/dt)^2$
i.e. $d^2X_t/dt^2 = f_{11} \times dG^2_{1t}/dt^2$

$$\text{i.e. } d^2X_t/dG^2_{1t} = \partial^2X_t/\partial G^2_{1t} = f_{11} \quad \ldots\ldots \ldots\ldots \ldots\ldots (7)$$

Similarly, by taking $G^o_{1t} = 0$ in eq. (6), we get

$$d^2X_t/dG^2_{2t} = \partial^2X_t/\partial G^2_{2t} = f_{22} \quad \ldots\ldots \ldots\ldots \ldots\ldots (8)$$

Thus, the slope coefficients of the functional relationship in eq. (4) of our model can be interpreted as the second order direct partial derivatives of the functional relationship between X_t and G_t provided that the variables G^o_{1t} and G^o_{2t} are measured so as to ensure that they remain constant over the relevant time interval.

As is well-known, the second order partial derivative of output (X) with respect to inputs (G_t) is interpreted as showing the behaviour of marginal returns to basic inputs. In our case, therefore, the slope coefficients of our function as described in eq. (4) can be interpreted as showing the behaviour of marginal returns to government efforts in different sectors. If the slope is positive, it implies increasing marginal returns; and if the slope is negative, it implies diminishing marginal returns; and if the slope is zero, it implies constant marginal returns. Thus, if our interest is in testing the direction of the marginal returns to government efforts through eq. (4), the most appropriate functional form for the equation would be linear. This is possible if we consider the real expenditure variable in such a way that the annual rate of change in the expenditure is zero. In order to ensure this, we have taken a simple arithmetic average of annual per capita real government expenditure on human capital (EHK) and physical capital (EPK) during 1970-80 and 1981-91 as our independent variables (see, Table 10.1). This would also eliminate purely short-term fluctuations in real per capita government expenditures and yet retain the basic feature of the change in the government effort on an annual basis.

METHODOLOGY FOR CONSTRUCTING THE BASIC WELFARE INDEX

The question which arises from the above framework is that if consumption of basic commodities, i.e. X can measure Basic Welfare (W'), and dX, i.e. change in X, can measure change in basic welfare (dW'), how should X be measured. Some studies have attempted to measure X through private expenditure or by considering government expenditure on public services as a proxy for consumption of essential commodities by the poor, or as index of social infrastructure, or combination of various social indicators (For details, see A. Dholakia 1990). But such studies can be said to have measured "efforts" or "inputs" provided for the consumption rather than actual output of basic commodities, i.e. X. Such studies may, therefore, grossly overestimate the extent of welfare, particularly when the available infrastructure is not utilised efficiently due to the constraints of demand or effective supply arising on account of the poor quality of public services, their ineffective delivery, corruption and lack of supplementary socio-economic inputs. In this context the PQLI approach is relatively better and appealing as it attempts to measure welfare through the indicators which are objective, reflect results or "output" rather than inputs, simple to construct and also easy to comprehend (see Morris *et al.,* 1979). However, it also has certain limitations. In the first place, its indicators are too few in number to give a comprehensive idea even about the minimum desirable welfare. Moreover, out of the three indicators, viz. infant mortality rate, life expectancy at age one and adult literacy rate, only two indicators relate to health. More importantly, these two variables are usually ill-measured in the LDCs (see A. Dholakia 1990). Secondly, the most important component of food and nutrition is conspicuously absent. These limitations make the PQLI more unstable, unreliable and less comprehensive. Lastly, the indicators chosen for PQLI are not selected on the basis of any systematic theoretical framework. On the other hand, the Basic Welfare Index (BWI) proposed by us is constructed out of those indicators.

Table 10.1: Average Annual Per Capita Real Government Expenditure for Sub-periods

State	*EHK*	*EHK*	*EPK*	*EPK*	*PCI*
	Rev. A/c	*Cap A/c*	*Rev. A/c*	*Cap A/c*	*Real*
	For the Period 1971-80				
Andhra Pradesh	68.47	8.14	47.06	35.06	627.00
Bihar	37.53	5.54	22.77	22.65	415.00
Gujarat	87.13	13.59	53.05	34.70	827.00
Haryana	74.95	14.64	93.20	64.54	960.00
Karnataka	76.35	8.79	66.04	34.46	698.00
Kerala	106.57	16.39	41.71	25.83	592.00
Madhya Pradesh	58.48	7.51	43.08	31.67	534.00
Maharashtra	95.60	12.10	67.38	42.04	808.00
Orissa	64.54	8.53	60.34	35.88	473.00
Punjab	101.31	14.77	80.90	37.82	1121.00
Rajashtan	76.77	12.60	50.41	34.30	560.00
Tamil Nadu	75.80	9.34	54.90	15.81	648.00
Uttar Pardesh	47.03	5.78	40.72	28.79	497.00
West Bengal	80.45	9.68	38.81	16.46	779.00
	For the Period 1981-91				
Andhra Pradesh	128.74	2.85	93.44	34.31	1380
Bihar	78.16	5.27	50.31	29.94	917
Gujarat	154.72	9.44	131.73	49.90	1940
Haryana	158.12	7.93	165.57	54.90	2370
Karnataka	131.88	2.50	102.06	42.63	1520
Kerala	153.87	9.34	63.47	29.65	1508
Madhya Pradesh	101.99	4.78	82.48	43.51	1358
Maharashtra	160.05	4.22	146.22	50.15	2435
Orissa	112.02	5.54	69.81	59.86	1314
Punjab	179.59	8.76	147.64	43.17	2674
Rajashtan	118.98	17.75	86.08	41.30	1222
Tamil Nadu	151.25	4.23	116.33	16.16	1498
Uttar Pardesh	85.70	3.97	69.68	35.19	1278
West Bengal	122.42	3.49	62.05	15.40	1773

Source: Various issues of RBI Bulletins and Economic Surveys.

(i) Which emerge from a theoretical model. (See A. Dholakia 1990);

(ii) Improvement in whose values invariably and infallibly implies improved consumption of basic commodities (X), whose marginal utility for the poor is very high and that to the non-poor is very low;

(iii) Which reflect output in terms of well-being rather than inputs;
(iv) Which have no ethnocentric biases and lend themselves to inter-state and inter-country comparison among LDCs; and
(v) Which represent all the three aspects of welfare, viz. health, education and nutrition.

In all nine socio-economic indicators identified by the above listed criteria are selected.

The final outcome of all the necessary inputs for health is measured through (i) Death Rate (DR), (ii) Birth Rate (BR) and (iii) Infant Mortality Rate (IMR). Consumption of basic educational inputs is measured through : (i) Male Literacy Rate (MLR) and (ii) Female Literacy Rate (FLR). To capture nutritional and other aspects like quality of housing, drinking water, etc. the N & O component index is constructed through selection of four indicators, viz. (i) Proportion of People Below the Poverty Line (PBP), (ii) Child Worker Participation Rate (CWPR), (iii) Females' Mean Age at Marriage (FMAM) and (iv) Male Participation Rate in Non-Agricultural Sector (MPRNA).

Ideally speaking, the NSS data on poverty should satisfactorily capture the nutrition and other aspects, but they do not. The correlation coefficients between the poverty rate and the remaining component index of N&O (excluding poverty rate) as estimated using the cross-section data of 14 major states for all the three periods (1971, 1981, 1991) are statistically insignificant at 5 per cent level (0.20, 0.27, 0.45, respectively). This confirms our belief that for capturing the true extent of basic welfare, the poverty rate can be one of the indicators but it alone cannot capture the general economic conditions of the poor in the population. Similarly, poor correlations between the BWI (consisting of all the three components of health, education, N&O) and the poverty index for all the three periods also suggest that the poverty data capture only a partial picture of the welfare and that they have to be supplemented with a set of other indicators.

Because the selected indicators are measured in different units they have to be first converted into indices. Moreover, they have to be made undirectional in order to meaningfully add them. The methodology adopted by us for constructing such indices is the same as followed for PQLI (see Morris *et al.* 1979). For each indicator the performance of an individual state is put on 0 to 100 scale where 0 represents an absolutely defined worst performance and 100 represents an absolutely defined best performance (see Table 10.2). Selection of

Table 10.2: Critical Values and Formulae for Indices

Indicators	*Best Value (=100)*	*Worst Value (=0)*	*Formula*
1. Male Literacy Rate (%) (Above age five)	100	0	$\frac{V - 0}{100} \times 100$
2. Female Literacy Rate (%) (Above age five)	100	0	$\frac{V - 0}{100} \times 100$
3. Infant Mortality Rate (Per 1000 Live Births)	7	263	$\frac{V - 263}{7 - 263} \times 100$
4. Birth Rate (Per 1000 Population)	79	60	$\frac{V - 60}{79 - 60} \times 100$
5. Death Rate (Per 1000 Population)			$\frac{V - 47}{6 - 47} \times 100$
6. Child Worker Participation Rate (%) $\frac{\text{Child Workers}}{\text{Child Population (5-14)}}$	0	30	$\frac{V - 30}{0 - 30} \times 100$
7. Male Participation Rate in Non-A Sector (%) $\frac{\text{Non-A Male Workers (Main)}}{\text{Male Population (5+)}}$	45	5	$\frac{V - 5}{45 - 5} \times 100$
8. Percentage of People Below poverty line (%)	0	75	$\frac{V - 75}{0 - 75} \times 100$
9. Female Mean Age At Marriage (Years)	24	12.5	$\frac{V - 12.5}{24 - 12.5} \times 100$

Note : V = Actual Value of the Indicator.

Source :(1) Dholakia, A. (1990) : *Benefits From Government Expenditure in India: A Welfare Indicator Approach*, Himalaya Publishing House, Bombay.

(2) U.N. Demographic Year Books.

(3) Morris, Morris David & Others(1979): *Measuring the Conditions of The World's Poor: The Physical Quality of Life Index.*

these values is based on the historical experiences of the Third World countries in the last 40 years. Thus 0 represents worst observed and not worst possible value. Similarly 100 represents either the best achieved or the targeted value of the indicator (see, *U.N. Demographic Year Books*). These indicator indices are then combined to construct component indexes. Within each component index the explicit weight attached to different indicator index is equal and similarly for construction of the BWI each of the three components is given equal weightage. Table 10.3 presents inter-state estimates of the three major components of Basic Welfare for the years 1971,1981 and 1991. The distance of each state and the country as a whole from the ideal value of indexes (=100) shows the shortfall in the basic welfare level in a state as compared to the ideal conditions already achieved elsewhere. Therefore, it shows the task lying ahead in different directions.

Table 10.3: Component Indices of Basic Welfare Index

State	*Health HI*			*Education EI*			*Nutrition & Others N&OI*		
	1971	*1981*	*1991*	*1971*	*1981*	*1991*	*1971*	*1981*	*1991*
Andhra Pradesh	61.01	70.76	77.66	28.38	33.95	41.15	41.72	52.21	59.17
Bihar	52.89	58.57	66.68	23.01	29.78	34.64	33.96	39.18	46.52
Gujarat	53.34	64.11	76.45	41.39	49.50	57.44	52.07	62.97	70.51
Haryana	66.59	65.79	74.10	30.90	40.58	51.07	52.40	62.34	66.50
Karnataka	67.68	76.82	77.15	36.54	45.53	52.21	46.56	56.48	60.39
Kerala	75.87	83.95	91.83	69.83	79.03	85.93	59.91	70.40	78.31
Madhya Pradesh	53.14	55.94	62.77	25.93	31.79	40.53	33.19	43.36	51.65
Maharashtra	67.22	74.82	79.93	45.20	53.15	60.71	50.06	57.47	63.60
Orissa	56.95	61.11	66.89	30.40	38.66	45.85	37.40	42.08	53.53
Punjab	65.76	73.69	79.40	38.07	45.80	54.85	64.24	71.85	74.54
Rajashthan	54.39	62.37	69.62	21.97	27.70	34.83	40.93	50.27	58.56
Tamil Nadu	63.00	72.20	82.86	45.23	52.50	59.79	54.75	59.01	66.75
Uttar Pradesh	41.42	52.96	65.34	24.53	30.44	37.43	38.67	48.85	55.30
West Bengal	59.88	69.88	78.34	38.06	45.65	53.65	51.57	55.58	73.16
India	*55.72*	*64.90*	*72.14*	*38.05*	*40.98*	*48.33*	*44.91*	*53.02*	*60.53*
Best or Targeted Value	*100*	*100*	*100*	*100*	*100*	*100*	*100*	*100*	*100*

Note: (a) Calculated by using formulae and indicators given in Table 10.1, (b) Data on the poverty rate relate to 1973,1983 and 1993. They are modified estimates of the expert group on poverty, (c) Data on health indicators for Bihar and West Bengal were re-estimated by using the probable extent of underreporting given in different SRS volumes.

Sources: (1) *Vital Statistics of India* (Various Volumes), (2) Census publications of 1971,1981,1991, (3) *Statistical Abstract of India* (Various Volumes).

Table 10.4 gives the estimates of Basic Welfare for all the states for the three benchmark years. Figures for all-India are also given to indicate the distance of each state from the national average and from the ideal value achieved at the international level. However, for policy purpose, we have to consider the change in the basic welfare rather

Table 10.4: Basic Welfare Index and (BWI) and its Disparity Reduction Rate (DRR)

State	*BWI*			*DRR*	
	1971	*1981*	*1991*	*1971-81*	*1981-91*
Andhra Pradesh	43.70	52.31	59.33	1.64	1.58
Bihar	36.62	42.51	49.28	0.97	1.25
Gujarat	48.93	58.86	68.13	2.14	2.52
Haryana	49.96	56.24	63.89	1.33	1.90
Karnataka	50.26	59.61	63.35	2.06	0.97
Kerala	68.53	77.79	85.36	3.42	4.08
Madhya Pradesh	37.42	43.70	51.65	1.05	1.51
Maharashtra	54.16	61.81	68.08	1.81	1.78
Orissa	41.58	47.28	55.42	1.02	1.66
Punjab	56.02	63.78	69.60	1.92	1.74
Rajashthan	39.09	46.78	54.34	1.34	1.52
Tamil Nadu	54.33	61.24	69.80	1.63	2.47
Uttar Pradesh	34.87	44.08	52.69	1.51	1.66
West Bengal	49.84	57.04	68.38	1.54	3.02
India	*46.23*	*52.96*	*60.33*	*1.33*	*1.69*
Best or Targeted Value	*100*	*100*	*100*	—	—

Note : (a) BWI is calculated by using the formulae given in Table 10.1.

(b) Formula for DRR is :

$$DRR_t^{t+n} = \frac{-[\{X^*_{t+n}\}^{1/n} - 1]}{X^*_t} x\ 100$$

Where DRR_t^{t+n} = Disparity Reducation Rate during the Period n.

$X^*_{t+n} = X_{t+n} - 100$ = Disparity between the actual welfare and the Ideal Welfare at the end of the period.

$X^*_t = X_t - 100$ = Disparity between the actual welfare and the Ideal Welfare at the start of the period.

X_{t+n} and X_t are the levels of Indexes X at time t+n and t.

Source: Same as Table 10.2.

than the level of the basic welfare as per our model. To measure the change in the Basic Welfare Index we have employed the tool of Disparity Reduction Rate (DRR) rather than the Percentage Growth

Rate for various reasons. (see Morris *et al.* 1979; Dholakia A. 1990). The DRR measures the rate at which the disparity between the actual value of an index and the ideal value of the index decreases per year. In other words, it indicates the rate of improvement or movement towards the ideal or the targeted value. The last two columns of Table 4 give the DRR the of BWI during 1971-81 and 1981-91. The DRR in the BWI is denoted by the DBWI here. As per the theoretical model discussed above, this DBWI becomes the dependent variable for both the periods.

ESTIMATION OF THE ECONOMETRIC MODEL

To test our model empirically, data on the 14 major states of India are considered. Multiple linear regression equations have been estimated by using the OLS method. As discussed earlier, the dependent variable for both the sub-periods, viz. 1971-81 and 1981-91 is Disparity Reduction Rate in Basic Welfare Index (DBWI). Independent variables are developmental expenditure or its components in terms of the social (human capital) and economic (physical capital) sectors (measured on the average annual per capita real basis) along with per capita real Net State Domestic Product (NSDP). The last one is introduced to capture the role of the level of developmental factors in the base period. In other words, it is a surrogate variable to all other exogenous factors not considered in the model explicitly. Hence, as per our model, we have to consider the evel of the NSDP rather than the growth in the economy.

In order to examine the structural shift in the slope parameters between the two sub-periods the technique of pulled regression with dummy variables is used. Dummies have been introduced for each parameter in the pulled regression equation. With a view to increasing the degrees of freedom and thereby the reliability of the estimates, Restricted Least Squares (RLS) method is also used by imposing the linear restriction of equality of parameters. (see Gujarati 1995)

We have tested the hypotheses with respect to the aggregative developmental expenditure and its social and economic components to find out whether the developmental effort per se is important or its composition and components are relevant to improve the DBWI. For this, alternative regressions are estimated by introducing combined developmental expenditure or its components and sub-components as independent variables in the model, results of which are presented in Table 10.5. Interestingly it emerges from the results that it is not the combined developmental expenditure but its allocation to different sectors which is relevant for the rate of improvement in the basic welfare. It is the component of expenditure on human capital (or social services) which is most crucial on margin and not the expenditure on physical capital or economic services. Regression fit of a model with aggregative developmental expenditure turns out to be poor for both the sub-periods, viz. 1971-81 and 1981-91. (see Equation 1 and 2 of Table 10.5) On the other hand when we consider the model with separate components of Expenditure on Human Capital (EHK) and Physical Capital (EPK) along with their revenue and capital categories as explanatory variables (both with and without dummies) the fit of the model significantly improves, and becomes statistically significant. (see Equation 3 of Table 10.5) The slope parameters of this equation show considerable stability between the two sub-periods as suggested by the statistical insignificance of all dummies. Even the Chow test also indicates the same situation. Because of this, for the final estimate of the model we dropped all the dummies to improve the reliability of the estimates of the pulled regression. (see Equation 4 of Table 5) insignificant dummy of intercept coefficient suggests that the net of changes in exogenous variables Z_1, Z_2, etc., was not significant on the slope or intercept parameters of our model. In order to find out whether the revenue and capital components of both EHK and EPK are separately required to explain the variations in the DBWI, we carried out the exercise of Restricted Least Squares. We put two linear restrictions on the parameters of the equation to test the equality between the slope coefficients of parameters for revenue and capital components of each of the two variables, viz. EHK and EPK. (see Equation 4 in Table 10.5) The required F test for testing the equality of restricted and unrestricted equations suggests that the restrictions put on the parameters are valid. In other words, instead of considering the revenue and capital expenditures separately, we can consider total expenditure on the EHK and EPK as explanatory variables in the model. This further implies that we can use restricted equation instead of unrestricted one to increase the degrees of freedom and thereby reliability of the estimates. Our final estimated equation thus arrived at is pulled restricted equation presented below: (Equation No. 6 in Table 10.5)

Table 10.5: Regression Results of the Model

Dependent Variable for all Regressions is Disparity Reduction Rate in Basic Welfare Index (DBWI)

Independent Variables

Equation No.	*Constant*	*Developmental Expenditure*	*PCI*	R^2	*F Value*
1	0.772	0.009	-0.004	0.120	0.600
		(0.885)	(-0.336)		(5,22)
Estimated	1.219	-0.0120	0.001		
Dummy	(0.992)	(-1.031)	(0.671)		
2 (Without	1.294	0.002	0.00008	0.062	0.832
Dummy)		(0.613)	(0.151)		(2,25)

Independent Variables

Equation No.	*Constant*	*EHK Rev. A/c*	*EHK Cap. A/c*	*EPK Rev. A/c*	*EPK Cap. A/c*	*PCI*	R^2	*F Value*
3	0.244	0.030	0.025	-0.006	-0.001	-0.001	0.671	2.968
		(1.375)	(0.217)	(-0.281)	(-0.027)	(-0.578)		
Estimated	0.177	-0.02	-0.007	-0.016	-0.012	0.001		
Dummy	(0.147)	(-0.67)	(-0.006)	(-0.648)	(-0.411)	(0.671)		
4 (Without	0.420	0.024	0.034	-0.020	-0.007	0.0003	0.632	7.270
Dummy)		(4.840)	(1.351)	(-2.722)	(-0.693)	(0.643)		(5,22)

Independent Variables

Equation No.	*Constant*	*EHK Combined*	*EPK Combined*	*PCI*	R^2	*F Value*
5	0.317	0.031	0.004	-0.001	0.666	5.705
		(3.392)	(-0.537)	(-0.823)		(7,20)
Estimated	0.337	-0.005	-0.150	0.001		
Dummy	(0.394)	(-0.441)	(-1.653)	(0.874)		
6 (Without	0.920	0.021	-0.016	0.0003	0.581	11.088
Dummy)		(5.133)	(-4.159)	(0.904)		(3,24)

Source: Based on Table 10.2 , 10.3 and 10.4.

$$DBWI = 0.920 + 0.021\ EHK - 0.016\ EPK + 0.0003\ PCI$$
$$(5.13)^* \quad (-4.16)^* \quad (0.904)$$
$$(R^2 = 0.581 \quad F(3,24) = 11.09^*)$$

*statistically significant at 1% level.

The results of the above equation suggest that out of the two components of the developmental expenditure, viz the EHK and EPK, the former increasing returns and the latter yields decreasing returns to government efforts. In other words, the EHK tends to increase the basic welfare (output) at an increasing rate but the EPK increases it at a decreasing rate given that other factors remain constant. As per these estimates, if the government increases the average annual per capita real expenditure on the EHK by Rs. 50, the disparity reduction rate of basic welfare (DBWI) would increase by 1 percentage point, on an average. While the same amount if diverted to EPK has a tendency to reduce the DBWI by one percentage point, keeping all other factors constant. What is important to note is that the accelerating impact of EHK on basic welfare was observed for both the periods, viz. 1971-81 and 1981-91. (See Equation 5 in Table 10.5). However, the government efforts on the physical capital or the economic sectors had constant returns during the seventies, but the deceleration during the eighties produced the overall diminishing returns over 1971-91.

It is interesting to observe that the slope coefficients of per capita real NSDP is statistically poor for both the sub-periods suggesting that the level of developmental factors did not have any influence on the rate of improvement of the basic welfare. They may be related with the *Level* of the welfare index but not the *Rate* at which it moves towards the targeted value. This has an important policy implication, that we cannot depend on the level of economic development of a state to take care of the basic welfare of its people.

As far as the budget allocation between the social and economic sectors is concerned, at the policy level, it is seldom a question of exclusive choice as noted earlier. It is always a question of according priorities to different items of expenditure ``on margin" and not of scrapping one to favour the other. The priority as discussed earlier depends not on the magnitude of the marginal returns but on the behaviour of the marginal returns. In this context our model suggests tilting the balance in favour of the EHK, i.e. expenditure on human capital as against the EPK. In spite of all inefficiencies, corruption and poor delivery of publicly provided social goods, the government does matter and has a major role to play in provision of social services to move faster towards the ideal level of basic welfare. This certainly does not mean that the private social sector is not important, but until we reach a certain threshold level of basic welfare, coexistence of the government with the former in the provision of social services is advisable.

SUMMARY AND CONCLUSION

Several measures have been developed in the literature to measure welfare of the people, like poverty rates, PQLI, LLI and HDI, to name a few. These measures are far from adequate in comprehensively measuring even the minimum desirable welfare in an economy. Moreover, they are also temporally and spatially unstable. We have suggested an alternative measure of welfare called Basic Welfare Index (BWI) to overcome some of the limitations of the above measures. BWI encompasses all the three components of minimum desirable welfare, namely, Health, Education and Nutrition and Others. It is constructed through nine indicators which are derived on the basis of the standard welfare theory. Moreover, these nine indicators are objective; measure output rather than efforts; have no ethnocentric biases; and do not assume any specific pattern of economic development. (see Dholakia A. 1990;1993).

In order to study the role of the government in this respect, a model hypothesizing of the relationship between BWI and government efforts is presented, specified and empirically tested with the data on 14 major states of India for the period 1971-81 and 1981-91. The dependent variable is Disparity reduction rate in Basic Welfare Index (DBWI) and the independent variables are average annual real per capita expenditure on development (or its sub-components) and per capita real NSDP (PCI). Results of the model suggest that an increase in the expenditure on human capital (EHK) by the government increases the basic welfare at an increasing rate and that on physical capital (EPK) increases the welfare at a decreasing rate, keeping other factors constant. It may be inferred from our results that at the policy level, where the choices are not exclusive but are only on the margin, tilting the balance in favour of the EHK would help achieve the targeted welfare level more efficiently than with the EPK. It emerges from the results that the level of economic development does not influence the rate of movement towards the targeted welfare (DBWI) and hence cannot alone be depended upon. In spite of the inefficiencies and corruption in the publicly provided social goods the role of the government in accelerating the basic welfare seems to have remained important in India.

NOTES

*1. In order to simplify the exposition, we assume for the time being that the new target of X_1 is such that it can be achieved by keeping the total rate of annual per capita real government expenditure the same as before.

*2. The new isoquant at X_1 may or may not belong to the same production function as Xo. Since X_1 is a target to be achieved over a period of time, it is possible to envisage changes in "other factors" held constant while drawing Xo. If these changes have taken place in a systematically predictable way, the argument in the text regarding the choice open for the policy-maker would not undergo any significant change.

*3. It should be noted here that point B representing the same rate of annual per capita real government expenditures in the two directions as before would be on the isoquant X_1 so long as we are assuming that the target of X_1 is achievable with the total government expenditure in real per capita terms remaining the same as before. If X_1 requires a higher expenditure rate, point B would lie below the isoquant X_1.

4 It is generally thought that if the magnitude of the marginal product of G_1 is greater than the one of G_2, the planner should increase the expenditure in the direction of G_1. Fan *et al.* (2000) also recommend budget allocation on these lines. However, our argument here shows that this would not necessarily be a logical recommendation. We should also consider the marginal costs for G_1 and G_2, which would compel us to consider the behaviour of r_1/r_2 rather than the magnitudes of r_1 and r_2.

REFERENCES

Aaron, H. and McGuire, M., (1970): "Public Goods and Income Distribution", *Econometrica*, Vol.38, November.

Chaudhary, Umadutta Roy, (1978): "Measurement of National Welfare for Developing countries : special factors for consideration", *The Journal of Income and Wealth*, Vol. 2, April.

Dholakia, A., (1990): *Benefits from Government Expenditure In India: A Welfare Indicator Approach,* (Bombay: Himalaya Publishing House).

Dholakia A., (1993): "Distributional Impact of Government Expenditure in India : A Suggested Model", in Y.K. Alagh, R.J. Mody and R.D.Desai (edi) : *Stability and Development: Essays in Honour of D. T. Lakdawala*, New Delhi : Har-Anand Publications.

Fan, S., Hazell P. and Thorat, S.K., (2000): "Impact of Public Expenditure on Poverty in Rural India", *Economic and Political Weekly*, Vol. 35, No. 40, September 30.

Gothaskar, S. P. (1978) : "Problems in Measurement of National Welfare", *The Journal of Income and Wealth*, Vol . 2, April.

Gujarati, D., (1995): *Basic Econometrics* (Tokyo : McGraw - Hill, Kogakusha)

Mishra, P.N., (1982): *Government Expenditure Policy on Social Services*, (mimeo), Indian Institute of Management, Ahmedabad, September.

Morris, Morris David *et al.*, (1979): *Measuring The Conditions of The World's Poor: The Physical Qualtiy of Life Index*, Washington D.C., Overseas Development Council.

Musgrave, R.A.; Case, C.E., and Leonard, H., (1974): "The distribution of Fiscal Burden and Benefits," *Public Finance Quartely,* Vol. 2, No. 3, July.

Wulf, D.L., (1975): " Fiscal Incidence Studies in Developing Countries : Survey and Critique," IMF *Staff Papers,* March.

Wulf, D.L., (1981): "Incidence of Budegetary Oultays: Where Do We Go From Here?" *Public Finance,* Vol. 36.

11

Health and Healthcare in Western and Central India

The Criticality of Public Finance

RAVI DUGGAL

The western-central region of the Indian subcontinent includes a mix of states with widely differing political economies. It includes some of the most developed states of the country like Maharashtra and Gujarat, which also form the axis of industrial India, and also some of the less developed ones like Madhya Pradesh, Chhatisgarh and Rajasthan. One need not emphasise that a very close association exists between economic development and health and healthcare, which is very clearly manifest in the health outcomes of these states. Maharashtra and Gujarat, besides being industrial centres, have also created agrarian wealth through sugarcane, cotton, groundnut and milk which has had a significant impact on the health outcomes of rural populations in these states. Another feature of this entire region is the large *adivasi* populaton. In fact, the tribal belt of India begins from south Rajasthan, traverses through north and south Gujarat, through north and east Maharashtra, the entire southern length of Madhya Pradesh and into Chhatisgarh and, of course, beyond it into Orissa, Jharkhand and right up to north-east India. This is important because when we look at the starvation pattern in India the tribal belts are often the most severely affected including those in the highly developed state of Maharashtra.

India lost the opportunity of creating a national healthcare system by not implementing the recommendations of the Bhore Committee (Bhore 1946). While it has made very poor investments in the public health sector over the years, the mid-seventies became a turning point for major investments, especially in rural India via the Minimum Needs Programme. The plan period between the Fifth and Seventh Plans may be regarded as the "golden era" of public health sector performance in India when not only public investments and expenditures in healthcare peaked but also health outcomes witnessed rapid changes (Tables 11.1 and 11.2).[1] Whereas Maharashtra and Gujarat supported by their economic development made early progress in health and healthcare, Rajasthan and Madhya Pradesh, because of inadequate economic development support, were slower on the uptake. This hypothesis gains greater significance when we look at intra-state differences, especially in Maharashtra and Gujarat. In both these developed states economic development (whether industrial or agrarian) is concentrated in some pockets and the high achievements of these pockets of growth undoubtedly skew the overall health outcomes. Madhya Pradesh and Rajasthan having fewer pockets of growth are unable to come up with health outcomes that are comparable to those in Maharashtra and Gujarat. An analysis of the health scenario and data from these states (Table 11.3) provide clear evidence that public financing of the health sector is critical in bringing about sustainable improvements in the health status of the people.

Health and Healthcare

The pattern of development of the health sector is closely linked to the political economy and the level of economic development. While economic development can create conditions for better access to healthcare as well as a better average standard of living and hence improved health outcomes, a political economy based largely on private healthcare financing can create major problems not only for the poorer sections of society but also for the middle classes. Thus the role of public financing is critical in both developed and underdeveloped economies. In most developed countries where healthcare access is near universal, public financing (whether through state revenues and/or social insurance) has been the critical component in realising universal access with equity (Roemer 1985; OECD 1990) In western and central Indian states one can see very clearly these associations in operation.

Table 11.1: Health Outcomes 1976-1996 across Rural and Urban Areas

	Total					*Rural*					*Urban*				
	1976	*1981*	*1986*	*1991*	*1996*	*1976*	*1981*	*1986*	*1991*	*1996*	*1976*	*1981*	*1986*	*1991*	*1996*
IMR per 1000 live births															
Gujarat	146	111	107	69	61	159	120	124	73	68	100	89	66	57	46
Madhya Pradesh	138	142	118	117	97	145	152	124	125	102	88	80	82	74	61
Maharashtra	83	79	63	60	48	91	90	73	69	58	61	49	44	38	31
Rajasthan	142	108	107	79	85	152	118	113	84	90	73	53	71	50	60
India	129	110	96	80	72	139	119	105	87	77	80	62	62	53	46
Mortality rate per 1000 population (0 - 4 ages)*															
Gujarat	58	41	37	23	20	66	44	44	26	23	37	31	23	18	16
Madhya Pradesh	53	61	50	45	34	56	66	56	49	36	36	28	26	24	18
Maharashtra	33	26	21	16	16	36	30	24	18	15	24	16	15	12	9
Rajasthan	56	50	41	31	31	57	57	45	33	34	25	19	25	21	20
India	51	41	37	27	24	55	46	41	29	26	30	20	21	16	14

Maharashtra is the most developed state in the country with the highest per capita income in real terms. Today, it has the best health outcomes among the central-western region of India and Maharashtra has occupied this position for many years. If we look at the historical data, we see that public financing and development of public health facilities played a critical role in giving Maharashtra an early lead in health outcomes. What was unique to Maharashtra was that health budgets were decentralised through zillah parishads right from the start for the development of the rural healthcare system. Maharashtra was perhaps the first state to realise the policy entitlements of one Primary Health Centre (PHC) for 30,000 population and one Community Health Centre for 5 PHCs. This was possible due to comparatively adequate investments and a higher level of per capita spending compared to other states in the region (Table 11.2).

Table 11.2: Public Health Financing Trends 1975-2002 and Selected Ratios

(in rupees crores)

	Chhattis-garh	*Gujarat*	*Madhya Pradesh*	*Maha-rashtra*	*Rajasthan*	*India*[#]
			Revenue Health Expenditures			
1975-76		**34**	**31**	**64**	**30**	**611**
% of NSDP[&]		0.92	0.86	0.83	1.20	0.98
% of govt. Expenditure		8.96	7.24	6.95	8.52	3.49
per capita (Rs.)		11.24	6.61	11.26	9.87	9.91
capital as ratio to revenue expend		0.02	0.05	0.03	0.03	0.10
1980-81		**64**	**69**	**125**	**57**	**1189**
% of NSDP		0.97	1.13	0.90	1.38	1.07
% of govt. Expenditure		7.11	6.77	6.53	8.28	3.29
per capita (Rs.)		18.83	13.18	19.94	16.61	17.35
capital as ratio to revenue expend		0.01	0.02	0.04	0.04	0.08
1985-86		**148**	**150**	**269**	**123**	**2715**
% of NSDP		1.20	1.25	1.02	1.60	1.32
% of govt. Expenditure		7.51	6.69	5.97	8.11	3.29
per capita (Rs.)		39.35	25.37	38.09	31.36	35.52
capital as ratio to revenue expend		0.02	0.07	0.03	0.03	0.09

(contd.)

Table 11.2 (contd.)

	Chhattis-garh	*Gujarat*	*Madhya Pradesh*	*Maha-rashtra*	*Rajasthan*	*India*[#]
			Revenue Health Expenditures			
1991-92		**284**	**275**	**527**	**280**	**5201**
% of NSDP		1.00	0.83	0.78	1.19	0.88
% of govt. Expenditure		5.42	5.78	5.25	6.85	3.11
per capita (Rs.)		67.25	40.40	65.13	61.76	60.13
capital as ratio to revenue expend		0.01	0.03	0.04	0.07	0.08
1992-93		**314**	**337**	**616**	**332**	**6204**
% of NSDP		0.83	0.91	0.73	1.19	0.92
% of govt. Expenditure		4.79	5.48	5.33	6.64	2.71
per capita (Rs.)		69.09	48.33	74.15	71.30	70.15
capital as ratio to revenue expend		0.01	0.03	0.03	0.04	0.04
1993-94		**356**	**404**	**698**	**385**	**7518***
% of NSDP		0.84	0.88	0.69	1.33	0.96
% of govt. Expenditure						3.33*
per capita (Rs.)		80.90	56.90	83.09	80.71	83.14
capital as ratio to revenue expend		0.01	0.03	0.03	0.03	
1994-95		**413**	**447**	**758**	**461**	**8217***
% of NSDP		0.74	0.89	0.65	1.25	0.90
% of govt. Expenditure		5.47	5.72	5.11	6.83	3.17*
per capita (Rs.)		91.98	61.23	88.65	94.27	89.13
capital as ratio to revenue expend		0.00	0.04	0.02	0.04	
1995-96		**468**	**463**	**890**	**515**	**10165***
% of NSDP		0.76	0.82	0.63	1.23	0.95
% of govt. Expenditure		5.33	5.07	5.18	6.18	3.47*
per capita (Rs.)		102.40	62.06	102.30	103.00	108.20
capital as ratio to revenue expend		0.01	0.04	0.02	0.12	
1996-97		**517**	**553**	**1004**	**591**	**11313***
% of NSDP		0.70	0.85	0.64	1.15	0.91
% of govt. Expenditure		5.03	4.82	4.81	7.01	3.47*
per capita (Rs.)		111.42	72.76	113.74	115.88	118.44
capital as ratio to revenue expend		0.01	0.05	0.02	0.11	
1997-98		**626**	**585**	**1097**	**625**	**12627***
% of NSDP		0.81	0.83	0.64	0.91	0.91
% of govt. Expenditure		5.16	4.99	4.79	6.96	3.39*
per capita (Rs.)		133.19	75.58	122.71	120.19	130.05
capital as ratio to revenue expend		0.02	0.05	0.02	0.15	

(contd.)

Table 11.2 (contd.)

	Chhattis-garh	*Gujarat*	*Madhya Pradesh*	*Maha-rashtra*	*Rajasthan*	*India*#
			Revenue Health Expenditures			
1998-99		**841**	**820**	**1160**	**820**	**16303***
% of NSDP		0.95	1.04	0.63	1.26	1.01
% of govt. Expenditure		5.39	5.77	4.52	7.08	3.6*
per capita (Rs.)		176.31	104.06	128.25	157.69	165.24
capital as ratio to revenue expend		0.04	0.04	0.02	0.05	
			Revenue Health Expenditures			
1999-00		**913**	**836**	**1354**	**858**	**17854***
% of NSDP		1.02	0.97	0.64	1.29	0.99
% of govt. Expenditure		5.21	5.18	4.58	6.39	3.45*
per capita (Rs.)		188.64	104.24	148.14	159.48	178.17
capital as ratio to revenue expend		0.04	0.05	0.05	0.04	
2000-01RE$	**95**	**899**	**844**	**1605**	**920**	**20090***
% of NSDP		0.96	—	—	1.32	0.97
% of govt. Expenditure	4.26	3.87	5.28	4.40	6.09	3.40*
per capita (Rs.)	45.89	182.72	139.97	172.03	167.88	197.44
capital as ratio to revenue expend	0.15	0.04	0.08	0.03	0.11	
2001-02BE@	**230**	**919**	**754**	**1666**	**990**	**22950***
% of NSDP						0.90
% of govt. Expenditure	4.55	3.18	5.13	4.55	6.10	3.52*
per capita (Rs.)	104.55	183.80	121.61	171.75	176.79	223.90
capital as ratio to revenue expend	0.07	0.02	0.07	0.04	0.03	

Note: Figures with* include capital expenditures;
for India income ratio is GDP at factor cost
& NSDP=net state domestic product;
$ RE=revised estimate;
@ BE=budget estimate

Health and Healthcare

The pattern of development of the health sector is closely linked to the political economy and the level of economic development. While economic development can create conditions for better access to healthcare as well as a better average standard of living and hence improved health outcomes, a political economy based largely on private healthcare financing can create major problems not only for the poorer sections of society but also for the middle classes. Thus the

Table 11.3: Overall Health Input and Outcome Profile, and Utilisation and Expenditure Patterns

	Chhatis-garh	*Gujarat*	*Madhya Pradesh*	*Maha-rashtra*	*Rajasthan*	*India*
		Input Indicators				
Beds per lakh population (1998)	N.A.	155	27	98	42	72
Registered doctors per lakh population		66.2	21.7	71.2	36.9	53.6
Per cent beds private (1998)		63.3	NA	47.9	N.A.	37.3
Per cent beds in urban areas (1998)		90.1	65.9	87.0	94.6	73.3
Health exp as a % of NSDP (1998-99)		1.0	1.1	0.6	1.3	0.8
Rev. exp on health as a % of total rev exp (1999-2000)	4.3*	5.2	5.2	4.6	6.4	3.5
Health exp per capita in rupees (1998-99)		183.6	107.8	131.1	162.4	134.4
		Outcome Indicators				
Crude Death Rate (2000)		7.9	10.2	7.5	8.4	8.5
Total Fertility Rate (1998-99)		2.72	3.31	2.52	3.78	2.85
Infant Mortality Rate (1998-99)		62.6	86.1	43.7	80.4	67.6
Life Expectancy rate (1992-96)		61.4	55.2	65.2	59.5	60.7
% pregnant women receiving full ANC		25.0	10.9	31.0	8.3	20.0
% children Fully Immunized		53.0	22.4	78.6	17.3	74.0
% Institutional Deliveries		46.3	20.1	52.6	21.5	33.6
% women with BMI below 18.5 kg/m2		37	38.2	20.2	36.1	35.8
% children with Weight by height below -2 SD		16.2	19.8	21.2	11.7	15.5
		Utilisation and out-of-pocket Expenditure Profile				
% using public OPD (1995-96)						
Rural		25(32)	23(33)	16(26)	36(56)	19(26)
Urban		22(19)	19(32)	17(25)	41(57)	20(27)
% using public IPD (1995-96)						
Rural		32(49)	53(79)	31(44)	65(80)	45(63)
Urban		37(59)	56(77)	32(46)	73(86)	43(60)

(contd.)

Table 11.3 (contd.)

	Chhatis-garh	*Gujarat*	*Madhya Pradesh*	*Maha-rashtra*	*Rajasthan*	*India*
Average Total Expenditure on OPD care (1995-96) Rupees per illness						
(a) Rural						
Public		76	104	90	198	129
Private		175	177	179	156	186
Total		157	155	165	192	176
(a) Urban						
Public		139	513	125	169	166
Private		230	279	195	223	200
Total		218	376	185	198	194
Average total expenditure on IPD care (1995-96) Rupees per hospitalisation						
(a) Rural						
Public		1465	2207	1529	2634	2080
Private		3245	3482	3836	3971	4300
Total		2663	2191	3089	3038	3202
(a) Urban						
Public		1897	1678	1439	2544	2195
Private		4185	3889	5345	4949	5344
Total		3327	2774	3997	3149	3921

Note: Figures in parentheses are 42nd Round NSS data; *figures based on revised estimates 2000-2001

role of public financing is critical in both developed and under-developed economies. In most developed countries where healthcare access is near universal, public financing (whether through state revenues and/or social insurance) has been the critical component in realising universal access with equity (Roemer 1985; OECD 1990) In western and central Indian states one can see very clearly these associations in operation.

Maharashtra is the most developed state in the country with the highest per capita income in real terms. Today, it has the best health outcomes among the central-western region of India and Maharashtra has occupied this position for many years. If we look at the historical data, we see that public financing and development of public health facilities played a critical role in giving Maharashtra an early lead in health outcomes. What was unique to Maharashtra was that health budgets were decentralised through Zila Parishads right from the start for the development of the rural healthcare system. Maharashtra was perhaps the first state to realise the policy entitlements of one Primary Health Centre (PHC) for 30,000 population and one Community Health Centre for 5 PHCs. This was possible due to comparatively adequate investments and a higher level of per capita spending compared to other states in the region (Table 11.2).

Gujarat's trajectory was similar to Maharashtra's. Being close behind Maharashtra in both industrial and agricultural development, Gujarat too had the necessary economic support to facilitate health development. But Rajasthan and Madhya Pradesh neither had this opportunity nor did their governments invest adequately in per capita terms in healthcare (Table 11.2). It must be noted that in terms of the per cent of government spending and as a proportion to the net state domestic product (NSDP), Rajasthan and Madhya Pradesh were on a par or even better than the developed states, but this high level is belied by their per capita expenditures. The higher ratios for the NSDP and government spending in the latter state are due to the low economic development and low income levels.

Further, health and development cannot be seen only in terms of state averages because all these states are huge and the intra-state differences are very pronounced. At one level, there are rural-urban hierarchies in the type and quality of health services available with the urban sectors appropriating most of the curative budget—often two to three times the resources in proportion to their proportion in the states' population. The rural areas receive mostiy preventive and promotive services like family planning, immunisation, ante-natal care and disease surveillance to some extent. At another level, there are sub-regional hierarchies in the form of pockets of growth like the sugar and cotton belts in Maharashtra, groundnut, milk and cotton belts of Gujarat and the industrial areas of Mumbai-Thane-Pune, Surat-Ankleshwar, Indore, Raipur, Kota, etc. Health outcomes in these privileged pockets are vastly different from those in the rest of the state's regions. Often public health resource commitments are also skewed in favour of these privileged areas.

Another difference between the developed and underdeveloped states of the region is the availability of private health services. Maharashtra and Gujarat have a well-developed private health sector, and this is largely due to the high level of economic development, which ensures purchasing power. In contrast, the relative lack of purchasing power in Rajasthan and Madhya Pradesh has inhibited large-scale growt of the private health sector. This is clearly seen in the larger levels of utilisation of public facilities in Rajasthan and Madhya Pradesh, especially for the more expensive hospital care. Further, when we look at the morbidity levels and hospitalisation rates and contextualise them within the utilisation pattern, it becomes clear why the poorer states at one level and the poorer classes at another level report lower morbidity and hospitalisation rates—the lack of purchasing power forces them to ignore and/or postpone paying attention to their illness (Table 11.4). Thus the healthcare development patterns and the political economy of health in the two different sets of states of this region are very different, in terms of both the trajectory of growth and their current standing.

Table 11.4: Morbidity Profile 1995-1996 NSS 52nd Round

	Chhatis-garh	*Gujarat*	*Madhya Pradesh*	*Maha-rashtra*	*Rajasthan*	*India*
15 day prevalence of morbidity per 1000 (rural)		46 (45)	41(43)	52(52)	28(24)	55(57)
15 day prevalence of morbidity per 1000 (urban)		36(37)	38(37)	48(51)	33(33)	54(58)
15 day incidence for acute per 1000 (rural)		25(26)	25(26)	27(27)	14(14)	30(30)
15 day incidence for acute per 1000 (urban)		20(21)	20(19)	25(27)	18(16)	29(30)
Daily morbidity (point prevalence previous day) per 1000 rural		25(24)	18(19)	30(30)	13(10)	29(30)
Daily morbidity (point prevalence previous day) per 1000 urban		20(21)	19(19)	25(24)	19(18)	29(30)
Hospitalisations per 1000 in last 365 days rural		14(13)	7(6)	19(18)	8(6)	13(13)
Hospitalisations per 1000 in last 365 days urban		21(20)	15(16)	26(25)	14(14)	20(20)
Hospitalisations bottom 10% rural		4(3)	2(3)	10(10)	1(0)	4(4)
Hospitalisations bottom 10% urban		17(21)	9(8)	17(18)	6(12)	12(13)
Hospitalisations top 10% rural		25(23)	25(22)	40(41)	18(14)	13(13)
Hospitalisations top 10% urban		39(29)	51(49)	39(34)	36(25)	20(20)

Note: Figures for females are in parentheses.

Threat to Public Spending

The achievements of the public health sector in improving health outcomes during the eighties received a setback with the economic crises of 1991 and the subsequent economic reforms which followed under the SAP strategy dictated by the World Bank. As mentioned earlier, between the Fifth and the Seventh Plan period public health services and public health investment were relatively robust. This was reflected in the faster improvements in health outcomes—to begin with in the developed states and later by the underdeveloped states (Tables 11.1 and 11.2). This received a setback at the turn of the nineties when resource commitments in the public health sector declined, especially in the developed states.

This is reflected at one level in the slowing down of the improvements in the health outcomes and the widening rural-urban gap of these outcomes (Table 11.1). At another level the public healthcare facilities are becoming incapacitated because the inputs necessary to run these facilities are not being adequately provided for (Table 11.5). The National Health Policy (2002) unashamedly acknowledges that the public healthcare system falls grossly short of the defined requirements, its functioning is far from satisfactory, morbidity and mortality due to easily curable diseases continues to be unacceptably high and resource allocations are generally insufficient:

> It would detract from the quality of the exercise if, while framing a new policy, it is not acknowledged that the existing public health infrastructure is far from satisfactory. For the out-door medical facilities in existence, funding is generally insufficient; the presence of medical and para-medical personnel is often much less than required by the prescribed norms; the availability of consumables is frequently negligible; the equipment in many public hospitals is often obsolescent and unusable; and the buildings are in a dilapidated state. In the in-door treatment facilities, again, the equipment is often obsolescent; the availability of essential drugs is minimal; the capacity of the facilities is grossly inadequate, which leads to overcrowding, and consequentially to a steep deterioration in the quality of the services. (MoHFW 2002: Para. 2.4.1)

Table 11.5: Adequacy* of Public Health Facilities RCH Facility Survey 2000 (Phase 1)

(figures in percentages)

	Chhatis-garh	*Gujarat*	*Madhya Pradesh*	*Maha-rashtra*	*Rajasthan*	*India*
		Primary Health Centre				
Infrastructure		73	6	88	26	36
Staff		71	31	60	32	38
Supply		11	15	87	47	31
Equipments		88	28	96	59	56
		Community Health Centre				
Infrastructure		82	26	97	75	66
Staff		12	2	28	16	25
Supply		2	4	8	9	10
Equipments		62	57	10	78	49
		First Referral Unit				
Infrastructure		96	49	100	84	84
Staff		25	16	34	26	46
Supply		8	7	50	32	26
Equipments		85	67	34	97	69
		District Hospital				
Infrastructure		100	92	90	100	94
Staff		93	75	80	66	84
Supply		21	17	20	33	28
Equipments		100	92	100	100	89

*Adequacy = having at least 60% critical inputs

This is largely caused by the compression of public spending in the health sector, and secondly due to allocative inefficiencies caused by unprecedented increases in the salaries as a consequence of the Fifth Pay Commission implementation (around 1996-1998). Non-salary components have shrunk considerably as budget increases do not factor for allocative efficiencies for an effective running of the public health system. This, coupled with the privatisation policies, including the introduction of user charges or an increase in them (if they have already been introduced), has taken the public health system to the brink of collapse. With greater dependence on the market for healthcare, access becomes more difficult.

The evidence for this is clearly brought out in the changes one sees across the 42nd and 52nd Round NSS surveys (NSS-1987 and NSS-1996). Over this decade, utilisation of private health services, especially in the hospital sector, has increased substantially, out-of-pocket spending gallops and indebtedness due to healthcare related expenses affects half the users; the proportion of non-utilisation also increases. And it is the developed states that are more adversely affected by the SAP policies because they have suffered a larger decline in public spending. Thus in the nineties Rajasthan and Madhya Pradesh showed relatively higher increases in public spending and hence health outcomes improved faster in these states in contrast to the developed states where the decline in the public spending led to stagnation in health outcomes (Tables 11.1 and 11.2) – yet more persistent evidence in support of the hypothesis that public financing makes a critical difference towards improving health outcomes even in the absence of significant economic development.

In fact, when we relate health outcomes with expenditures we see that in comparison to similarly developed countries like China, Sri Lanka, Malysia and South Korea, India's performance is the worst despite her having one of the highest total health expenditures among these countries.[2] This is largely due to the fact that in India the spending is mostly out-of-pocket because there are very few public resources. In a scenario of poverty such a mechanism of financing will never show up good health outcomes because out-of-pocket health expenditures for the poor as well as the not-so-poor means forgoing other basic needs, or worse still, getting into indebtedness. National surveys show that taking of loans for healthcare is the number one reason for families, especially the poor ones, getting into indebtedness (in the category of consumption loans).

Another dimension of the reform process is that of disinvestments by the state in economic activities. This is supposed to release resources for a larger role of the State in the social sectors—the "human face" in the reforms/adjustment process. While divestment of public sector undertakings has been taking place, there is no evidence of increased support to the social sectors like health and education. This is perhaps due to the simultaneous shrinking of state revenues due to cuts in tax rates, excise duties, etc., which reduces the state's share in the national income leading to a declining tax : the GDP ratio (from a peak of over 16 per cent in the mid-eighties down to 13 per cent presently) (DEA 2003). This trend in itself is a threat to public spending because not only the promised additional resources are not available for the social sectors, but also some support which was available through public sector enterprises has now diminished. This is already being reflected in the increased unemployment ratios which are up from around 2 per cent in the eighties to over 7 per cent presently (DEA 2003).

The social sectors, which are of primary importance for human resource development, are critically dependent on public financing. The latter becomes even more important in the context of poverty because such support creates equity even with high levels of income poverty. Three-fourths of the people live below or at the subsistence level. This means 70-90 per cent of their income goes to food and related consumption. In such a context, social security support for health, education, housing, etc., becomes critical. Ironically, India has one of the largest private health sectors in the world with over 80 per cent of ambulatory care being supported through out-of pocket expenses (Table 11.6).

Table 11.6: Out of Pocket Burden to Seek Healthcare 52nd Round NSS-1995-96

	Gujarat	*Madhya Pradesh*	*Maha-rashtra*	*Rajasthan*	*India**
Hospitalisation (Rs. crores)	205.22	186.25	698.36	122.28	4824
% of NSDP**	0.33	0.33	0.50	0.29	0.45
per capita burden (Rs.)	44.91	25.17	80.27	24.46	51.35
Outpatient care (Rs. crores)	778.50	1482.52	1813.66	582.31	22085
% of NSDP	1.26	2.62	1.29	1.39	2.05
per capita burden (Rs.)	170.35	200.34	208.47	116.46	235.07
Total Out of pocket burden (Rs. Crores)	983.72	1668.77	2512.02	704.59	26909
% of NSDP	1.59	2.95	1.79	1.68	2.50
per capita burden (Rs.)	215.26	225.51	288.74	140.92	286.42
ratio to public expenditure	2.10	3.60	2.82	1.37	2.72

* For India the income ratio is GDP at factor cost;
** NSDP=net state domestic product

We have seen earlier that the public health services are very inadequate. The public curative and hospital services are mostly in the cities, and in this region between 20 to 40 per cent of the population resides in the cities. Rural areas have mostly preventive and promotive services like family planning and immunisation. The private sector has virtual monopoly of ambulatory curative services in both rural and urban areas and over half of the hospital care. Further, a very large proportion of private providers are not qualified to provide modern healthcare because they are either trained in other systems of medicine (traditional Indian systems like *ayurveda*, *unani,* and *siddha*, or homoeopathy) or worse—they do not have any training. These are the providers from whom the poor are most likely to seek healthcare. In the underdeveloped states the proportion of unqualified or inadequately trained practitioners is much higher. This adds to the risk faced by the already impoverished population. The healthcare market is based on a supply-induced demand and keeps growing geometrically, especially in the context of new technologies. The cost of seeking such care is also increasing. This means that access to healthcare, which is already difficult, is getting worse affecting severely not only the poor but also the middle classes.[3] Thus despite its poverty, India has a large, unregulated, poor quality, and expensive private health sector which is dominant, and an inadequately resourced, selectively focused, and declining public health sector. The former has curative monopoly, and the latter carries the burden of preventive services.

Economic reforms towards liberalisation began in the early eighties. It is important to make a note of the date because often there is a tendency to look only at the post-1991 period. Data available up to now clearly shows that economic performance of the eighties far outweighs that in the nineties. And the underlying fact about this is that in the eighties there was no structural adjustment or World Bank dictates. The classical "Hindu" rate of growth in the eighties had doubled from 3 to 6 per cent, without much inflation and with declining levels of poverty. Thus we were already liberalising our economy and speeding up growth without the World Bank running the show.

In fact, the post-1991 reform period slowed down growth, increased poverty[4] and inflation, and reversed many trends of the eighties. No doubt it caught up towards the mid-nineties, but it has not yet surpassed the achievements of the eighties. Thus in the eighties India was developing rapidly with a gradual globalisation process and with the advantage of its inner strength which insulated it from global shocks. In the nineties there was rapid globalisation that exposed India to global fluctuations; if India survived the Asian shock, which destroyed Indonesia and other Southeast Asian economies, it was because of its sheer size and the strengths of its own local markets.

Another fact to contend with is that over two-thirds of our population depends on agriculture and 70 per cent of it lives in the rural areas. Since the larger impact of macro-economic reforms is on the urban-industrial sector, which integrates globally with much ease, the rural population is still relatively protected from the global impacts. Further, it is the consistent good performance of agriculture that has helped ward off the severities of the SAP, which many other countries have faced. In addition, India's strong investments in the past in rural development, especially employment guarantee programmes and agricultural subsidies, aided in reducing the adverse impact of the SAP. And this is not likely to change thanks to the strong farm lobby that is in fact demanding greater investments and subsidies for the rural economy. Thus at one level, India and the states in this region are exposed to the global market with increasing vulnerability. But at another level, they continue to enjoy an inner strength and autonomy because of sheer size, large rural-agricultural population and a large local market of its own, despite the fact that politically the situation is very fluid. This background is important for understanding the impact and changes in the health sector.

Moving towards a New Paradigm[5]

The question often raised is "Why invest in health?" One argument is that investment elsewhere often has a positive impact on health which is true, provided such health-impacting investment is available! India's social infrastructure is inadequate and poor across the board. Whether it is education, sanitation, drinking water, rural transportation, electricity supply, or water harvesting, they are as bad as if not worse than the public healthcare services. Over the years public health services have deteriorated. If one reviews the health plans and policies, one finds that the state is heading clearly in the direction of abdication of its responsibility. From comprehensive basic care we have moved towards a programme-based approach (much like fire-fighting), and now we are becoming selective even about the programmes and the recipients of these services. This approach of the State has created favourable conditions for the private health sector to grow from strength to strength, often aided by public resources (Duggal 2000).

The other argument that investing in healthcare is gilt-edged because it has wide-ranging spin-offs in the overall economy is also very credible. Kerala in south India is a very good example. Kerala is economically less developed but has the best health profile in the country. This is because of its long history of public investment in healthcare services in both rural and urban areas. Conversely, with declining investment in the last decade we see degeneration in Kerala's health profile. Similarly, metropolitan areas like Mumbai, Delhi, Chennai, Bangalore, Ahmedabad, and Indore have seen vast investments in public health services and these are reflected in reasonably good health outcomes. In recent years one can see deterioration because of reduced investments and expenditures which is forcing people to access healthcare increasingly from the expanding rapidly private sector. Also these prime public health services have come under the purview of privatisation and user fees have been introduced across the board with the consequence that a large number of the poor who were the main users of these services have moved away from them.

With such a health system in the country, the health of the people cannot be any good. There is no dearth of evidence to show that India's health indicators are one of the worst in the world. In fact the latest Human Development Report shows a downward trend in India's global ranking.[6] Thus there is a crying need to reorganise the country's healthcare system. The future lies in creating an organised and regulated healthcare system, which is responsive to the people's needs and accountable to them. While reorganisation will be a long-term process, beginnings will have to be made by rationalising the existing healthcare system. For example, primary care (especially first line curative) services needs to be strengthened, a referral system needs to be organised for secondary and tertiary care, and resources have to be reallocated on a more equitable basis.

Operationalising the New Paradigm

Post-independence, India had committed itself to a comprehensive healthcare for all irrespective of the capacity to pay. We even had an elaborate national health plan in the form of the Bhore Committee Report. But as we have seen earlier, over the years there has been a clear process of dilution of the basic healthcare package. And the basic healthcare has to be viewed as a right. Today the world has moved beyond regarding only political rights as fundamental; increasingly social and economic rights are acquiring such recognition.

Thus we would like to view healthcare in the right perspective and frame priorities accordingly.

Basic health care, or primary healthcare as it is referred to today, must begin with family physician services and have an adequate support of referral services for speciality and hospital care, including special services for the disabled. This should be under an organised system, which, in today's given reality, best exists as a public-private mix. Curative and preventive services have to be integrated so that the existing dichotomies are removed. Pharmaceutical services also need to be regulated and organised, especially given the World Trade Organisation's anticipated impact. With drug price control virtually coming to an end, the rising prices are already creating a crisis in healthcare in both public and private domains.

A system based on a public-private mix would be most suitable for the realities in India. The state has to play a central role in helping develop an organised system of healthcare as against the prevailing *laissez faire* approach. The existing healthcare services will have to be restructured under a defined system and its financing organised and controlled by an autonomous body. To facilitate such restructuring a well-defined system of rules and regulations will have to be put in place so that minimum standards and quality care are assured.

There will be a great deal of resistance to implementing such a system, and it is here that the state will have to show its determination. Experience across the world shows that wherever near universal access exists, the system is a public-private mix organised under a single umbrella, which is well regulated and the fiscal control rests with a monopolistic and autonomous agency or a group of agencies. The best examples are Canada, Britain, Sweden, Germany, Costa Rica and South Korea, among others.

Public spending on healthcare is barely 1 per cent of the GDP as it stands today and in some states in this region it is much lower. This, in fact, is a decline over the earlier years, especially the mid-eighties when it was 1.32 per cent of the GDP at the national level and higher in some states of this region. Nearly 70 per cent of the state spending goes to urban areas, mostly for hospitals. The balance 30 per cent is spent in rural areas, mostly on family planning services, immunisation and selected disease surveillance. Organised information about private out-of-pocket expenditures on healthcare is not available.

At best, estimates can be made based on sample surveys of household expenditures and indirectly by extrapolating on the basis of the strength of the private health sector. Today this expenditure is estimated to be over 4 per cent of the GDP, more than double the estimates available for the sixties and seventies.

A restructured public-private mix would need fewer resources. Estimated basic healthcare package, including existing public secondary and tertiary services, would cost around 3 per cent of the GDP. This would mean a large saving amounting to 40 per cent of what is spent overall now. In addition, the quality of care will be much better and services more effective. As far as sharing of costs is concerned, the public share would definitely have to go up. Private resources would be channelised through employers, employees, insurance funds, or other collective mechanisms of pooling resources as non-governmental organisations and unions have demonstrated. The state would have to raise additional resources through earmarked taxes and cesses for the health sector. This would mean a greater burden on those with capacity to pay but there would be an overall saving of out-of-pocket expenses for all, especially for the poor.

Thus the new strategy should focus on strengthening the state sector, and at the same time also plan for a regulated growth and involvement of the private sector. There is a need to recognise that the private health sector is huge and has cast its nets far wider than the state sector health services. Through regulation and involvement of the private health sector, an organised public-private mix could be set up which can be used to provide a universal and comprehensive care to all. The need of the hour is to look at the entire healthcare system as a whole to evolve some sort of a national system. The private and public healthcare services need to be organised under a common umbrella to serve one and all. A framework for a basic minimum level of care needs to be spelt out in clear terms and this should be accessible to all without any direct cost to the patient at the time of receiving care.

Today we are at the threshold of another transition which will probably bring about changes such as regulation, price control, quality assurance and rationality in practice. This is the coming of private health insurance that will lay down rules of the game for the providers to suit its own motives. While this may improve the quality and accountability to some extent, it will be of very little help to the poor and the underserved, who will anyway not have access to this kind of a system. Worldwide experience shows that private insurance only pushes up costs and serves the interests of the haves. If equity in access to the basic healthcare must remain the goal, then the State cannot abdicate its responsibility in the social sectors. The state need not become the primary provider of healthcare services but this does not mean that it has no stake in the health sector. As long as there are poor, the state will have to remain a significant player, and interestingly enough, as the experience of most developed countries shows, the state becomes an even stronger player when the number of the poor becomes very small![7]

While reorganisation of the health sector will take its own time, certain positive changes are possible within the existing set-up through macro-policy initiatives. Some examples of setting priorities within the existing system for its improvement are presented in the box.

Priorities for Making it Work

To reorganise the healthcare system we need a policy statement to begin with. There has to be a political will to carry out such restructuring and reorganisation as well as the strength to overcome resistance from the vested interests.

While the ideal would be to see an organised system in place with an Act of Parliament, the reality is that the political will is missing because healthcare as a right is not a priority issue in civil society as yet. However, there is adequate interest and concern to take up piecemeal reforms and here the priorities are clear. Improvements and accountability of the existing system in both public and private domain are emerging on the agenda of reforms. People are demanding quality care and with the consumer courts on their side are increasingly confronting bad medical practice. The medical profession has also been awakened to the existing mess and is working to put its house in order: minimum standards, continuing medical education and accreditation are clearly emerging as items on their agenda.

In the public domain there is pressure for privatisation via introduction of user charges. Civil society groups in a number of places are fiercely resisting this. This battle has the potential of taking healthcare into the arena of a rights perspective and expediting the process towards an organised system of health care.

Policy Measures to Improve the Existing Healthcare System

Some Examples

The medical councils should be directed to put their house in order by taking the following steps:

1. Ensure that only those qualified and registered practise medicine.
2. Make continuing medical education compulsory and link renewal of registration to it.
3. Make it compulsory for medical graduates passing out of public medical schools to put in public service of at least five years, of which three years must be at PHCs and rural hospitals. This should be ensured not through bonds or payments but by providing only a provisional licence to practise under supervision in state healthcare institutions. The right of admission to.pursue post-graduate studies should be granted only to those who have completed the three years of rural medical service.
4. Regulate the spread of private clinics and hospitals through a strict location policy. The local authority should be given the right to determine how many doctors or how many hospital beds they need in their area using norms for family practice and ratios of practitioner to population and bed to population. Fiscal incentives may be provided for remote and underserved areas and strong disincentives and higher taxes for urban and overserved areas.
5. Assure the quality of care provided by hospitals and practitioners by setting up minimum standards to be followed.
6. Put in place compulsory health insurance for the organised sector employees. Restructure the existing Employees' State Insurance Scheme and merge it with the common national healthcare system where each employee has equal rights and cover but contributes according to his earning capacity. For example, if an employee contributes 2 per cent of his earnings and the employer adds another 3 per cent, then nearly Rs.100 billion could be raised through this alone.
7. Levy special taxes and cesses to generate additional resources. For instance, 1 per cent tax on sales turnover of alcohol and cigarettes and 1 per cent value tax on the asset for property owners and vehicle owners could bring in substantial resources.
8. Rationalise allocation of existing resources through preserving acceptable ratios of salary to non-salary spending.
9. Set up a referral system for secondary and tertiary care.

To establish the right to health and healthcare with the above scenario the following steps are necessary and should be taken first:

1. Equating Directive Principles with Fundamental Rights through a constitutional amendment.
2. Incorporating a National Health Act (similar to the Canada

Health Act) which will organise the present healthcare system under a common umbrella organisation as a public-private mix governed by an autonomous national health authority which will also be responsible for bringing together all resources under a single-payer mechanism.
3. Generating a political commitment through building a consensus on the right to healthcare in civil society.
4. Development of a strategy for pooling all financial resources deployed in the health sector.
5. Redistribution of existing health resources, public and private, on the basis of standard norms (these would have to be specified) to ensure physical (location) equity.

As an immediate step, within its own domain, the state should undertake the following:

1. Allocation of health budgets as block funding, that is on a per capita basis for each population unit of entitlement as per the existing norms. This will create redistribution of current expenditures and reduce substantially inequities based on residence.[8] Local governments should be given the autonomy to use these resources as per local needs but within a broadly defined policy framework of public health goals.
2. Strict implementation of the policy of compulsory public service by medical graduates from public medical schools and mandatory public service of a limited duration for those who are seeking admission to post-graduate education. This will augment human resources in the public health system substantially and will have a dramatic impact on the improvement of the credibility of public health services.
3. Return to price control over essential drugs (90 per cent of them are off-patent) as per the World Health Organisation list, or make production of volumes needed for domestic consumption compulsory to ensure availability of such drugs at affordable prices and within the public health system, or both.
4. Adoption of location policies by local governments for setting up of hospitals and clinics as per the standard acceptable

ratios, for instance, one hospital bed per 500 population and one general practitioner per 1,000 persons. To restrict unnecessary concentration of such resources in areas, fiscal measures to discourage such concentration should be instituted.[9]

5. The medical councils must be made to ensure that only licensed doctors practise and practise what they are trained for.[10] Such monitoring is the core responsibility of the council by law which they are not fulfilling, and as a consequence are failing to protect the patients who seek care from unqualified and untrained doctors. Further continuing medical education must be implemented strictly by the various medical councils and licences should not be renewed (as per the existing law) if the required hours and certification is not accomplished
6. Integration of Employees' State Insurance Scheme (ESIS), Central Government Health Scheme, and other such employee based health schemes with the general public health system so that discrimination based on employment status is removed. The integration will help in a more efficient use of resources. For instance, ESIS is a cash rich organisation with large funds collected from employees (which are invested in debentures and shares of companies!), and their hospitals and dispensaries are grossly underutilised. The latter could be opened up to the general public
7. Strictly regulate the private health sector as per the existing laws, but also an effort to changes these laws to make them more effective. This will contribute towards improvement of the quality of care in the private sector as well as create a degree of accountability.
8. Strengthen the health information system and database to facilitate better planning as well as audit and accountability.

Strategies and Approaches

An organised and universal healthcare system is possible only under a rights perspective. Right to health and healthcare is a fundamental social and economic right recognised by the International Covenant on Economic, Social and Cultural Rights. But the demand to recognise healthcare as a right is not on the political agenda in India. The People's Health Assembly initiative (called *Jan Swasthya Abhiyan* in India)[11] has voiced such a demand but this requires a widespread awareness campaign and participation of many more civil society groups.

At the other end of the spectrum, the medical profession needs to be educated not only about self-regulation and the need to assure minimum standards for quality healthcare, but also about the benefits of an organised public-private mix in the healthcare system.

Only such an approach can lead us closer to a system that guarantees universal access. Healthcare will have to be viewed in the context of social security. The latter becomes even more urgent under the changing political economy. Additional resources will be needed to finance these new public management systems and innovations in healthcare. From the standpoint of both equity and sustainability, it is critical that the financial support comes through a mechanism of public (collective) financing.

We are at a stage in history where the political will to do something progressive is conspicuous by its absence. We may have constitutional commitments and the backing of international law, but without the political will, no changes can take place. To reach the goal of the right to healthcare discussed above, civil society will have to be involved in a very large way and in many different ways.

The initiative to bring healthcare on the political agenda will have to be a multi-pronged effort, taken up at different levels. The idea here is not to develop a plan of action but to indicate the various steps that will have to be taken and the different parties that will have to be involved to build a consensus to make access to healthcare a matter of right. We make the following suggestions:

1. Policy level advocacy for the creation of an organised system for universal healthcare.
2. Research to develop the detailed framework of the organised system.
3. Lobbying the medical profession to build support for universal healthcare and regulation of medical practice.
4. Filing a public interest litigation on the right to healthcare to create a basis for constitutional amendment.

5. Lobbying the parliamentarians to make the Directive Principles justiciable.
6. Holding national and regional consultations on the right to healthcare with a wide array of civil society groups.
7. Running campaigns on the right to healthcare with networks of people's organisations at the national and regional levels.
8. Bringing the right to healthcare on the agenda of the political parties and to have it incorporated in their manifestoes.
9. Pressurising international bodies like WHO, Committee of ESCR, UNCHR, as well as national bodies like NHCR and the NCW to demand accountability from the Indian state and to monitor effectively the Indian state as it fulfils its obligations.
10. Preparing and circulating widely shadow reports on the right to healthcare to create international pressure

The above is not an exhaustive list. The basic idea is that there should be a widespread dialogue, awareness raising campaigns, research, documentation and legal and constitutional discourse.

To conclude, it is evident that the neglect of the public health system is an issue larger than government policy-making. The latter is the function of the overall political economy. Under capitalism only a well-developed welfare state can meet the basic needs of its population. Given the backwardness of India, the demand of public resources for the productive sectors of the economy (which directly benefit capital accumulation) is more urgent (from the business perspective) than the social sectors, hence the latter gets only a residual attention by the state. The policy route to a comprehensive and universal healthcare has failed miserably. It is now time to change gears towards a rights-based approach. The opportunity exists in the form of constitutional provisions and discourse, international laws to which India is a party, the potential of mobilising civil society, and creating a socio-political consensus on the right to healthcare. Great many small efforts towards this end are being made all over the country but what is really needed is to synergise these efforts so that the people of India can gain the right to health and healthcare (Duggal 2002b).

NOTES

1. Most of the data used have been compiled from the CEHAT Database. The assistance of T.R. Dilip and Rajeswari Balaji in compiling some of the data is gratefully acknowledged.
2. Health Outcomes in Relation to Health Expenditures

	Total Health Expenditure as % of GDP	*Public Health Expenditure* as % of total	*U-5 Mortality*	*Live Expectancy*	
				Male	*Female*
India	5	17	95	59.6	61.2
China	2.7	24.9	43	68.1	71.3
Sri Lanka	3	45.4	19	65.8	73.4
Malaysia	2.4	57.6	14	67.6	69.9
South Korea	6.7	37.8	14	69.2	76.3

Source: ICRIER 2001

3. The 52nd Round NSS data reveals that for in-patient care 46 per cent of poorer classes and 34 per cent of the richer classes either sold assets or took loans to pay for treatment. Secondly, those using private hospitals were 16 per cent more likely to get into indebtedness than those using public hospitals (NSS-1996 2000).
4. The poverty ratio is much debated and there are different estimates of the ratio. The official line is that the poverty ratio declined considerably in the nineties and stands around 27 per cent. However, if we move away from the numbers game and look at the character of poverty, its increasing severity with starvation deaths is most striking. In the eighties one had stopped hearing of starvation deaths.
5. The discussion from here onwards is contextualised for the country as a whole but is relevant for all the states in the western and central region.
6. India's human development index rank is down from 115 in 1999 to 124 in 2000, though still better than the 1994 rank of 138. India is on the fringe of medium and low HDI group of countries. The improvement in India's HDI in the last 25 years has been marginal from a score of 0.407 in 1975 to 0.577 in 2000—this works out to an average increase of 1.6 per cent per annum. The slowing down of growth is shown in the table below:

	1975	*1980*	*1985*	*1990*	*1995*	*2000*
HDI score	0.407	0.434	0.473	0.511	0.545	0.577
Annual % increase over previous period	—	1.3	1.8	1.6	1.3	1.1

Source: UNDP various years

7. Data from OECD countries clearly shows that the state is a major player in health financing and over three-fourths of the resources for the health sector in these countries, except the USA, comes from the public exchequer; even in the USA it is over 40 per cent. But in India the state contributes less than one-fifth, the balance coming out of the pockets of the households (OECD 1990).

8. To illustrate this, taking the Community Health Centre (CHC) area of 150,000 population as a "health district" at current budgetary levels under block funding this "health district" would get Rs. 30 million (current resources of state and central government combined are over Rs.200 billion, that is, Rs. 200 per capita). This could be distributed across this health district as follows: Rs 300,000 per bed for the 30 bedded CHC or Rs. 9 million (Rs.6 million for salaries and Rs. 3 million for consumables, maintenance, POL, etc.) and Rs. 4.2 million per PHC (5 PHCs in this area), including its sub-centres and CHVs (Rs. 3.2 million as salaries and Rs. 1 million for consumables etc.). This would mean that each PHC would get Rs. 140 per capita as against less than Rs. 50 per capita currently. In contrast, a district headquarter town with 300,000 population would get Rs. 60 million, and assuming Rs. 300,000 per bed (for instance, in Maharashtra, the current district hospital expenditure is only Rs. 150,000 per bed) the district hospital too would get much larger resources. To support health administration, monitoring, audit, statistics, etc., each unit would have to contribute 5 per cent of its budget. Of course, these figures have been worked out with the existing budgetary levels and exclude local government spending which is quite high in larger urban areas (Duggal 2002a).
9. Such locational restrictions in setting up practice may be viewed as a violation of the fundamental right to practise one's profession anywhere. It must be remembered that this right is not absolute and restrictions can be placed in the interest of the public good. The suggestion here is not to have compulsion but to use fiscal measures. In fact, in the U.K. under the National Health Service, the local health authorities have the right to prevent setting up of clinics if their area is saturated.
10. For instance, the Delhi Medical Council has taken first steps in improving the registration and information system within the Council and some mechanism of public information has been created.
11. *The People's Health Campaign* is a unique grassroots-to-global movement for *Health for All*, a campaign for better health. This innovative campaign has been active since July 1999, to enquire into the current state of health services and to demand better healthcare. The background to this campaign is a global wake-up call being given to governments around the world, reminding them of their promise and pledge made in 1978 to provide "Health for All by 2000 AD". India took the lead in this campaign and over 1,200 health, science, women's, and other organisations and NGOs, including nineteen national networks, in twenty states are involved in the Peoples Health Assembly (PHA) process.

REFERENCES

Bhore, Joseph, (1946): "Report of the Health Survey and Development Committee". Volumes I to IV. Delhi: Government of India.

DEA, (2003): "Economic Survey 2002-03". New Delhi: Government of India.

Duggal, Ravi, (2000): "The Private Health Sector in India: Nature, Trends and a Critique". New Delhi: Voluntary Health Association of India.

Duggal, Ravi (2002a): "Resource Generation without Planned Allocation". *Economic and Political Weekly* (January 5).

Duggal, Ravi (2002b): "Health and Development in India – Moving Towards Right to Healthcare". Draft paper for Harvard School of Public Health Initiative on Right to Development.

ICRIER (2001): "Changing the Indian Health System: Draft Report". ICRIER.

MoHFW (2002): "National Health Policy 2002". New Delhi: Government of India.

NSSO, (1987): "NSS-1987-Morbidity and Utilisation of Medical Services, 42nd Round, Report No. 384". New Delhi: National Sample Survey Organisation.

NSSO, (2000): "NSS-1996: Report No. 441 52nd Round". New Delhi: National Sample Survey Organisation.

OECD, (1990): "Health Systems in Transition". Paris: Organisation for Economic Cooperation and Development.

Roemer, Milton, (1985): "National Strategies for Healthcare Organisation". Health Administration Press.

UNDP, "Human Development Report". various years.

12

Human Resources for the Twenty-First Century

The Contribution of Traditional Birth Attendants (*Dais*)

MIRAI CHATTERJEE

Strengthening our human resources is surely one of the greatest challenges of the twenty-first century globalisation. As trade barriers are lifted, markets open up, and capital crosses the national borders, the task of ensuring that all workers, especially the poor, also enjoy the fruits of the new economic environment looms large.

Our grassroot-level experience reveals that unless the poor, and especially informal, women workers are organised, their skills are upgraded and enhanced, and markets are made accessible to them, it will be difficult, if not impossible, for the working poor to weather the changes brought about by globalisation and liberalisation, leave alone benefit from these. It is in this context that we need to discuss capacity-building or human resource development.

Capacity-Building at SEWA

Over 30 years of organising the poor, self-employed women workers has taught us that capacity-building or human resource development is one of the four pillars or strategies for the removal of poverty. This, along with capitalisation of the poorest people, especially women; building social security and collective strength; and voice or representation; has constituted the core of the Self-Employed Women's Association's (SEWA) strategy to support women's struggle against poverty.

Our human resource development efforts have been grounded in the belief that everyone has some potential and ability. Adequate opportunity, exposure and nurturing allow this potential to develop which leads to creative action. Most of all, we have faith in the immense potential of the poor, working women of this country who have shown time and again that they are ready to learn and seize new opportunities, not only for themselves but also for their families and communities. They are prepared to give their time and energy to the task at hand; they are also ready to demolish the age-old myths about their abilities to grow and develop. Finally, in building their capacities, their primary goal is not merely to forge ahead as individuals and develop their own careers, but also to serve their villages and *mohallas* as best as they can.

SEWA's on-going work provides than opportunity for our members and organisers (staff) to grow and develop in many ways including as strong leaders. The day–to-day demands of organising and building economic organisations of the poor, whether their own bank, village-based producers' group, or *dai* or child-care cooperative, are the best laboratories for human resource development. In addition, through our various training programmes, including classroom sessions and exposure visits, or just learning-by-doing, we strengthen our members' knowledge, skills and capacities to:

- run their own activities independently whether they pertains to savings and credit, insurance, nursery-raising, craft, dairying, health- and child-care, or something else;
- use, manage and control their own village or *mohalla* group and district-level organisation; and
- organise, develop and run their own organisations, movements and campaigns whether they are state-level federations, national-level unions, or national and international campaigns or movements for greater visibility, recognition and economic rights.

Capacity Building at Grassroots

Capacity building at SEWA takes many forms. Over time, various methodologies have been evolved, based on our members' needs.

Learning-by-Doing

When poor women themselves run their own economic activity, group and even organisation, they become strong, confident and articulate. Hitherto-hidden potential and even skills develop. This has been our experience time and again. Hence, at SEWA, opportunities are created whereby women actually run their own organisations. The following few examples indicate the range of their activities.

1. Every month women from the same occupation meet in their own trade committees and discuss work-related issues such as how to organise for minimum wages or increased income, how to create more employment, or how to ensure social security.
2. They plan, implement and monitor their own campaigns—be it for full rights as home-based workers, to assert their claims on water, or to put land, forests and nurseries in women's hands.
3. For each economic activity and service, spearhead teams have been developed. These teams comprise mainly our members and a few full-time organisers (staff). These teams meet every month in each of the 11 districts where SEWA works. Women take the lead in planning, implementing, monitoring and evaluating their activities.
4. SEWA-promoted cooperatives and DWCRA groups have their own elected executive committees which meet regularly and run their own activities, including overseeing and managing all financial transactions and interactions, with their group members as well as with the outside world.

Learning-by-doing is a long but fruitful journey for our members. In contrast to mere classroom learning or theoretical discussions, in learning-by-doing they are involved in the day-to-day implementation of plans, in solving problems and in developing vision and direction for their own economic activities.

Technical Training

For women to run their own economic activity and reach their ultimate goals of full employment and self-reliance, several technical inputs—based on their needs and existing knowledge and skills—are required. This technical information is shared with women with the help of experts by SEWA organisers and leaders. Exposure visits are also arranged for the same purpose both within SEWA and outside. Over the years, thousands of women have participated in technical training in diverse fields, including:

- savings and credit (financial services);
- craft, embroidery, patchwork, beadwork, tie and dye and block-printing;
- agriculture, nursery and plantation;
- water harvesting, conservation and watershed development;
- dairying including para-veterinary training;
- video production;
- health to be barefoot doctors; childcare and nutrition; and
- housing.

These are but a few examples of the numerous technical training programmes offered to SEWA members. The training programmes are as diverse as our members and their occupations. But all aim at strengthening them economically and promoting self-reliance among individuals and groups.

Encouraging Grassroot Leaders

SEWA is both an organisation and a movement. Every movement requires an ideological framework and a clear direction: the framework must be understood by all and the direction must be clear to all. All participants in the movement must have a common understanding of the vision and the strategy. The messages of the movement must be taken to the public, to policy-makers and to those persons whose help the movement needs. A movement also needs leaders. In SEWA's case, most of the leaders are working class women from the rural and urban areas.

A SEWA Academy was started in 1991 with the objective of offering training to SEWA members to prepare them to be leaders in their respective fields of work as well as in the SEWA organisation.

The SEWA Academy is now our capacity-building and research organisation. Our members call it "SEWA University".

Human Resource Development: The Case of *Dais*

If our members are to meet the challenges of the new economic scenario and enjoy its benefits, their health and well-being, what we may call their health security, must be attained. Indeed, for the poor being healthy means being productive and able to work and earn. Our members often explain this by saying, "Our health is our only asset."

Unfortunately, even in a relatively economically advanced state of Gujarat, we have a long way to go in attaining health security. In fact the health indicators of Gujarat are average at best; indeed some areas such as infant mortality rate, sex ratio, and HIV/AIDS are a cause for concern. The state government acknowledges that improving our citizens' health calls for efforts from all quarters: government and non-government, private and people's initiatives. Importantly, it calls for human resource development on a massive scale as supporting efforts towards health security are necessarily a labour-intensive process.

Although we have invested in human resource development for health care, most of the personnel are concentrated in urban centres and do not serve the poorest of our citizens. In fact, at the international level, a commission to study human resources in the health sector has begun to identify serious shortfalls, in terms of both quality and quantity.

For several years now, we have seen that our traditional birth attendants or *dais*. If properly trained, provided with opportunities for skill up-gradation, and given continuous back-up support (by way of refresher training, provision of the latest health and medical information, referral linkages and other connections with government health services) they can be very effective and enthusiastic barefoot doctors of their villages. And their range of knowledge, skills, and services need not be restricted to obstetrics. Our early insights into their potential as care-providers and healers came from a study undertaken by us jointly with the Foundation for Public Interest in the early eighties. We learnt that not only did they enjoy tremendous trust and confidence among their communities, especially among women, they were also performing a number of health-related tasks and activities which remain unrecognised and undocumented for the most part. And, needless to say, all of these services were carried out without any fee or remuneration. While *dais* traditionally obtain some payment in kind (foodgrains, coconuts and sometimes a sari), they do not receive anything for ensuring that the village's children were immunised or for assisting auxiliary nurse midwives in ante-natal check-ups, family planning services, or even emergency referrals, for that matter.

These revelations prompted us to link up with the government for special skill up-gradation training and even to develop some of our own in-house skill up-gradation curriculum with the help of obstetricians and gynecologists. We received an overwhelming response to our initial efforts, which encouraged up to set up a special *Dai Shala* (Mid-wife School) for these traditional birth attendants in April, 2000, with an experienced obstetrician-gynecologist leading the effort. Information about the number of *dais* trained is given in Table 12.1.

Table 12.1: Number of *Dais* Trained

Year of Training	*District*	*Number trained*
2000	Ahmedabad/Gandhinagar	40
2000	Ahmedabad/ Gandhinagar	38
2001	Mehsana	32
2001	Ahmedabad	38
2001- 2002	Sabarkantha	28
2002	Gandhinagar	29
2002	Anand/Kheda	30
Total	Six Districts	235

An impact study of the contribution of trained *dais* to the health of women and others is in progress. However, in these three years, significant lessons have been learnt some of which are outlined below.

1. *Dais* are eager to learn the modern ways of delivering babies and to put them into practice. In fact, there are some women, both young and old, who have not worked as *dais* but would like to taking the course and learn.
2. *Dais* are willing to take time off from their routine for

attending the training. The course runs for three months, and the attendance at the training is high and regular. In fact, the commitment of the *dais* to the training is remarkable as the story in the Box depicts.

3. Illiteracy does not have to be a bar to learning and strengthening one's knowledge and skills. In the course of the training, some women's literacy skills are revived, and others begin to sign their names and write simple words by copying them down from the blackboard.
4. In terms of pedagogy, it was realised that when teaching illiterate and semi-literate women, it is necessary to go at a slow pace so that the information is properly absorbed by them. There is also a need to repeat and revise whatever is taught so that the women retain what they have been taught.
5. Use of visual teaching aids, such as posters, charts, models and videotapes are very helpful for communicating information. Role plays also work well.
6. While women have a high degree of motivation for learning, it is important to encourage them constantly. The sensitivity, patience and attitude of the trainer are critical to the success of the training.
7. One of the subjects highly valued by the *dais* was anatomy. None of the previous trainings they had attended had provided them with any information on anatomy. For instance, they learnt for the first time that the uterus is separate from the stomach! They now use their knowledge to dispel several myths about pregnant women. They also appreciated learning about how X and Y chromosomes determine the sex of the foetus.
8. Equipped with enhanced knowledge and skills, *dais* have emerged as strong and capable local leaders and are increasingly recognised as such in their villages. Many are asked to stand in the election as a *sarpanch* of the village. They continue to provide services as *dais* and also as responsible leaders of the Panchayati Raj.

Dhaniben and Shardaben

It was the monsoon season and sowing was in full swing in the fields. Despite this, the *dais* (students of the school) came regularly. "We want to study – to learn. We will go for sowing in the next monsoon. It does not matter if we lose wages—Rs. 100 per day", said Dhaniben Ambaram Parmar of Dhadrodi village in Ahmedabad district.

After the examination of the December 2002 batch of the *Dai Shala* in Anand was over, everyone was sitting together. Dr. Renuka Patwa, the Director of the *Dai Shala*, asked the women what were their feelings about the course and about the examination now that it was over. "We learnt a lot, and we are very thankful to you for teaching us so much. The course has meant a lot to us."

One of them pointed to Shardaben and said, "Her mother-in-law died this morning, yet she came today for the examination". Shardaben (from Dalapur village, Umreth taluka, Anand district) said in a quiet voice, "I told my family that I had to go for the examination today". This is a testimony not only to the women's commitment but also to the commitment of their families to the advancement of their women members.

Dais graduating from the *Shala* not only take up the additional responsibilities as health educators for primary health care, they also disseminate information about HIV/AIDS and actively campaign against sex determination tests. They are also raising issues pertaining to their rights such as being issued with an identity card so that they are both visible and are considered *bona fide* service providers. Most importantly, they have been organising in larger numbers than before. In fact, almost 6,000 *dais* have now joined SEWA and 500 of them have also been organised into their own district-level cooperatives in Ahmedabad, Kheda, Mehsana and Gandhinagar districts. One of the cooperatives, the *Lok Swasthya* cooperative, which was originally operating in Ahmedabad city and district, now operates statewide. It has already taken the responsibility of implementing TB and AIDS control and education programmes in two wards of Ahmedabad city and in the district. The other *dai* cooperatives will be shortly following suit.

Our experience with capacity-building of *dais* leads us to suggest that they be considered essential human resources and key providers of health services. We may begin by entrusting a few health-related activities to them and then add other activities at a later date in a phased manner. In this way, we are likely to move closer to our goals of achieving health security for our people and at the same time build local human resource pools. But we need to do this through a planned effort. One way to achieve this is through *Dai Shalas* at district, if not taluka, levels. We have the infrastructure. It is more a question of revitalising, re-visiting and reorienting our approach.

Another important contribution from the above efforts is the generation of income. SEWA-trained *dais* are now able to ask for and obtain some user fee for their services. Though the supplementary income of about Rs. 200 per month on average is modest, it is useful for them; many of whom are widows and are very poor, landless, agricultural labourers.

While these are still new and developing experiences, the potential of providing employment in the health sector to *dais* and other local-level health workers is enormous. The effort may well serve to fill the human resource gap in the health sector, especially since the city-based personnel rarely opt to serve rural areas where the majority of the poor people live. According to a recent Confederation of Indian Industries-McKinsey study of the health sector, "this sector can increase employment by generating jobs for 2.5 million people by 2012, in addition to 4 million already employed in this sector" (Khorakiwala 2003).

But the road to supporting *dais* and other local health workers through capacity-building inputs is likely to be long and difficult. *Dais* and others are labelled "unskilled", or even worse, "quacks". Thus programmes and initiatives to promote them not only lack support, they are viewed with suspicion or even disapproval.

And the disapproval of *dais* is globalised! Some research in the universities overseas has found that a *dai's* training does not help reduce the maternal mortality—as if this is the sole responsibility of *dais*. And there is not much discussion yet on widening their roles to include a broader spectrum of health work. Unfortunately, many multilateral aid agencies and other donors have taken this view.

On the other hand, several policy-makers, doctors, people's organisations, and NGOs who have first-hand experience with *dais*, argue that the of and other local health workers can make a difference between health security and insecurity, between death and survival in the traditionally underserved communities. *Dais* are present in villages night and day and enjoy the trust of their communities. In addition to SEWA, several other community-oriented service providers all over the country have found that their experiences with *dais* hold out a promise for solving the problem of human resources implementation plaguing our health system.

Without going into the "for" "against" and debates, our plea, based on empirical evidence over the past two decades of actively working with *dais,* is that we should explore the real potential of these committed and hard-working women with an open mind. The commitment has to be buttressed with ear-marked resources for training, back-up support and better referral and service linkages with government and private health-service providers. We see *dais* as a case in point in our discussions on developing human resources and health security, for the 21st century with people, especially women, leading the process and also remaining at the core of these efforts.

REFERENCE

Khorakiwala, Habil, (2003): "Healthy, Wealthy and Wise", *Hindustan Times,* New Delhi, February 26.

13

Liberalisation and Labour in Indian Industry

TIRTHANKAR ROY

India's closed and over-regulated economy began to be liberalised and market-oriented from 1992 onwards. How has this structural adjustment benefited the working masses? In general assessments of the economic reform process, it is often too readily presumed that the return of free market has benefited capital more than labour. The idea that the elite and middle classes gained while the workers, barring some exceptions, probably experienced deterioration pervades a large body of work on the subject. Overarching statements, indeed, abound in this discourse, dominated by public lectures and newspaper articles rather than serious research. Consider, for example, a very recent advertisement for a talk by Mario Rutten at the H-Asia Discussion Group on the net: Prof. Mario Rutten discusses the contradictory effects of globalisation on Indian society. While the interests of the working poor in India have deteriorated, operating in the new globalised economy has created increasing opportunities for the emerging middle class. Their global outlook has made them even more indifferent to the plight of the Indian poor.

Needless to add, the perspective from which this was written is nowhere more common than within India itself. If indeed the outcome of the reforms was so starkly contradictory, the reforms cannot be sustained without incurring massive social and political costs. It makes the reform process a fundamentally contested one, rather than one based on consensus and cooperation. Manufacturing labour, which has experienced stagnation in real wages after the economic reforms, and has for some time been engaged in a grim battle for maintaining *status quo* in the labour laws, would seem to be an obvious example of the costs of reforms. The war between the government and the national trade unions over the changes in the Industries (Disputes and Regulation) Act would seem to represent one of the many fronts where conflicts are breaking out.

The widespread perception that the market-reforms had an elitist bias is partly coloured by the recession of the late-1990s, the effects of which were especially bad on the manufacturing workers. These effects linger on. The job market has not returned to the buoyancy that it saw in the early 1990s. "Work harder for less" is still a norm in many sectors that briefly saw a boom in the mid-1990s. But essentially, this perception is based on the belief that deregulation withdrew considerable state support formerly extended to the weaker party in the employer-employee relationship, and that this relationship is basically a contradictory, a zero-sum one.

Looking more closely at the data, it would seem that the perception that on the whole labour has been hurt is simplistic. Economists are often persuaded by the media focus on the more visible conflicts into thinking that the whole relationship is conflictual. In fact, no overall assessment in terms of gains and costs is possible unless we segregate the working classes. Two divisions are particularly relevant.

The first distinction is between the formal and the informal sectors. In the formal or "organised" sector, a contradiction in the capital-labour relation did arise, partly from a latent contradiction. The formal sector operated in regulated labour markets but protected product markets. In this sector, therefore, there was a latent tendency for substitution of labour with capital. This contradiction had already manifested itself in a conflict before the reforms started. India's political economy in the pre-reform phase was strongly committed to forestalling any serious confrontation at the work-place. This political economy had accumulated tremendous strain, and had become unsustainable before the market reforms started.

On the other hand, in the overwhelmingly larger informal sector, where the social and economic distance between capital and labour has always been rather small, there was never a zero-sum game at work in the first place. In these tiny firms that operated in unregulated markets both capital and labour worked generally with a poor asset base and their interests were closely tied to the fortune of the whole industry. In these highly labour-intensive and low-investment firms, employers could not easily replace labour and, therefore, there was a fundamental compatibility in labour-capital relations. If the market improved for capital, it improved for the labour as well. Capital and labour floated and sunk together. Nowhere is this more evident than in the case of the textile industry after the reforms, where an estimated one million jobs were created in the course of an export boom, nearly all of it in the informal sector. Needless to add, great many of the new firms and new jobs were wiped out in the 1997-2001 recession.

The second distinction is between the old and new firms. The reforms ushered in new businesses like never before. The reforms hurt primarily the old firms in the formal sector, where the contradiction between capital and labour had already opened up and became a battleground after the reforms. But the reforms came as an opportunity for new firms in the formal sector, which did not have to treat labour and a strained relationship as an overhead cost. A substantially new working class took shape in and via the new enterprises after the reforms. In the informal sector too, key elements of the reforms, such as access to export markets for labour-intensive goods, benefited labour and capital. On the other hand, globalisation of consumer preferences hurts capital and labour in many traditional industries. Thus old and new firms faced very different-uneven-sets of issues in the industrial relations and adjustment to free markets.

In this essay, I develop the notion of a variable impact of market reforms on employment and industrial relations. Both distinctions–old-new and formal-informal–will be used as key devices. I shall also argue that the perceptions of changing industrial relations in India can be biased if we focus too much, as the media has a tendency to do, on the old firms and old labour in the formal sector, and neglect the new firms, the new labour and the informal sector. The weight of the last is increasing in the labour market. And yet, new labour remains very much a neglected field of enquiry.

The rest of the paper has five sections: (i) a brief survey of the reforms, (ii) a political economic overview, (iii) the formal sector, (iv) the informal sector, and (v) conclusion.

BRIEF SURVEY OF THE REFORMS

Partially from the mid-1980s, and generally from 1991-92, economic reforms were initiated in India with the explicit aim of improving efficiency. In the first 40 odd years since independence (1947), India followed a development policy which relied on the domestic market (tariffs, quotas and overvalued exchange rate made import and export both difficult), and on the planning philosophy, by which I mean rationing of investment funds via fiscal, monetary and regulatory policy instruments.

While these strategies did create a large domestic industrial base, they had many weaknesses echoing the problems of transitional economies the world over. Lack of international contact had made the Indian industry fall behind in technology. Lack of competition both at home and abroad had compromised quality and efficiency. In turn, consumer goods markets stagnated due to high cost or poor quality. Planning often directed investments to low-return fields. Capital cost had to be lower to compensate for such a policy. Both strategies led to wastage of scarce resources.

In the first phase of the reforms, relative factor prices changed mainly via trade policy changes (making the exchange rate market-determined, reducing tariffs and partially withdrawing quotas). Given that India has an abundance of labour, one would expect the world prices of Indian labour-intensive manufactures to fall, and become competitive, as a result of the devaluation that followed. Given that India has a relative scarcity of capital and was technologically backward, imported capital-intensive manufactures should become competitive due to the tariff reduction. Devaluation partly taxed that price reduction, but only partly. Withdrawal of quotas substantially reduced the transaction costs of imports of items formerly subject to licensing. Both these effects, export of labour-intensive manufactures and import of technology-intensive products, did materialise. Further, domestic deregulation in respect of licensing and direct fiscal support to specific sectors made it easier for firms to utilise economies of scale and reduce their start-up costs. These moves, in turn, greatly encouraged new enterprises and new entrants.

For a few years after 1991-92, the growth rates in employment, real income and real output per worker, and the rates of investment tended to be exceptionally large. As expected, the major gains occurred in the labour-intensive informal-sector-based consumer non-durable industries. On the other hand, the rates of real wage growth slowed down considerably in the post-reform period, suggesting that the labour market functioned more freely in this period. That particular change helped the formal sector. The major industries experiencing growth were textiles and clothing, leather, gems and jewellery, processed food, plastics and plastic intermediates, machine tools, etc. The Major industries in decline included engineering, metallurgy and textile intermediates in large mills.

The formal sector or the organised sector in India is defined as factories covered by the Factories Act. The unorganised sector consists of production units not covered by the Act. The distinction is crucial in the explanations of employment trends because regulation and politics affect hiring and firing of labour. Despite the gains mentioned earlier, employment in the unorganised sector fell marginally in the period 1989-94. This, in fact, is an average between the rapid growth in the exportable sectors like garments and leather products and fall in the old-style utilitarian handicrafts like handloom weaving and pottery. Employment growth in the formal sector accelerated rapidly in the mid-1990s, but fell sharply thereafter. Table 1 captures, once again, an average experience between considerable job-loss in the old firms and growth of jobs in the new firms. To understand the former process, we need to understand the political economy of the Indian labour better.

POLITICAL ECONOMY OF ORGANISED LABOUR: 1950-1990

The political-economic regime that remained in place from 1950 until the beginning of the 1990s incorporated several types of implicit contracts between the government, on the one hand, and the major constituents of the manufacturing sector on the other. This was an era when the average firm, large or small, rationalised its existence by citing the number of jobs it created. The organised sector came under laws that protected wages and employment. It received protection in the product market, especially in the relatively capital-intensive sectors such as the manufacture of machinery and intermediate goods, in return for giving up the flexibility to adjust labour costs, as it were. Given protection in the final market, the average firm could bear excess labour cost (that is, sustain labour productivity below internationally competitive levels), afford over-manning to some extent and wages above the market rate. By thus expanding employment they became a party to the effort to attain economic growth and social justice.

In this arrangement, the government was committed to intervene in dispute settlements. Accordingly institutions were set up and laws framed that involved the government as a powerful third party even in a small dispute. Such involvement demanded macro-level collective bargaining. Therefore, the counterpart of the government institutions was not the firm itself, but the national trade unions affiliated to the major political parties. In some cases, special laws awarded monopoly to one of these.

The informal, unorganised, or small-scale sector was already highly labour-intensive and operated in an unregulated labour market. As long as there was a large wage-gap between India and the industrialised world, the sector did not need a similar sheltering from world competition. But it did need protection from the organised sector because the wage-gap between the organised and the unorganised sector within India was narrow and tended to disappear in a certain range. A policy of reservation of industrial goods for small-scale industry, and the more focused and aggressive textile policy, extended this protection to the unorganised sector, with the hope that this sector will continue to be pivotal in employment generation. By 1990, the reservation policy covered close to one thousand product items.

Already in the "industrial stagnation" of the late 1970s and through the great strikes that followed it, the contract between the government and the organised sector was showing signs of strain.[1] Protection in the final market was proving to be not enough compensation for the loss of flexibility in the labour market. A great many of the large firms faced saturated or slow growing home market. In the contemporary leftist view, the sluggish home market reflected inequality and exploitation. But, according to another view, the sluggish home market was a result of an innovation paralysis, which resulted from the lack of competition and access to technologies (Roy, forthcoming). In 1982, faced with a near-zero employment growth rate, labour demanded more concessions. But the capital had had enough. This was the background of the fierce strikes of 1981-84 in the textile, engineering and jute industries. These were also the circumstances that led to the "jobless growth" of the mid-1980s.[2] All this was still only a prelude to the complete collapse of the implicit contract. When a liberalised trade regime was sort of forced upon the government, the disparity in competitiveness between many old, organised sector firms, and the NIE capability, became exposed. All of a sudden, the extent of accumulated overmanning was discovered, above-market-wage became a serious issue, and the labour regime began to hurt, fatally in many cases.

In the liberalised trade regime that unfolded slowly from the 1980s and more rapidly after 1992, the average firm rationalised its existence by the amount of foreign exchange it earned, and not by the number of jobs it created. It became increasingly apparent that surviving in the world market and the framework of implicit contracts, drawn up with the home market in view, did not hang together. This changed mindset was not only a cause, but also a symptom of a gradual process of losing faith in the implicit contract that had begun earlier.

In the unorganised sector, there were no clear battlelines. After 1992, the ground for upholding the old understanding between the small-scale industry and the government was receding. The connection between the unorganised sector and employment generation was not obvious any more. Given the big reshuffles that were going on within the unorganised sector, the net employment implications were not clear at all. Economists and policy analysts did not tire of pointing out that the reservation policy interfered with competitiveness by hindering emergence of the efficient scale. Effectively, the reservation policy divided the small firms into two sets. One set consisted of industries with low economies of scale in production or marketing or the "naturally small" firms. The other set consisted of industries with potentially larger economies of scale but where government policy created a bias for remaining small, or the "artificially small" firms. Whereas the former did not need reservation, the argument for identifying and de-reserving the latter set was strong. In some cases, where production economies remained small, but marketing economies large, some form of ancillarisation developed. But there was no way of knowing whether these arrangements were natural (market-driven) or artificial (policy-driven). Reforms here did begin to happen as a matter of course, but were stalled and delayed by adverse circumstances.

By 1990, this sector had segmented into at least three large clusters. The first consisted of the older artisanal industries. These industries by and large represented a declining political force. By 1990, a fairly large segment among them had already become a "basket case" due to the changes in the consumption pattern.[3] When fiscal pressures began to be unbearable, the artisans receiving some form of state aid were the first to be sacrificed. On the other side, entrepreneurs who benefited from reservation and other promotional measures had emerged as a powerful vote bank with a considerable say in state politics. The influence of these small capitalists was not concentrated in individuals or associations, but was widely diffused in the body politic and that much more difficult to deal with. After trade liberalisation a yet third group came to the fore in the form of the successful exporter of industrial goods. The subsequent export boom was largely led by small firms. Although their comparative advantage derived from low labour costs vis-à-vis the world market, these small firms were not very securely placed relative to the potential competitors in the organised sector. The wage-gap was not wide enough. Many had to live with a poorer infrastructure and public services than what their organised sector counterparts enjoyed. Also they did not have a secure place in the competitive world market as the constant comparisons on firm-size and efficiency between India and China suggested.

Despite the rents that the small-scale policy had created, there was no strong lobbying against policy reform. The reservations continued more out of inertia and fear of economic collapse than any well-defined political resistance. Export sectors and the garment industry saw the first round of de-reservation. More recently, in 2002-03, a further series of de-reservations has been proposed or approved. The list of reserved items is still long enough, but with these step-by-step changes, the share of "naturally small" industries is rising in this list.

For the formal sector, the fundamental problem in the economic reform process was that it reduced protection but did not suitably change the labour laws. The dice was loaded in favour of the new firms in new industries that had the benefit of access to export markets and imported technologies, but did not have a labour overhead to deal with. Existing firms shared the gains too, but unequally. Some went down in the new competitive regime, some survived and did well. However, nearly all had to find ways of dealing with the labour overheads. New business was shared between informal and formal, informal on the strength of crude labour costs and formal on the skilled labour costs. But in the old firms, the social contract broke down.

The formal sector now wanted de-protection of jobs and of the informal sector, where there were potentially strong advantages of skilled labour or economies of scale. Jobs and reservations were the new stakes in a three-cornered contest—the three antagonists being formal sector capital, formal sector labour and, to a small extent, informal sector capital—in which the state acted as a not-so-convincing referee.

THE FORMAL SECTOR

Old Firms and Old Labour: Obsolescence, Exit, Disempowerment

Throughout the 1990s, a few major industry groups in the formal sector stagnated or their employment and profitability declined. The most important examples include cotton spinning and weaving in mills, jute spinning and weaving in mills and synthetic textiles. A few groups within the machinery and metallurgy declined too, chiefly ferrous metals. But in almost the all major non-textile groups, the first half of the 1990s was generally profitable.

In the synthetic textiles and engineering, the decline was quite clearly attributable to tariff reduction. But the in cotton and jute textiles, reforms marginally worsened the long-standing decay. On the other hand, in all these industries, deregulation of technology import offered a few firms that were better managed, more credit-worthy, and already technologically advanced, the chance to globalise with success. The reforms as such, thus, had the effect mainly of a sharp inter-firm polarisation even within the so-called declining sectors.

At the end of 2000, 1.9 million workers were on the rolls of the factories that had registered themselves with the Board of Industrial and Financial Restructuring (BIFR), the government body in charge of reviving firms on the road to bankruptcy, a condition known in India as "sickness". A little less than half of this number was employed in textiles and engineering. The figure is exaggerated, in that a great many of these workers had long left these sick firms. Sickness redressal and bankruptcy proceedings take such a long time that many on the BIFR rolls existed only in name.

A substantial number, possibly 250,000 out of the 500,000 engaged in sick textile firms, had been already out of these jobs in 1991. Throughout the 1980s, the rate of employment growth was very slow in the formal sector, it was called "jobless growth". The apparent slow growth rate in employment actually conceals the fact that *jobs were lost on an exceptionally large scale in the 1980s.* Gross jobs lost amounted to almost a quarter of the employment level in 1980. What appears as jobless growth reflects the effect of *closures* of whole clusters of firms in specific industries, the most famous examples of which occurred in the textiles and engineering. By contrast, in the first half of the 1990s, large-scale pan-industrial closures became rare, closures in individual firms occurred in a somewhat more isolated way. Gross jobs lost made up only about 2 per cent of the 1991 employment.

The shift from industry-wide closures to firm-specific closures suggests that bargaining institutions changed in the 1990s. Industry-wide unions were in decline all through the 1980s, making way for firm-specific bargaining. In turn, this was a reflection of new firms' determination to steer clear of the national trade unions. At the same time, the Central and the State governments had implicitly adopted a "hands-off" policy with regard to collective bargaining and dispute settlement. The net result of both these processes was the retreat of the national trade unions into old firms and old labour segments. This process of losing relevance, power, and spread is what I have called *disempowerment* of the organised labour.

Disempowerment indirectly benefited the new firms. It benefited those old firms that could restructure and survive. It came too late for the old firms that were already sick. In this segment, disempowerment did hurt labour and worsened industrial relations. These new trends can be illustrated with two examples, cotton textile mills and jute textiles.

Cotton: A Case Study

Between 1985 and 1996, 111 mills, of which 52 were composite spinning-weaving-processing mills, closed down. By a rough estimation, about 272,000 persons—over 200,000 of them in western India—lost their jobs in this period.[4] There is now a substantial literature on the effects of the mill closure on workers.[5] This literature shows how the "unofficial" closure–closure not notified to nor contested by the trade unions and the authorities – hurt labour more badly than official closure would have.

The first signs of closure are irregularity in the payment of dues. Many private mills in western India followed a simple course—they stopped paying electricity bills until the electricity connection was cut and operations ceased. Such *de facto* closure was accompanied with non-payment of workers' dues. The matter ended up in court. If the court decided on a legal closure, the whole process to liquidation might take several years. On the employers' side, physical assets remained locked up in the mill premises, unless they were stealthily removed with the help of the underworld. Rarely was any compensation paid, and when it was paid, it was very little.

That said, the adjustment process is quite a disparate one. A series of studies on the effects of the closure on workers reveal certain common conclusions:

1. Levels of unemployment due to job-loss vary between surveys. Most surveys find a minority (about a quarter) of workers remaining unemployed even after a year. There is often a long period of initial unemployment, which is partly due to search costs and preferences. At first, workers look for old-type factory jobs. The length of the period depends upon the extent of help received from relatives.
2. Age is a barrier to re-employment and retraining.
3. New employment has the following general characteristics:

   - informalisation, or greater extent of participation in the informal sector,
   - departure from permanency, return to job-security being extremely rare,
   - greater extent of self-employment, that is, a general departure from wage-work,
   - on average much reduced levels of earnings and welfare provisions, and

4. Usual new occupations include factory work, operating small

trades and shops, agriculture (in rural districts), security services, transport and casual labour.

5. Compensation is generally small and rarely given. When available, it plays almost no role in facilitating re-employment. Usually it is used for payment of debts, or construction of a house. Full legal compensation is rare. Voluntary Retirement Scheme (VRS) exists only in the case of closure of public sector mills
6. Loss of job is a multiple social loss: it is a loss of community, credit, dignity and self-respect. For workers getting a mill job used to mean a major improvement in their economic and social status, correspondingly closure meant social decline. Children might give up studies. Marriages had to be postponed. Spouses needed to look for work. The usually very small prior work-participation of adult women in the mill-hand families of Gujarat heightened the costs of job-loss. In that respect, job-loss and social practices join hands in making it harder for the workers.

How did the national trade unions respond to unofficial closures? Both Mumbai and Ahmedabad have, by law, monopoly unions, but the monopoly had lost its legitimacy and was in practice broken up at least twenty years back. The few surviving and profitable mills invariably broke away from these unions and devised decentralised bargaining institutions. For the closed and sick mills, the unions have generally played a non-interventionist role in the prevention of closure; their role has been confined to fighting for compensation after the closure takes place. However, in Ahmedabad, the steady loss of membership seriously constrained the main union even in this battle. The battle could not be fought for long by the labour simply because the industry was almost bankrupt and public support for mill workers had more or less eroded in the 1990s.

Jute: A Second Case Study

In the cotton textile mills, adverse industrial relations resulted from the widespread sickness that had roots in the textile policy. In contrast, in the jute industry, adverse relations had roots in the history and structure of the industry. There are 73 jute mills in the country, of which 59 are situated in West Bengal. These jute mills employ around 194,000 regular workers. There are many casual workers, but their exact number is unknown.

In the early 1980s, jute tended to be written off as an industry without future. However, the industry has not declined any further thereafter. The production volume of jute goods has fluctuated widely around an almost constant average of 1.3 million tonnes between 1985 and 2000. But the composition of jute goods has changed. The main product has all along been material for packaging. Domestically, the demand is artificially maintained by a government order making it mandatory for some bulk commodity producers to use jute bags. There has been a lot of resistance to this order, and some industries completely stopped following it. But there is also an increasing preference for jute bags because of its eco-friendly qualities. Further, new products made of jute have fared quite well in the consumer market. The export market is growing due to both diversification and environmental awareness. The year 1995 was a turnaround year for jute.

As in the cotton textiles, the direct effect of the reforms on jute was encouragement to export and modernisation. Consequently, a set of mills were renovated and became fully export-oriented in the 1990s. These mills manufacture high quality yarn/twine, jute decorative fabrics, fine hessian cloth, jute bags and blended fabrics. By and large the industry manufactures material for various types of packing bags. The majority of the mills continue to function more or less along the old lines: traditional products with traditional machinery, high labour cost, low productivity and fluctuating profits. When they come under pressure, these mills squeeze labour.

As in cotton textiles, the reforms have had an indirect effect on labour—disempowerment of unions. Central trade unions command less and less following in jute. Unions have decentralised and fragmented. Every major incident of dispute such as the industry-wide strike in 2000 has hastened this process further. In 2001, it culminated in a spate of mill-level disputes which turned exceptionally violent. This was not unexpected, given the generally strained nature of industrial relations. Inter-union fights worsened the situation.

Again, as in cotton textiles, in jute, industrial relations were strained in the 1980s, and there was a major strike in 1984. Thereafter, the threat of closure was perpetually present, or strategically used, by many vulnerable mills to extract wage concessions from workers. There was widespread disillusionment with the central trade unions. In the early 1990s, two cases of closure became highly publicised, the Kanoria Jute Mill, which was managed by a worker cooperative following closure, and the Titagurh Jute Mill, whose closure led to several deaths and suicides. From the mid-1990s, even though the general prospect of the industry improved, costs have been highly variable due to the fluctuations in the jute prices and erratic power supply. Since 1998-99, the problem of cost has become especially serious. Most mills do not have the reserves to tide over these fluctuations. The import of cheap jute products from Bangladesh and the collapse of the government scheme for mandatory use of jute added to the uncertainties. The outcome is extreme vulnerability. Most mills have not modernised, and they carry a large labour cost as overhead. If they are to reduce costs, they have to target labour.

Contract labour provides some flexibility in adjustment. Given the seasonality of jute production, there has always been an incentive to employ contract labour in the manufacturing process. Further, some mills routinely close down in summer, though each closure is technically illegal. But the ever-present uncertainty over the material costs means that often dues are not paid to regular workers. On top of this, thanks to its location in the heart of the left-ruled West Bengal, jute has always had strained industrial relations, with or without support from the government in power. Given this combination of managerial failure, history of militancy and political backing to labour, and high price-cost uncertainty, industrial relations in jute are a powder keg.

In 2000-01, relations were especially strained, and violent incidents became more frequent than usual. The incidents occurred in a number of jute mills along the east and west banks of the river Hooghly. The provocations were non-payment of wages, actual or threatened closure, attempted negotiations for voluntary retirement, inter-union fight for control, etc.

Jute needs modernisation and retrenchment through negotiated means. But neither has been easy in this industry which survives by and large on short-term profits. As for the workers, there have not been significant gains or costs due to the reforms. Employment has been almost stationary. However, there has been a change in the dynamics of violence. Violence has become decentralised, and possibly more intense, with the disappearance of industry-wide unions and divisions among the employers.

The Profile of New Labour

New industries and firms spawned a completely different labour regime, meaning a different set of bargaining institutions, and even a different profile of labour. In the very few firms that started after 1992 was there a presence of the national trade unions, even any trade union at all. Knowledge-based industries such as pharmaceuticals and software did not involve a large shop-floor, and thus did not fit the traditional model of a space for labour organisation and action. Many firms in cotton yarn or food processing started in semi-rural areas, outside labour agglomerations. In these various ways, the ground from beneath the national trade unions shifted, and disempowerment followed. In today's political world, a strident battle-cry of the trade unions is far from a show of strength; it displays weakness and insecurity.

Nevertheless, in the scholarship on labour after the reforms, there has been a remarkable neglect of forms of labour in new firms, industries and locations. The change in the bargaining institutions has been noted, but the underlying change in the profile of capital and labour has largely remained unstudied.

Labour and State: Attempts at Change in Law and Labour Resistance

What factors block a quick and transparent bankruptcy and exit policy? Many would answer, the legal overhang of the implicit contract regime. Under the Industries (Development and Regulation) Act of 1947, employment in the organised sector is subject to 47central laws relating to hours, security, wages, safety, lay-off, etc. Any firm with at least 100 workers on its rolls and wishing to downsize or close down must first seek permission from a third party, that is, government labour courts and other bodies. Such permission is rarely given and if given, seldom quickly. In the views of the industry, many economists, and sections within the government, the legal regime is responsible for a number of distortions.

1. Labour legislation, for instance, provides no flexibility for downsizing. This has led to entrepreneurs adopting expensive labour-saving equipment and keeping the employee numbers at the lowest levels possible.
2. It is designed to protect the existing employees. It creates a strong insider protection, resulting in equally strong outsider discrimination. It is inherently iniquitous.
3. It makes closure difficult. This has led to a large amount of non-viable assets being kept out of the market; neither are they giving returns nor can they be liquidated. By a conservative estimate, such unproductive capital amounts to almost 2 per cent of the GDP.
4. It forces employers to adopt unfair or harsher terms of employment than otherwise. Contract labour is one of these. In the case of contract employment, no severance pay is mandatory.

In the first 10 years after the reforms began, labour law did not or could not emerge as a priority. In the early 1990s, when the job market was booming, it was not necessary to worry about labour laws. In the next five years of job-loss and recession, it was not possible to do so. But by then, the industry was impatient.

The first Finance Minister of the National Democratic Alliance government announced soon after taking office that the government had embarked on "second generation" reforms, with an accent on reforming labour laws. If the first generation reforms focused on globalisation or on ending India's isolationist trade and investment policies, the second generation was to focus on more micro-economic issues such as enterprise reforms, privatisation and giving greater say to capital in the matter of enterprise restructuring. The Minister also stated that success in this phase would be heavily dependent on political consensus and cooperation from the state governments. This emphasis on cooperation was a new one, and underscored the fact that the second-generation reforms touched the lives and livelihoods much more directly. Not surprisingly, this effort has largely failed to generate political consensus.

The government faltered at more or less the very first step. In his budget speech in February, 2001, the then Finance Minister announced that a new labour relations bill will be introduced soon in

Parliament making it easier for any firm to close down or retrench surplus labour. Currently, under Section 5B of the I (DR) Act, firms with 100 or more employees have to seek the government's permission to either close down or retrench. The proposed bill was to raise this limit to 1,000. The budget was enthusiastically welcomed in the corporate circles and by economists. In a subsequent Cabinet meeting, the amendment to the act was accepted "in principle".

The bill, however, never materialised due to opposition which arose from three sources. First, thère was dissension from the Ministry of Labour, which is conventionally regarded as being "pro-labour" (as opposed to the Ministry of Finance's pro-reform—widely seen as pro-capital—world-view). In view of the opposition, the bill was reportedly watered down; the proposed limit on the number of employees was reduced to 300. Even that change did not see the light of day. Second, there was resistance from the main opposition party, the Congress, which had a majority in the Upper House of Parliament. Third, there was apposition from the trade unions of all the major political parties, including the largest party in the ruling coalition. The fact that the then Finance Minister made himself unpopular with the middle classes with his badly timed austerity drive did not help matters either. His next and last budget speech was profoundly silent on labour.

In 2001-02, the Prime Minister himself took up the cause of labour law reforms and replaced the non-compliant Labour Minister with a new one. A comprehensive new commission of enquiry (the Second National Labour Commission) was to report on labour law reforms, which it did in September, 2002. The Commission was broadly pro-reform and recommended modification of laws to facilitate lay-off and retrenchment of labour and closure of industrial units. In October, the Prime Minister, inaugurating the 38th session of the Indian Labour Conference, made a strong commitment to the continuity of the reform process and implementation of the recommendations of the National Labour Commission.

Apparently, this was the first occasion when the employers' bodies, the government and the unions met to thrash out their differences on globalisation, privatisation and laws on closure and retrenchment. At the end of the two-day meet, there was a reasonable agreement on a few issues, the most important being the constitution of a national social security authority to cover all sections of workers. On the other issues, however, the meet ended in a virtual stalemate. Subsequently, the Ministry of Labour has been holding a series of dialogues with the unions to bring them round to a deal, hoping that if that works, the Congress will be forced to soften its opposition. Another ray of hope is a lack of consensus on reforms within the Congress leadership, leading to some kind of a rift between its Parliamentary party and the trade union body.

Labour and Capital: Disempowerment

Disempowerment is an indirect result of the reforms. It has derived from three changes in particular. First, modernisation which is a major imperative for restructuring a firm Second, the entry of new firms and new industries enabled substantially new forms of contract and institutions to come in place. Third, a reformist mentality was ushered in by the policy changes and their quite dramatic effects in the early 1990s. In the past (the early 1980s, for example) there was no serious questioning of the labour laws, trade unions tended to be seen as weapons of the weak rather than as powerful distributional coalitions,[6] and the implementation of labour laws involved a broadly shared concern for job security. In the 1990s, that mindset disappeared. Labour laws were now seen as a problem by almost everybody except the central trade unions themselves. The Press takes a generally reformist stand. The government as well as the judiciary played a broadly non-interventionist role in respect to job-loss and enterprise restructuring in the nineties. And the organised labour is more easily seen as groups fighting for sectional interests at the cost of national interest.

How Did Old Business Adapt? Voluntary Retirement and Ancillarisation of Services

While formally employment practices in the organised sector continue to be bound by rigid laws, many firms have shed labour via voluntary retirement, a course that would have invited a great deal of resistance from trade unions a decade ago. All large and profitable firms have reduced their core, that is, permanently employed (unionised) labour force. The work formerly done by the core work-force is now being done either by other firms (outsourcing) or by contract labour. (In some cases, outsourcing and contract labour are identical.) The unionised component of work-force has thus shrunk, and the nature of the unions themselves has changed. In different contexts, this process of disempowerment of labour has been called *casualisation, informalisation* and *feminisation* (the last when gender aspect is involved).

To increase flexibility of the labour market and yet reduce its social costs, the government announced the start of National Renewal Fund (NRF) in 1992-93. The fund was to support retrenchment, retraining, redeployment and compensation due to closure. For the unorganised sector, the NRF was also meant to finance employment generation schemes. The experience of the NRF in the period 1993 to 1998 showed that:

1. Rs 18 billion was spent on various schemes, 89 per cent on VRS packages for about 100,000 public sector employees,
2. The number of persons covered under the NRF steadily fell,
3. Budgetary provisions also fell and were considered grossly inadequate,
4. Other programmes such as counselling, retraining and redeployment involved about 50,000 workers,
5. All other schemes such as soft loans for restructuring and employment generation schemes were more or less ignored, and
6. The International Labour Organisation (ILO) found that until 1995, a majority of those under the VRS were public sector employees of the managerial cadre, which made the compensation unsustainably high for the government.

After 1995, the NRF became wholly associated with the divestment process in the central public sector undertakings. Whereas until mid-1998, only about 100,000 public sector workers opted for the VRS under the NRF, the ILO estimated the total redundancy in the public sector at 3.4 million, and redundancy in the public sector undertakings at 0.4 million. The VRS coverage, in other words, was less than 25 per cent of redundancy. In October, 2000, the NRF was abolished and replaced with a scheme to supply direct budgetary support to individual ministries according to their VRS requirements. In the private sector, voluntary retirements have been implemented on a wider scale, though the exact magnitudes and costs are unknown.

In the 1990s, major changes took place in the modes of employment and collective bargaining to allow for greater flexibility. The roots of some of these changes went back to the turbulent 1980s. The most important options were:

- contractual employment,
- voluntary retirement,
- ban on recruitment, and
- outsourcing.

A number of large firms have implicitly banned recruitment in manufacturing since the 1980s. Voluntary retirement schemes have been implemented in almost all the major firms, with a minimum or no resistance from labour.[7] A large number of firms have been subcontracting previously integrated processes and services to other firms, in the process shedding permanent work-force.[8] The employers resort to reduction in the permanent (unionised) component of work-force, or "off-loading" labour,[9] because it offers the prospect of achieving a smaller and more amenable core work-force, and they believe that in the non-core work, having a unionised permanent labour force will result in a waste of the bargaining energy. Contract employment means subcontracting parts of factory work, not usually related to the manufacturing process, to other firms (usually labour supply agencies). Typically, such intra-factory services as running a canteen and providing maintenance services are routinely contracted out. This has become a universal practice in western India. Contract employment not only reduces the possibility of resistance (since contract workers are non-unionised), it also saves the employer money which otherwise will have to be spent on benefits. Subcontracting, however, is not limited to such intra-factory employment. It also includes an ever-increasing practice of acquiring parts and processes from outside. Industries that were formerly not heavy users of subcontractors such as pharmaceuticals due to central trade unions have now become so.

In the 1990s, both the state-backed industry-wide unions and industry-wide bargaining declined.[10] Outside the public sector, such unions are considerably weaker now. In the public sector, the de-linking of wage issues from the budgetary support in the early 1990s effectively ended industry-wide bargaining on wages. Their increasingly close identification with bankrupt public sector firms has contributed greatly to political isolation of the central trade unions and weakened their legitimacy in the public eye as representatives of labour in general. "Labour regime" is a phrase used to characterise labour market institutions, especially labour's power to influence its own absolute and relative economic situation. The literature on this subject notes that the Indian labour regime is decisively changing. It seems to be changing from a pluralist regime, where unions can play a role in the national politics via their dependent relationship with political groups, to a truly decentralised regime where unions have little or no relationship with political groups.[11]

If this is the general picture of the 1990s, declining industries differ from it somewhat. They do employ contract labour heavily to achieve an extra measure of flexibility. On the other hand, industry-wide unions have survived somewhat more in the declining industries, and play a more active role. This feature owes its existence partly to the presence of the public sector in some of them such as the National Textile Corporation in cotton textiles, or the National Jute Mills Corporation in jute. Partly it is a result of an internal paralysis; many firms in the declining sectors cannot exit or negotiate a profitable solution with labour. The greater role for industry unions is also partly a matter of history and regional politics. In cotton mills, officially, there is still a single representative union of the workers (whose monopoly the workers effectively rejected in the famous 1982-83 strike). In the jute textiles, on the other hand, the leftist government of West Bengal and the trade unions have traditionally played an activist and interventionist role.

On the other hand, the firms which have survived within the declining industries aggressively pursue contract employment and plant-level bargaining. For this reason, intra-industry variations in wages, employment security, permanent-contract proportion, and modes of bargaining tend to be especially wide in the declining industries.

THE INFORMAL SECTOR

The effect of market opening has been mixed on the informal sector as it has been upon the formal sector. Some industries declined, and others survived. The reason for the decline was not the excess labour cost; small firms do not carry excess labour. The reason for the decline was change of taste and fiscal tightening that led to withdrawal of some subsidies. In an indirect way, the change in taste was hastened, if not caused, by globalisation. Plastics replaced earthenware in a variety of uses and western style casual-wear replaced handloom garments, for example. On the other hand, having low labour costs and not having labour overheads was a big advantage for the informal sector firms that found an export market for the first time.

In the organised sector, the post-reform period has seen a distinct improvement in performance and efficiency. The unorganised sector presents a more complex picture. If we confine ourselves to employment, income, or output, it is a picture of decline. If we look at labour productivity, the unorganised sector has enhanced its efficiency just as impressively as the organised sector has. Even the handloom industry, which saw the largest decline in employment, saw a rise in the productivity per worker. While segments of the unorganised sector saw shrinking markets, other segments witnessed adjustments to improve efficiency and competitiveness. In these segments, furthermore, there was increasing employment of wage-labour in place of family labour and greater urbanisation.

Export opportunities came as a boon for specific segments inside the organised as well as the unorganised sector. The biggest exporters—garments, leather, jewellery and even cotton spinning to a large extent—flourished in the informal sector. But the experience of exporting also uncovered serious weaknesses of the supplier firms, weaknesses that arose out of inexperience, massive asymmetric information, absence of regulation, poor infrastructure and chances of fraud.

We do know that substantially new forms of labour have emerged in the informal sector. We can surmise that the extent of migrant labour has increased, based on impressions from major export craft clusters. There has also been *feminisation* of the work-force. For example, many garment factories employ women. In turn, feminisation implies a deeper transition in the industrial organisation. Traditionally, women manufacturing workers displayed a strong preference for working from within the household. Or, the proportion of women in the industrial labour and the proportion of labour employed in the household industry have been correlated. This is clearly changing. *Feminisation* of the work-force is now correlated with a break-up of the household as a working unit. However, looking again at the profile of a major cluster of informal enterprises such as the Dharavi region in the city of Mumbai, it would seem that the household is changing in character rather than declining. In Dharavi, nearly everyone is employed and nearly every bit of space is used commercially. Whole families do something or the other, from inside the home or outside. Such forms of household enterprise, however, are different from the old forms of household enterprise one would encounter in the artisan families in two ways. First, in the latter, members of the family worked in the same industry, gender and age distribution in the family coalesced with permissible divisions of labour in a single manufacturing unit. In the Dharavi type of family enterprise, such coalescence may not be found. Second, in the artisanal set-up, family members worked for the household enterprise. Today, members of the working family are more often employed on wages by an outsider.

Table 13.1: Employment in Manufacturing

(in millions)

	1989	*1994*	*1999*
Unorganised	35.0	33.4	35.1
Organised (excluding electricity and gas)	8.2	8.2	8.6
Total	43.3	41.6	43.7

Source: National Sample Survey Organisation, 45th, 51st and 55th Rounds; Central Statistical Organisation, "Annual Survey of Industries".

CONCLUSION

How did India's market reforms affect jobs and employment in manufacturing? There is, first of all, an identification problem here that we need to be careful about—the effects of the late 1990s recession often prejudice assessments of the reforms. In principle, we should be able to keep the late 1990s aside in studying this question.

This paper has argued that, in answering this question, it is important to keep in mind the differences between existing firms and new entrants, and between formal and informal sectors. The former distinction is important because the existing firms in both formal and informal sectors were party to an old, implicit contract with the state that began to break down from the 1980s. The reforms, introduced in this state of collapse of understanding, imposed a cost upon both capital (the situation made the old firms weaker compared to new entrants) and labour (new entrants chipped away the ground beneath the organised trade unions) in the formal sector, a process we have called *disempowerment*. These conditions, with the impact of the recession added on them, intensified political conflicts in the formal sector that now threaten to put a brake on the labour law reforms.

The second distinction is important because the formal and informal sectors produce different goods and operate in different labour markets. Insofar as labour is a source of comparative advantage of Indian manufacturing, the informal sector can exploit this advantage better than the formal sector. But the informal sector also contained a large traditional industrial segment that has partially lost markets due to globalisation and change of taste, and it has lost state support due to fiscal tightening. In both sectors, in other words, there was a sphere of decline and difficult adjustment involving the old firms, and a sphere of growth and dynamism. The difficulties faced by the old firms and old labour were largely due to the withdrawal of the state (along with age). But equally, new entry and new jobs derived from withdrawal of the state.

The economic challenge is to redress the divisions and anomalies that have arisen due to the vestiges of the old regime. The challenge for analysts is to study more closely some elements in this transition that have received little attention in a largely media-driven discourse. The most important among them is the labour regime and bargaining institutions that are taking shape via the new entry in both formal and informal sectors.

NOTES

1. Between 1970 and 1975, industrial growth in India decelerated. The positions taken in the literature trying to explain included inequality and underconsumption,

reduction in public investment, increasing allocative inefficiency due to planning and regulation, and agricultural stagnation. For a selection of the papers on the subject, see, Nayyar 1994.

2. "Jobless growth" refers to a phenomenon of very slow rates of employment growth but healthy output growth which took place during much of the 1990s. The conflicting positions on this basically debate the significance of a fairly rapid real wage increase at the same time. Did employers decide to replace militant labour that could extract a lot of concessions from them, or was it a coincident that such trends in wage and employment growth happened together? For a selection of writings, see, Ahluwalia 1991; Nagraj 1994; Ghose, 1995; Bhalotra 1998; Ramaswamy 1999; and Goldar, 2000.
3. A section of the handloom industry, for example, was heavily dependent on government support for its survival.
4. No direct estimate of job-loss in the cotton textiles is available. This estimate is based on the following figures: the number of workers on the roll in 1995 was 1.023 million and the number of workers employed in active factories was 0.578 million. The difference between the two must be workers in closed factories which numbered 181 in 1995 ("Annual Survey of Industries" 1995). This gives us an average of 2,456 workers per closed mill, or 272,000 workers in the 111 closed mills.
5. Roy Chowdhury 1996; Howell and Khambhampati 1999; Noronha and Sharma 1999; Desai 2001; B.B. Patel 2001.
6 The term "distributional coalition", a group that in effect tries to capture a larger share of the common product without necessarily contributing to the size of the common product, owes its origin to Olson, 1982.
7. For a discussion of cases, see Candland 1996 and Noronha, 1996.
8. For figures on the rise in the extent of contracting in the organised sector, see the essays by Uchikawa and Ramaswammy 2001.
9. I borrow the term "off-loading" from Singh and Mukhopadhyay 2001.
10. For an overview, see Bhattacharjee 2000.
11. For a discussion of the literature, see Candland 1996.

REFERENCES

Ahluwalia, I.J. (1991): *Productivity and Growth in Indian Manufacturing*. Delhi: Oxford University Press.

Bhalotra, S.R. (1998): "The Puzzle of Jobless Growth in Indian Manufacturing". *Oxford Bulletin of Economics and Statistics* 60(1).

Bhattacharjee, Dabashish (2000): "Globalising Economy, Localising Labor". *Economic and Political Weekly* (October 14).

Candland, Christopher (1996): "Labor Institutions and Industrial Restructuring in India". IRIS-India Working Paper No. 24. College Park, MD.

Desai, Kiran (2001): "Workers of Closed Textile Mills: A Case of South Gujarat". Paper prepared for the seminar on Collective Care Arrangements among Workers and Nonworkers in the Informal Sector, held in Hyderabad.

Ghose, Ajit (1995): "Economic Restructuring, Employment and Safety Nets". ILO-ARTEP, *Social Dimensions of Structural Adjustment in India.* Delhi: International Labour Organisation.

Goldar, B.N. (2000): "Employment Growth in Organized Manufacturing Growth in India". *Economic and Political Weekly* 35(14).

Howell, Jude, and Khambhampati, Uma (1999): "Liberalization and Labor: The Fate of Retrenched Workers in the Cotton Textile Industry in India". *Oxford Development Studies,* 27(1).

Nagraj, R. (1994): "Employment and Growth in Manufacturing Industries: Trends, Hypotheses and Evidence". *Economic and Political Weekly* 29(4).

Nayyar, Deepak (ed.) (1994): *Industrial Growth and Stagnation: The Debate in India.* Delhi: Sameeksha Trust and Oxford University Press.

Noronha, Ernesto (1996): "Liberalisation and Industrial Relations". *Economic and Political Weekly* (February 24).

Noronha, Ernesto, and Sharma, R. N. (1999): "Displaced Workers and Withering of Welfare State". *Economic and Political Weekly* (June 5).

Olson, Mancur (1982): *The Rise and Decline of Nations. Economic Growth, Inflation, and Social Rigidities.* New Haven: Yale University Press.

Patel, B.B. (2001): "Socio-economic Marginalisation of Displaced Textile Mill Workers in Ahmedabad, Gujarat, India". Paper prepared for the seminar on Collective Care Arrangements among Workers and Nonworkers in the Informal Sector, held in Hyderabad.

Ramaswamy, K.V. (1999): "The Search for Flexibility in Indian Manufacturing: New Evidence on Outsourcing Activities". *Economic and Political Weekly* 34.

Roy Chowdhury, Supriya (1996): "Industrial Restructuring, Unions and the State. Textile Mill Workers in Ahmedabad". *Economic and Political Weekly* (February 24).

Roy, Tirthonkar, forthcoming. "Economic Reforms and the Textile Industry in India". In S. Gokarn, S.; Sen, A.; and Vaidya, R. (eds.) *The Structure of Indian Industry.* Delhi: Oxford University Press.

Singh, Kavaljit, and Mukhopadhyay, Nilanjan (2001): "Globalization and India. The Other Side of 'Success': Bayer in India". Delhi: Public Interest Research Group.

Uchikawa, Shuji and Ramaswammy, K.V. (2001): [Various essays]. In Shuji Uchikawa. (ed.) *Labor Market Institutions in India: 1990s and Beyond.* Tokyo: Institute of Developing Economies.